THE POWER OF PARLIAMENT

The Power of Parliament

by Ronald Butt

Foreword by KARL LOEWENSTEIN

Walker and Company ✺ New York

TO MARGARET

Acknowledgments

My first thanks are to the Warden and Fellows of Nuffield College, Oxford, for electing me to a Research Fellowship. During the year of my Fellowship a large part of this book was written and I was enabled to cover much more ground than would otherwise have been possible. My debt to the conversation of my colleagues at Nuffield is too widespread for it to be possible for me to name individually all those who in one way or another stimulated and helped me. Nevertheless, I must record my special thanks to Phillip Williams, Fellow of Nuffield, for his generous help as the book was being written. He read the greater part of the manuscript, often in more than one draft, and, giving his time and his thoughts unselfishly, enabled me to make improvements in several chapters and saved me from a number of errors.

I should also like to thank, for reading various sections of the book, Dr David Butler, Fellow of Nuffield, Mr T. S. G. Hunter and Dr Eric Taylor, Deputy Principal Clerk of the House of Commons. Professor May McKisack kindly read a longer manuscript of mine on the medieval Parliament which was the basis of the short passages covering this period in the first chapter of the book. All helped me to correct some errors of fact or judgment; for those that remain, as for the general theme of the book, I alone must take responsibility.

I should also like to thank Michael Pinto-Duschinsky for referring me to relevant passages in Lord Salisbury's writings and for valuable help at other points in the book.

My thanks are also due to the politicians and other public servants who helped me at various stages during the writing of the book but who would not wish to be named—and to the many more whose conversation over the years provided much of the basis on which the second part of the book is built, and contributed to the formulation of the idea behind it.

Equally, I owe thanks to many colleagues in journalism. I am grateful to Sir Gordon Newton, the Editor of *The Financial Times*, for his agreement to the period of my absence at Nuffield. I am also indebted to my colleagues in political journalism for their characteristic professional generosity and especially to Francis Boyd, the political correspondent of *The Guardian*, for many insights into politics.

I would like to thank Anne Duncan-Jones for helping me to put the final manuscript in order, and the Hon. John Jolliffe, of Constable, for his patience in dealing with it.

Finally, I am grateful to my wife, Margaret, and to my children, Bridget, Oliver, Edmund and Elizabeth, all of whom, according to their several dispositions and ages, enthusiastically and stalwartly accepted the neglect imposed on any family by over three years devoted to a book of this nature.

London,
June, 1967

Contents

Foreword

When members of this House divide
If they have brains and cerebellum too
They have to leave their brains outside
And vote just as their leaders tell 'em to.

But then the prospect of a lot
Of all MP's in close proximity
All thinking for themselves is what
No one could bear with equanimity.

—The sentry before Westminster in
W. S. Gilbert's "Iolanthe."

(i)

Of all instruments of government in existence today, the American Constitution of 1787, as the oldest, is the most venerable. Fourth of July oratory habitually describes the form of government it established as the "best ever invented by man." However, at no time within memory and, as a matter of fact, not since the War between the States, has the patriotic claim of the superiority of our political institutions been unchallenged. Is it indeed "limited government" and does it really guarantee the "rule of law" instead "of men"? At the present time, the war in Vietnam has sharpened our constitutional introspection—and this far beyond academic circles—when it is realized that the Presidency has involved the nation in the third costliest war in its history, in conflict with the explicit provision of the Constitution (Article I, Section 8, Clause 11) to the effect that "Congress shall have the power . . . to declare war." Doubts concerning the wisdom of American political institutions multiply when certain specific aspects are considered: the near-unlimited and practically illimitable expansion of Presidential powers; the inability of President and Congress to provide for constructive solutions of the urban imbalance and racial tensions; the impediments built into the legislative process by constitutional custom such as the seniority rule for the chairmanship of the committees; the filibuster in the Senate; the selective morality of Congress, in spite of feeble efforts to write a code of ethics; the unrestrained power of the lobbies—one of which, to cite a particularly glaring instance, successfully frustrated reasonable gun-control legislation that, in the light of the recent assassinations of public figures, the vast majority demands; the exorbitant costs of running for a democratic office, recently underscored by the abolition of the ineffective statutory ceilings. And, in this Presidential year, one may point to the stark obscenity of the party conventions, unknown to the Constitution, manipulated at will by the party professionals and often in conflict with the democratically expressed will of the voters; and the blatant absurdity of the Electoral College, which permits a minority President to attain office and which may even throw the final determination of the Chief Executive into the House of Representatives where—one can hardly believe it—the vote would be taken by states!

All these defects of our Constitution, grave as they are, are dwarfed by the crucial dilemma that, in this technological age, the Presidency has become wholly unmanageable as a one-man job. Four of our last five Presidents were stricken by grave illness during their incumbency; in the case of President Eisenhower, two irresponsible private individuals—Sherman Adams and James Hagerty—governed the nation. Only a fundamental reform aimed at creating a kind of collective Presidency could remedy the dangers of the situation. In short, the American nation has survived, not because of the excellence, but in spite of the defects of our political institutions. No wonder that a large and responsible segment of the population experiences an ever-increasing alienation from an obsolete document that was written two centuries ago.

In view of these widespread misgivings, it is understandable that responsible studies are under way on how to adjust the Constitution to the requirements of the technological age. Congress is engaged in a major investigation of Presidential elections. The Center for the Study of Democratic Institutions in California is trying its hand at the attempt of completely rewriting the document.

An indispensable prerequisite, however, for better understanding the effects and defects of our political system is reliable and unbiased information on the political process of other democratic nations. Considering our common Anglo-Saxon heritage, it is natural that Great Britain offers herself as the primary source of comparative knowledge. On closer inspection, it could be shown that the British have been able to avoid most of the pitfalls of the

American political process that have been referred to before, and that more than any other contemporary nation they have succeeded in combining the unchallenged authority of political leadership with the rule of law and the preservation of citizens' liberties.

Such an investigation, however, encounters serious difficulties, which derive partly from intellectual misconceptions, partly from emotional prejudices. While it is generally known that the British pattern of government is parliamentary, the public image of parliamentarianism is conditioned by the French variety: an allegedly omnipotent assembly rent by party pluralism and party dissensions that result in unstable and fickle majorities which, in turn, frustrate stable government and consistent national leadership. But even if the more knowledgeable public is able to grasp properly the British version of parliamentary government as the leadership of the Prime Minister and his Cabinet, unconditionally supported by the majority party, the didactic value of the British pattern of government has been diluted in this country by the undeniable fact that, since the Second World War, Great Britain, allegedly through faults of her own, has lost her status as a world power and has become a second-rate power, from which after all we cannot learn much. For our own political ills, we would have to develop our own remedial solutions.

Studies on the reform of the American Constitution have rarely, if ever, gone so far as to recommend the introduction of British parliamentarianism in this country. To this, a near-insurmountable obstacle exists in the provision of our Constitution (Article I, Clause 6, Sentence 2) to the effect that "no person holding office under the United States shall be a member of either House during his continuance in office." This prohibition makes the essence of British parliamentarianism, as it has evolved over the centuries, inapplicable to this country because the members of the British Cabinet and the Prime Minister are also simultaneously members of the parliament. Thus, the adoption of the British pattern by the United States would be tantamount to a complete recasting of our Constitution. For this there is not the slightest prospect in the forseeable future. Nonetheless, when circumstances compel public opinion in this country to rethink seriously the fundamentals of our political existence at the same time more accurate information on the British political process may seem a prerequisite for the revaluation of our institutions. From this viewpoint, the book by Ronald Butt, *The Power of Parliament,* now submitted to the responsible American reader—and there is hope that more of this species exist than current best-seller lists suggest—is a most welcome contribution to the realistic understanding of how the British Government operates, and this particularly because it stresses an aspect—to be discussed later—that is more or less obscured by the customary cliché thinking on the subject.

(ii)

There has also existed in Great Britain—and this is one of the things we may learn from the book—for some time a tangible malaise about the efficacy of the traditional British institutions, not dissimilar to, and even more acute than, the discomfort about ours in this country. The national self-confidence of the British people has been severely bruised by the failure of the protracted effort to maintain the position of a world power with a far-flung empire that belied the reduced resources of a land so poor in natural endowment. The present Labour government is confronted with the hard economic and educational task of reconciling the nation to its inferior status as a second-rate power. This sense of frustration could not fail to rub off on the national political institutions. After two centuries in which the British served as the worldwide political model, they have discovered tangible defects at home. One demand, raised in the thirties and vigorously renewed at present, is the reform of the House of Commons which, if we believe the experts, has suffered a visible decline in prestige and power. The reform of the House of Lords, so much debated a generation ago, is no longer on the agenda. Having been pushed on a political sidetrack by the statutory reforms of 1911/1949, the Lords meanwhile has undergone a process of modest revitalization, particularly by the creation of life peers under the legislation of 1958, and is generally useful for handling nonpolitical, technical bills with more leisure than the Commons could afford.

Among the desiderata for the Commons reform are: the need for better working conditions for the members of Parliament (MP's) who at present do not have an office, or a secretary, or even a telephone of their own. Only a new office building in Westminster would remedy these grievous defects; while under consideration for years, it is still a long way off. The business conduct and working habits of the Commons are under fully justified attack: the interminable night sittings; the absence of reasonable voting techniques which, in the case of a slim majority, make government by ambulance a constant practice; the number of, and waste of time by, irrelevant divisions in noncontroversial matters anyway agreed on beforehand by the party leaderships; the general committees to which at present all bills are assigned, instead of specialized or topical committees capable both of expert discussion and of educating members to become experts themselves; the old-fashioned and cumbrous procedure which basically has not changed for two centuries. Equally important may seem the splendid isolation of the "mother of parliaments" which, without a public relations office or service of its own, has to rely on the reporting in the press, radio, and television. While a number of these reforms at least have been tackled by the recent Labour Cabinets, such as morning sittings twice a week, the establishment of certain specialized committees, and some modest streamlining of the procedure, much remains to be done to restore to the Commons the vitality and efficacy which are said to have been lost.

There is a point, however, at which the signs of marginal inefficiency in the present parliamentary process assume a deeper significance. There is no scarcity of qualified candidates for a seat in the House of Commons. As much as ever, it is most desirable as a status symbol and for the opportunity it affords to do worthwhile things. Yet in this technological age, the recruitment of parliamentary personnel has to compete with other attractive civilian careers in the laboratory, in the academic lecture hall, in the board room of leading business corporations and, last but not least, in the civil service. Genuine leadership talent, perhaps, is in shorter supply than in previous generations. But this, rather than being the fault of the institution of parliament as such, is a universal phenomenon acutely observable also in the United States.

(iii)

Yet, in spite of such blemishes on the parliamentary image, the British have reasons to count their political blessings. The British nation had the good fortune of being able to develop their political and social institutions peacefully. For more than three centuries, they were spared violent upheavals, civil wars, bloody party strife and—thanks to their powerful navy—foreign invasion and occupation. Without interruption, they enjoyed constitutional government in which civil liberties were earlier and better protected than in any other country. All this was due to the general political climate developed by parliamentary institutions which bestowed on the British people several immense advantages. One: access to political power was—and still is—possible only through the parliamentary career. No outsider, whether an adventurer, a demagogue, or a victorious general, was ever admitted to political leadership except through membership in the parliament. Parliament has become the ideal training ground for politics. Two: the parliament, through the traditional and periodic swing of the pendulum between alternating power groups, provided the frame for mutual compromise. No party could force its policies on a reluctant nation because, sooner or later, the outs would become ins and reverse the trend. Three: the institution of parliament provided the British with the visible focus of legitimacy for the exercise of political power. The fiction of parliamentary sovereignty—and it has been a fiction for a century and more, adhered to today only by the textbooks and the courts bound to accept the parliamentary statute as the unchallengeable law of the land—instilled into the ruling classes as well as into the masses the rock-ribbed conviction that parliamentary decisions are the will of the state to which all have to submit and on which, be it noted, the liberties and freedoms of the citizens and the respect for the courts depend. Four: parliamentary government proved itself eminently adaptable to changing political, social, and economic conditions, thus making violent revolutions unnecessary. Parliament served as the frame for the transfer of power from the monarchy and the aristocratic congeries affiliated with the Crown to the propertied bourgeois upper and middle classes, and from them, by a gradual process, to the fully democratized mass electorate. By its very existence and its ready response to changed conditions, parliament has given the British the invaluable sense of continuity whose outward reflection is sometimes the adherence to seemingly obsolete traditions and rituals that other nations would not tolerate. Parliament, thus, has evidenced a staying power no other human institution—be it the civil service or the military establishment—could achieve.

Compared with these benefits that parliament has bestowed on the British, the discontent with its present operation is of relatively small importance. Ronald Butt's book is a timely reminder, by an experienced and astute observer with a considerable degree of historical perspective, that the British parliament is a unique and nontransferable institution deserving, if not blind admiration, at least a closer study than Americans are in the habit of giving. To find the proper mooring for the author's thesis, a summarizing review of the British political process may be welcome.

(iv)

1. The present-day operation of the British Constitution—unwritten, in contrast to the American, though a great deal of constitutional law is in statutory form—may conveniently be described as resembling a pyramid of political power. Its basis is formed by the electorate. Elections for the House of Commons are held regularly upon, or close to, the expiration of the legislative term (since 1911, five years), or before that date after a dissolution decided on at the absolute discretion of the Prime Minister. In the general election, the voters decide which of the two—and only two—alternating parties, once Tories and Liberals, now Conservatives and Labour, will be the government majority for the coming legislative period. The leader of the winning party is entitled, by constitutional convention, to be asked by the Crown to assume the office of the Prime Minister and to form a Cabinet.

The next level of the power pyramid is occupied by the House of Commons, divided into the majority and the minority—the opposition— parties. Within the dynamics of the political process —and this is the aspect most readily misunderstood abroad—the Commons is the least important factor. Its function consists primarily in translating the policy decisions of the Prime Minister and his Cabinet into legislation. Consequently, the Commons is mainly an organ of policy execution.

At the apex of the pyramid stands the Prime Minister and his Cabinet. With the Cabinet as his principal instrument in arriving at the policy decisions, he dominates the political process.

2. The Prime Minister draws his paramount authority, not from an action of the majority in parliament, but from the fact that the electorate, for at least a century (since 1867), determines by its vote the person of the party leader who is to assume office in case his party wins the election. Although the general election formally is a contest between the competing parties, it actually assumes the character of a plebiscite on the person of the future Prime Minister. The voter, when casting his ballot, knows that the leader of the winning party unfailingly will become the next Prime Minister, whether the present holder of the office continues or whether he is replaced by the leader of the opposition party.

3. Elections are conducted, as is the case in the United States, by straight majority contests in single-member constituencies. The candidate who wins the relative majority of votes cast in his election district obtains the seat. The issue of apportionment that has plagued the United States for generations and is now being adjusted to conform to more or less equal population figures of the election districts no longer arises in Great Britain, since after the last war boundary commissions for England, Scotland, and Wales were established, which periodically adjust the constituency boundaries to the population fluctuations. Election expenses in the constituencies are limited by scrupulously observed and rigidly enforced statutory ceilings. United States, please take note.

The straight majority system, however, is somewhat vitiated by the fact that in numerous districts a third party—mainly, the Liberals—participates in the electoral contest, the so-called triangular elections, with the not-infrequent result that the winning candidate may have obtained only the minority of all votes cast. The Liberals, as the present third party, were able to obtain only twelve seats in the last election of 1966, though their share in the total vote cast was substantially higher. This shortcoming the British consider—and not without justification—only a minor disadvantage when compared with more sophisticated electoral techniques such as proportional representation or the alternative vote, because the relative majority guarantees the distribution of the seats obtained among two, and only two, parties and, thereby, ensures a stable majority government. By-elections are bound to occur frequently with a parliamentary personnel of (at present) 630 MP's; they are considered a useful barometer of electoral opinion. But even if consistently adverse to the party in power, they do not compel the government to resign or, by dissolving the House, to call for a new general election. In England the change of government is possible only as the result of a general election. In the United States, with fixed terms for both the President and the members of Congress, by-elections for the House of Representatives do not attract much public attention.

4. The fulcrum of the British political process is the Prime Minister. Anointed by the democratic oil of the general election, he actually has become what may be called a monarch elected for a time. Since, as has been mentioned before, the leader of the victorious party has the vested right to be appointed by the Crown to the position of the Prime Minister, the manner in which he has become leader of his party is of very considerable importance. The leadership of the Labour Party is obtained through election by the Parliamentary Labour Party; that is, all Labour members in the House of Commons. If Labour is out of office, he has to submit to reelection every year. Among the Conservatives, until recently, a rather fortuitous and haphazard system had prevailed by which the leading politicians among themselves designated the person of the party leader, without any genuine democratic participation of the rank-and-file of the party members or even the Conservative MP's. This was replaced, in 1965, with a reform of the bylaws or statutes of the 1922 Committee—an influential party organ—by a formal election through the Conservative members of the Commons whereby an intricate procedure of several secret ballots aims at creating the potential unanimity of the MP's on the person of the party leader.

The technique by which a determinate party leader automatically and without any additional action on the part of the parliament becomes the Prime Minister is preferable to any other mode of investiture—for example, as in France, through election by the majority of the National Assembly—because it guarantees the elevation of the recognized party leader to the position of the leader of the government.

5. The essence of the British political process is the undisputed and unchallengeable supremacy of the Prime Minister over all other organs of government. As long as he commands the support of his party in the Commons, he is as irremovable from office as the

American President with his fixed term of four years. Consequently, the British system of government has recently sometimes been spoken of as Prime Ministerial instead of Cabinet government, though the appellation is not likely to gain general acceptance. The approximation of the position of the Prime Minister to that of the American President has been much noted lately. There exists, however, a fundamental difference. The President, constitutionally separated from the Congress, does not require the continued or even the initial confidence of the majority of Congress, or even only of his party in Congress. This would, in any event, be impossible in those cases in which the President does not belong to the party holding a majority in Congress or when the majorities in the Senate and in the House of Representatives differ. In Britain, by contrast, the Prime Minister and his Cabinet permanently require, and frequently seek, the confidence of the Commons or at least of their party in the Commons. Votes of confidence, moved by the opposition party, are among the great moments in the Commons. Invariably, they result in the positive endorsement of the conduct of office by the majority of the Commons. Not since the last decade of the nineteenth century has a Prime Minister been defeated in open battle in the Commons. At the present time, it is unthinkable that a Prime Minister would be compelled to resign because his party has defeated him. Consequently, while an American President has to rely on the doubtful devices of opinion polls to assess his popularity, the British Prime Minister at any time while in office can be sure of the continued support of his party.

6. The government consists of the Prime Minister, as head of the Cabinet, the Cabinet proper, and the ministry. The actual policy-making group is the Cabinet, a group of about twenty people who are the actual governing body, while the ministry comprises the less important government positions. All members of the government, without any exception, have to be and are members of one of the two houses of parliament. No person without parliamentary qualification can attain governmental office.

The Prime Minister forms his Cabinet at his discretion, whereby he will see to it that the different wings of his party are being represented. His selections of Cabinet and ministry members are automatically executed by the Crown, as are his decisions to dismiss a person from ministerial office. In passing, it may be mentioned that the manner in which Cabinet decisions are arrived at is among the weakest points of the British political process, and this in spite of a certain streamlining that was undertaken during the First World War by the establishment of a Cabinet secretariat and by the taking of minutes of Cabinet meetings which nowadays are made accessible also to the monarch.

7. Turning now to the crucial issue of the relations of government and Commons: Is it true as is often contended abroad that the government is able to force on the Commons whatever policy or statute it deems in the national interest, and even ram it down the throat of a recalcitrant parliament? With this question we are approximating the principal topic of the book under review. Once again, reality has to be divorced from myth. Undeniably, Prime Minister and Cabinet dominate and control the Commons to a degree unheard of in the United States with its separated, though allegedly coordinated, powers. By virtue of reforms of the Standing Orders introduced as long ago as the last third of the last century and the first decade of the present one, the government disposes of the time and the timetable of the Commons. For a century and more, the Commons has been laboring under the pressure of business to be attended to. Government business, therefore, has absolute priority over all motions and bills introduced by the rank-and-file of the members. Practically all legislative proposals brought before parliament are government bills drafted by the experts of the ministerial bureaucracy, again in contrast to the United States where government proposals are initiated, on behalf of the President, by individual members, or originate from the members themselves, or, through them, are initiated by interest groups. By various devices inscribed in the Standing Orders, the government is in the position to impose restrictions on the debate of the House as well as (since 1945) of the committees, such as the "guillotine" and the "kangaroo"; the former cuts off debate after a predetermined time limit has expired, the latter—resorted to in extreme cases only—determines which parts or clauses of a bill will be discussed while all others have to be voted on in the form the government has submitted them. Government spokesmen are guaranteed priority in being heard. In financial matters—in Britain always considered the core of government activity—the Commons is doomed to complete impotence. A motion involving expenditure can be lodged—and

this since the early eighteenth century—only by a minister of the Crown. Appropriations are granted exactly in the form submitted by the Chancellor of the Exchequer in his budget. The many days the Commons spends year after year on Ways and Means and Supply are, in effect, merely official opportunities for voicing criticism of the opposition toward the government policies,[1] without ever leading to so much as a penny cut from government appropriations. In short, the government proposes and, at the same time, it disposes. Certainly, to the outsider it looks like governmental dictatorship, but a dictatorship of a special kind.

v

How is this apparent emasculation of the House of Commons achieved? The principal device for the governmental control over its majority party is the institution of the whips. Its underlying psychological motivations, however, are party loyalty and party solidarity—qualities rather mysterious for foreign and, particularly, to American observers.

The whips are salaried members of the government party. They exist also for the opposition party where the chief whips in the Commons and in the Lords are likewise salaried (since 1965). Their primary function, in addition to arranging by mutual consent the timetable, is the enforcement of discipline among the members of their respective parties. Voting discipline, of course, is more crucial for the majority than the opposition party because a serious breach of party solidarity could endanger an individual legislative proposal, or even threaten the stability of the government in power. Each MP receives a statement, also called "whip," from the whips' office—incidentally, the office of the government whip is located next to the Prime Minister's residence, at Number 12 Downing Street—announcing the divisions that are to be taken. If a forthcoming division is underlined once, it indicates that the member should be present and vote for the party line, but his absence may be condoned. A two-lined whip implies that he is duty-bound to appear and vote as prescribed. If he has urgent reasons for being absent, his whip will find an absent opposition member for "pair-

[1] For an enlightening chapter on the role of the opposition see pp. 293*ff*.

ing." If an MP feels that, in good conscience, he will not be able to vote for the motion, he may obtain from his whip permission to abstain which, as a rule, is granted, though reluctantly and after arguments. In the case of a whip three times underscored, there is absolutely no chance of being permitted to abstain unless on account of grave illness. If the government operates on a slim majority, as was the case of the first Wilson Cabinet (1964 to 1966) when the government majority at times was down to four or even three, it may become necessary for an invalid member to be carried by his friends through the lobby on a stretcher—the famous and highly undignified "government by ambulance."

At this point it should be emphasized that, in cases of adverse voting behavior, a vote with the opposition against the government is considered the crime of lèse majesté. An unforgivable sin, it could lead to what in parliamentary jargon is called the "withdrawal of the whip"—that is, exclusion from the parliamentary party. The inevitable result is that, unless the ban is rescinded in time, the rebel will lose the support of his party at the next general election. If running as an "independent," his chances of retaining the seat are negligible. Voting against one's own government has become so rare for a generation and more that it is no longer considered a viable protest of an individual MP against his government's policies. About the last time it happened on a mass scale was in May, 1940, when, after the Norwegian disaster, Conservative members voted against granting Neville Chamberlain a vote of confidence, or abstained—a defection on such a scale that it forced the Prime Minister to resign and make room for Winston Churchill. Rebels among Labour are more frequent than among the Conservatives; the most distinguished was the fiery Welshman Aneurin Bevan, possibly Labour's greatest political talent of the last generation. Even Desmond Donnelly and Woodrow Wyatt of the Labour right wing, who were opposed to steel nationalization and the Prices and Incomes Act of 1966, never went so far as to vote with the opposition agianst the Labour Cabinet.

In the United States no such unconditional identification of a Representative, let alone a Senator, with his party exists. Southern Democrats can be counted on to desert the party on any issue remotely touching on their alleged privileges, particularly on civil liberties issues. Under normal conditions, Republicans as well as

Democrats are expected to maintain the party line, by and large. Statistics over the years, however, prove that the voting behavior of about 20 percent in the House and of a somewhat larger percentage in the Senate—the exclusive club of one hundred prima-donnas—cannot be counted on in advance, making forecasts on the outcome of a vote difficult. The group does not invariably consist of the same members, but the volume of opposition to the party line is rather constant.

What, then, are the motivations underlying party loyalty and party solidarity? Obviously there exist tangible reasons of political self-interest. Who kicks against the party prick must risk losing the party whip, and with it the party support at the next general elections. As mentioned before, independents find little favor with the constituency electorate. In the late thirties, Sir Stafford Cripps could afford to stand as an independent in his constituency in Bristol and be reelected, since the Labour Party refrained from setting up an official candidate. Three Conservatives who in the fifties left the party and stood for reelection, were sunk without trace. In every case, the independent had to compete with an official candidate behind whom the party threw its full support.

Moreover, the breach of party solidarity on vital issues is deeply resented by the constituency party organization which, in the first place, was responsible for choosing the candidate. This was clearly demonstrated by the fate of a mere handful of party rebels against Eden's Suez adventure who, in the decisive division in December, 1956, had abstained, if for different reasons—some of them because the campaign had been undertaken at all, others because it had been conducted incompetently or abandoned prematurely. Most of them, disowned by their constituency associations, either resigned or, when standing for election in 1959, were unsuccessful, although the Conservatives were able to increase their overall majority considerably. If the party leadership may forgive party disloyalty, the voters usually do not.

But the fear of losing the seat—the parliamentary mandate is still today a status symbol and much coveted as a public distinction—is not the whole story. The British MP believes in his party and obeys its commands, even though on occasion—and contrary to public belief such occasions are not too numerous—loyalty to his party may involve an intellectual sacrifice on his part; in such cases

Foreword

the permission to abstain may assuage his conscience. Party loyalty in Britain is a deeply ingrained psychological attitude for whose explanation mercurial motivations are insufficient. Change in party affiliation—"crossing the floor" in parliamentary lingo—has become exceedingly rare. A Churchill could afford it, though with the risk of being permanently considered unreliable. Party loyalty and party solidarity, hence, are part of the peculiar mystique of British parliamentarianism.

Party solidarity, however, differs insofar as the majority or the opposition party is involved. No MP—whether Conservative or Labour—would ever violate the parliamentary canon to the extent that his adverse vote would endanger his government. Conversely, a member of the opposition party, knowing full well that it will be beaten in the division regardless of what he does, may be more inclined to disregard the party orders carried to him through the whips and follow his own conscience. Different attitudes are observable here between Conservatives and Labour and also concerning the subject matter of an individual division, whether referring to domestic or to foreign policies.

vi

This leads to the main issue with which the book under discussion is concerned. It deals with the generally little-explored subject of the attitude of the rank-and-file in both parties—the so-called backbenchers—toward their party. The distinctive merit of the book would appear to be that it combats the misconception generally held abroad that the individual member is nothing but the docile slave of the party managers. The situation requires an antecedent discussion of the position of the individual MP within the frame of the British political process.

Officially, all MP's who do not belong to the governing group in Cabinet and ministry and who are not included in the "shadow cabinet" of the opposition, in permanent readiness to assume the government, are spoken of as the "private members," more colloquially as the backbenchers because they sit behind the front benches to the right and the left of the Speaker which are occupied by the leading government and opposition figures, respectively. Since the government personnel, including the parliamentary secretaries and other functionaries, at present number more than 100, to which some twenty members of the shadow cabinet have been added, the total number of private members runs somewhat above 500, that is, five sixths of the present number of 630 of the members of the House of Commons. It is uncontested that, in general, the political power of the rank-and-file of the Commons has decreased in the measure that the power of the Prime Minister and his Cabinet has increased. The impotence of the private members has been deplored—and more or less in vain—for several generations. As early as the eighteenth century, when British parliamentarianism was in its puberty, the sharp-eyed Rousseau could declare that the British people are free only on the day when they elect their parliament and that, thereafter, they were slaves without liberty; and this although he knew nothing of rotten and pocket boroughs and the immense corruption of the electoral process at his time. The complaint about the humiliating subordination of the rank-and-file to the dictates of their leaders has been vigorously articulated ever since. Walter Bagehot, in his classic, *The British Constitution* (1869), sardonically observed that "any well-trained poodle could do most of the duties of the average member of parliament." And the biting verse at the head of this introduction penned by W. S. Gilbert shortly thereafter (1881) is in the same vein. Contemporary observers express their evaluation of the influence of the backbenchers in even more drastic terms. The question, therefore, has been raised ever since whether the stability of the British Government, conditioned by the enforced party discipline, has not been bought at too heavy a price; namely, the loss of intellectual self-determination of the rank-and-file. Frequently the political disfranchisement of the private members is identified with the alleged decline of the House of Commons at large, a contention which obviously ignores or minimizes the inevitable ascendancy of the Prime Minister in the British political process.

The recurrent lament about the political emasculation of the backbenchers is justified. A distinction, however, has to be made between the day-by-day conduct of the political process on the one hand, and the overall impact of the party members on the political leadership on the other. In general, the range of the political and particularly the legislative action of the private members is very limited. The mass of them are completely barred from any participation in the policy-formation process monopolized by the Prime Minister in consultation with trusted members of his Cabinet and certain dignitaries of the party hierarchy. All the private member is called on to do is to vote on the government proposals and bills that incorporate the policy decisions. His own legislative initiative is most severely restricted. Practically all legislation coming before the parliament is government-sponsored and goverment-drafted. At the beginning of each session a lottery is held to designate a limited number of Friday afternoons—when, as part of the weekend, the attendance of the House is meager—on which a private-member bill is given the chance of a second reading. But the lucky winner is by no means out of the woods. The government is in the habit of claiming even these afternoons for government business. And the private-member bill is assured success only if and when the government supports it or even takes it over as a government bill. However, one of the recent cases in which a private member-bill finally reached the statute book was Sidney Silverman's Murder (Abolition of Death Penalty) Act of 1965 which he had pressed indefatigably for many years.

The rare opportunity that the rank-and-file can make their own legislative decision comes when the whips of both parties permit the so-called free vote. All of them, without exception, pertain to controversial matters of a nonpolitical character; examples were the amendment of the Anglican prayer book which has to be voted on by parliament; the opening of cinemas and other places of public entertainment on Sundays; the permissibility of medical abortion; the alleviation of criminal penalties for homosexuality; and similar socially significant measures. Such occasions, however, are infrequent; even for the transition from the sterling to the decimal system (1967) the whips were put on by the Wilson Cabinet although a free vote would have resulted in an adequate majority.

Nonetheless, the contention that the private members are driven like sheep through the division lobbies by their whips is exaggerated. On closer analysis the private member has considerable opportunity for making himself seen and heard. In the daily question time, which the ministers and their civil servants take very seriously, he has practically the monopoly of criticizing the administration. He also frequently uses the so-called ten-minute rule after question time to call the attention of the Government and the public to legislative gaps or administrative grievances. Moreover, his talents are given free rein in the committees to which in the course of the legislative process each bill is being sent. In the technical discussions, clause by clause, he can show his mettle; government bills are frequently changed and amended in committee. He also may serve as one of the "added members" who, because of their technical knowledge, are attached to a specific committee. In short, he is not barred from making valuable contributions to the legislative process as well as to efficient and fair administration, and by doing so he may attract the attention of the party whips and the ministers with the result that, having earned his spurs, he may later be called on to fill a vacancy in a minor government office as the first rung of the ladder to political leadership. The recently introduced institution of the ombudsman, called Parliamentary Commissioner, may prove his usefulness to his constituency. If it is true, hence, that the private member is the foot-slogging soldier under the command of the party generals, no battle can be won by the generals alone. Subordinate the private member may be, yet he is indispensable. To this may be added that the parliamentary personnel of today is of a high educational and intellectual caliber. At least two thirds of the men and women in both parties have academic diplomas or their equivalents. The average MP is intellectually not inferior to his French or German counterpart and possibly superior to many of his American colleagues.

Moreover—and now we are entering the special plot our author has chosen to cultivate—the political and legislative omnipotence of Prime-Ministerial government is limited by the willingness of the rank-and-file of the government party to go along with the government policies. The whips serve as a two-way street; not only do they convey to the MP's assigned to their tutelage the instructions of the party leadership, they also report back the opinions, the doubts, and the objections of the rank-and-file. Britain is a small country with excellent rail and air communications. Most MP's are in the habit of the weekend visit with their constituencies to discuss current events with officials of their party and also with members of other parties. What they learn by such grass-roots contacts they refer back to the whips who, in turn, keep the party leadership informed. This is quite different from the United States where the relations between the Congressman and "his" electoral district are, at best, tenuous and intermittent, often maintained only by "letters to your Congressman," and these frequently are initiated by a pressure group. Who reads the Monday morning column: "How Congressmen from this area voted last week"?

Similarly, the periodical party caucuses to which ministers are invited serve as an outlet for responsible party opinion which even a government with a large majority is well advised to heed. In addition, the private members of each party are organized in informal working groups, charged with discussing specific topics such as trade and industry, defense, or foreign policy. Those of the government party are in frequent contact with the minister in charge of a bill. No political or legislative surprise can be sprung on the rank-and-file since agenda and timetable are invariably arranged between the whips of both parties. Consequently, if the government plans a legislative action which it finds, through the whips and other channels, to be very obnoxious to the rank-and-file, it will either meet substantial objections by concessions or, in extreme cases, drop the proposal altogether.

It is this aspect of mutual give-and-take between government and majority party that constitutes the bulk of Ronald Butt's book. The process is spelled out by chapter and verse. For example, the Shops Bill, introduced in 1956 by a Conservative government, aiming at a uniform regulation of the closing hours for retail stores, was fully endorsed by the retail trade associations, but had to be dropped by the government in the face of the resistance of many of its own backbenchers.[2] One of the most telling episodes of backbench opposition in recent years was the Resale Price Act of 1965[3] which dealt with what is known in this country as fair trade legislation: to wit, whether manufacturers of brand-name merchandise, amounting in Great Britain to 40 percent of all retail trade, are legally entitled to maintain a uniform retail sales price. The issue was, and remains, economically double-edged. While increased competition is generally considered desirable, release from administered prices would benefit the stores with a large turnover but would hurt the small shopkeeper whose protection is a traditional

[2] See pp. 220 *ff.*
[3] Pp. 251 *ff.*

Conservative policy. The passage, if with certain concessions, was secured only when the minister in charge, Edward H. Heath, threatened to resign.

This was an authentic "revolt of the backbenchers," a situation any government, regardless of how large its majority may be, fears and tries to avoid at any cost. This phenomenon is understood to be a collective resistance of a sizeable group of government supporters, possibly led by older, respected members, which makes its opposition to a government policy or bill known to the party leadership through the whips, the party caucus, and other means of communication. In an institution whose climate favors the compromise between government and opposition as well as within the government majority, such situations are relatively rare. But in the past they have occurred, leading, for example, in 1886 to the split of the Liberal Party over Home Rule for Ireland; in the early twenties to the break between the Lloyd George and the Asquith Liberals from which the Liberals have never recovered; and in 1931 to the desertion of Prime Minister MacDonald by the entire Labour Party, with the exception of ten. Even today, with strengthened party discipline, a revolt of the backbenchers may still occur even though it will no longer lead to a substantial defection of government backbenchers because the government will always blunt it either by making concessions or by putting its foot down.

A most characteristic episode occurred recently in the second Wilson Cabinet which, it will be remembered, was returned in the election of 1966 with a majority of over 90. Faced with repeated attacks on his policies, particularly in foreign affairs—retrenchment east of Suez and British support for the American war in Vietnam —Mr. Wilson, in the party caucus in July, 1967,[4] offered a blunt warning to his followers in the form of the now-famous illustration of the "biting dog": every dog is entitled to one bite, but from a persistent biter the license would be withdrawn. The taste of this simile may be doubted, but it was effective: Members are sent to Westminster on the party ticket to vote for the government, and any opposition has its limits. In extreme cases the government may stake its continuation in office on enforcing party solidarity. This happened even during the last war when a majority composed of all

[4] See p. 291

parties voted for equal pay for women. On the next day Churchill made the repeal of the resolution a matter of confidence, and it was repealed.

Even the most cursory review of recent British history will demonstrate the power of the rank-and-file of the government party to force a change of the leadership of the party and, thereby, bring about a change in the leadership of the government. The famous Carlton House meeting of the Conservative MP's in 1922—the origin of the 1922 Committee, still today an important organ in the Conservative Party organization—insisted on the installation of Bonar Law in the place of the discredited leadership of Austen Chamberlain–Arthur Balfour. After the infamous Hoare–Laval agreement that sold out Ethiopia to Mussolini, the backbenchers were instrumental in forcing the resignation of the Foreign Secretary, Sir Samuel Hoare (1937). The massive defection of the backbenchers—the government majority fell from 240 to 81—compelled Neville Chamberlain to make room for Winston Churchill (May, 1940). In 1957, Anthony Eden, after the failure of the Suez adventure, resigned though reasons of health were given as the official explanation. The master tactician, Harold Macmillan, was able to weather the storm of the Profumo scandal (June, 1963), but his position was so shaken that an impending operation (October, 1963) was a convenient cover for his retirement from the Prime Ministership, to be replaced by Sir Alec Douglas-Home.

Whether sustained reverses of the Labour Party, as evidenced by disastrous by-elections in March, 1968, will compel a change of leadership in the Labour Party—Roy Jenkins is being spoken of as the heir-presumptive—may seem moot at this juncture. Though diminished, Wilson's majority is still over 70, with the legislative term not expiring before early 1971. By that time much water will have flowed under London Bridge.

vii

The attitude of the rank-and-file, the private members or the backbenchers of both parties, constitutes the primary subject of Ronald Butt's meritorious study. Throughout the author, well versed in political theory and constitutional history, proceeds from the assumption that Burke's famous hypothesis of the parliamentary representative as being a free agent, not bound by instructions from his voters, if ever it were true, has been replaced by the much stronger bondage of the MP to the interests and the injunctions of his party; to disregard these as an allegedly free agent he is no longer capable. Perhaps the only parliament in the world in which the classic Burkean concept of free representation is still alive today is the American Congress, and it may be by no means accidental considering the simultaneousness of Burke's and the founding fathers' political philosophy. However, the submission to the party commands even today is not unconditional. One may argue with the author that the title of his book, *The Power of Parliament,* is an overstatement of the situation. It might have been preferable to speak of the "influence" or the "impact" of parliament which, of course, is rather less than power.

It is fortunate that the subject of this research has found so well qualified an author. Now in his late forties and with an Oxonian First in History, he was successively political correspondent, political editor, and editorial writer of the London *Financial Times,* and is widely known as a political columnist. At present he is the assistant editor of the respected *Sunday Times.* An expert in constitutional history, to which the book abundantly testifies, he was given in 1965 a research fellowship in Oxford during which time the major part of the book was written. What gives the book its specific flavor is the inside information, what actually happened, which the author was able to elicit from personal interviews with government and party leaders as well as with individual participants in backbench opposition. What we have, therefore, is less a learned treatise on constitutional customs and political practices than an unusual picture of what has been going on in what may be called the parliamentary mind, that mysterious collective compound of many and different individual capacities.

The author has divided the parliamentary history of the more recent past and present into time periods to find out how far and with what results parliamentary opposition has manifested itself. After a survey of parliament in the nineteenth century—the contemporary political process actually begins in 1867—these periods are discussed: 1918 to 1931, the crucial year in which, with the breakdown of MacDonald's second Labour (and minority) government, the entire structure of the functioning parliamentary institutions was placed in jeopardy, to be rescued—if this is the proper term—by a Conservative rule (under Stanley Baldwin). Conservative ascendancy, with the short interval of Labour (1945 to 1951), was to last all told thirty-four years. The influence of the backbenchers is presented in the subsequent key chapters dealing, respectively, with the periods from 1931 to 1945 (Prime Ministerships of Baldwin, Neville Chamberlain, and Winston Churchill); 1945 to 1951 (Clement Attlee); 1951 to 1956 (Churchill and Anthony Eden); 1956 to 1964 (Harold Macmillan and Sir Alec Douglas-Home); and 1964 to 1966 (first and second Harold Wilson Cabinets). Added to this core are illuminating chapters on the "independent" MP—today *avis rarissima;* parliament and opposition; parliament and civil service (Whitehall); and finally on the public relations of parliament from which this writer learned a good deal without being convinced that our author sees the whole picture. In the handling of its "image" through the cultivation of public relations, the "mother of parliament" is still among the most backward institutions of its kind, dependent on the goodwill of the reporters in the press, the radio, and on television. Much of this is old-fashioned, often incompetent and inferior, in comparison, for example, with the coverage of parliamentary affairs in France or Germany or, for that matter, even in the United States.

The book deals with events and material up to 1966–67, but reports from Great Britain almost daily focus on the author's theme of how the individual MP's are able to reconcile their personal views with the party injunctions on the one hand, and the pressures exercised by their constituencies on the other. A case in point is the racial dilemma that suddenly has emerged and is splitting both parties right down the middle. The MP is torn between the imperative of his conscience that requires fairness toward all citizens regardless of color of skin, and the aversion of his constituency to the influx of "colored," by which term the British mean high-grade Pakistanis and Indians as well as authentic Negroes from the West Indies and Africa, an aversion that is particularly pronounced if a locality is already burdened with a colored population. Step by step public opinion has forced the parliamentary parties to enact legislation restricting further immigration, first with the Immigrants Act of a Conservative government (1962), setting annual quotas. Subsequently, Labour further reduced immigration and finally closed the door to the Pakistanis and Indians left stranded by the nationalist legislation in Kenya, this despite the fact that they carry British passports. The immorality of the humiliating measure was deeply felt by responsible members of both parties, but the act was passed. And the conflict of conscience is repeated in the most recent bill for fair housing and equal employment. The members may sincerely be willing to grant it, but the constituencies, emotionalized by the altogether unreal fear of a "colored" Britain, are strongly opposed, as was dramatized by the intemperate speech of the Conservative leader Enoch Powell. Yet the measure could not fail to pass, although with substantial modifications in committee.

To summarize the findings of a book for the reader cannot be the purpose of an introduction. All it can do is to whet his appetite. It fulfills its proper function when it is able to point out the position the author takes within the general frame of British parliamentarism, a task which the book's last two chapters also serve. But it can be predicted with a good deal of conviction that the attention the American reader may pay to so unique a political institution as the British parliament will be rewarding.

KARL LOEWENSTEIN

Amherst, Mass.
May 15, 1968

THE POWER OF PARLIAMENT

Introduction

This book is an attempt to assess the place of Parliament in the practice of contemporary politics. It seeks to understand what Parliament actually does in the politics of the mid-twentieth century and to show how far it still fulfils the same sort of functions as those it performed when parliamentary influence was allegedly greater. Does Parliament retain, if not the same, at least a roughly equivalent utility in the political community? Has Parliament lost power? What sort of power does it now have? What has been the essential nature of parliamentary 'power'—and is 'power' the right word?

For purposes of comparison and as a help towards understanding the essential characteristics of Parliament, the first sections of this study are historical, but they make no claim to be constitutional history in the ordinary sense. Further, the book is not a mechanistic account of how Parliament functions as an institution, nor is it a study of procedure. Such works are already liberally available. Finally, although one purpose of this book is to provide a background of practical parliamentary politics against which some of the contemporary criticisms of Parliament can be assessed, it does not offer schemes of reform: these are already plentiful to the point of excess, not to say repetition. By providing an insight into Parliament's essential function, however, the study does seek to make it easier to judge the validity of allegations that Parliament has declined and the relevance of particular schemes of reform.

It is primarily to see whether it is possible to discern any essential and continuing political function for Parliament, underlying all the changing forms and constitutional fictions, that the historical sections of this book have been written. The essay on the origins and development of Parliament up to the eighteenth century and the chapter on the nineteenth century which follows it have not been inspired by romantic antiquarianism but by the belief that a long perspective

1

provides a clearer understanding of the essential nature of parliamentary activity. It may be argued that I am straying in the realms of ontology; that Parliament, despite its long institutional history, has had no consistently essential historical function; that the idea of any essential nature is a meaningless concept. But if so, then it is also beside the mark to accuse Parliament of having declined. Moreover, although it would be foolish to defend Parliament on the ground that it was antique, it is undeniable that its antiquity is an essential element contributing to its authority. We respect an institution the more because it has not been improvised to meet a political expediency: because it antedates contemporary problems and can be expected to outlive them: because it passes on the accumulated techniques of government, acceptable in a particular community, from one generation to the next. No political institution has ever owed more to the evolving attitudes of an unusually cohesive nation and less to the political theorists than the British Parliament. For this reason alone, students of its contemporary function cannot entirely ignore its history.

No constitution, written or unwritten, is worth more than the political temper of the community allows it to be worth. The best of paper constitutions is worthless if applied to an unstable, divided, or intolerant community. The worst of paper constitutions can evolve into something better in the right political atmosphere. It would be wholly wrong to suppose that a written constitution was inevitably more static than an unwritten one or that an unwritten constitution was necessarily the more capable of growth. The most superficial knowledge of American and British history demonstrates that the capacity for constitutional development depends, not on whether a constitution is written (the American) or unwritten (the British) but on the political spirit of the nation.

For this reason, I have thought it worthwhile to start with an account of the political attitudes of the community in which Parliament originally evolved and to follow this up by relating the growth of the institution to the successive political situations to which it responded. The historical political persona of Parliament has lent zest to research into its origins and development, yet a narrow institutional view of Parliament can be a distorted one. It can give the impression that our political attitudes have been entirely created by Parliament whereas (although Parliament has fostered their growth) it might be equally true to say that our political attitudes have created Parliament. Moreover, a strictly institutional view of Parlia-

2

ment—and it is in this that the romance is perhaps to be found—may leave the wholly inappropriate impression that Parliament, in some teleological way, was working throughout its history towards a kind of final perfection which, once attained, was the fount of all our civic and political virtue. A common myth has been that this perfection was reached in the nineteenth century and that Parliament has steadily declined in potency since then. The truth is rather that, whether Parliament is more or less influential than it was, its place in politics and its evolution in any particular period depend on the hard political facts of that period and the way in which the inherited political character of the nation—which included inherited parliamentary attitudes—digests them. This is as true of the twentieth century as it was of the nineteenth, the seventeenth or the thirteenth.

Sir Kenneth Pickthorn, a constitutional historian who was himself a Member of Parliament, observed very aptly that 'procedure is all the Constitution the poor Briton has'.[1] Obedience to parliamentary procedure; the agreement of majorities and minorities to work within it as a method of dealing with their daily problems, are together the essence of British liberties. But this is only so because procedure can be changed and adapted to meet new problems. What is important about procedure is the underlying political spirit that particular rules and conventions embody: the idea of political method that procedure expresses in a changing way as circumstances change.

For all these reasons, I have leant heavily on the historical approach in the 'contemporary' as well as in the 'historical' sections of this book. In the historical first part of the book, I have followed the short account of Parliament's political rôle in earlier centuries with chapters which take us up to the end of the Second World War, where, for the purposes of this book, I have taken history to end and modern politics to begin. It will be obvious that, for the earliest sections of the book, I have relied greatly on the historical scholarship of others, though I have extensively consulted printed original sources and, for the nineteenth and twentieth centuries, have sought to trace from the printed records of the period what rôle Parliament seemed, to the eyes of contemporaries, to be playing. The scale of the first historical sections of the book is inevitably telescoped but, as the study moves into the twentieth century it gradually spreads out. In a study primarily directed to the understanding of contemporary politics this seems plainly to be the right proportion. Similarly,

[1] H.C. Deb., Vol. 617, col. 70, February 8, 1960.

because the focal point of the book, as a whole, is contemporary politics, I have taken Parliament for the purposes of this study to mean essentially the House of Commons. The House of Lords is referred to in the earlier chapters only incidentally where it is relevant to the main objective of the book.

In the second half of the book I have largely continued with a historical narrative approach since it seemed that only in this way could any attempt be made to show convincingly what Parliament does now: what its influence really amounts to. But for these later chapters of the book, my sources are of a different kind from those on which I drew for the earlier sections. Primarily, I have relied on my own acquaintance, as a political journalist, with the political and parliamentary history through which we have recently passed. Of course, there is always a clear distinction between 'old' history and 'contemporary' history. Each has its advantages and disadvantages. The conventional historian has the advantage of perspective: he has the papers but cannot meet the people concerned. The student of contemporary history can draw upon the people concerned but he cannot generally see the papers. The contemporary historian, however, often has another disadvantage. He is sometimes obliged to consult persons who are his sources wholly after the event, by which time they have had time to rationalise the position they took up at the time they were actively engaged in the affair under discussion. Of course, the danger of error arising from this tendency can be minimised by extensive cross-checking, but there is a limit to how far this corrective can be applied. Moreover, the contemporary historian is also flooded (and this will make the task of future historians much more difficult) with the memoirs of politicians, each of whom has arranged and presented his case. In writing the chapters of this book which deal with Parliament for the last decade, however, I have tried to add a fresh dimension by drawing on my own knowledge of what people said at the time (as distinct from what they say now) and on private and naturally non-attributable conversations with many of the chief political figures concerned. But in no case have I relied entirely on the knowledge I acquired on the day or even in the month concerned. No one is more conscious than the journalist of the inevitable margin of error which may arise from his close perspective, the speed of his work, the lack of time for all the cross-checking he would like, and the vulnerability he has to any of his sources who may wish to tell, in any sense, less than the truth, which is something he cannot always know until after the event. I have therefore cross-checked my own knowledge of particular episodes with the written work of others: the written record of parliamentary and governmental proceedings; conversations with some of the participants after the event: and above all, where I could, with those who were concerned in the events with which I have dealt and whom I believe to be able and willing (whatever their private views about the merits of a particular political argument) to make a dispassionate assessment of its relevance to my theme and who have the special knowledge to be able to do so. My experience is that British government, in the widest sense, is not so closed as is often suggested; that to those who do not abuse confidences and who are prepared to read the fairly liberal documentation of political events much knowledge is readily available. Using these techniques I have examined in some depth one or two specific instances of parliamentary influence in the mid-twentieth century in the belief that this may add a dimension of understanding of what Parliament effectively does in the large issues of politics. In the process, I hope that I may also have added a little to contemporary political history in a wider sense.

Criticism of Parliament has a long history. In this century it has been almost incessant since parliamentarians were depressed, after the First World War, by a sense of lost independence and by the encroachments of bureaucracy and government action. Such criticisms have become particularly strong in recent years, however, and since the focus of this book is on the contemporary rôle of the House of Commons, I take as my point of departure the criticisms of parliamentary efficacy made in the last decade.

After the 1959 General Election, which brought Harold Macmillan's Conservative Government back to power with an increased majority and which seemed, to many politicians and observers, to presage the break-up of the Labour Party,[1] or at least its

---

[1] See Sir Ivor Jennings, *Party Politics*, Vol. II: *The Growth of Farties* (Cambridge, 1961), pp. 378–9: 'The emergence of a dominant personality, though this seems unlikely in the early sixties, would fundamentally alter the situation. A major international event, too, would have a profound effect on British politics. If, however, the present lines of development could be projected into the future, the next ten years would probably see a gradual decline in the fortunes of the Labour Party. It has attained its true objectives, the Welfare State, and is finding difficulty in attuning its organisation and methods to the social and economic structure of the United Kingdom.'

banishment from power for another decade, criticism of Parliament became insistent and strident. Articles in learned journals and news-papers poured forth to demonstrate the impotence and low calibre of parliamentarians: the frustration of life at Westminster: the inadequacy of Parliament as a modern instrument of government unless its procedure were drastically reformed. Politicians themselves joined vigorously in the analysis of the problem of Parliament, and television and radio programmes swelled the chorus of discontent.

It was manifestly part of a national mood of introspection in which hardly a single established institution escaped criticism. Funda-mentally, perhaps, this may have been the nation's psychological response to the difficulty of adjusting itself to its reduced international status in the post-war world. For a time, the affluence of consumers and the new prosperity of the middle classes had staved off dis-illusion. But soon after 1959 it became clear that the nation had failed to solve its fundamental economic difficulties. For whatever reasons, industry appeared to be failing to modernise itself fast enough to provide the country with a balanced economy. The new recruits to the middle classes, people without either benefit of capital or of public school education, were showing themselves im-patient with traditional class divisions: lip-service to the idea of a classless society began to be paid by supporters of all parties. It was argued that the 'old-boy net' had a stranglehold on every branch of British communal life, from the board room and the City to the traditional recruits to politics and the Civil Service. Envious eyes were being cast across the Channel at the rapid expansion of the Common Market countries: Britain, it was argued, had lost her momentum because her institutions had fallen out of date. A 'What's wrong with Britain?' mood prevailed and this was undoubtedly heightened by the growing disillusion with the performance of the Conservative Government under Macmillan in the first years of the 1960s. Inevitably the question was asked 'What's wrong with Parliament?'—a question which appeared as the title of one book in a series, published by Penguin, each of which asked what was wrong with one aspect or another of British life and institutions.[1] In a mood of national masochism, the British people lashed themselves with the whips of odious comparisons: why were other countries

[1] Andrew Hill and Anthony Whichelow, *What's Wrong with Parliament?* (Penguin, 1964). The authors are believed to be Clerks of the House of Commons using pen-names.

apparently doing so much better than ourselves? An almost uniform answer was that we were mesmerised by our past to such an extent that we were failing to concentrate on the challenge of the present: we were, it was said, too much attached to ancient monuments and antique ceremonials and insufficiently interested in the automation of our factories and in planning the life of the nation. The Conservative Party was so pervaded by the mood of self-doubt that it was even prepared to go over to a form of planning in obeisance to the current demand for modernisation. Many of the criticisms of institutions were facile: historians, as they study the search for institutional panacea in the 1960s, may ask why the British people were so convinced that the fault lay in their institutions rather than in themselves and in their social and economic habits.

No effective institution in British government is more ancient than Parliament: none has more jealously preserved the outward and visible signs of antiquity. This very fact was an affront to some modernisers who, themselves, seemed to fall into the trap of paying too much attention to the formalities of parliamentary life and too little to the real place of Parliament in politics. Anyone who reads extensively the bibliography of parliamentary criticism will be struck, first by the repetitious nature of much of the limited array of criticisms and remedies: secondly, by the fact that many of the criticisms appear, when subjected to analysis, mutually irreconcilable.

Criticisms of Parliament have been made by academics, journalists and by politicians themselves, inside and outside Parliament. The House of Commons has appointed a series of Select Committees on Procedure since the Second World War to consider what might be done to improve the efficiency of the House. The latest of these Select Committees heard evidence and reported in the Parliaments of 1964 and 1966. Some reference will be made in later chapters to the more important suggestions for reform made in these reports, in so far as they are relevant to the broad functions of Parliament, although the House, during the writing of this book, had not completed its decisions on the findings of the Select Committee.

Much of the general criticism of the House of Commons has been rational. On the other hand, some of the attacks on it have been too exaggerated to carry conviction with anyone who gives them serious thought. Unfortunately, criticism of Parliament has, in recent years, become so fashionable an intellectual position that even the wildest accusations seldom provoke correction. Conditioned, therefore, by the incessant drip of unanswered scorn that falls upon Parliament, the public may be in danger of lumping together the reasonable and the unreasonable criticisms of the House of Commons, accepting both as equally valid. In particular, the widespread obsession with the ceremony of the House and its forms of procedure is such that there is a widespread tendency to believe that the anachronisms to be found in both are a greater hindrance to genuine parliamentary influence than is really the case. The purpose of this book is to try to present enough evidence of the part that the House of Commons now plays, and has played, in politics for it to be possible to separate the real from the superficial shortcomings of Parliament. At the outset, it is convenient to sort into broad categories the most important charges against the efficacy of Parliament.

Decline. Although the most rational critics of Parliament have been careful to deny any intention of suggesting that Parliament has fallen away from some golden age, the notion of decline runs through virtually all the criticisms and, indeed, the word itself has been freely used. For example, in an editorial article entitled 'The Decline of Parliament', the *Political Quarterly* (July–September, 1963) discussed what it regarded as 'at best' the 'below-average quality' of the 1959 Parliament but asserted that the problem was not, unfortunately, just one of the previous four years. 'The signs are that Parliament itself is in decline—losing in popular esteem, losing in the degree of control it should exercise over the government, failing to adapt itself to the complexity of the tasks the quickened tempo of modern life has thrust upon it.' A year later similar arguments were put forward in a further article in the *Political Quarterly* by one of its editors, Professor William A. Robson (Professor Emeritus of Public Administration in the University of London), on 'The Reform of Government'. It was again argued that 'the status of Parliament has declined to a serious extent during the post-war era: and if this tendency is to be reversed the House of Commons must be prepared to assert its right and authority more forcibly than it has done in recent decades. After all, the *power* of Parliament is intact: it is the will to exercise it which is lacking. No Government, whatever its political complexion, is going to make the first move towards enhancing the status of Parliament: the initiative must come from the House of Commons.'

Few of the critics were precise about the period and nature of Parliament's decline, but the authors of *What's Wrong with Parliament?* were prepared to be specific. They contrasted the decline of

8

Parliament in public esteem with its status at the end of the last war. 'In 1945 the reputation of the British Parliament stood as high as ever before in its long history', the authors stated and they cited the vigilance of the Commons during the war, when the Prime Minister and the Government had been provided with extraordinary powers for the purpose of defending the realm. These authors also deduced a decline in the public's interest in Parliament from the evidence of a sharply declining sale in the number of copies of *Hansard* between 1945 and 1963. They further illustrated the disillusion of Members of Parliament themselves by citing a list of men of calibre who had left the House of Commons in the years before 1963.

One of the most comprehensive statements of the case for reform from an academic writer was made by Professor Bernard Crick.[1] He specifically stated that he had no sympathy with the argument that Parliament had declined from some golden age in which it had 'governed' or for the idea that the rule of 630 independent minds would either be possible or preferable to party government. He regarded party as essential; indeed, one of the main reasons why Professor Crick wanted to see Members of Parliament, rather than external bodies or officials, involved in the job of scrutinising the evolution of Government policy was precisely because he resisted the contemporary urge to take governmental problems out of the hands of politicians and put them in the hands of judges, Royal Commissions and other neutral bodies or individuals. 'This is really the root of the *malaise* in contemporary British government—the belief that is growing up in Downing Street and Whitehall that if anything useful is to be done, it must be taken out of politics. . . . There has grown up a cult of "Wise Men" who are to be consulted if anything "goes wrong", distinguished public figures, but never politicians, all with an aura of "very responsible fellows indeed" about them, to hide how politically irresponsible they are.' For political decisions should be made by politicians, who can be held responsible by the electorate, not by distinguished figures who cannot be.[2]

Yet Parliament was, according to Professor Crick's diagnosis, failing to do the job which was the only realistic job it could do in modern conditions—informing and alerting the public on matters

[1] Bernard Crick, *The Reform of Parliament* (Weidenfeld & Nicolson, 1964).

[2] Ibid., p. 176. See also, Bernard Crick, *In Defence of Politics* (Weidenfeld & Nicolson, 1962).

which would influence its vote. He accepted the need for strong government, but argued that strong government needed, but was not getting, strong opposition and criticism. He conceded that there was nothing new in the dominance of House of Commons procedure by the Executive. But there was now an attitude of mind that parliamentary proceedings were a waste of Ministerial time. He denied both that the real opposition was provided from within the governing Party and that the swing of the pendulum was guaranteed to provide us with governments of alternating parties. For these reasons, liberty was in danger. Members of Parliament had become, because they seemed happy to be so, 'rubber stamps'. To Professor Crick's account of what was wrong and what should be done to put it right I shall refer again, but his statement that Parliament had become a rubber stamp seemed to postulate that it had declined from something better.

But academic writers held no monopoly in arguing that there had been a decline. As though some entirely new disaster had burst upon Parliament in the preceding few years, politicians and journalists produced article after article along similar lines. Some were uncompromising in their pessimism and all-embracing in their dismissal of the House of Commons as a political organ. Mr Humphry Berkeley, the Conservative Member for Lancaster (who subsequently lost his seat in the 1966 General Election) stated bluntly: 'Well, it's dead. Nobody attends debates, and this gives a general atmosphere of lifelessness about the whole place. Of course, power has now by-passed the House of Commons; it's exercised by other bodies by and large, such as Neddy, Nicky, the Trade Unions and, of course, the Cabinet itself.'[1] Mr Grimond, the Leader of the Liberal

---

[1] Mr Berkeley was speaking in a television symposium on Power and Parliament, an enquiry broadcast by the BBC on June 20, 1963. Readers may need to be reminded that 'Nicky' was the short-lived National Incomes Commission which was widely recognised as a political non-starter soon after its inception. It was instituted in 1962 as part of the then Conservative Government's attempt to obtain some influence over the rise in incomes. 'Neddy', the National Economic Development Council, also a creation of the Macmillan Government, remains (in 1967) as an adjunct to the Labour Government's planning machinery, though before coming to power Labour had intended to abolish it. But the 'power' of 'Neddy', in the sense of producing the National Economic Plan, whatever that may be worth, has passed to the Government's Department of Economic Affairs. While 'Nicky' is no more and 'Neddy' is down-graded, Parliament, on the other hand, is still with us.

Party, on the same occasion, said simply: 'Power has left it.' He went on: 'What the Employers' Federation, or the Trade Unions or other pressure groups may say to the government in private is probably of much more importance in determining policy than what is said across the floor in the House of Commons. What is said in Party Committees in private, again secretly, is of more importance than what is said in public in the House of Commons. The House of Commons is becoming a place in which there is a gladiatorial display between the front benches followed very often by a lot of backbenchers reading things into their local newspapers.' Implicit in Mr Berkeley's observation that the House of Commons was dead was presumably the belief that it had once been alive and that there had been a decline. Implicit in Mr Grimond's statement that power had left it was the belief that it had once had 'power', by which Mr Grimond appeared to mean power exercised on, or across, the floor of the House. It will be one purpose of this book to discern how far its traditional power was of this nature and how far it has been lost.

But the politicians of both major parties also examined (apart from the Select Committees of the House) the problem of Parliament's decline far more formally than on television and in newspapers. In 1963, a group of Conservative Members of Parliament concerned with industry produced a pamphlet which set out to decide what was wrong with Parliament and how it could be improved.[1] The starting point of their argument was the Government's involvement in an increasingly vast and complicated network of detailed and highly technical activity, notably concerned with the economy, which it was difficult for Parliament, as at present constituted, to scrutinise, control, or even understand. Parliament no longer had the capacity to oversee the Executive that it had once possessed. In advance of the General Election of 1964, a group of Labour Members also discussed what had gone wrong with Parliament and produced their plan for reform.[2] But before referring to these and other remedies, I turn from the general notion of 'decline'—which we shall be able to

[1] *Parliament and Government in Our Industrial Society*, by a group of Conservative Members of Parliament, published by the Conservative Political Centre, 1963. The Chairman of the group was Sir William Robson Brown: its drafting committee was under the Chairmanship of Mr Airey Neave. The group, which was not an official Party body, took advice from industrialists, trade union leaders and others.

[2] *Three Dozen Parliamentary Reforms by One Dozen Parliamentary Socialists* (Socialist Commentary, 1964).

check against the historical section of this study—to a more specific account of what is alleged to be wrong with Parliament now, whether or not this represents a falling away.

Parliament and the Executive. The most serious of the charges against Parliament is that it has ceased to have any serious influence over the Executive. The House of Commons now, so it is often alleged, is little more than an electoral college through and from which the nation elects the Cabinet or, more specifically, the Prime Minister. Once in its place, the Government, backed by a majority of the House of Commons, cannot be shifted and is free to pursue what policies it likes. For the Government makes every issue of any importance a matter of confidence and its followers will never desert it in effective numbers on a vote if doing so means defeat in the House, the overthrow of the Government and the handing of office to their political opponents. To the extent that the rank and file of a governing Party can persuade their leaders to give them an occasional sop, they exercise such powers of persuasion as they have inside private backbench Party Committees and not on the floor of the House where (so it is implied) it is proper that they should be exercised. 'The position of a Member of Parliament in Opposition is now difficult enough, but the position of a backbench Member of Parliament supporting a government in power has become almost absurd', wrote the future Editor of *The Times* and former Conservative candidate, William Rees-Mogg, in a pamphlet after the Conservative defeat of 1964.[1] His argument summed up the fashion in contemporary criticism of Parliament in the following passage: 'The ordinary Member of Parliament is by-passed on every side. He is by-passed by the relationships between the Executive and television and the press. Ministers will as a matter of course submit to questioning by lobby correspondents[2] which they would not submit to in the House of Commons. They will answer questions on television which they have actually evaded or refused to answer in the House of Commons. This is matched by the relationship between the Executive and the big power groups in the country. The Trade Unions expect to deal direct with

[1] William Rees-Mogg, *Liberty in 1964* (Conservative Political Centre, 1965). The author was at that time Deputy Editor of *The Sunday Times*.

[2] Lobby correspondents are accredited political journalists who are provided with facilities at Westminster by the Serjeant-at-Arms to enable them to discuss political matters with Ministers and Members of Parliament, either as individual journalists or collectively—and normally on a 'non-attributable' basis.

12

Government and regard the trades union Members of Parliament as a quite unimportant adjunct to their power. In ordinary cases the trades union Members of Parliament are men who have not made their way to the top of the trades union movement. They are the movement's second best where they are not actually its pensioners. Business deals direct with Government and does not even bother to seek representation in the House of Commons, though the occasional business will have a retired Minister as an adviser on its board. When important matters of policy come to be discussed, Parliament is often left out of it altogether.'

But why, more specifically, is the House of Commons so impotent before the Executive? And before precisely *what* Executive is it impotent? The question, and the relevant answers that are now often given may be sub-divided as follows:

The Commons and party organisation. The growth of party and party organisations has destroyed the possibility of independent Members finding a place in Parliament. That much is self-evident, though the development is less recent than is sometimes supposed. But the argument is now commonly taken further. It is said that the growth of party and of party organisations has destroyed the possibility of any independence for the average Member who belongs to them and has reduced him to the position of a subservient cog within the wheel of his great, disciplined, mass Party. Correspondingly, the Prime Minister of the day is seen as the chief beneficiary of the power that is bestowed by party organisation. Much of the comment on the subservience of the backbencher to his Whips and his Party has taken its tone from the observation of a former Member, Christopher Hollis, who saw the modern Member of Parliament as no more than the 'obedient servant of the Party machine' tramping through the Division lobbies. Mr Hollis thought it would be simpler and more economical to keep a flock of tame sheep and drive them through the lobby in the appropriate numbers.[1]

Some critics allow that the backbenchers of the governing party have some influence in private: others do not: still others have a somewhat ambivalent view of this. Thus Professor Crick observed that 'much of the most effective parliamentary control of the Executive takes place in the committees of the Government Party itself, not in the official proceedings of Parliament'. Yet Professor

[1] Christopher Hollis, *Can Parliament Survive?* (Hollis & Carter, 1949), p. 64.

Crick also described as 'procedural or antiquarian-romantic' anyone who thought that informal checks on the Executive would arise elsewhere than on the floor of the House—'for instance, in the private meetings of the parties themselves'. Professor Crick added: 'We were beginning to hear it said that the real opposition is always within the Government Party. All this is at best a dangerous half-truth. More often it is a piece of plain man's metaphysics, a subtle version of the old mechanistic theories of heaven-sent "checks and balances"....'[1]

One frequently heard argument is that party keeps its control through the exercise of patronage—the honours and offices at a Prime Minister's disposal. Another is that the party organisations have an increasing hold over the choice of candidates and over those who succeed in getting into Parliament—a control which arises from the simple fact that only the major political parties have the funds to support a modern electoral battle of mass communications. The authors of the article on 'The Decline of Parliament', already quoted on page 8, regarded this control as the real sanction behind the excessive use of the Whip. And the excessive use of the Whip was responsible for reducing independent expression so far that 'Parliament has been deprived of one of its most important functions, the scrutiny of government policy without fear or favour, and has also largely lost its power of initiative'.[2]

Yet it is also argued that the backbench Member is subservient, in his constituency, to his party caucus and this criticism is sometimes expressed in terms which, if they are correct, somewhat diminish the contention that the power of the party organisation is all-pervasive. The authors of 'The Decline of Parliament' touched on the difficulty in asserting that the average Member was of poor quality. This they believed to be partly due to the haphazard selection of candidates followed by the main political parties—which, if it is true, hardly suggests the influence of the central organisation, at the beck and call of the Prime Minister, is as all-pervasive as is sometimes suggested. Indeed the authors of this article pointed out that one way of achieving the selection of better candidates might be to strengthen the powers of the central party organisations to influence the choice of candidates. But this, they recognised, would create another problem,

[1] Bernard Crick, *The Reform of Parliament*, p. 30.
[2] 'The Decline of Parliament', *Political Quarterly* (July–September 1963), p. 236.

14

since central party organisations were already said to be too strong. To the argument about the quality and selection of candidates I shall return. It is enough to say here that, with a few exceptions, there is a general concensus among the critics of Parliament that the average Member quails before the Executive when his Party is in power. When in Opposition, he is said to be impotent to influence the Government and still, very largely, at the mercy of his own Whips and party organisation.

Parliament and the bureaucracy. But it is not only before the political Executive and before the menacing bosses of the party organisations that the backbencher is supposed to be powerless. He is also, it is alleged, generally incapable of influencing or investigating the Civil Service within which (it is frequently said) the 'real' decisions are taken in modern Britain. The argument here takes on two rather different shades of emphasis. In one form, it suggests that the British Civil Service is a feeble instrument, whose inadequacy is concealed by secrecy and by the false doctrine of Ministerial responsibility. Parliament, because of this doctrine, and because it lacks adequate facilities to question Government departments, cannot expose these shortcomings. This was the argument put by Professor Chapman in a monograph analysing the failure of British institutions and beginning, significantly: 'I take it that there is little doubt that Britain has now reached her lowest point in international prestige for many a long year.'[1]

Professor Chapman took 'Britain's haughty exclusion' from the European Common Market by General de Gaulle as the culmination of a disastrous period in British foreign, economic and military policies in which Britain had declined, relatively, as a European power. The British Civil Service was compared unfavourably with the French bureaucracy. Discussing British institutions of government, he suggested that good policy is 'a function of the quality of the information on which it is based, and on the quality of the men who are formulating it'. The closed Civil Service in Britain was lacking in men with the appropriate talent. It lacked the 'imagination, experience, and knowledge' that are 'the prerequisites of good government in modern society'. These attributes were supposed to be the function of the political system in Britain. 'And yet comparatively speaking the mother of Parliaments is a very weak old lady', wrote

[1] Brian Chapman, *British Government Observed* (Allen & Unwin, 1963), p. 7.

Professor Chapman. 'No other legislature in Europe works under such bad conditions of service and pay or under rules of procedure which are in practice so heavily weighted in favour of the Government.'

Another version of the bureaucratic argument lays less emphasis on the poor quality of the Civil Service than on its uncontrollable power against which, not only Members of Parliament, but also the Government itself, can do little. In this version, it is said that Ministers can do little more than rubber-stamp Civil Service decisions: that the Cabinet is, for the most part, no more than a body for giving formal approval for decisions made inevitable by the processes of argument inside Government departments. It is argued that the essential decisions in, say, defence and economic policy arise from the way in which Whitehall departments present the options to Ministers. Such decisions are taken in a closed circle from which Members of Parliament are wholly excluded. Similarly the House of Commons finds it increasingly difficult to fulfil its traditional rôle as guardian of the liberties of the subject against bureaucratic infringement.

It may seem that this picture of the dark, hidden power of the bureaucrats, to which Ministers and Members of Parliament alike are subject, accords a little uneasily with the account of a Presidential-type Prime Minister or an all-powerful party organisation as the main reasons for the impotence of backbenchers. Indeed, it is clear that there is no unanimity about where the 'power', which is said to be wholly excluded from Parliament, is now to be located. However, it is possible to reconcile the 'power of the Prime Minister' theory with that of the 'power of the Civil Service' and (before himself becoming a Minister) R. H. Crossman provided a popular version of this reconciliation.[1] Describing the decreasing parliamentary control over the Executive, Mr Crossman also alleged that power was being concentrated in fewer and fewer hands. He argued that, just as Parliament had been reduced to a 'new and more submissive rôle by the modern party machine, so the powers of the Cabinet have been eroded by the growing ascendancy of Whitehall'. He took the view

[1] R. H. Crossman, Introduction to Walter Bagehot, *The English Constitution* (Collins, 1963). Mr Crossman was Minister of Housing and Local Government in the Labour Administration of 1964 and he became Lord President of the Council and Leader of the House of Commons in August 1966.

16

that Cabinet Government had passed away as state activities had grown and he cited the ending of Cabinet informality, in World War I, by the creation of a secretariat, and a small War Cabinet, as the first big stage in its passing. After the First World War, Cabinet informality was restored—but not for long. It finally disappeared under Sir Winston Churchill's war régime. 'Once Sir Winston had accepted the leadership of the Conservative Party, his ascendancy became unchallengeable', wrote Crossman. 'As Prime Minister and Minister of Defence, he was the apex of a pyramid of power, exerting a personal control over the whole of the war effort through a vastly expanded Cabinet Secretariat, and a network of Cabinet Committees, under the chairmanship of Ministers who had become his agents.' After the war, Mr Attlee ensured that there was no 'return to normalcy' and a 'well-organised system of centralised decision-taking replaced the rather haphazard personal autocracy of Sir Winston'. According to Mr Crossman, the 'point of decision' was now transferred from the Cabinet upwards to the Prime Minister or downwards to the powerful Cabinet committees. Moreover, the Whitehall bureaucracy itself had become increasingly homogeneous and was closely controlled from the centre—the Treasury. Unification and centralisation of the Civil Service made it 'even more difficult for departmental ministers to get their way against their senior officials'. It also (because of the responsibility to Downing Street) brought an 'immense accretion of power to the Prime Minister', wrote Crossman. 'He is now the apex not only of a highly centralised political machine, but also of an equally centralised and vastly more powerful administrative machine.'

Thus, according to the 1963 Crossman version (a different one may well be available after Mr Crossman's tenure of office), the Prime Minister and the Civil Service are wrapped together in a nexus of power before which the backbencher can do little.

Another frequent allegation is that the bureaucracy gains immense power from the contact between Government departments and interest-groups in the country—in which process Parliament is altogether by-passed. Consultations about proposed legislation take place with affected interests before Bills are drafted and presented to Parliament. The employers associations, the Trade Unions, trade and professional associations, welfare associations—all have their private access to the appropriate government department. In addition there is the growth of quasi-governmental bodies, committees of

17

inquiry and Royal Commissions, all of which may be more influential in determining Government decisions than the House of Comm s and none of whom can be regarded as politically responsible to the electorate.

Parliament and the Purse. But it is not only by the Executive, the party organisations and the bureaucracy that the ordinary Member of Parliament is said to be deprived of power. Behind all these, according to some accounts, is an even more crucial deprivation—the loss of parliamentary control over public spending.

It is, of course, accepted as a truism of English constitutional history that Parliament's control over monarchs and governments was won because it was in control of the purse. What precisely 'control of the purse' has implied can be left to appear in the body of this study. In this context, it is enough to refer to two characteristic critics who have made this loss the main point of their criticism against Parliament. Thus Dr Paul Einzig, basing himself on the premise that Parliament's early development was owing almost entirely to its control over government finance and taxation, has argued that the Executive's present grip over finance was so great that effective parliamentary control over public finance was now incomparably weaker than in any other democratic country.[1] Dr Einzig was especially critical of the weakening of parliamentary control over the Estimates and the use of parliamentary time which is nominally provided for their scrutiny for the purpose of discussing some general political topic.

In their *What's Wrong with Parliament?* Hill and Whichelow diagnosed the 'root of the evil' similarly. They cited, in particular, the way in which the Labour Government of 1945–51 committed the country to make nuclear bombs without consulting Parliament. This was possible because the House yearly voted sums of money for 'research', which were then used on building the bomb. These authors concluded that now the House had abandoned what they regarded as its traditional rôle, 'the only curb on Government expenditure today is—the Government'. But since Government control over its own expenditure is ineffective, the public puts the blame for the state of the economy (so argued the authors) on Parliament as well as on government policy. Thus the '*raison d'être* of Parliament is called into doubt'. Backbench Members were no longer

[1] Paul Einzig, *The Control of the Purse: the progress and decline of Parliament's financial control* (Secker & Warburg, 1959).

vigilant, as they had been in the nineteenth century, to challenge government expenditure: the Treasury, since 1962, had given the Commons less detailed information about Estimates: less time had been devoted to the scrutiny of Supplementary Estimates since the session of 1947–8, when new financial procedures were agreed to, despite the fact that the amount of these Supplementaries had increased very considerably. The House had improved its effectiveness as a debating machine at the expense of controlling the detailed Estimates which it voted.

But though Dr Einzig and Messrs Hill and Whichelow started from the same critical position, they advocated different remedies, to which I shall refer later.

Parliament and Procedure. The backbench Member of Parliament as an individual, and the House of Commons as a body, are said also to be defeated by their own procedure. The criticisms fall into two main categories. First, procedure is said to be antiquated, time-wasting, irrelevant and incomprehensible. In this category, one may group the following objections to existing procedure. Parliament is often nominally fulfilling one function when it is actually performing another—as, for instance, when it uses time allowed for dealing with Supply for discussing foreign affairs. Much of the 'ceremony' of the House is regarded as pointless and time-wasting; so is the long and tedious process of voting in the Division lobbies. The House not infrequently indulges in all-night sittings in which Members have to hang about simply to record their vote. When the parties are narrowly balanced, the sick must be dragged down to Westminster to vote from an ambulance or a wheel-chair. Yet proxy-voting is not allowed. It is convenient to record, under this section, the familiar complaint that Members are under-paid (this has been remedied since the 1964–6 Parliament): that they lack proper accommodation and adequate research facilities.

The second main category of criticism of procedure is that it is overwhelmingly weighted in favour of the Government which has now usurped control of the major part of parliamentary time—and that the House of Commons spends far too long doing things that it cannot, by their nature, do well. Private Members, it is said, not only lack adequate time for their own Bills: they are, for the most part, unable to get such Bills as they do produce through the House if the Government is determined to stifle them. The House is also over-worked and it cannot deal adequately with the weight of Government legislation put before it. Frequently, a Session ends with a Government having to shelve two or three fairly important Bills for which there has proved to be no room in the Parliamentary time-table. At the same time, the House is said to be deprived of the ability to express its view quickly on urgent topics of the day: it is not easy to obtain the Speaker's ruling that a subject falls under Standing Order Number 9 which allows a motion for the adjournment of the House to debate a 'definite matter of urgent public importance'.

Within this compendium of complaints against existing procedure, however, there are some which plainly contradict others and this contradiction arises from differing views on what should be the essential function of the House. Is its primary commitment to help the Government to get its legislation through quickly and efficiently so that the administration keeps pace with changing needs? Or is its first duty to subject legislation, administration and public policy to as deep a scrutiny as possible—if necessary at the expense of the Government's time-table? Further, how far is the House to involve itself in the formulation of policy and administrative method: how far is it to confine itself to being a critic, mostly after the event? How far is it to be outside: how far a partner inside the 'establishment' of government?

One of the main objections to existing procedure is that the proceedings on the Floor of the House become clogged with discussion and divisions over legislative technicalities in which few Members are interested. On the other hand, the House must continue to scrutinise such technicalities by some means if it is to be a watchdog over government activity. Professor Crick argued that Parliament spent relatively 'far too much time discussing the details of legislation and far too little examining and publicising the conduct of administration'.[1] He believed (unlike many other critics) that the House was at its best in general debates: these were invaluable occasions for forcing the Government to explain its policies and actions before a partly hostile audience which can gain the maximum publicity. But, on legislation, he found it hard to believe that criticism from the floor of the House could be informed or even moderately effective unless MPs had some sources of knowledge at least remotely equivalent to that of the civil servants who drafted legislation.

Nor does the device of Question Time, by which Ministers are called to answer a Tabled Question, which may be followed by

[1] Bernard Crick, *The Reform of Parliament*, p. 27.

Supplementary Questions, escape criticism. Although this has been widely regarded as one of the most valuable parliamentary defences of the liberty of the subject, it is also attacked as the 'ritual exchange of non-information' in which the British Civil Service practise (by the form in which they prepare the Ministers' answers) the art of concealment at which they are adept.[1] Another argument is that the current dominance of the Prime Minister (of any Party) at Question Time twice a week has changed the character of Questions. It is suggested that policy Questions 'cannot possibly be answered satisfactorily except at length: they inevitably lead to an attenuated kind of debate rather than to the cross-examination which Question Hour used to be'. The time set aside for the Prime Minister to answer Questions gives him 'a regular platform from which to give his views in short, bright and easily digested answers on the main issues of the day'.[2]

On the other hand, it must be mentioned here that the decision in July 1961 to set aside a quarter of an hour for the Prime Minister to answer Questions after 3.15 on Tuesdays and Thursdays arose from a very different complaint by the House itself—that the Prime Minister's Questions were often not reached because the Questions to other Ministers were going so slowly owing to the number of Supplementaries asked.

Parliament has been highly introspective about its procedure ever since the Reform Act of 1832 and Select Committees have repeatedly been put to work on it in this and in the last century. Many reforming proposals have been accepted by the House but most of the more radical suggestions have failed to command the common consent of the House, after repeated scrutiny, because it has been felt that, in the end, they might diminish rather than increase the scope of the House and the rights of minorities.

The quality of the House. Disillusion with the House of Commons because of its lack of power and its time-wasting procedures are said to have lowered the calibre of men and women prepared to be Members in modern circumstances. The front rank of industry and trade unionists are not in the House: for instance, the executive of the Transport and General Workers Union made clear their view, after Mr Frank Cousins' resignation from the Labour Government in July 1966, that they did not consider he could combine his duties as

---

[1] Leader in *The Guardian*, July 10, 1964.
[2] Andrew Hill and Anthony Whichelow, *What's Wrong with Parliament?*, pp. 32–3.

their General Secretary with his duty as a Member of the House. Moreover, it is frequently alleged that the quality of general debates is poor (though Professor Crick was one who did not think so). The authors of *What's Wrong with Parliament?* accused the House of Commons of avoiding debate on unpalatable subjects and they quoted a speech by Jo Grimond, the Liberal Leader, in which he asserted that strikes were rarely discussed in the House because neither the Conservative Party nor the Labour Party wished to talk about them.[1]

The authors of 'The Decline of Parliament'[2] considered that in both main parties there was a shortage of 'really good men'. The contest for the Leadership of the Labour Party with its 'narrow field' was cited as an instance of this and the authors asked: where were the successors to the 'great names of the 1945 Labour Government'? Some Members, this article stated, had left Parliament out of sheer frustration to do things that seemed more worthwhile. Others had tried to enter but had failed because of the haphazard way in which parties chose their candidates. Others, though of good parliamentary calibre and sound ability, had not sought to enter Parliament at all because of the conditions they knew they would find there. Yet not every critic asserted that MPs were of low calibre. Professor Crick was one who argued that the public was not let down by the kind of man who was sent to Westminster nor by his lack of political independence, but by the use made of his time.

The function of Parliament. So much for the broad categories of criticism. The remedies proposed naturally depend on the view held of the functions of the modern Parliament. Most critics now agree that it does not exist to make or unmake governments. Although one of the chief grievances of the newer Members of the 1960s was that they did not participate enough in the formulation of policy, most critics would agree that Parliament does not exist to usurp the job of the Executive. What, then, do the critics believe that it exists for?

To Professor Crick, Parliament appeared as primarily a forum of publicity. 'Its real functions are those of alerting and informing the public on matters relevant to the decision which way (or whether) to vote.'[3] He dealt sharply with the theory of parliamentary sovereignty

---

[1] Andrew Hill and Anthony Whichelow, *What's Wrong with Parliament?*, p. 33. See also Jo Grimond, *The Liberal Challenge* (Hollis & Carter, 1963), pp. 80 et seq.   [2] *Political Quarterly*, July–September, 1963.
[3] Bernard Crick, *The Reform of Parliament*, p. 27.

which, for practical purposes, existed only when 'the function of government is held to be reduced to one overwhelming consideration: survival'—of which war was an obvious example. For the rest, governing had become a 'prolonged election campaign' and the Conventions of the Constitution are really 'the agreed devices by which *the continuous election campaign* of the whole life of a Parliament is fought'.[1] Parliament today, according to Professor Crick, influences the electorate which controls the Government: the electorate does not influence Parliament which controls the Government.

Yet behind most of the arguments for reform, there seemed to lie some idea of parliamentary influence, of a kind distinct from that normally exerted on party leaders by their followers, over the administrative decisions of the Executive and over the evolution of policy. One sees this more clearly when one comes to examine the main remedies proposed.

Parliament and the cure. The cure most widely advocated is an extension of the Committee system of the House as a means of keeping a constant eye on the administrative acts and policies of the Executive. For many, Parliament is at least a potential 'adviser' on policy: indeed, Professor Hanson, in a discussion on 'The Purpose of Parliament'[2], thought it more profitable to consider the rôle of Parliament as an 'advisory body' than as one seeking to control the Executive. 'If the relationship between the legislature and the Executive is thought of in terms of conflict, as the use of the term "control" inevitably implies, then resistance by the Executive to the establishment of new parliamentary committees is only natural and the chances are that its actual relationship with such committees will be one of suspicion and hostility.' But if the advisory aspect was stressed, the Executive's fears would be diminished—and Professor Hanson considered that hardly anyone had ever suggested that the Committees' functions should be more than advisory. Professor Hanson argued that, despite their Party and other special interests, a *group* of Members represents a cross-section of the community who can be regarded as 'exponents of something called the "national interest" '. He drew a sharp distinction between the sort of function such House of Commons Committees would perform in 'advising a ministry on current policies and methods' and the rôle of the party committees in 'advising a frontbench on the "party line" '. 'The

[1] Ibid., p. 26.
[2] *Parliamentary Affairs*, Vol. XVII, No. 3 (Summer 1964).

problem to be solved', Professor Hanson wrote, 'is that of making parliament a more effective channel through which a stream of democratic influences may be brought to bear on the administrative process, in order to stem the growth of that arbitrariness which is the occupational disease of bureaucracy.'

One suggestion has been a revival of the nineteenth-century practice of setting up *ad hoc* Select Committees to investigate particular problems: this would return to the House of Commons consideration, in a political context, of some of the subjects now delegated to impartial Committees of Enquiry and Royal Commissions. But the greatest weight of support has been for the establishment of specialist, functional Committees, each of which would be detailed to scrutinise the activities of a particular government department or group of departments. Almost every critic whose views have been cited in this short summary (and many more besides) was an advocate of some form of extended Committee system and most also regarded the Select Committee on Statutory Instruments and the Select Committee on Nationalised Industries as useful models. On the other hand, there are differences about the form such Committees should take. Professor Robson argued that since one of the most necessary changes is for Parliament to take a close and continuing interest in the Civil Service and Central Government Organisation, the House of Commons should set up Select Committees on these twin subjects to which the Government could hardly object. But he accepted that functional committees to discuss such topics as defence, foreign policy, Commonwealth affairs, social services and so on were likely to meet much more opposition from the Government. 'I doubt whether it would be possible to confide frankly to a Select Committee all the considerations which influenced defence policy.'[1] Others had no such inhibitions, though supporters of a more thoroughgoing Committee system differed among themselves as to the precise functions to be assigned to Committees. Mr Grimond advocated Standing Committees of between twenty and forty Members of Parliament, which would meet regularly and before which the appropriate Ministers should appear not only to make statements but to answer questions. These Committees should also be able to interrogate civil servants, since the function of the Committees would be 'to get at

[1] William A. Robson, 'The Reform of Government', *Political Quarterly*, April–June, 1964.

what was happening and bring the influence of informed discussion to bear on the subject in hand'.[1]

Besides performing the traditional function of the Commons in examining what the Executive had done, the Committees would also 'supervise current decisions and in this regard would be a new departure'. Recognising that to call civil servants before such Committees would be contrary to the tradition of ministerial responsibility, Mr Grimond argued that it had become a myth that a Minister could be responsible for everything that happened in his department. It had become necessary to 'probe into the policy-making machinery and have a right to examine the people who really do the business'. Mr Grimond also argued that 'the House of Commons has lost all control over public expenditure', since party governments were committed to expenditure demanded by the electorate.[2] Although he did not see the Committees which the House should establish as 'congressional-type inquiries', he did suggest that 'if MPs are to go on to become experts on some subject, exerting pressure on the Executive over its legislative and managerial functions, then indeed they will need assistants, secretaries, offices, as American senators do'.[3]

But how far should such Committees deal with policy: how far only with the administration of policy? Could a clear distinction be drawn between the two? The Labour authors of *Three Dozen Parliamentary Reforms* thought the Committees should provide a check on the administration of policy and also help formulate the 'long-term framework within which policy is later argued on the floor of the House'. The authors of *What's Wrong with Parliament?* (who objected to Party backbench committees on the grounds that they inhibited the development of a House of Commons 'view') suggested Specialist Committees of Inquiry into administration which might later be given the task of dealing with the Committee stage of Public Bills. This latter suggestion hardly fitted with their contention that Specialist Committees in Britain would bear no resemblance to those in the US or in France—an argument also strongly put by Professor Crick. The structure of politics here was so different from that in the US that there was no danger of their 'controlling the Executive', Professor Crick believed.

[1] Jo Grimond, *The Liberal Challenge*, p. 84.
[2] Ibid., p. 92.   [3] Ibid., p. 104.

As for the form of the extended Committee system, Professor Crick was inclined to recommend that the existing Standing Committees might be left to continue their work of considering Bills on the Committee stage, though more Bills might go to those Committees and fewer to Committees of the Whole House. Quite distinct would be the Standing Committees of Advice, Scrutiny and Investigation, which would have a resemblance to the Select Committees dealing with Estimates, Public Accounts and Nationalised Industries. They would last the lifetime of a Parliament and would enable their members to specialise on groups of departments, or single departments, as seemed most practicable. They might be used 'more and more by Ministers, both as sounding-boards for future legislation, and as partners in investigating the efficiency of sections of the administration'. They would also be better qualified than the present Committee to scrutinise annual departmental Estimates.[1]

The arguments of parliamentarians and civil servants over a possible extension of the Committee system are most conveniently found in the 4th Report of the Select Committee on Procedure, 1964–5, to which I shall refer later.[2] But one other difference of opinion must be mentioned here. Some who are anxious to restore Parliament's control of the purse believe it can best be done by referring, *inter alia*, the Finance Bill (which annually implements the Budget) to a Standing Committee on the ground that so technical a Bill could only properly be discussed by specialists. On the Floor of the House, it was a 'time-wasting operation for all but those interested in the technicalities of particular clauses and amendments'.[3] The Select Committee of 1958–9 had recommended that part of the Finance Bill should be taken 'upstairs' but the House had rejected the proposal. On the other hand, Dr Einzig was vehemently against removing the Bill from the Committee of the Whole House on the argument that to do so would weaken parliamentary control of expenditure still further: indeed he was critical of the extent to which the House already uses time allowed for the scrutiny of the Estimates for the discussion of general topics which do little to

[1] Bernard Crick, *The Reform of Parliament*, p. 199.

[2] See, in particular, the Memorandum submitted by the Study of Parliament Group (Appendix 2) and the oral evidence of Professor Hanson and Professor Wiseman.

[3] *Parliament and Government in Our Industrial Society*, by a group of Conservative Members of Parliament (Conservative Political Centre, 1963).

influence policy. 'On the Committee stage of the Finance Bill, on the other hand, a well-led Opposition can secure some important concessions', he argued.

Other 'cures' for parliamentary ills have included more 'professionalism' of Members, more modern voting methods, and morning sittings. It appears to be beyond argument that the conditions in which Members of Parliament work and the facilities accorded them drastically need improvement. But I do not propose to deal at all with this aspect of the problem, which seems to me to be largely irrelevant to the main issue. For one thing, it is not peculiar to Parliament. Running institutions on a shoe-string and a contempt for auxiliaries runs through British life and it is something that Parliament itself can cure without any great argument if it has the will. It has nothing to do with the real problem, which is, not how Parliament should be physically equipped but what is and what should be its place in politics. Is the House of Commons little more than a forum for electioneering, as Professor Crick argued?

Almost all the reformers stress the informative side of Parliament —suggesting that its influence on policy can most usefully be exerted through its advice to the government on the quality of administration. Few, if any, lay emphasis on the Commons' capacity to influence 'political' policy directly through the pressures that the majority party can exert on the Government or (on rarer occasions) by means of the ability of the House as a whole to represent public opinion to Ministers in such a way that they cannot afford to disregard it. Views expressed by Members about *political* issues, either on the floor of the House or in informal exchanges with Members of the Government, are regarded as of slight significance compared with the influence that Committees of the House can (or could) bring to bear on the Government through oversight of administrative processes. Even Professor Crick, a strong advocate of *not* taking government decisions out of politics, appeared to assign to the House of Commons no important political rôle beyond its Committee work and the conduct of an electoral battle in general policy debates.

Of course, everyone knows that the result of most Divisions in the House is calculable in advance and is almost invariably a Government victory. This is one reason why many reformers advocate dropping the convention by which most Divisions are regarded as votes of confidence. But does the House (apart from Committee work) exercise no important influence over the *immediate* conduct of

27

the Government? Can it be no more than a congeries of Committees of Inquiry supplemented by periodical conversion into a publicity-seeking debating chamber in which the object of the arguments is not to affect policy *currently* but to influence the *next* General Election? In this book, I try to answer these questions, not in the form of an argument, but by presenting a practical narrative account of what the Commons have done and still do. I hope that, at the end, the answers to some of these questions will have suggested themselves: my own general conclusions I have tried to exclude until the final chapters.

Part I: The Historical Background

Chapter One

The Foundations of Parliament

Parliament arose from the need of early English rulers to consult with their more influential subjects. Indeed, through seven centuries the one constant function of Parliament has been to provide for consultation between successive English Governments and those sections of the community, or their representatives, which have mattered in terms of political power. Parliament, of course, has been much more than this. It originated from the King's Court where law was declared and administered and it has retained some aspects of a court in the judicial sense. Parliament has also, for much of its history, been a legislature and it would not have been capable of exercising an influence on the Executive if it had not quickly developed the status of a law-sanctioning assembly. Parliament has also virtually always been a tax-granting body and from this function has flowed much of its power. Nevertheless, the deepest roots of Parliament are not to be found in legislation, nor even in the supply of finance, but in the broad consultation over acts of government between the executive monarch and the political nation of the day. Tolerably efficient and viable rule by the king needed some process, however rough and ready, by which he could obtain the consent, or at least the acquiescence, of the influential sections of the people to his acts of government. At first the King's Court, or Council—and later Parliament—provided the means by which the king could take the advice and seek the support of those sections of the community with power to assist or to frustrate his executive actions.

The parliamentary idea of consultation is older than Parliament as an institution and the seniority of the parliamentary idea is a useful reminder that institutions of government depend for their character and evolution not primarily on procedural rules and mechanisms but on the political climate in which they arise. If the parliamentary idea ceased to carry conviction, Parliament would quickly atrophy, despite the authority it derives from its history as the decisive organ of British government and for all the protection it (and the community) receives from traditional conventions and procedures which have gained common consent. It is therefore relevant to recall the emergence of Parliament from a primitive society in which the parliamentary idea was particularly deep-rooted, for this early English community practised political habits of lawful government which were the powerful progenitors of our own attitudes. Centuries before there was any body which could properly be called Parliament, a polity of consultation existed among the free elements in the Anglo-Saxon communities where reverence for commonly accepted political practices and for the law was expressed through a non-arbitrary and quasi-elective kingship. Indeed, consultation was a characteristic of most European communities at the time; pure despotism has been a comparatively rare and painful phenomenon in western European history. The rulers of most primitive societies found it necessary to consult subjects of strength, wisdom and reputation before taking important actions so that their rule should not be undermined by the hostility of the governed. But this characteristic took firmer root here than in many other European communities and was to produce in Parliament a singularly efficient and durable means of responsible government.

Much of this was owed to political habits bequeathed by the Anglo-Saxon community. Together the king and Witanagemot constituted the highest authority in the 'nation'. In the Witanagemot, the law was declared or codified, justice might be done and taxation levied—all within the framework of community customs which gave to every man and every class lawful rights. Though not elected, the Witan spoke, in some sense, for the wider community and, like the Anglo-Saxon organisation of the shire, which linked local communities administratively with the king, and from which the first knights were eventually to be sent to Parliament, the consultative habits of the Anglo-Saxon community prepared the ground for parliamentary government. Indeed, one of the most eminent of Anglo-Saxon historians has gone so far as to assert that the Witan, for all its weaknesses, gave, in however narrow a form, the character of a constitutional monarchy to the Old English state.[1] Of course the Witan was an aristocratic and not a democratic body and one of

[1] Sir F. Stenton, *Anglo-Saxon England* (Oxford History of England, 1947), p. 546.

variable constitution. But so was the Norman King's Council which followed it and from which Parliament itself developed.

Like their Anglo-Saxon predecessors, the early Norman kings recognised that they had a practical obligation to consult their 'natural' counsellors. 'I commit myself and the people of the whole Kingdom of England to your counsel and to the counsel of those who ought to advise me', wrote Henry I to Archbishop Anselm. Naturally the kings only accepted the obligation so far as they needed to and in the early years of post-Conquest military occupation the need was not overwhelming. Yet the Norman kings found it politic (if only as a bulwark against the pretensions of their own powerful magnates) to insist on their acceptance of the old English law and institutions. They repeatedly swore to rule according to the law and they consulted (in theory) their whole baronage in the Great Council on important occasions. They were also limited by the notion implicit in the feudal relationship that if the king broke his political contract with his barons, they might break with him. Magna Carta established more clearly than before that the community of the realm—then represented only by the barons—must be consulted.

The political history of the Middle Ages was in essence a struggle for the balance of power between the king, who was the natural policy-maker, and his 'natural counsellors', the baronage. There was no idea that anyone except the king should rule; yet he was expected to rule acceptably to his most powerful subjects. Medieval eyes looked ambivalently upon kingship. The king was the Lord's anointed, yet he could be deposed on grounds of inadequacy; his right was inherited—yet strict hereditary right could be by-passed if politics demanded. This was the political society from which Parliament emerged some seven centuries ago. 'Parliament', which meant discussion or conference, was a progression from the Great Council of the baronage—and the baronage was effectively the political nation in early medieval England. It cannot be too strongly stressed that though the king was expected to govern himself he was supposed to do so within a framework of the law of the community which he formally 'declared'; he was not a despot who made the law according to his own will. The Council was the natural setting in which the king might, after consultation, discover and declare the law. Magna Carta, effectively a treaty between the king and his barons, antedated Parliament but was in a real sense a parliamentary document. For it established, if not the right, at least the unremitting claim of the community of the realm to be consulted on matters of high policy and the demand that no extraordinary taxation (as distinct from customary feudal dues) should be levied without consent. Thereafter, the political history of medieval England was largely a struggle between the barons, basing themselves on Magna Carta, to bring the kings into consultation with them and pursue policies of which they approved. Wise and strong kings provided leadership and policies which, if they were not all the barons wanted, were at least acceptable; such kings took account of the views of the great men in the nation and thereby strengthened their own power. Foolish and weak kings who ignored the necessary minimum of consultation, found themselves pressed by the barons to yield more than they would have otherwise had to. Thus by falling foul of the baronage, Henry III provoked his magnates even to seek to control his choice of advisers (or ministers) and to force him into regular 'Parliaments' with the barons; this was in addition to the demand that extraordinary taxation should only be levied after consent. (The medieval king, except in extraordinary circumstances, was expected to pay for his government and personal household from revenues received from his own estates and from feudal dues.)

Consultation before taxation was not merely in the interest of the taxpayers: it was also of practical importance to the king, who needed to know how much he could expect to raise. The function of tax-assessment in the shires was part (though not the primary part) of the reason for the initial association of the knights of the shire—the ancestors of the House of Commons—with Parliament. In 1254, two knights from each shire had been summoned to report on the amount of aid their communities were able (or willing) to grant. Yet for all the barons' claims to taxation only by consent, it cannot be asserted that *parliamentary* assent to taxation had any reality before the reign of Edward III. When Simon de Montfort called not only knights but also *burgesses* representing the towns during the baronial wars against Henry III, he was simply seeking reinforcements for a partisan baronial Parliament in opposition to the king's cause. Edward I's summons to the Commons' (or Communities') representatives might more accurately be regarded as the origin of the House of Commons. Yet even he established a habit rather than a system and the presence of the Commons was not yet invariable.

In Edward I's Parliaments the representatives of the Commons stood humbly on the side-lines playing no part in the discussions of high policy. Moreover, their presence was required neither to assent to financial aid nor to deliver petitions. The Commons were called to hear what was said and to receive full power to carry it out so that nobody in their shires could say they lacked authority, especially for tax-collecting.

Edward, of course, did respond to petitions in his Parliament and he may be regarded as the founder of Statute Law. But there is no evidence that it was yet the function of the Commons to present the petitions which might form the basis of a new Statute. Edward I's Parliaments and his law-making by Statute were designed to strengthen the king's authority and prerogative; they were not weapons used against him. This reign provides an early and absolutely clear illustration of one of the constant features of English parliamentary government—that Parliament exists to uphold a strong Executive, not to create a weak one, provided that the Executive is reasonably responsive to the political nation, whether narrow or wide, which Parliament represents.

Inevitably the political nation was widening in the later Middle Ages and as it did, the presence of the Commons' representatives at Parliament took on a new significance. In the troubled reign of Edward II their presence became regular and both the king and barons, in revolution and counter-revolution, sought the Commons' support and found their formal approval of successive *coups d'état* worth having. Although at every stage in medieval history it was the magnates and not the Commons who were decisive in politics, the Commons slowly enhanced their status. The practice of presenting common petitions (as distinct from individual petitions) as a basis for statutory legislation grew up and in the reign of Edward III the redress of grievances by the king in response to common petitions was sought by the Commons in exchange for their grant of taxes. The demands of Edward III for extraordinary taxation to defray the cost of his wars were to be the foundation of parliamentary influence with the Executive exerted through control of the purse. Yet for the most part, this king got what he wanted and had no trouble with his Parliament—barons or Commons—because Parliament was in general sympathy with what he was doing. Thus as early as the fourteenth century another of the cardinal aspects of parliamentary history—which has remained true in every century—was clearly revealed. Parliament did not mind then, and seldom has minded finding money for policies of which it approved. In modern times, it has concerned itself with the efficiency of Government spending, and even in the Middle Ages there were examples of its interest in the appropriation of taxation. Yet its prime concern was, and is, not with the detailed spending of money but with the broad policies being pursued by the Executive.

In the earlier centuries of parliamentary history, concern to influence what one might call the *high* policy of the king was a matter for the baronage or later for factions of the nobility. The Commons' business was primarily with securing redress of unsatisfactory administrative or fiscal processes or social grievances, even though their approval of what had been done by the great men in Parliament was increasingly sought. In the later Middle Ages, factions of the magnates both dominated Parliament and also determined who should be the occupant of the throne. Yet the desire to present in legal terms even the most arbitrary actions of power politics never died; indeed, as politics became more factional there seemed to be an even greater desire to use Parliament to confer legality upon political changes imposed by force. Parliament had been used to approve the deposition of Edward II. In the reign of Richard II, after the *coup d'état* of the Lords Appellant, the Merciless Parliament was the scene of the punishment inflicted on the king's friends and, in turn, of the king's revenge upon his enemies when he counter-attacked. After Richard's deposition, the accession of Henry IV was registered, if not in a Parliament proper, at least in a quasi-parliamentary assembly of Estates. Successive Acts of Parliament were produced to declare where the succession to the throne was supposed to lie during the struggles between the Houses of Lancaster and York. In all this the Commons were acquiescent to the deeds done by the magnates, yet it was important to parliamentary development that their assent was considered worth having. The purpose and the authority that Parliament had gained among a law-desiring people in an age of lawless power politics was never put better than in the Act of Parliament which recognised the succession of Richard III in place of Edward IV's deposed children. After stating Richard's inheritance as of right by the laws of God and nature, the Act pronounced him king because

> ... the court of Parliament is of such authority, and the people of
> this land of such nature and disposition, as experience teacheth,
> that manifestation and declaration of any truth or right ... in
> Parliament, and by authority of the same, maketh, before all other

things, most faith and certainty; and, quieting men's minds, removeth the occasion of all doubts and seditious language.

While the Commons were acquiescent to the power politics of the magnates in the later Middle Ages, they steadily built up their parliamentary privileges. The fifteenth century brought the Commons the privilege of freedom from arrest in Parliament-time and a broad acceptance by the king that they had freedom of speech in their own 'House'—though, of course, only the Speaker could utter on their behalf before the king in Parliament. From this period also dated the Statute which, to ensure the 'respectability' of electors, limited the right of electing knights of the shire to Forty Shilling freeholders—a provision which astonishingly endured until 1832. After this period, the Commons' control over extraordinary taxation is undeniable.

Yet as the fifteenth century moved on, Parliaments diminished in frequency, the number of Statutes declined and those that were passed now generally originated from the king, not the Commons. The practice began of granting the king the customs dues, 'tonnage' and 'poundage', for life and this lessened his need to call Parliament for other supply. The paradox of the period is that the Commons were both establishing their rights more firmly than ever and yet were far less politically active. It is not difficult to explain why. The Commons were largely, if not 'packed' by, at least subservient to the dominant faction which was therefore perfectly happy to grant them their privileges. Like the eighteenth century, this was an oligarchal period in which the prevailing faction dominated both Parliament and the throne. Opposition politics had gone out of Parliament which increasingly ceased to concern itself with matters of national policy. The Commons in Parliament had no quarrel with the régimes which succeeded one another and therefore they could consolidate the two cardinal aspects of medieval parliamentary activity—the supremacy of Parliament in the making of new law and its control over the extraordinary finance needed by the king. From these two 'rights' the modern 'sovereign' Parliament emerged in the reign of Henry VIII.

(ii)

Judged by the infrequency with which the first Tudor king, Henry VII, summoned Parliament, it might have been a declining body. In other European countries, parliamentary assemblies did decline before the power of nearly despotic kings in the sixteenth and seventeenth centuries. In England, however, Parliament reached maturity by the will of a king. By making Parliament the instrument for implementing a revolutionary policy, Henry VIII gave it a new status and, at the same time, further emphasised the tradition that Parliament existed to uphold a strong Executive (provided broadly acceptable policies were pursued), not to create a weak one. Henry built on the medieval tradition of Parliament's supremacy in the making of new law to give legal sanction to his nationalisation of the church in England. More specifically, he used the Commons in matters of high policy as they had never been used before and in doing so he laid the basis for their later insistence that no matter was too high for them to deal with.

Yet it was understandable that Henry should rely especially on the Commons in Parliament to legalise the ecclesiastical revolution which was both to give him the divorce he wanted and free him from a humiliating dependence upon Rome. The upper 'House'—the Lords who had been Parliament proper—had been diminished in numbers and authority by the dynastic wars and contained too many ecclesiastical and other conservatives. The Commons, on the other hand, represented the aspirant gentry who might be expected to be sympathetic to the king. The 300-odd Members of the 'House' of Commons (which was still, in a sense, extraneous to Parliament proper) did not seek entry in order to oppose the Crown but rather to be near the centre of authority and perhaps qualify for a successful political or administrative career. It was a perfect instrument for a king who wished to introduce laws to establish that his acts were lawful, however revolutionary they seemed. The king knew that he could rely on anti-clerical sentiment to support a policy which could be presented as anti-papal but not anti-Catholic. The Commons were not asked to accept too much.

The Long Parliament which began in 1529 and which effected the ecclesiastical revolution by successive Statutes made Parliament a more permanent and less occasional institution. With repeated prorogations, it lasted for seven years and eight sessions instead of the customary few weeks and thus its Members learned to work together. The new Statutes did not purport to make changes but rather to state (much as medieval kings declared the law) what the law already was—and then enforced it by statutory penalties. Nevertheless, no

Parliament, and certainly never the Commons, had dealt with such high matters before.

Henry's notion of Parliament, like that of Edward I, was to enhance his own prerogative. As he acknowledged in a famous case of privilege, the king at no time stood

> ... so highly in our estate royal as in the time of Parliament, wherein we as head and you as members are conjoined and knit together into one body politic, so as whatsoever offence or injury (during that time) is offered to the meanest member of the House is to be judged as done against our person and the whole Court of Parliament.

He could afford these lofty sentiments. This king and his Parliaments were as much agreed on the fundamentals of policy as a modern British Government is with the majority party in Parliament which supports it. Yet the king had created a potentially revolutionary situation which could not remain as he left it. Parliament's status was enhanced not merely by the ecclesiastical Statutes but by being asked to pass three successive Statutes determining the succession. Though these were passed at Henry's will, they were an ominous precedent which could in future be turned against the Crown.

What Parliament could do once, it could do again. The Erastian revolution of Henry VIII was, by means of Parliament, turned by a dominant minority into a Protestant revolution under Edward VI. Even dogma and the meaning of things eternal now needed to be sanctioned in Parliament. It was appropriate that in the reign of Edward VI the former collegiate chapel of St Stephen should be made over to the Commons as their 'House' which it remained until it was burned down in the nineteenth century. Then, under Mary, Parliament was the necessary means of approving the return of England to the Roman obedience, though the pious queen would have had it otherwise. But this time Parliament was showing signs of independence. The men in the Commons now had a vested interest in the new social and economic order and they were adamantly opposed to the return of church lands now in their possession. They had their way. The consensus between throne and the middle-class gentlemen who dominated the Commons was breaking down. So also were the distinctions between the nobility and the gentry. The gentry were enriched by the distribution of church lands, and their ranks were constantly enlarged in this period by recruits from the well-off merchant classes who bought themselves gentility through land. In later Tudor England, the two classes were by and large combined in a single interest, linking Lords and Commons, and based in the shires. It was an interest far too potent for any monarch to overcome as continental monarchs had overcome their feudal nobility.

The country gentlemen, closely linked with the nobility, not only had wealth; they were the government in the shires and in this lay their ultimate power. Families which sent Members to Parliament in the reign of Elizabeth were still doing so in the eighteenth and nineteenth century—a few even in the twentieth. Such men not only represented the counties; they also took over the boroughs in place of the burgesses, ignoring the requirement for residential qualification. They packed Parliament to preserve their own interest. At the end of Mary's reign, men in Parliament were beginning to form an Opposition anti-Catholic party which met in Arundel's tavern in Poultney Lane. By the end of Elizabeth's forty-five years on the throne, the Commons had repeatedly forced the queen to meet them more than half-way over matters of high policy which she believed were reserved for her prerogative. These were the first signs that Parliament would sooner or later move against a monarch whose policies no longer represented the interests of politically effective sections of the population. There were two logical solutions: the elimination of a free Parliament and the abandonment of an ingrained tradition of government by consultation, or an Executive responsible and acceptable to Parliament.

Elizabeth was not in love with Parliaments. In forty-five years she called only ten Parliaments whose sittings barely totalled 140 weeks. Yet in this period, the modern Parliament established its independence from the Executive and demanded successfully to have a say in the determination of high policy. Elizabeth sought to establish a compromise church which might attract Catholics as well as Protestants. But the 'Protestant gentlemen' (as she called them) in the Commons forced her to make the religious settlement far more Protestant than she had intended. They pressed her to marry (which she regarded as no business of theirs) so as to secure the Protestant succession; in this, however, she evaded their pressures. They badgered her to execute Mary, Queen of Scots and, in the end, she felt obliged to let this happen. The Puritan Party, to the queen's fury, tried to use her financial dependence on Parliament to force her to accept their views on policy. They insisted on stiffer anti-Catholic legislation and sought to reform the Prayer Book. As the reign progressed, the Puritan movement became more distinctly anti-episcopalian and by the 1580s it produced a system, based on the local Puritan 'classis', of national and provincial synods. This was the forerunner of political party organisation. Through it the Puritans sought to get their men into the Commons, they promoted Bills and they persistently lobbied Members. This particular threat was beaten off but at the end of the reign, the Commons scored two major victories. In the earlier part of the reign, as under former Tudor sovereigns, the initiative in introducing legislation had been with the Crown. Few Bills had originated from (as distinct from in) the Commons. In Elizabeth's last years, however, the Commons themselves took the initiative in producing a series of Bills dealing with the social and economic problems of dearth and unemployment. Secondly, they forced the queen to introduce corrective legislation to deal with abuses created by her sale and gift of monopolies. This second episode demonstrated the skill of Elizabeth in knowing when to yield. Her personality and the affection the Commons bore her helped to bind queen and Parliament together but an even stronger bond was their common interest in broad policy. In many respects (*mutatis mutandis*) the mutual responses of Crown and Commons under Elizabeth anticipated the relationship of a modern Cabinet and its own party in Parliament. Elizabeth was something like a party leader of the Commons as a whole and, like other party leaders since, found herself pushed by extremists farther than she wanted to go. But equally, her Commons would never—not even the extremists— endanger the hold on the Crown of one they accounted their greatest protection. The result was a series of compromises.

Again, as in modern times, it was the rule for the queen's Ministers to have the initiative in Parliament. They dominated the time-table and introduced Bills with supporting speeches. It followed that when some outside interest wished to promote a Bill (in some matter of trade or some tax concession for instance) the method normally chosen was direct dealing with a 'Minister' of the Queen's Council— though on occasions individuals or corporate bodies who wished to press or promote Bills might approach a Member and even give him an expense allowance for his pains on their behalf. This general preference, even in the sixteenth century, for dealing direct with Whitehall is of some interest in the second half of the twentieth when it is commonly asserted—with the apparent implication that this is something new—that Members of the House are being by-passed by direct dealings between Government departments and interested parties. There is no evidence that it has ever been substantially otherwise.

In view of the twentieth-century predilection for an increased use of parliamentary Committees, it is of some interest to note that the House of Commons Committees to which legislation was referred under Elizabeth I were greatly influenced, sometimes dominated, by the Privy Councillors who, in the intimacy of a small Committee, could more easily impress ordinary Members by dropping confidential and friendly hints of the queen's views than they could in open Parliament. A modern Member could hardly be cajoled by intimations of a Minister's views in the same fashion. Nevertheless, a critic in any age who is brought up against the essential *reasonableness* of almost any official position and confronted with the expertise of administrators in a close committee may be less persistently critical than he might be in the more open atmosphere of the floor of the House where he might hope for the support of the uncommitted. At all events, the parallel is sufficiently close to tempt one into a comparison with the observation of the Labour Member of Parliament, Michael Foot, in a House of Commons debate on procedural reform in 1965. On the subject of specialist committees he observed: 'Any Minister worth his salt knows how to diddle a Committee of that nature. . . .'[1]

(iii)

The relationship between Tudor monarchs and Parliament was viable because the fundamental objectives of policy were generally the same for both. As the Commons felt their power under Elizabeth, and the Crown, faced with heavier expenditure and shrinking revenue, became more dependent on Parliament for supply, this accord was frequently strained. Parliamentary management became a necessity and by it the Crown had been able to guide and to respond to parliamentary opinion. In the seventeenth century, this accord broke down. The Commons (as they made clear to James I) would not stand from the tactless foreign Stuarts what they had stood from Elizabeth. Maladroit handling of the English Parliament by both James I and Charles I contributed to the breakdown of the constitution.

Yet the fundamental reason for the clash between king and

[1] H.C. Deb., Vol. 718, col. 209, October 27, 1965.

Parliament, which erupted into Civil War, was that the objectives of the king's policies no longer suited the interests and the political notions of the classes represented in the House of Commons. It is sometimes argued that better parliamentary management by the Stuarts could have averted the Civil War and indeed it might have helped to do so. But in the seventeenth century the clash of economic interest, social ambitions and religious beliefs, as well as of political ideas, was too great for parliamentary management alone to have effected a cure. Parliamentary management could succeed under Elizabeth, as in the eighteenth century, because on all basic issues, the *political* nation was united. In the early seventeenth century, there was no such unity. The underlying causes of the conflict, how much they were matters of belief and how much matters of interest, lie outside the present discussion. It is enough to note that Parliament's antipathy to the Government of the Stuarts did not primarily arise from reluctance to provide money nor even from the fight for parliamentary privilege. The root causes were, first, a clash over religious, foreign and economic policy; second, the growing apprehension that the Stuarts (in order to have *their* way over policy) were departing from the ancient tradition of consultation with the community and resorting to arbitrary government.

The Commons were at odds with the king from the start of James's reign. They fought him first over their privileges, and over abuses arising from feudal dues. They used delaying tactics to undermine the king's plan for a union with Scotland. They fought the king over non-parliamentary taxation (impositions) to which he resorted to make good his financial deficiency and they resisted making an adequate allowance, in lieu of the resented feudal dues, for fear of making the king independent of Parliament, as foreign monarchs had become. They fought him, above all, over religion and foreign policy, which James, like his forebears, claimed to be outside their proper competence. They petitioned the king to take up the sword on behalf of Protestantism against Catholic Europe and appealed for the marriage of the prince to 'one of our own religion'. To this the king replied with a command that they should not meddle 'in deep matters of state'. The Commons insisted, to the contrary, that

> ... the arduous and urgent affairs concerning the king, state and the defence of the realm, and of the church of England, and the maintenance and making of laws, and redress of mischiefs and

grievances which daily happen within this realm, are proper subjects and matter of counsel and debate in Parliament. . . .

In other words, the Commons were claiming that there was no aspect of policy too high for them to deal with. It almost amounted to the total claim of the modern House of Commons to have the Executive pursuing policies within broad lines approved by Parliament. In one sense this was an historical, in another an innovating claim. It was historical in that the ancient Great Council had always claimed to be consulted on high policy in the medieval period. It was unhistorical in that such a claim had never been made (except hesitantly under Elizabeth) by the Commons who had never been part of the Great Council, for all their growing influence. Although Henry VIII had used the Commons to change the organisation of religion, the legislation they passed was on his initiative and, in any case, it simply declared what the state of things was already supposed to be, appending punishments for infringement, rather than creating something new. Under James I, however, the Commons were virtually claiming to be part—perhaps the most essential part—of the 'Great Council' which should be the forum of national debate on policy. This claim, if strictly unhistorical, represented the facts of political life under the Stuarts. The Commons, together with their allies in the House of Lords, were effectively the king's natural counsellors because, as representing the political nation of the seventeenth century, they had the power to oblige him to consult them.

The smoother relations which James achieved with his Parliament at the end of his reign themselves testified to the new influence of the lower House of Parliament. For the improvement was the direct result of James's adoption of the Commons' anti-Spanish policy. The Commons therefore made a grant of money conditional on the king's 'public declaration' that he had adopted policies in respect of Spain and the Palatinate 'in pursuit of our advice therein'. What is more, the money was appropriated for the war which was supposed to follow. The Commons would pay for a policy of which they approved.

All this was the work of a deliberately organised Opposition Party in the Commons which represented something new in parliamentary history. Although this Opposition was in some degree a development from the Puritan extremists, who had been so pertinacious in organising themselves during the previous reign, any idea of a consistent

Opposition Party would have been considered an outrage under Elizabeth. After 1604, however, the year in which the Commons, in their famous 'Apology', set about teaching a foreign king what they alleged to be the rules of the political game in England and instructing him in the privileges of Parliament, there existed a durable Opposition Party which was recognised as such by contemporaries. Sir Francis Bacon recognised its existence in some revealing words which he addressed to the king just before the 1614 Parliament:

> The opposition which was the last Parliament to your Majesty's business, as much as was not *ex puris naturalibus* but out of party, I conceive to be now much weaker than it was. . . .

Bacon was, perhaps, right in this diagnosis of weakness for the time being; nevertheless there remained enough of a cohesive and organised Opposition not merely to continue its activities in swaying the House as a whole for the rest of the reign but to hand on the torch of their tradition to the far more powerful opponents of Charles I.

The active Opposition—indeed, the active Membership—of the Commons was, of course, a small proportion of the House as a whole. Of 461 Members, between sixty and eighty did most of the work and of these a small leadership cadre dominated the decisions of the House. They used changing procedural techniques and they gave the House the 'leadership' formerly supplied by the Privy Councillors. In particular, after 1607 they used the newly developed procedure of Committee of the Whole House (which freed them from the 'chairmanship' of the Speaker, then in principle still primarily a royal servant) to escape from royal control. The small committees of the Elizabethan Parliament, which did much of the detailed legislative work, had been dominated by Privy Councillors. Now, however, most major issues were referred to the Committee of the Whole House where, for instance, one of the 'opposition' lawyers might suggest a Bill which would then be drafted in a sub-committee of lawyers. In this way, the House of Commons was coming to take the initiative in major national legislation to a degree it never had before.

Legislative initiative by the Commons, however, has been the exception not the rule in parliamentary history and at this stage in the seventeenth century it reflected the beginning of the breakdown in a viable relationship between the Executive–Crown and Parliament. In due course, when a normal relationship between these two arms of government had been restored, though on a different basis, the initiative in policy and legislation naturally returned to the Executive. But before this revival, the nation was to fall into revolution and civil war which culminated in the temporary abolition of the monarchy itself. The reign of Charles I was, in most respects, an extension of the problems which had faced his father. The new king was at odds with Parliament over religion (his Arminianism against their Puritanism); over foreign policy and the claims of the Crown to find by extra-parliamentary means taxation to support the king's policies for which the Commons refused to find adequate supply; and over parliamentary privilege. In the early years of the reign, moreover, one aspect of the king's quarrel with the Commons reflected both the very roots of the constitutional problem and presaged the ultimate solution; this was the Commons' distrust of Buckingham, the king's chief Minister, and of his management of foreign and military policy. Buckingham's position was something like that of a modern Prime Minister—but, unlike a modern Prime Minister, he was responsible not to Parliament but to the king. Moreover, Charles adamantly refused to 'allow any of my servants to be questioned amongst you, much less such as are of eminent place, and near unto me'. The attack on the Minister Buckingham was a first step towards the revolutionary situation which developed later when Parliament sought to call the king himself to account and to dictate the policies adopted in his Council. The ultimate solution would be to make Ministers responsible to a Parliament, the majority of which sanctioned their general policies. This would enable them to enjoy the sort of executive discretion which, during the constitutional breakdown of the seventeenth century, Parliament came near to denying to the Government of Charles I.

Three general points about the constitutional struggle in the first half of the seventeenth century must be made in any general discussion of the historical rôle of Parliament. First, in the early years of Charles I, the Opposition in Parliament took up what seemed to them to be a conservative position, seeking merely to restore the constitution to what they conceived to have been its proper balance under Elizabeth. To the king, on the other hand, the Commons were innovators and according to the strict letter of the law he was right. In seeking to participate in policy-making the Commons were innovating. In a deeper sense, the king was wrong for the Commons were embodying the tradition of government by consultation with the political nation which had since the earliest English society run through the nation's political life.

Secondly, the constitutional struggle of this period demonstrated the nature, the necessity and the limitations of parliamentary management. As the relationship between king and Parliament deteriorated, the Commons came under new management and the former conservatism of the parliamentary Opposition fell to shreds. In the Short Parliament called to meet the Scottish crisis in 1640 by the king, after eleven years without a Parliament, John Pym became the effective leader of the House of Commons. He used a knowledge of parliamentary procedure gained in six previous Parliaments to outwit the Court Party and operated an Opposition far more ruthless than ever before. By now he and his closest friends probably realised that they were set on a revolutionary course. The mass of Members, however, cannot be said to have belonged either to the Court or the Country Party and, indeed, such parties had no existence in the sense of being large organisations of Members with clear objectives. But the essential Opposition, the comparatively small group which fought for the allegiance of the Commons, was organised. Like the Court Party, they sought to get their supporters returned to the Commons. Moreover, a long-standing common interest in a particular commercial venture, the Providence Island Company provided them with an organisation and common meeting ground for their political activities. The Providence Island Company, which controlled Caribbean settlements, included as shareholders and officials many of the leading Puritans, some of whom were also interlinked by family ties, such as Lord Saye and Sele, Lord Brooke, Hampden and Oliver St. John. Pym was the company's secretary. This association is alone enough to dispose of the myth that the Puritans were low-class, canting sour-faces. The Providence Company epitomised the essential nature of the Puritan movement, consisting of men of an austere religion and robust and commercial enterprise—men, both of the aristocracy and country gentry, who were jealous of their political rights. The first English revolution was possible because this minority gave leadership to the uneasiness and discontent felt by the more passive mass of English parliamentarians. On the other hand, the parliamentary management of Pym and his friends could not have made a revolution had there not been deeper political causes than a failure by the king to 'manage' Parliament.

The activities of the Puritan Opposition within the organisation of the Providence Company illustrate the third general point—that the Opposition of these years organised itself and co-ordinated its strategy off the floor of the House itself—much as a modern political party does. Thus Charles dissolved the Short Parliament on May 5, 1640, having heard of a meeting of leading Opposition Members which had privately agreed the night before on a motion, to be moved in the House by Pym, asking the king to come to terms with rebellious Scotland. To avert this danger, Charles hastily dismissed his Parliament and his doing so (like so much else in this reign) illustrated the extent to which men in government recognise the desirability of operating within existing institutions, and seek to win their strategical points within a framework of agreed rules. Otherwise, Charles might have simply allowed the motion to be passed and have attempted to overrule it. In this period as a whole, both sides felt obliged to adhere to existing procedures up to the last moment, however much they twisted them to their own advantage. Charles' dismissal of his Parliament on more than one occasion was a tacit recognition that, though they commanded no army, his enemies were really potent (and only potent) when they assembled in Parliament. Conversely, the Commons' reverence for the forms which signified their authority was demonstrated more than once. In 1629, when the king sought to adjourn the Commons, they forcibly held the Speaker in his chair and refused to deliver up the mace rather than continue to sit without the symbols of their authority and legitimacy.

In the years before the outbreak of war, the Opposition and the king fought for command of the majority of the House. As Pym's movement was increasingly seen to be revolutionary, the constitutional moderates who had previously sided with him rallied to the king so that when the Grand Remonstrance, which attempted to undermine the king's authority by condemning all the earlier misdeeds of the reign, came before the House, it was passed by only eleven votes. The issue thereafter was one of authority and legitimacy —which to most men in those days meant monarchy—as well as of the liberty of the subject and the privileges of Parliament. What was now at stake was the monarchical element in the English constitution.

(iv)

The death of the king and the abolition of the monarchy was followed by the only brief period of executive rule by 'Parliament' (or what was left of it) that England has ever known. The executive Council of State was elected by the Rump of the old Long Parliament and under it there operated a number of smaller parliamentary committees. The experiment was not a success. In 1653 the Rump was dismissed by Cromwell, who ironically came to accept that a government with 'something monarchical in it' was probably the best. Thereafter the various experiments of the Protectorate, moving towards government by a 'single person', were tried. England gravitated back to a quasi-monarchical method of government—but one which lacked the authority of legitimacy and which ultimately rested on military force and Cromwell's personal ascendancy over the army. Cromwell's personal failure with his Parliaments has been ascribed to his back-bench mentality and his total failure to manage Parliament with an efficient frontbench as the Tudors had done. Yet, as with the Stuarts, this was not the only reason for, under Cromwell too, there were deeply divisive instincts in the body politic as well as strong differences over foreign policy and taxation between the Crom-wellian Government and Parliament. The balance of power between Parliament and the Executive was not settled yet and it was hardly likely to be settled under one who was being pushed by events towards a monarchical government without any authority, except that of the army, for his position. The Restoration of Charles II was an attempt to renew both legitimacy in government and the old, balanced, pre-Stuart constitution (as hindsight envisaged it) in place of military rule.

Charles II received back his throne without formal strings. Except for the prerogative courts, which had been abolished in 1641, the old institutions were restored. Yet the situation had now fundamentally changed. For one thing, it was obvious that after the breakdown of monarchical awe in the 1640s no future king could be unmindful of the fate of Charles I. For another, extra-parliamentary taxation was now, once and for all, outlawed. The king still had in his hand the weapon that Parliament depended on him for its existence and its duration. Only by the king's will could Parliament be summoned; a pliant Parliament (supposing there were to be one) could be kept in being indefinitely; there was no limit to the term of years between Parliaments. On the other hand, the king (unless he could assure himself of funds by some such extraordinary means as Charles II did in taking a pension from Louis XIV) must depend on Parliament for money. That meant that there must be Parliaments, and that the king's and Parliament's *basic* policies must be in general accord. Under Charles II they were not and thus the last phase of the tension between Crown and Parliament began. The king sought to rule as he thought fit and Parliament, while accepting that he was the Executive, tried by using the power of the purse to prescribe his policies for him. Once again, the essential issues were foreign and religious policy— and taxation. The solution, which Charles II himself came reluctantly to apprehend, could only be that the king should be assured of a majority in Parliament. The question still to be settled was whether the king should be the 'nominee' of a majority Party or whether the king should be able to contrive a pliant parliamentary majority for himself.

From the hard politics of the reign of Charles II, party began to emerge in something like the modern sense. Both the Tory (loyalist) and the Whig (opposition) parties arose from the crisis caused by the attempt of the Opposition to exclude from the succession the Catholic Duke of York. In the successful revival of his authority at the end of his reign, which was partly made possible by reaction against Whig excesses, Charles managed to rule without calling another Parliament. But he showed his awareness of the Crown's future dependence on a viable relationship with Parliament by trying to arrange for future control of the House of Commons by the Court. This could only be done by controlling elections and Charles therefore called in borough charters and issued new ones which gave the Crown control of civic appointments—and therefore of municipal government and parliamentary elections. By so rooting out the Whig and Dissenting governors of the parliamentary boroughs, he remodelled the electorate in the hope that future Parliaments could be arranged in the interest of the Crown.

These were the years in which coffee-houses began to serve as party headquarters and the Whig Green Ribbon Club was founded. Charles II's tactics were a recognition of the fact of party and an admission of the king's appreciation that tension between Crown and Parliament could only be avoided in future if both could again follow the same 'interest' and the same broad policies as they had in Tudor times. But whereas there had been a genuine identity of basic interest between Crown and Parliament under the Tudors this simply could not exist under the Stuarts. The divergence between the Stuarts and the predominant classes of their subjects on the fundamentals of policy, religion and the *idea* of how government should be conducted were fundamental. Any accord could therefore only be created artificially by manipulating the structure of the electorate.

Even so, there was a limit to what such manipulation could achieve. Charles had triumphed because he had come to accept, if reluctantly, the position of leader of the Tory–Anglican party. It was a good deal less than the position he had originally sought and was far from amounting to monarchical freedom. The position he bequeathed to his brother James was strong but far from despotic and the new king destroyed his inheritance by seeking to restore the royal authority on a personal basis and in the interest of a religion hateful to the majority of both parties. By his actions, James so alarmed Tories as well as Whigs that both parties united to call in William of Orange, whom the Tories reluctantly (having recourse to historical fictions in order to preserve the idea of monarchical legitimacy) and the Whigs avidly installed as king.

The years between the Glorious Revolution and the arrival of the Hanoverians in 1714 were not Whig years in practice. Both parties participated in government. Sometimes they joined in mixed ministries; later they alternated in power. Until the death of Anne, the Tories could still claim that they were supporting a legitimate monarch—and the idea of legitimacy was fundamental to the old Tory position. Party battles were real and elections were more often and more bitterly contested in those post-Revolution years than was to be the case later. Yet the future lay with the Whigs. Tory morale had been punctured and it gradually declined. The Whig hold on the rising wealth of the country through both the mercantile and the land interest was strengthened. The *raison d'être* of the old Tory position had been undermined because the fundamental argument between an independent Crown and Parliament had gone out of politics. The basic religious issue as between Protestant and Catholic was settled (whatever the remaining differences between the established church and the Protestant sects). The monarchy was clearly re-established on a new basis. After 1689, the occupants of the throne had less reason to collide headlong with Parliament because Parliament had given them the throne and, owing their throne to Parliament, the sovereigns immediately after 1689 had their own peculiar sort of strength. There was certainly no idea that they should be political ciphers—simply that they should pursue politics in consultation with Parliament.

Logically the position after 1689 was made for the Whigs but they did not finally take over until 1714. Many Tories had a conscientious objection to the Hanoverians but the Whigs, strong in wealth and in the victory of their political idea, were single-minded. In the following years they built up their position in alliance with the new monarchy which could itself help them in controlling elections—but much more successfully than Charles II could ever have done because there now existed a community of interests. The Government, which meant the Crown and the Ministers of the day, had a rising tide of patronage to dispense, as government departments and the services multiplied. There were more and more officials and more and more of them sat in the House of Commons; the outcry against placemen was a constant feature of politics in the first half of the eighteenth century. In the constituencies, local corporations became more venal, the number of voters in many boroughs diminished, the hold of the borough patron grew tighter, elections became more expensive—and therefore fewer elections were contested. The discredited Tory Party died, or went underground. Though there is room for interminable dispute of an almost theological character about the meaning of 'party' in the eighteenth century, it was the Whigs, of one or another faction, who engrossed British politics in the middle decades of the century. There were independent 'country' backbenchers of whom some might be described as Tories of a sort, though many of the independents (who by their nature were not themselves seekers of office) deemed it their duty to support the king's Government of the day. There were also the placemen—the nominees of the Court and of whatever faction of the Whigs was in power—whose support was normally necessary to maintain an administration. The Government could also normally rely on the support of the Scottish seats. For the rest, the active Members of the House, the seekers after office, were divided into those who supported and those who did not support the administration of the day. A high proportion of the Members owed their places either to patronage, influence or place. At the accession of George III, about half the representation of the English borough seats were under patronage of some sort, according to Namier's analysis. Borough patrons, however, were far more influential than the government as such and the influence of government corruption has been exaggerated. A total of 111 borough patrons determined or influenced the election of 205 seats whereas only thirty seats were under direct government management.

But however 'party' allegiances are described in this period, there was a fundamental homogeneity in politics; a common interest based on property and the conservation of an existing social and political order which transcended smaller clashes between political factions. These factions were largely about who should govern, though they could also involve particular differences on particular policies. But until Burke came to defend party as a proper and legitimate means of organising political opinion, any notion of sustained opposition was frowned on as unpatriotic. The former Opposition had enthroned itself after 1714 and it was catholic enough to claim to stand for the nation.

The political world of Hanoverian Britain was a small, enclosed society in which the strings of power and economic influence were tightly held in a circle small enough to have an inner coherence, and comprehensive enough to withstand outside assaults, so long as it still controlled the wholly unrepresentative electoral system. On the other hand, the Whig hegemony had its own ethos; and that included a genuine belief in the freedom of expression and the rule of law, however harsh the law might be. It embodied the notion of a balanced constitution and different spheres of influence. In the first three-quarters of the eighteenth century Britain could do without party because the big issues, if not dead, had been buried alive. Or, to put it another way, all were united in a Whig harmony in which court and country, government and 'opposition', had their place. In this harmony, one of the functions of the Crown was to use its patronage to determine the political balance, and this was considered perfectly respectable.

During the eighteenth century, the House of Commons as a corporate body reached the height of its prestige. Yet, as its resistance to the reporting of its debates and the public communication of its proceedings showed, it regarded its business as nothing to do with the public. The very firmness of its base and the internal cohesion of its Members created a corporate spirit and corporate manners which it bequeathed to Parliament in a democratic age. The procedures followed by the Commons in the eighteenth century were substantially the same as those of the seventeenth but they were now lovingly nurtured and amplified by Members who had come to reverence the House and its forms not as a means of government but as a bulwark against arbitrary rule. The old forms were developed to give Members the most intricate control over legislation and discussion. Procedural devices existed to enable any Member to bring up any question at any time and for so long as he liked. Legislation was equally slow and the point came when no less than eighteen questions had to be put to the House (each involving a division) on the passage of a Bill—quite apart from Committee work. The time-table was haphazard and the individual Member had the widest scope to intervene; as the century progressed, speeches by the leading lights of the House lengthened—often to more than two hours. But this leisurely pace, this club-like atmosphere did not matter—for government activity was negligible. Whig Britain acted on the maxim of Lord Shelburne that 'Providence has so ordered the world that very little government is necessary'. There was hardly any major Government legislation; what there was arose out of the financial provision for the major policy issues of foreign affairs and defence. The tightened control of the Commons over spending since the Revolution drew Executive and Parliament into closer communion over policies and the cost of them. Under William III the foundation of a permanent Commons system of estimate, appropriation and audit was the price paid by the Government for parliamentary support for the war against France. Navy, army and ordnance estimates were considered and the appropriation of supply became regular. Moreover, the Crown became dependent on Parliament not only for extraordinary but for ordinary taxation too and the Civil List replaced traditional revenues.

What, then, was the function of Parliament in this close, stable, oligarchical world of Hanoverian England? Plainly, the House of Commons did not control the composition of the Government in any modern sense; the reverse was often nearer the truth. For a Ministry which had the Crown's support could always be assured of winning the election of a new Parliament; indeed, no eighteenth-century Government lost an election. Nor did Ministers necessarily resign on suffering the defeat of one of their Bills, even if it were a major measure, provided they had the general confidence of the House. The Younger Pitt, for instance, carried on as Prime Minister after the Commons had defeated his Reform Bill of 1785, which was not his only piece of proposed legislation to be rejected. Sometimes Ministries resigned when the particular groups and political compacts which had constituted them fell assunder: only rarely did this take the form of an actual defeat in the House. The favour of the Crown, on the other hand, was an indispensable requisite of office-holding, at least during the first three-quarters of the century. What can be said is that no Ministry, even with the Crown's support, could survive an outbreak of opposition on the part of the 'independent' Members of the House of Commons. It was, for example, their withdrawal of confidence which forced Lord North out of office and, as North informed George III, he believed that the sense of the House against his Ministry also represented the sense of the 'Nation at large'. On the other hand, the independent Members struck but rarely, deeming it their normal duty to support the Ministry of the day, which was more likely to disintegrate from internal reasons than under attack from the Commons.

The eighteenth-century House of Commons cannot be described as a great legislature. Appropriately (for a body primarily representing a class concerned with the defence and exploitation of property), the bulk of the Commons' legislative work consisted of passing an incessant stream of private Bills authorising, for instance, the enclosure of land, the setting up of turnpikes or the building of canals. Though much of this legislation was of national importance, it was not regarded in this light and was enacted with a view to the requirements of a private world—and by the initiative of private Members. Such Members of Parliament might be tied to patron or Government by interest or place. On the other hand, the influence of the 'independent' Members could be decisive at moments of political crisis and even rotten boroughs could have the advantage of sending men of talents to Westminster with greater independence of mind and action than is normally possible under a system dominated by party. Moreover, the House was not bound to the Government as it now is, since Governments did not change as a result of elections and, in electing Members to the Commons, the electorate of those days was in no sense choosing a Government.

Was this, then, the great age of the private Member as such—especially bearing in mind his capacity to take control of the parliamentary time-table? The claim could hardly be sustained. The majority of Members took little part in debate; attendance in this 'golden age' was frequently poor and a quorum often lacking. The great oratory was left then, as later, to the giants; the country Members remained taciturn when they were not applauding or jeering the speeches of leaders of the competing groups of the oligarchy. Nor was the backbench Member 'independent' of outside pressures. For the majority, after all, 'independence' was undermined by 'influence', which was the eighteenth-century Ministry's alternative to party discipline. In the twentieth century there has been criticism of the relationship between MPs and outside pressure groups with which they have some private connection, or of the extent to which the Member is by-passed by the dealings of interest groups with the Executive. Both features were prominent in the eighteenth century. Strong bonds existed between Members and their patrons. A Member was honourably bound to pursue a policy of which his patron, usually a peer, approved and much of the private legislation was on behalf of outside interests with which the Member was personally linked. The economic predominance of the House of Lords (of which most Ministers were members) had a pervasive influence over the Commons. The eighteenth century also saw the growth of external political, religious and social associations operating not only through pressure on MPs but in direct relationship with the Executive.

With the backbenchers mostly mute and under external pressures; with opposition reluctant and Parliament dominated by a minority of great figures, what was left to the House of Commons now that the Whig harmony had replaced the genuine political clashes of earlier times? Was it no more than a facade? In fact, it had a genuine contemporary rôle and it also left a valuable bequest to the future democracy. Its contemporary rôle was to hold the balance of the Constitution. Respectful towards the Executive which was the nominee of the prevailing class (or a faction of it), Parliament was also vigilant to ensure that executive power was not extended. Its opposition to Walpole's excise scheme was an example of its vigilance. Walpole's scheme had aroused such antipathy, on the ground that it might lead to unlimited encroachments on liberty by the taxmen, that his majority in the Commons began to fall away and he withdrew his Bill after second reading. Similarly, Dunning's famous resolution of 1780 alleging that 'the influence of the Crown has increased, is increasing and ought to be diminished' was carried in an exceptionally full House by 233 to 215 votes. This resolution, passed at the height of the parliamentary attack on Lord North's Government and seeking to restore parliamentary 'freedom', demonstrated the sort of issue which stirred the eighteenth-century Commons.

While defending the Constitution in this period of harmony and 'non-politics', the House of Commons built its prestige to an importance never reached before and created an institutional atmosphere which had a life of its own. It was a sort of sanctified club with an inner harmony and code of behaviour achieved precisely because it had a narrow, integrated membership which could accept the common rules. Its manners and its institutional self-confidence were bequeathed to the new parties and classes which were later to enter the House of Commons. If its manners are not quite so casual now as in the eighteenth century, when Members stretched themselves on their benches, cracked nuts and ate oranges, while cheering good and harrying poor speakers, they are still informal enough to startle many an overseas visitor. The informality is the mark of the self-confidence of the institution and the common bond of its members. The historical persona of the House and its prestige as guardian of the Constitution were to ensure that when party broke out again, it should be within an accepted constitutional framework.

In the last three decades of the century, the House of Commons entered into a state of tension with the country outside—with a new, potential electorate. From this tension party emerged in a new sense. The case of the radical John Wilkes (a former MP who had been expelled by the Commons) and the electors of Middlesex marked the beginning of a new sort of politics. In 1768 and twice thereafter, Middlesex elected Wilkes to Parliament and as many times the Commons expelled him. In a fourth election, the House declared the runner-up elected thus precipitating a significant argument. On the one hand, the House of Commons had always guarded its independence from pressure from the electorate: on the other, some of Wilkes' supporters would have had their Members pledged to certain policies. In other words, they would have turned the MP into a mandated delegate instead of maintaining him as a (nominally) free representative in the old tradition. This, indeed, the Commons might reasonably resist: but could they claim to determine who should sit among them? Could they continue to shut the door against representatives of a broader electorate?

The Wilkes case was a symptom of a wider malaise than that created by the Middlesex elections. The country was knocking at the door of Parliament and demanding electoral reform. It was also increasingly demanding public knowledge of the proceedings of Parliament. In 1771, the Commons entered into a struggle with the printers of the London newspapers over their 'right' to publish debates. Under standing orders, reporting the proceedings of the House was forbidden but the order had been generally ignored. The Wilkes affair inspired the House to try to enforce it but the attempt at prosecution failed. Though the House did not abandon its right to exclude reporters, and still from time to time had them excluded under the standing order forbidding the presence of Strangers, the Commons tacitly relinquished their claim to enforce this 'right' by prosecution.

The new public interest and the wider reporting of Parliament made people outside better politically educated and, for all its corruption, the unreformed House of Commons became increasingly sensitive to public opinion. The abolition of the slave trade in 1807 and Catholic emancipation in 1829 were both results of the pressure of public opinion. Finally, in 1832, public opinion forced Parliament to reform itself. But political reform had been slow in coming and, largely out of the combat between radical-reformers and the conservers of the Constitution, political parties were reborn.

In the 1780s, at a low point in the standing of Lord North's administration (at the time, indeed, when Dunning moved his famous resolution), the demand for reform errupted in a concerted movement of petitioners from the counties, seeking an increase of 100 in the number of county and independent Members as against the unreformed boroughs. The Younger Pitt himself was associated with this movement and when Prime Minister he introduced in 1785 a modest measure of reform to increase the country members, abolishing an equal number of rotten boroughs. The measure was defeated and, after the outbreak of the French Revolution, the demands for reform were crushed under a new defensive conservativism in the 1790s. Indeed, the French Revolution entered into British politics on both sides. For the radicals, it was a symbol of advancement and enlightenment, though more and more Whigs came to fear the excesses of revolution. For Pitt and his followers, however, the prime aim must be the winning of the war with revolutionary France and the defence of the Constitution by holding potential subversion in check at home. Pitt the Younger, himself once a reformer and now pledged to carry on the king's Government and to overcome faction, would have called himself a Whig; but from his followers a new Tory Party was born. Against him were the radicals and the Foxite Whigs. In the early years of the new century it was again becoming possible to speak with some meaning of Tory versus Whig politics—with the Radicals on the extreme 'left'.

The Whigs themselves, for all their vested interest in maintaining the social and economic *status quo*, found themselves driven forward

58

on a tide of opinion which they could not control to put Parliament on a more rational, if still narrow, electoral franchise in 1832—a franchise, however, at least as firmly related to property. In so doing, the Whigs took the first step towards opening the parliamentary 'club' to democracy. They also raised in a new form the old question: how could a strong Executive be reconciled with a *free* Parliament which could no longer be controlled by influence and containing parties of strong and combative opinions and interests? The answer was to be the evolution of 'party' organised with a thoroughness never known before. When this system reached its peak in the twentieth century and well-drilled phalanxes faced each other under organisations that appealed directly to a mass electorate, the question was again to be asked: what effective and independent rôle now remained for the House of Commons?

Chapter Two

The Nineteenth-century Parliament

The Reform Act of 1832 gave the House of Commons greater influence over the formation and the political complexion of governments than it had possessed at any time since Walpole had established the Whig hegemony over party politics. From now on, the composition of the House of Commons was to be decided largely by an electorate which could not be controlled, instead of through the exercise of Crown patronage on behalf of one or another faction of the dominant Whig Party.

Of course, 1832 did not bring about an overnight transition from corrupt patronage to perfect electoral freedom: the process of change had started before the Reform Act and continued after it. The influence of the Crown over the House of Commons by means of patronage had already so diminished that it had become impossible before 1832 to use it as a means of determining the majority of the House. Moreover, even after the Reform Act some of the characteristics of eighteenth-century politics persisted for a time. The influence of the landlords over the return of Members for rural areas remained strong until the introduction of the secret ballot in 1872. Even the remnants of Crown influence lingered on for some years and one contemporary politician, Charles Arbuthnot, reckoned that after 1832 the support of the Sovereign was still worth between twenty and thirty votes at a General Election.[1] If this was so, it meant that Queen Victoria won the General Election of 1837 for the Whigs, who were returned with only a small majority. Arbuthnot said: 'If the late King had lived, we might have turned them out, but with the young foolish Queen against us we can have but little hope.'

Nevertheless, even allowing for these qualifications, the fact

[1] Arthur Aspinall, Introduction to *Three Early Nineteenth Century Diaries* (Williams and Norgate, 1952). See also Norman Gash, *Politics in the Age of Peel* (Longmans, 1952), Ch. 14.

remains that the Reform Act did mark the clearest point of distinction between the phase of British politics in which Crown influence could largely determine both the membership of the House of Commons and the way many of its Members voted; and the period of party-based nineteenth-century politics in which a free electorate, however limited, decided the complexion of the House and therefore of Ministries.

The end of the rotten boroughs and the creation of new, larger constituencies whose parliamentary representation could not be bought meant that the Crown must in future accept Ministers appointed by a House which it could no longer control. It was not long before William IV learned this lesson. Giving expression for the last time in 1834 to the king's traditional right to change his Ministers, he dismissed Melbourne at the suggestion of the Prime Minister himself, who was having difficulty in reconstructing his Cabinet. William did so because Melbourne's suggestion coincided with the king's own wishes. Peel, the Tory leader, briefly held office in a House of Commons where he had no majority and even continued for a few months after a General Election had failed (though Melbourne's majority was reduced) to give him one. Only when defeated in the House over the Irish Revenues did Peel resign. But the important point, constitutionally, was that, despite the wishes of the king, he had to abandon office because the House of Commons was against him, and could no longer be dissolved and reconstituted in any Ministry's favour.

The episode illustrates both the older view of the relationship of the monarch to his Ministers and to Parliament—and also the new impotence of the Crown when faced with the hard facts of the House of Commons statistics. The older view of the sovereign's rights was again to be demonstrated in 1839 when, after Melbourne had resigned on being defeated in the House, Peel was invited by the queen to form a Government, but failed because the queen would neither grant him a Dissolution nor agree to the appointment of some Tory ladies to the Royal Household. But again, parliamentary statistics in due course had their way: though Melbourne returned to office, his Government was more or less impotent as his majority in the House fell away. Peel took office with a more than adequate majority in 1841.

The need that governments now had to secure stable majorities in the House of Commons led to the growth of party political organisations which began to evolve soon after the Reform Act: when this process was completed it would be possible to argue (though not, I think, convincingly) that the House of Commons was in a subordinate position to the Executive: that it had become no more than a mechanism for giving the Cabinet plenary powers based on a majority of 'Whipped' MPs. But the first effects of the Reform Act were rather different. Deprived of the 'discipline' of Crown influence, and with parties in an embryonic stage, the House of Commons (as Peel and Wellington had feared) entered upon more than three decades of making and unmaking governments by its votes in the Division lobbies: of political allegiances so shifting as to seem potentially anarchical.

It was not that the membership of the new House of Commons was startlingly different from that of the old. No great new Radical Party was formed and, as for working-class representation, the new property qualifications actually diminished the working-class vote in some constituencies. Though the property-owning middle classes were taken into junior partnership with the landowners, it was the latter who still predominated numerically in the House. There were some 500 MPs representing the landed interest in 1833 and 400 in 1865. Nor, perhaps, would the Reform Act alone have created such inchoate politics in the House of Commons had it not been passed when so many other major political and social changes were the subject of debate. It was, after all, as part of a much wider movement of public opinion that the Commons had been persuaded to reform themselves and reform generally remained the theme of politics after 1832. One of the main results of the Reform Act of 1832 was that politics became rather less a conflict of interests and more a conflict of opinions: and the House of Commons was the forum in which opinions on a number of issues of (more or less) principle were argued out.[1] Of course, interest remained a fundamental—perhaps the fundamental—condition of politics and was often concealed within arguments of principle—as in the matters of protection and slavery. Nevertheless, the change of emphasis was important for the character of the House and it was perhaps this *moral* attitude to politics (however much it may be debunked) which really marked the nineteenth century as the 'golden age' of the House of Commons. As a Radical, John Stuart Mill argued that Parliament should be a

[1] A. H. Birch, *Representative and Responsible Government* (Allen & Unwin, 1964), pp. 52–3.

'Congress of Opinions': as a Conservative, Disraeli contended that it should be a 'mirror of the mind as well as the material interests of England'.[1] It is arguable that the House of Commons attained, in the second half of the century, a desirable balance between interest and opinion: party discipline and independence of expression. The basis for this balance was established in the years between the first and the second Reform Acts when, for all the cross-voting and independence of Members, the Party system was established in Britain. But the road the House of Commons travelled until the second Reform Act of 1867 was a hard one which, to the eyes of some contemporaries, was also discreditable.

(ii)

The years between 1832 and 1867 which put the House of Commons into a new position as a maker and unmaker of Ministries may conveniently be looked at in two separate periods. From 1832 until 1846 there was, in fact, a surprising stability of government. Although individual politicians changed sides, the Whigs were in office (apart from the short interlude of Peel's Prime Ministership in 1834) until 1841. Thereafter, Peel's Conservative Government held power strongly until the Prime Minister split his Party in 1846. The second inter-Reform Act phase that then began presented a very different appearance. With former party allegiances broken, Britain was ruled by a series of coalitions and minority governments. Contemporaries now saw very clearly the difference between the reformed and unreformed House of Commons. The later Lord Salisbury, who himself became Prime Minister in 1885, was one of them. He had entered the House of Commons as Lord Robert Cecil in 1853 when political confusion was at its height and in 1861, reviewing the political diaries of Lord Colchester (a former Speaker), Salisbury took the opportunity to discuss the House of Commons' failure to make proper use of the new power it had gained over Governments.[2]

[1] Quoted in A. H. Birch, *Representative and Responsible Government*, p. 53.

[2] Anonymous article by Salisbury in the *Saturday Review*, February 2, 1861. Salisbury's writings in the *Saturday Review* are identified as his by a list of 607 published by Dr J. F. A. Mason, Librarian of Christ Church, in an article in the *Bulletin of the Institute of Historical Research*, 'The Third Marquess of Salisbury and the "Saturday Review"', May 1961.

[The House of Commons] was far, in those days, from being the powerful body it has since become. Governments did not then depend exclusively on its favour. . . . The influence of the Crown, both upon the elections and the votes of members, was so enormous, that matters very rarely came to the pass that the House of Commons forced a minister upon the Crown. During the fifty years which intervened between Lord Shelburne's resignation, and the accession of William IV, ten Administrations successively rose and fell; and not one of them left office in deference to an adverse vote of the House of Commons. . . . The House of Commons went for little or nothing in all these changes and passively accepted the leaders whom accident, caprice, or intrigue imposed upon it. If we recollect that, since the Reform Bill, every Ministry that has fallen, with the single exception of Lord Grey's, has fallen in deference to an adverse vote of the House of Commons, the change that has taken place in its position will be manifest.[1]

Salisbury drew the conclusion that the House was strengthened by popular support but that, in another sense, it was shackled by its responsibility to the electorate.

However, so long as parties had remained intact, as they did until the disintegration of the Conservative Party in 1846, the power of Parliament was 'bridled'. After 1846 fights between the factions which now composed the House reduced it, in Salisbury's words, to a 'formless chaos'. To Salisbury's view of the situation in the fifties and sixties and his remedies, I shall return in context, but it is logical to look first at the years between 1832 and 1846 when the idea of organised parties, which was to develop in the second half of the century, really took root.

The first election after the 1832 Reform Bill had given the Whigs what was on paper a big majority. There were 360 of them, supported by seventy Radicals and seventy Irish Members as against only 150 Tories. In fact, the majority was neither so great nor so assured as it might seem. Party relationships were fluid, even before the total disintegration of the Tory Party through Corn Law Repeal: an example was the resignation from the post-Reform Act Whig Ministry of Lord Stanley, a member of an old Whig family, over Lord John

[1] One of the pre-Reform Act Ministries, that of Addington in 1804, did resign out of deference to House of Commons feeling, and as a result of a shrunken majority, but *before* it was defeated.

Russell's appropriation of Irish Church revenues for Roman Catholic education. Stanley, who took a number of other prominent Whigs with him, formed for a time something like a third party and his progress in crossing the floor all the way to the Tories was a slow one. But he got there in the end to become Disraeli's Leader, after the break with Peel, and three times a Conservative Prime Minister. This, however, was only one element in the decline of the old Whigs which went on in the post-Reform Act decade.

After the curious 'bedchamber episode' had sent Peel back to Opposition, the Whigs, though in government, lost their grip on politics. They might have expected the Reform Act to make the political world safer for them and it had been widely heralded as meaning the death of the Tory Party. In fact, it was the old Whigs who were at risk: their sort of politics, based on land and personal connections, had a diminishing place in the new order. By 1840, their majority in the Commons was little more than nominal and Disraeli, in *Coningsby*, expressed their plight thus:

> Though it was circulated among their friends, as if from the highest authority, that 'one was enough' [the phrase was, of course, used by Harold Wilson when Prime Minister in the 1964 Parliament and also by Winston Churchill in his post-war government] there seemed daily a better chance of their being deprived even of that magical unit. For the first time in the history of this country since the introduction of parliamentary sovereignty, the Government of England depended on the fate of single elections; and indeed, by a single vote, it is remarkable to observe, the fate of the Whig government was ultimately decided.[1]

During these declining years of Whig government Peel, though in Opposition, was the dominant figure in British politics. Immediately after the Reform Act, he had set about fashioning out of the old Toryism a new, pragmatic Conservative Party which both demonstrated its willingness to accept change while carefully refusing to give hostages to fortune by committing itself in advance. Peel himself had done much to make the Reform Act work by taking up the posture of a responsible Opposition leader and, in the Tamworth Manifesto of 1834, he not only made history by addressing to the electors a statement of the general principles on which a Conservative government would act, but also specifically accepted the Reform Act.

[1] Benjamin Disraeli, *Coningsby*, Bk. VIII, Ch. I (first published 1844).

What is more, the defeated Tories under Peel had set about building a party organisation designed to see that Tory voters were registered in their constituencies. The Carlton Club was formed in 1832 not merely as a social meeting-place for Conservatives but as the head-quarters of the Party's parliamentary and political organisation. The Whigs, in turn, followed by establishing the Reform Club in 1836. But it was the new Conservatism which was making the pace in these years.

> There is a perfectly new element of political power—namely, the registration of voters, a more powerful one than either the Sovereign or the House of Commons. That party is the strongest in point of fact which has the existing registration in its favour. It is a dormant instrument, but a most powerful one in its tacit and preventive operation,

wrote Peel. Of what use, he asked, was the prerogative of dissolution with an unfavourable registry—and the fact of its being unfavourable known to the world?[1]

Peel's concept of the new Conservative Party was of one which would accept necessary change but which would not compromise with certain basic principles for the sake of power. Peel's attitudes were the foundation of modern Conservatism. Yet out of them also came the disintegration of the Party in 1846 when Peel, who had headed a notably strong Government, broke his Party by repealing the Corn Laws with Whig help. He did it because he believed it necessary. Yet his pragmatism could be looked at in a less favourable light. 'The Tamworth Manifesto of 1834,' wrote Disraeli,

> was an attempt to construct a party without principles. . . . There was indeed a considerable shouting about what they called Con-servative principles; but the awkward question naturally arose, what will you conserve? . . . Conservatism assumes in theory that everything established should be maintained; but adopts in practice that everything that is established is indefensible.[2]

When the Corn Laws were repealed, only 112 Conservatives voted with Peel. Immediately afterwards, Whigs and Protectionist Tories combined to defeat him in the House and force him to resign. Not only was the Conservative Party shattered but most of its able men

[1] C. S. Parker, *Sir Robert Peel* (John Murray, 1899), Vol. II, p. 368.
[2] Benjamin Disraeli, *Coningsby*, Bk. II, Ch. V.

went with Peel. Of the men of stature, only Disraeli and Bentinck remained with the Protectionist Tories. So began the phase of 'formless chaos' which was only ended by the second Reform Bill, the amalgamation of the leading Peelites (after Peel's death) with the Liberals and the drift back to the Tory fold of most of the Peelite rank-and-file. Until then, neither of the main Parties could retain office without Peelite support.

From the Corn Law Repeal until 1852, the Whigs (under Lord John Russell) held office, with the support of Peelite votes, though the number of Peel's followers in the House had been sharply reduced in the General Election of 1847. Even when the Derby–Disraeli Tories abandoned protection, personal bitterness was too sharp to allow reunion. Lord Derby (the former Whig Lord Stanley) was now the Tory Leader, with Disraeli leading the Party in the Commons. (Not until 1868 was Disraeli reluctantly accepted as Leader on Derby's resignation through ill-health: there was no one else.) In 1852, Derby, with Disraeli as Chancellor of the Exchequer, formed a brief minority government which lasted for ten months on sufferance. In the same year, after its fall, the Whig–Liberals formed a coalition with the Peelites under the Peelite, Lord Aberdeen. This, in turn, was followed by the administrations of Palmerston, who dominated English politics and remained in office, with one intermission, from 1855 until his death in 1865. In this Palmerstonian decade, the Tories, again under Derby, had a few months of government in 1858. These were the years in which the new Liberal Party, which Gladstone was to lead so triumphantly, finally emerged from its Whig, Radical and Peelite forebears. Yet the many breaks and changes and the persistence of minority rule made this a sour and disillusioning period in politics and the prestige of Parliament suffered.

Once again the question of parliamentary reform had arisen. First one and then another government tried and failed to bring in an acceptable measure and it was the Conservative administration, under first Derby and then Disraeli, from 1866 to 1868, which finally succeeded— though they had previously defeated a Liberal Reform Bill brought in by Palmerston's successor, Lord John Russell. Even now, when the Peelites' leaders had been finally absorbed into the Liberal Party,[1] there was a devastating symptom of the potential fragility of party allegiances when the Liberal Reform Bill was defeated by the

[1] Other Peelites drifted back to the Tories.

Tories with the aid of a band of dissident anti-Reform Liberals—the 'Adullamites' under Robert Lowe's leadership.

In these unstable years, it seemed as though party, in the old sense, was dead. Though the ranks of the Whigs and the Tories were broken no more, the Peelites, the Radicals and the Irish persisted as more or less independent groups. Both Whigs and Tories angled for the votes of the small groups and the Peelites, for want of issues big enough to force them to take a position, were slow to amalgamate with other parties. Yet, though the parliamentary chaos was real enough in these years, one detects, looking back, a certain underlying unity between the period immediately before and that which followed the disintegration of the Conservative Party.

In the first period, the foundations of the future party system were laid not merely in organisational terms but because of the polarisation of opinion over a number of basic issues between the one side and the other. Despite the cross-voting, contemporaries had no doubt about the reality of party divisions in the early post-Reform Act years, and Professor Gash has shown that, despite the Protection issue, what distinguished the new Conservatism of Peel was less an attachment to economic dogma or particular social policies than a united determination to preserve the Constitution.[1] For this the gentry and the clergy formed a natural base for a party which was to outlast the troubles ahead.

Similarly, the post-1846 parliamentary 'chaos' perhaps did less harm to the notion of Party than might be superficially supposed. The disorganisation of these years, in fact, probably intensified the British attachment to firm Party discipline in the Commons. After Gladstone had formed his Liberal Ministry in 1868, domestic British politics again became stable. One 'golden age' of Parliament, which had given shifting factions of Members of the House of Commons maximum scope for changing the Executive, was over: a new sort of 'golden age', based on the stability of great parties, was to follow.

(iii)

To most contemporaries, the disintegration of party in the mid-nineteenth century brought discredit on the House of Commons and was wholly foreign to the British parliamentary tradition. The chorus

[1] See Norman Gash, *Reaction and Reconstruction in English Politics, 1832–1852* (Oxford University Press, 1965), pp. 126–9.

of disapproval from men inside and outside Parliament was almost unanimous in regarding the breakdown of party ties as weakening to government and conducive to inefficiency. Before citing some of the contemporary opinions on these points, however, one must note that the parliamentary conditions after 1846 did not even produce the freedom for the individual Member that is sometimes spoken of as a nineteenth-century characteristic.

Parliament between the Reform Acts was not in any sense democratic. The franchise was strictly limited and a large number of constituencies were uncontested. Less than half the constituencies were contested in the 1841 election when the Whigs were replaced in office by Peel.[1] The affairs of Parliament were of concern to a very narrow political nation and within the close political community of Westminster 'Whipping' had become accepted as perfectly normal. If it was not as stringent as it was later to become, it could still be pretty ruthless. This was so even in the early years after the 1832 Reform Act. Though a tradition of independence survived through these years to erupt into indiscipline after 1846, party bonds between the first two Reform Acts was a reality.

Party influence is so defined that there are few, if any, floating voters who are sufficiently independent or unprejudiced to be gained by any sudden convictions; so decidedly are the minds of all made up on the subject before the discussion takes place,

noted a contemporary.[2] So much for any notion of a Parliament of independent Members, all thinking more or less intelligently for themselves. The expected Division figures supplied to the political leaders often showed a surprisingly small number of 'doubtfuls'. Russell, in 1837, Greville in 1839 and Peel in 1840 calculated the doubtfuls as only five, five and eight respectively.[3] Of course, on many issues Party lines were not as rigid in the mid-nineteenth century as they were to become later. Many more important matters, especially those involving social legislation, were then open questions and over these the reins of party could be loose. Furthermore, men were more willing to change their allegiances and to put party unity at risk on

---

[1] Norman Gash, *Politics in the Age of Peel*, pp. xix and 441.

[2] Journal of T. Raikes (1851), quoted in Norman Gash, *Reaction and Reconstruction in English Politics, 1832–1852*, p. 127.

[3] Norman Gash, *Reaction and Reconstruction in English Politics, 1832–1852*, p. 127.

some major issues. Nevertheless, party lines could be drawn very tightly on occasions vital for the life of a Government and generally the intentions of MPs were calculable well in advance of a public airing of the arguments.

Political leaders were often prepared to act as they thought fit regardless of their followers (for whose attainments they had no great regard anyway) and they sometimes clung less to office than their modern counterparts do. But just the same, the nineteenth-century Whips were kept busy taking the temperature of backbench opinion and pressing Members into the lobbies. No reader of Trollope, an acute recorder of the parliamentary atmosphere, could doubt it. The ordeal of that ancient piece of Whig lobby-fodder, Sir Everard Powell, at the hands of the Whips is graphically described in *Phineas Finn*: no Whig, however old, was allowed to escape coming down to the House for a certain vital Division. ' "Poor Sir Everard!" said Lord Brentford. "It will kill him no doubt, but I suppose the seat is safe." ' On the crucial night, for a Division which did not take place until after 3 a.m., Sir Everard was there, 'in his bath chair at twelve, with a doctor on one side of him and a friend on the other in some purlieu of the House, and did his duty like a fine old Briton as he was'. Soon the news spread that he was dead of the gout. ' "By —— yes; as dead as a herring," said Mr Rattler' the Whip, who defended his ruthlessness on the ground that no one complained if 'a fellow dies leading his regiment' and Sir Everard had done more for his country than that. When Mr Rattler presently heard that old Sir Everard was not dead, because the journey to the House 'did him a world of good', the Whip's single-minded comment was: 'Then we'll have him down for every division.'

Nor was this piece of fiction far-fetched. Gladstone in his old age reminisced about the skill of the Whips in the forties who 'somehow seemed to know more precisely than they do now how a division would go'. It was 'positively known', he said, that in the division which turned out Melbourne in 1841 there would be a majority of one: the only doubt was on which side it would be. This was the famous 'one is enough' Division to which Disraeli had caustically referred, and Gladstone gave his own account of one Opposition Member who was almost at death's door. 'He *was* dead', Mr Gladstone added emphatically,

except that he had just a little breath left in him. The question was, could he be brought to the House? The Whips said he must come, and so they carried him down. He was wheeled in a Bath-chair. To this day I never forget the look on his face. His glassy eyes were upturned, his jaws stiff. We, a lot of young Conservatives clustered round the door, seeing the Bath-chair, thought at first they had brought down a corpse. But he voted, and the resolution which turned out Lord Melbourne's government was carried by a majority of one.[1]

Bagehot reported a politician's comment on the long row of 'fresh and respectable looking' country Members: 'By Jove, they are the finest brute votes in Europe!'[2] The notion of the Commons as a body of high-minded independent gentlemen was also given short shrift by Salisbury, who was convinced that freedom to overturn Ministries was a symptom not of independence but of the irresponsibility of factions. Palmerston, Disraeli and Russell, by bidding for Radical votes, had (Salisbury considered) led the House to complete demoralisation by the end of the 1850s. Without fairly strict Party divisions, the House of Commons was no more than a 'chaotic, unorganised mass'. The remedy must be strong party government and he expounded his views in an article, 'Party', as follows:

On the conduct of the next few legislative campaigns will depend the issue whether the future government of this country is, or is not, to be party government. We shall ascertain whether we are to be ruled by an aggregate of minute factions, almost irresponsible from their obscurity, or by the representatives of broader national phases of opinion; for between these the choice must lie. There is no alternative. The independent-member theory—the notion of 653 men, each studying every question for himself, and voting on his own judgment of its merits without bias or favour—is an inspiration from Laputa.... Combinations there must be—the only question is, whether they shall be broad parties, based on comprehensive ideas, and guided by men who have a name to stake on the wisdom of their course, or obscure cliques, with some narrow crotchet for a policy, and some paltry yelping shibboleth for a cry.

It seemed clear to Salisbury that since 1846,

[1] Henry W. Lucy, *Later Peeps at Parliament* (1905).
[2] Walter Bagehot, *The English Constitution* (Watts Edn., 1958), p. 158.

votes are given for selfish or sectional ends. Private gratitudes or grudges, the promotion of some local interest, or the glorification of some parochial notability, have replaced the old fidelity to a party banner.[1]

The view that party was essential to viable parliamentary government was expressed on all sides. As early as 1848, Disraeli delivered a long, bitter attack on the inefficiency with which the business of the House was being conducted—forty-seven Bills abandoned, withdrawn or postponed in the previous six months in consequence of time wasted—but insisted that it was not the fault of the House itself. The fault he said, pointing to the Treasury bench, was there: 'I see there a body of men who acceded to power without a parliamentary majority.' It was a Cabinet without conviction that measures would be carried: success depended on an aggregate of small parties. Measures were altered to suit all needs and ended by suiting no-one—and Disraeli stated categorically: 'I trace all this evil to the disorganisation of party.' He then went on:

I know that there are Gentlemen in this House who affect to deprecate party government. I am not now going to enter into a discussion respecting party government; but this I will tell you . . . that you cannot choose between party government and Parliamentary government. I say, you can have no Parliamentary government if you have no party government.[2]

A few years later, the *Economist*, likewise, contrasted the contemporary parliamentary chaos with 'the glory' of the old days of parliamentary government: the days of Walpole, Chatham and Pitt when the parties were marshalled against each other like two battle arrays and when absence from division required leave and desertion was 'visited by ignomony'. In those 'halcyon days' not only were there no third or fourth parties 'to embarrass action and set calculation at defiance' but independent members were 'about as rare as the sea-serpent and as mythical as the unicorn'. Even before the Reform Bill there had been a change but now, in addition to the breakdown of party, a number of 'really independent members' had found their way into the House, politicians without allegiance. Gloomily, the *Economist* observed: 'It is obvious that the real strain and trial of the

---

[1] *Saturday Review*, May 9, 1857.
[2] H.C. Deb., Vol. 101, cols. 205–6, August 30, 1848.

British Constitution which has been staved off for generations has come now.' Intrinsic faults in the Constitution were now breaking through and as a result the *Economist* found cause to worry for the survival of parliamentary government altogether.[1]

The *Spectator* also pleaded the cause of party discipline[2] and Bagehot believed that, as the House of Commons lived in a state of perpetual choice, 'party is inherent in it, is bone of its bone, and breath of its breath'.[3] If this is accepted then, indeed, it might be argued that, in Aristotelian terminology, the period before 1867 represented a perversion, not a glorification, of parliamentary government.

There was also a widespread contemporary agreement with Disraeli that the Commons were an inefficient body, partly because the rift in the party structure had disorganised the business of the House. In 1856, the *Spectator* devoted an article to 'the phenomenon, noted of late very generally as a decline in the efficiency of Parliament'.[4] It was sceptical about further electoral reform as a cure: and asked whether the falling off was attributable, not to the way Members were selected, but to 'causes that lie deep in the stage of social development through which the whole nation is passing'. (The thought is worth consideration in regard to contemporary criticisms of Parliament in the middle of the twentieth century.) The comparison was not, said the *Spectator*, made with the period before the Reform Bill: the complaint was of a falling off since Corn Law Repeal. But what big questions had there been since then to divide the Commons into broad opposing armies, asked the *Spectator*? It concluded that there had been none. Political leaders had had a hold on their followers when there were big issues to be settled.

All that has changed since the Conservative Leader demonstrated in his own person that the real tendencies of the age are not to be resisted by any combination, however powerful in great names, in traditional renown, in territorial influence,

said the *Spectator*, in something like an echo of Disraeli's comment on the Tamworth Manifesto. Parliament could be nothing except a reflex of public opinion.

[1] *Economist*, April 23, 1853.
[2] *Spectator*, July 12, 1857.
[3] Walter Bagehot, *The English Constitution* (Watts Edn.), p. 158.
[4] *Spectator*, 'Parliamentary Inefficiency', November 8, 1856, pp. 1186–7.

If public opinion is decided, clear and well-marked into broad divisions, Parliament will be so too; if public opinion is doubtful, sceptical of all political principles, living from hand to mouth as it were, Parliament will not exhibit the opposite characteristics.

An examination of the politics of this period, together with contemporary views of the state of the House of Commons, suggests that Parliament only managed to do its job in its state of confusion because that job was comparatively unexacting: because of the lack of great divisive issues. This is not to say that there were lacking important issues which ought to have been dealt with: only that they were not so explosive as to concentrate the minds of the politicians. In 1857, the *Spectator*, complaining of 'political stagnation' and of the failure of Party to revive, observed: 'If the House of Commons mechanically preserves the habit of restlessness on secondary questions, to real political influences, it is torpid.' Once-familiar voices were silent, those of Gladstone, Cobden and Lord John Russell among them. A number of questionable Bills, the article continued, demanded money for doubtful, or even unexplained objects. 'The still small voice of the private Member' occasionally called these duties to mind, but the call fell flat. Ministers replied in conciliatory manner that it was 'all right' and every question was hushed. The material silence was exceeded by a sort of moral silence: you could hear, said the *Spectator*, 'a Bill drop'.[1]

Salisbury also had no doubt that only the paucity of issues enabled Parliament to manage in its state of internal anarchy.

At the distance of a very few years its protracted sittings will seem to the historian to have been an objectless waste of labour. . . . It has eminently been a session of little things. . . . Nothing has been on a great scale except the length of the speeches,

he wrote in 1861. Parliament's independence, its scope for unlimited, undisciplined discussion represented, in Salisbury's eyes, no Golden Age: he stated categorically that he considered it to be in decline.

So much for the 'stature' of the House and its new 'independence'. What, then, of the quality of the individual MP in the nineteenth century? The *Spectator*, in the article on 'Parliamentary Inefficiency' already referred to, was outspoken. It considered that, if Parliament was indeed inefficient, reform of the electoral system was as such no cure, and the picture of the Membership given to support this

[1] *Spectator*, June 1857, p. 625.

argument is convincing, and not, perhaps, unfamiliar to the twentieth century.

Fluent lawyers with their personal ends to serve, jobbing directors who regard Parliamentary honours as at once a convenient badge of social distinction and an instrument of commercial speculation, nincompoop lords with local influence, or even without it, are quite as likely to be selected by people who pay five pounds a year for house rent as by those who pay ten or twenty.[1]

Lord Salisbury, in the *Saturday Review* of July 4, 1857, gave an even more scathing account of the Members (pseudonymously referred to) he had watched in a Commons' Committee[2]: Sir Tunbelly Turnbull 'noted for his success in fatting pigs, and a great connoisseur in middens'; Mr O'Blunderbuss, an Opposition-minded Irishman; Mr Muddle, a small country grocer; and a 'scamp of a Life-Guardsman whom his aristocratic mother had sent into the House as the sole chance of making him steady'. Several millions of pounds hung on the words of this 'strange collection of varieties'. Why had they been selected when the House was supposed to contain some of the best businessmen in the country? Salisbury was told why by a knowledgeable friend:

Oh, none of the members are employed on this work except those who have nothing else to do. . . . Therefore these committees, which within the last few years have disposed of money more than equal to half the national debt, are almost invariably composed only of men whose time is worth nothing to themselves and whose opinion is worth nothing to the political world.

Nor was the House, as a general rule, filled with enthusiastic Members, eager to do their duty, however pedestrian. Then as now, it was crowded on the great occasions in which the Commons were passionately interested—and the greatest of all had been Corn Law Repeal, which had reduced the House to unparalleled wildness and bitterness. But after 1846, the House fell into a new torpor. In the sluggish days of Palmerston's administration, count-outs were frequent. On private members' nights in the 1860s the House was frequently cut short for lack of the quorum of forty Members. A certain Mr Thomas Collins, a Member of three Parliaments in the

---

[1] *Spectator*, November 8, 1856.
[2] For discussion of the nineteenth-century committee 'system' see below, p. 78.

sixties, earned the title of 'Count Collins' from his hobby in trying to count the House out whenever he saw a chance. 'He seemed to hold the opinion that the House of Commons was most usefully engaged when it was not sitting', wrote a contemporary observer in the Press Gallery.[1]

Between the Reform Bills, Parliament still reflected a small political and fundamentally aristocratic society. It was itself, in spirit, a club: its Members, whatever their divisions, responded to the club atmosphere which bound them together. The House has, indeed, through all its history been notable for its skill in adapting the most rebellious outsiders to accept its collective standards and habits. But behind the 'club' which was the House of Commons, there were also other clubs. This was the age of club government: as Professor Norman Gash expressed it,

> It would be true to say that the period between the first and second Reform Acts was as much the golden age of the political club as of the private member.[2]

The developing independence of the House of Commons accelerated by the Reform Act of 1832 had forced politicians to think about political management in a new form in order to correct the dangers of parliamentary independence. The clubs were their answer: they were the origin of modern party organisation. The meeting together of more or less like-minded members on club premises meant, in practice, that political decisions were more often than not taken there and not on the floor of the House. The clubs were like the back-bench meetings of today. The bulk of party members belonged to them and club membership became a badge of allegiance.[3] The political novels of the period give a clear picture of the manœuvring before divisions and the extent to which cases were not considered on the arguments in the House. The clubs led to organisation and concentration and they played their part in destroying the individualism of the Radicals. In the club system surely lay the explanation of Gladstone's assertion of the foreknowledge the Whips had of division results. The chaos between 1846 and 1867 shows how far Parliament fell short of a true party system. Statesmen still thought their first duty was to preserve the monarch's government rather than

[1] William Jeans, *Parliamentary Reminiscences* (1912), p. 3. The author spent forty-five years in the Press Gallery.
[2] Norman Gash, *Politics in the Age of Peel*, p. 395.
[3] Ibid., p. 398–9.

77

keep their party together. But the clubs did temper the prevailing 'anarchy' with political manipulation which was to lead on to more solid political organisation. As for the House of Commons, it is enough to say that it was the leaders of parties, not the rank and file, who were normally responsible for those decisions which were taken against the interest of party for the sake of what were deemed to be broader considerations of government. This, however, was only natural. Except in a national emergency, there are few major changes of party policy which arise primarily from rank and file Members of the House acting independently of their leaders.

(iv)

The first half of the nineteenth century, which led up to several decades in which the House of Commons was at its least effective as a political and legislative body, was also, as it happened, the high-tide of parliamentary committees in Britain. They were not normally used for the scrutiny of public legislation: this was still a duty of the Committee of the Whole House. But they were extensively employed for two important functions which together took up more of Members' time in those days than the consideration of Public Bills. The first of these functions was to inquire into and investigate particular public problems, when parliamentary committees performed much the same task as Royal Commissions and other independent inquiries have done in the twentieth century. The second function was the scrutiny of Private Bills which, at that time, constituted the bulk of legislation. In neither of these fields was the use of committees regarded by contemporaries as satisfactory.

In his speech attacking the inefficiency of Parliament and government as a result of the breakdown of party, Disraeli listed, in August 1848, the rash of committees that had been functioning during that Session. There had been forty-five public committees, with an average of fifteen Members on each. Of these public committees, that on commercial distress sat for thirty-nine days, one on sugar and coffee planting for thirty-nine days, another on navy, army and ordinance expenditure for forty days, yet another on miscellaneous expenditure for thirty-seven days. There were also twenty-eight election committees, with five Members on each; fourteen groups on railways, with five on each; seventeen groups on Private Bills (five on each) and 111 other committees on private business.

Such was the passion of the Commons for setting up committees of inquiry that Salisbury commented mockingly in 1860: 'When the Emperor of the French does land at last, we shall no doubt have a committee appointed to examine the Horse Guards.' More elaborately he described this habit of the House as follows:

Scarcely an evening passes in the House of Commons but somebody moves to refer something to a Select Committee. Our taxation, our colonies, our poor law, our navy and half a dozen other things besides have been sent upstairs to feed the appetite of these insatiable inquirers. At last the guardians of the Constitution have become frightened. The Prime Minister actual, and the Prime Minister expectant, and *The Times*, which domineers over both, have sounded the alarm that the House of Commons is invading the rights of the Executive. . . . One would imagine from all these timid alarms that there was something very powerful and very terrible in a Select Committee.

In fact, there was, Salisbury believed, nothing to worry the Executive in such committees. Ministers, though they did not like committees, found it easy to foil them and government departments could mystify 'the meddlers' by sending down 'a history, a correspondence of all accounts for the last century, and a cohort of witnesses. . . .' Every Member on the committee would have his

own little mare's nest to look for, and questions each witness about it. The rate of progression therefore will probably be very satisfactory to the departments who will look upon the Committee as a convenient peg on which to hang up any disagreeable question for a year or two.

Salisbury gave three main reasons for dismissing committees of inquiry as useless to control the Executive—the incompetence and laziness of the MPs who sat on them; the inability of a committee lacking technical knowledge to grasp such complicated matters as those referred to them; the fact that the committees received no publicity (a point of some interest a hundred years later when there is a general assumption that the press no longer gives serious government reports the attention it once did) so that even if matters of interest were revealed, the achievement would be ineffective.

These ideas were by no means peculiar to Salisbury. Parliamentary inquiries were widely regarded as both expensive and unproductive.

They were also accused of evading their duty by simply recording the evidence in huge reports that offered no solutions or conclusions. The Government was said deliberately to use such committees to shelve problems, not to solve them. 'The blue book does not satisfy curiosity but palls it—overwhelms it', commented the *Spectator* sourly on one occasion and it cited as an example the Committee on Transportation. This had provided no extracts of the information latent in the evidence and after all the expense of time and money, the result was 'a folio volume of more than 700 pages of evidence, prolix, entangled, incoherent, crude. . . .' So much for the futility of blue books which were never read—though it was conceded that occasionally, when the chairman was master of his subject, there were some good reports. For this reason, every committee should have the help of a competent secretary.[1]

Committees of investigation, which had the power to send for persons, records and papers, inquired into a wide range of social and economic subjects, including education, the poor laws and problems affecting particular trades and industries—for example, the hand-loom weavers. Sometimes legislation followed from such enquiries; for though it was not the job of the committees to produce positive proposals which could be turned into legislation, they provided information on which a Bill might be based. After 1836, the number on such committees was fifteen (it had previously been twenty-one) but five was a quorum and the committees were often badly attended. As is customary with fashionable contemporary outcries against institutions of government, the mid-nineteenth-century allegation of uselessness directed against House of Commons committees of investigation was probably overdone. Parliamentary blue books played a part in the movement for reform in the first half of the century. Nevertheless, their weaknesses, which were plain to contemporaries, are of some interest in the mid-twentieth century when a different demand is made of Parliament: that it should revert to *ad hoc* committees of enquiry or establish new investigatory committees which would bring departments under Commons' supervision.

As the century progressed, such parliamentary committees, which had originally been more or less constituted without reference to party considerations, became increasingly composed of MPs in accordance with the relative strength of parties in the House. Partly

[1] *Spectator*, October 11, 1856, p. 1,079.

for this reason, the Government now began to turn increasingly to the use of Royal Commissions in order to obtain non-partisan advice —and also because it was possible to include experts in non-parliamentary inquiries. The two methods continued side by side in the second half of the century and it was only in the twentieth that parliamentary *ad hoc* Select Committees to inquire into particular problems were really displaced by other forms of independent inquiry. Just the same, in the second half of the nineteenth century most major reforms were based on the findings of Royal Commissions rather than parliamentary inquiries.

Even more consuming of parliamentary energies than investigatory Select Committees in the first half of the nineteenth century were Committees dealing with Private Bills—that is to say, Bills affecting some private interest and seeking the enactment of a special law to give authority for a particular project. Such legislation as had passed Parliament in the eighteenth century had largely been in the nature of Private Bills dealing with enclosures, turnpikes, and canals. But it was in the first half of the nineteenth century that the flood of these Bills reached its height as leave was sought for the construction of new railway lines. The importance of the use of committees for these important measures is that they were, in effect, being employed on a species of legislation which, though then 'private', would in a later age have been regarded as of national concern—and therefore as public business.

Private Bills originated with a petition (which included estimates of the expected cost of the project). After the Bill was presented it came before the House for a second reading—which might be refused if the Bill's opponents could muster enough general support to secure a majority. Assuming the Bill passed, it would then be handed to a Private Bill Committee whose procedure was in many respects comparable to that of a court of law. There now took place, in the Committee, a trial of the argument between the proposers of the project and the opponents. Intense lobbying, often conducted by parliamentary agents, was customary and each side was represented by counsel. Private Bill Committees were made up by Members selected under the Speaker's List system. Alongside each county in the list were grouped adjacent counties, towns and boroughs and, in any case affecting a particular county, all who represented the places listed as adjacent could attend, together with other Members named by the introducer of the Bill. In total, a Committee might amount to

120 Members in all, though only a fraction of them attended. After 1854, however, a general committee on railways and canal Bills was created which referred Bills to a small subcommittee, the chairman of which it selected from its own ranks, the other members being chosen by the Committee of Selection.

This study is not concerned with details of the reform of Private Bill procedure but some note must be taken of contemporary complaints against so important a branch of parliamentary activity at this time. There was, for instance, the general disadvantage that a local authority must promote a *Private* Bill to do its *public* duty in obtaining, say, land for building a street. It was increasingly realised that the matter of Private Bills was frequently of great public concern. But the system was even more vulnerable to charges of corruption and jobbery—which were, indeed, levied generally at committees, including those of investigation, at this period. Thus in 1845, the *Spectator* attacked corruption on the committee on the South Eastern Railway transactions, citing a Member who acted as counsel for a party (and received £300 cash) in a case where he was supposed to be judge.[1] In 1844, however, the House had decided to require members on committees considering railway Bills to sign declarations of non-interest and in 1854, as we have seen, local representation on opposed Private Bill committees was ended. Gradually the number of Private Bills began to fall away and, in their place, public legislation increased in the second half of the century. The 'committee system' was subject to piecemeal reform and in 1882 a plan of Standing Committees was adopted which remained the basis for future committee development.[2] With detailed procedural changes this study is not concerned. It is enough to notice that at a time around the middle decades of the century, when the House of Commons was making and unmaking governments, when the breakdown of party allegiances made its political job almost impossible, the House relied heavily for some of its main work on committees and was generally criticised for the manner in which it did so.[3]

[1] *Spectator*, 1845, p. 687.   [2] See below, p. 88.

[3] For a general account of House of Commons Committees in the nineteenth century see A. L. Lowell, *The Government of England*; J. Redlich, *Procedure of the House of Commons*; F. Clifford, *A History of Private Bill Legislation*. For an interesting short account of aspects of railway and canal politics, see S. H. Beer, *Modern British Politics*, Ch. I. I am grateful to Professor Max Hartwell for letting me read a draft paper on 'Committees of the House of Commons, 1800–1850'.

(v)

The nineteenth century, which has understandably been regarded as the great age of the House of Commons, was also the century in which Members steadily lost control over their own time. This was a natural development now that both the Executive (unlike the old 'independent' Crown) and Parliament were linked in responsibility to the same electorate. The House of Commons was no longer 'in opposition' as it had been when it had seized the legislative initiative in the seventeenth century. Now that an accord had been restored between the Executive and the majority of the House by means of direct ministerial responsibility to Parliament, it was both logical and essential that the Government should once again lead the House in its legislative activity as it had not done since the age of the Tudors. The legislative output now rose to an unprecedented flood in the age of reform; only the Government could manage it—and for its management drastic procedural changes were needed in Parliament.

Since the end of the seventeenth century procedure had barely changed in essentials and during the eighteenth a day's business was at the mercy of any individual Member's whim. But since, apart from Private Bills which occupied little time on the floor of the House, the process of law-making had become stagnant, this standstill in procedure had not greatly mattered. By the beginning of the nineteenth century, it was obvious that some method of organising the business of the House was needed. Though Private Bill legislation was, as we have seen, far from decreasing, government business was proliferating so rapidly that it became essential for Ministers to feel certain that they had charge of a given portion of the time of the House for matters they must put before it.

The change began even before the first Reform Act. In 1806 it became the rule that notices of all motions, except those that were purely formal, must be given not later than one day before they were to be brought up.[1] Secondly, about the same time, the House began, for the convenience of the Cabinet, to reserve one or two days a week for government business by giving orders of the day precedence. It now became the job of the Government to lead the House: gradually, the old freedom of individual Members to discuss what they wished withered away.

After 1832, the tone of the House of Commons changed, even

[1] J. Redlich, *Procedure of the House of Commons*, Vol. I, p. 70.

though its social composition had altered little. It became more businesslike and even showed signs of preferring information to oratory. Even before the Reform Act, the change was noted by contemporaries as the House got to grips with the duller business of money and commodity regulation. After the parliamentary franchise was reformed, legislation to extend reform to other aspects of life heightened the seriousness of the House of Commons. The length of sessions increased and more papers were printed by order of the House. What is more, the Commons, to the disapproval of some of their number, became more responsive to public opinion. In these years, there was a fourfold increase in public petitions.[1] This was a sign of the new demands made on Parliament—but it was also the occasion for one of the most important reforms in procedure. The presentation of these petitions had become an excuse for unlimited debate which totally disrupted the organisation of business. In 1832, therefore, the House decided to discourage such discussion and, a few years later, to abolish it outright, except where immediate action was needed. Yet, if the disorganised discussion on the petitions was in the eighteenth-century mode, the rise in their volume was essentially a symptom of the new interaction between the Commons and public opinion. When the young Mr Gladstone complimented the Speaker on the time he had saved by stopping discussion on the presentation of petitions, the Speaker's reply, noted in Gladstone's diary for 1838, was instructive.

> He replied that there was a more important advantage; that those discussions very greatly increased the influence of popular feeling on the deliberations of the House; and that by stopping them he thought a wall was erected against such influence—not as strong as might be wished. Probably some day it might be broken down, but he had done his best to raise it. His maxim was to shut out as far as might be all extrinsic pressure, and then to do what was right within doors.[2]

Gladstone was one of the new Members of the reformed Parliament: he first took his seat in 1833 and in later life recorded his first impressions of this 'august' assembly—and 'the prosaic character of its entire visible equipment'.

[1] Between 1875 and 1879, 880 petitions were presented; between 1839 and 1843 the number was 94,292: E. L. Woodward, *The Age of Reform, 1815–1870* (Oxford History of England, 1938), p. 88.

[2] John Morley, *Life of Gladstone* (Macmillan, 1903), Vol. I, p. 150.

What I may term its corporeal conveniences were, I may observe in passing, small. I do not think that in any part of the building it afforded the means of so much as washing the hands.[1]

The next year, the old House of Commons was burned down and though so much of the intimacy and custom of the old was translated to the new chamber, there is a sense in which the new building marked a change in the attitudes of the House. After the fire, a reporters' gallery was provided in the new temporary premises in 1834 and in 1836 Division Lists were published regularly—both symptoms of the new responsiveness to public opinion.

Moreover, the need to reform the procedure of the House was appreciated immediately after the Reform Act. Arrangements were made for daily sittings: private business was from noon until 3 p.m. followed after an intervening adjournment by public business at five. Apart from tightening the arrangements for presenting petitions, the House set up a Select Committee in 1837 which was charged with considering how to improve the regularity and despatch of business. One of the findings of this first Select Committee was that a considerable part of the two days allotted 'by courtesy of the House' to the Government had been usurped by discussion of other subjects. This had arisen from the right of any Member to move any amendment he felt like moving on any occasion. Such amendments were, as a result of the Select Committee, ruled out of order except when the question was whether to go into Committee of Supply or Ways and Means.

Select Committees on Procedure followed regularly throughout the century—in 1848, 1854, 1861, 1869, 1878 and 1886. But the House of Commons suffered from a constant delay in its business. Legislative progress was hampered by protracted proceedings and a lengthening in debates.

The leisurely, fashionable young men who had been nominated for the rotten boroughs had been succeeded in many cases by a more earnest, if not necessarily more brilliant type. They insisted on their views, and those of their constituents, being heard at length. In 1849, Sir Erskine May, the Clerk of the House, noted the enormously increased desire to speak. Delay and even obstruction were not necessarily illegitimate parliamentary weapons: they could be a way of collecting the opinions of constituencies and the public. For the future (May noted) on important legislative proposals, long debates

[1] John Morley, *Life of Gladstone*, Vol. I, p. 101.

might always be reckoned on; to meet these new circumstances, antiquated rules needed to be revised.[1]

Apart from the increase in business, the confusion was also partly caused, Speaker Shaw-Lefevre told the Select Committee of 1848, by the number of important discussions under debate all at the same time and the intermingling of various adjourned debates on various subjects. Motions to adjourn the House on various matters irrelevant to the subject due for discussion were one of the main causes of this confusion and the Speaker suggested that debate should not be allowed on motions for adjournment and that before resuming debate on an adjourned subject, it should be possible to move that the debate should not be *further* adjourned. These suggestions were rejected as too drastic but various changes were made which shortened the procedure on Bills. The first reading of a Bill was to be entirely unamendable and undebatable. Further, under what became known as the 'rule of progress' it was made impossible for Members to re-open the basic issues of a Bill when the House went into Committee on it.

These are only some of the landmarks in the reform of procedure[2] which took place in the nineteenth century. It was, in fact, a slow business. MPs remained jealous of their rights. There had been protests at the beginning of the century when the Government was granted a stated time for its business. Subsequently the custom had grown up of recovering some of this time by the device of moving amendments, when the question was put that the Speaker should 'leave the chair', so that the House could go into Committee of Supply. Several Committees considered the question of changing the procedure to remove this abuse, but it was not until 1882 that the ancient privilege of the House to raise its grievances before granting Supply was finally removed. The problem was a substantial one. It was possible to delay the Commons from going into Committee while Members raised a series of issues on the question 'That Mr Speaker do now leave the chair' while the Government would be prevented from answering all the subjects raised because no member of the Government could speak twice on the same question.

Several Committees considered the question but failed to agree to

---

[1] Quoted in J. Redlich, *Procedure of the House of Commons*, Vol. I, p. 81.

[2] For a full account, see J. Redlich, *Procedure of the House of Commons*, Vol. I, p. 73, 'The Reform of the Antiquated Procedure'.

recommend reform. The Select Committee of 1861, on which Disraeli, Palmerston, Bright and Stanley sat, emphasised that the chief object of reform was to achieve daily certainty for Members about the business to be transacted. Although the Speaker proposed the extension of the 'rule of progress' to the Committee of Supply, the Select Committee on Procedure could not bring itself to accept this. Agreeing that these preliminary motions were an obstacle to the business of the House, the Committee nevertheless pointed out that 'the statement and consideration of grievances before supply are among the most ancient and important privileges of the Commons, and this opportunity of obtaining full explanation from the Ministers of the Crown is the surest and the best'. This Committee's rather conservative general view was that the old rules were the 'safeguard of freedom of debate, and a sure defence against the oppression of overpowering majorities'. It considered that the House should help the Speaker to resist attempts to encroach upon the rules: 'Common consent is the best security for their maintenance.'

The conflict was between the efficiency in the conduct of a rising tide of Government business, brought forward in the national interest, and the rights of the House to sift and examine what questions it would. But not until 1882, when Irish obstruction was at its height, was the House forced by the hard facts of politics to lay down that the motion for the Speaker to leave the chair should only be moved when the House first went into Committee on the major (service) Estimates. Later it became the practice to hold debates on these in the Committee itself and then the old opportunity to raise grievances before Supply ceased to exist. Yet it is arguable that, in the new parliamentary democracy being born in the nineteenth century, the nation had its real opportunity to secure the remedy of its grievances when it sent a majority party to Parliament—and therefore elected a particular government committed to a particular programme of action. The nineteenth-century changes in procedure may denote a loss to the House of Commons which was more apparent than real.

The struggle for the parliamentary time-table between the Executive and the House continued throughout the century. Since the early years of the century, it had been the custom for Government business (ordered business) to have precedence on Mondays and Fridays. In 1846 a definite order fixed Mondays and Thursdays as Government days and in 1852 the Government obtained three days. But the sternest checks on the private Member were imposed to save Parliament from a menace which nearly destroyed it—the attempt of the Irish Members to bring all business to a halt. Obstruction was not new but the systematic obstruction now practised to stop even the most uncontroversial business from making progress threatened the whole parliamentary fabric. For the Irish were misusing the rules of the game—and therefore the rules had to be changed. Gladstone was considering some form of devolution as a remedy for obstruction even before the final crisis in January 1881, when a sitting lasted from 4 p.m. on a Monday until 9 a.m. the next Wednesday. The sitting was only ended by the closure being moved by the Speaker himself on his own authority, and this crisis made drastic changes in procedure essential. In 1882, Gladstone introduced procedural reforms which represented the watershed between the old and the new government-managed Parliament. Motions to adjourn the House, which had given Members the right to raise issues as they wished, were restricted to matters accepted by the Speaker (and then only after Question Time) as of definite and urgent public importance. The Speaker was able to oblige a Member who was being deliberately repetitive to end his speech and the 'closure', most radical of all the new devices, was introduced to bring obstructionist debates to an end. Subsequently, the 'guillotine' was introduced which enabled the Government, by the weight of its majority, to name a limited time-table for a Bill over which the House was taking too long. In 1882, standing committees for legal and trade Bills had been introduced to save the time of the House and, after a period in which it lapsed, the standing committee system was extended in 1907 to all public Bills (except Finance Bills) unless the House ordered otherwise. In 1888, the procedural reforms were systematised and a stated hour for the automatic adjournment of the Commons was introduced. In 1896 the number of days for discussing Supply were limited to twenty, when the Opposition had the right to discuss business. Thereafter, these days were normally allocated for general rather than strictly 'supply' debates. In 1902, Balfour introduced a further comprehensive scheme which included Government precedence, except for the latter half of Tuesdays and Wednesdays and the whole of Fridays. The supremacy of the Executive over the parliamentary time-table now seemed to be complete. Yet it was also true that the majority had been released from the tyranny of the minority and Parliament enabled to continue, albeit with difficulty, to deal with the rising flood of national business.[1]

(vi)

In the second half of the nineteenth century, party allegiances tightened and Members of the Commons increasingly cast their votes according to the party line. It has been calculated that in 1836 the percentage of divisions where both parties cast 'party votes' (a 'party vote' being regarded as one in which 90 per cent of the Members who voted in a Division were on the same side) was only 22·65 per cent. This diminished to 6·22 per cent in 1860, when the fragmentation of parties was greatest. Thereafter the percentage of party votes rose almost uninterruptedly to 76·03 per cent in 1894, with a slight fall-back to 68·95 in 1899. But by 1899, the number of Divisions in which neither side of the House cast a party vote almost vanished—with a percentage of only 2·28.[2]

Two great parties, the Conservatives and Liberals, now dominated the House of Commons and alternated in government from 1868 to 1885—after which the Conservatives (with two short intervals) held power until 1905 as a result of the Liberal split over Irish Home Rule. Despite the political upheavals of these years and the threat which the Irish directed at the constitutional procedures of Britain, this was indeed political stability. When Governments were in office they were genuinely in power and, save for the big splits on issues of principle, their followers were increasingly operating in the Commons within party lines.

If party ties and the loss of parliamentary time by backbenchers inhibited the 'independence' of Members in the House, the status of the MP might also seem to have been diminished by the increasingly direct relationship of the parties (as such) and of their leaders with the new democratic electorate. It was a sign of the times that, immediately after being defeated on the new franchise in 1868, Disraeli resigned without waiting for a defeat in Parliament. It was the first open recognition of the Government's new dependence on a

[1] For a detailed discussion of the reform of procedure see J. Redlich, *Procedure of the House of Commons*, Vol. I; for an excellent concise account see Kenneth Mackenzie, *The English Parliament* (Pelican, 1963); Edward Hughes, *The Changes in Parliamentary Procedure, 1880–1882* (Essays presented to Sir Lewis Namier, Macmillan, 1956).

[2] A. Lawrence Lowell, *The Government of England* (Macmillan, New York, 1924), Vol. II, pp. 77 et seq.

widening electorate to which it could appeal but which it could not control. There was now a sense in which the electorate—because in voting it was choosing the Executive itself—was more important than the House of Commons. For the first time the electorate could not be managed by patrons and had to be wooed by parties.

The Conservatives after their defeat of 1868 and the Liberals after their rejection in 1874 both reformed and extended their organisations in the country in recognition of the new political climate. The constituency party caucus was taking on a new meaning and the improvement in communications was tightening the relationship between the MP and his local organisation. Members who had so recently regarded public attention to their proceedings in Parliament as an intrusion now sought publicity in a new responsiveness to public opinion. In their rôle of loyal party members they naturally looked rather less like independent representatives acting on their own discretion at Westminster. The new public relations of politics also brought the party leaders into direct contact with the voters as never before. Gladstone's stump oratory in his Midlothian campaign of 1879 was a new departure. Although it did not take place during an election campaign, it was a model for future direct appeals by party leaders to the people.

As the decades passed, policy was increasingly first 'floated' in the country before being announced in the House and this caused resentment among Members. In 1866, Robert Lowe objected to the partial conduct of the debate on reform outside the House. Gladstone, he complained, had first delivered his reasons for bringing in the Bill to a Liverpool audience instead of giving them first to the House on first or second reading.[1] (It is a familiar complaint by critics who complain that the House is *now* by-passed a hundred years later.) Similarly, in 1902, Joseph Chamberlain first publicly proclaimed his faith in imperial preference in Birmingham—and repeated it in the House a few days later.

As the two great parties alternated in power between 1868 and 1885, their leaders Gladstone and Disraeli presented the nation with a battle of giants. In the stature of the leaders, in their parliamentary duels and in the stability of politics—marred only by the growing Irish threat to order and even to the very institution of Parliament—this was perhaps a golden age of the House of Commons. The new

[1] Robert Lowe, *Speeches and Letters on Reform* (2nd Edn., 1867), p. 122 (April 26, 1866).

rule of party was certainly preferable to the chaos that had preceded it, but it was hardly a stimulus to independent action. For the most part, the backbenchers displayed an awesome reverence towards their leaders. Even the resignation of the Gladstone Government in 1885 as a direct result of defeat in the House of Commons by 264 votes to 252 cannot convincingly be construed as evidence of the deliberate exertion of the Commons' authority to dismiss a Ministry.

The defeat was on an amendment to the Budget moved by Sir Michael Hicks-Beach for the Conservatives. Two points were at issue. The first was the increased duty on beer and spirits which was being proposed by the Government without a corresponding increase on wine. The second was an increase in the duty on real property which was unaccompanied by any relief for ratepayers. In the Division, four Liberals, four Irish Liberal Home Rulers and thirty-nine Irish Nationalists (the Liberals' allies) joined the Conservatives in voting against the Government. Seventy-six Liberals (of whom only fourteen were paired) abstained. Gladstone resigned.

There is some room for argument about the extent to which this Government defeat was the result of accidental mismanagement by the Whips and how much it was by the design of the rebels. Gladstone himself told the queen that it was only just before the Division that he was first told of the likelihood of a defeat, remarking that his supporters had received none of those imperative adjurations to return after dinner that are usual on solemn occasions, else there could never have been seventy-six absentees.[1] A large number of absentees afterwards said that they had not realised that the debate was vital. *The Times* reported that the issue of the vote came as a complete surprise to most Members and it ascribed the defeat of the Government to 'defective party management'.[2] The carelessness of the Whips was generally blamed for what had happened; according to the *Spectator*, it was heard everywhere that if they had whipped better, the collapse would not have taken place.[3]

Yet it is also true that the Cabinet was losing its cohesion and its morale was already impaired. The death of Gordon and the defeat at Majuba had greatly lowered the standing of the Government in the country and in Parliament. Contemporaries were quite clear that indisposition and absence would not have been so common among

[1] John Morley, *Life of Gladstone*, Vol. III, p. 202.
[2] *The Times*, June 11, 1885.
[3] *Spectator*, June 13, 1885.

Liberals had morale been higher and, in that case, the feebleness of the Whips would have been much less dangerous. Moreover, not only the Irish but also many radical Liberals were disposed to prevent the renewal of the Irish Crimes Act and certainly the decision of the Irish Nationalists to vote with the Tories was influenced by the belief that a Conservative Government would not reimpose that measure. Even in the Cabinet, there was a considerable radical element opposed to the Irish measure and, as the *Spectator* put it, if the Prime Minister had decided to go on with this, he would have had to do so 'without colleagues who represent great sections of the constituencies, with a fourth, perhaps, of his party discontented, and with his own heart but half inclined towards his work. . . . His party was honeycombed with latent disaffection.'[1] Moreover, Cabinet unity was jeopardised by discontent from the opposite wing also. Owing to the attitude of Sir Charles Dilke and Joseph Chamberlain to the future government of Ireland, a disruption of the Ministry was, if not imminent, at least probable. Indeed, it seemed to *The Times* that the Budget defeat had at least enabled the Government to pre-serve until the end the appearance of unanimity.[2]

The truth is that the Liberals who abstained or voted against the Budget on the Conservative amendment did so because of their general disillusion with the Government's performance and that the accidents of mismanagement by the Whips were symptoms of a deeper malaise. In one sense, this incident—the last occasion on which a Government resigned as the direct result of its defeat in the House —demonstrated the responsiveness that any Government has to majority feeling and the way in which a Government can fall by failing to hold together its followers, whether or not it is actually brought down by a vote. On the other hand, this episode cannot be seen simply in terms of rejection of the Government by the Commons for the reason that the Government was itself as split over many current issues (including the renewal of the Crimes Act) as its fol-lowers were. To some observers, the Cabinet seemed deliberately to have courted defeat at a convenient moment to itself.[3] It can, perhaps, be acquitted of such deliberate subtlety. Nevertheless, it is undeniable that many Cabinet members were far from displeased by their fall and, as the Duke of Argyll put it: 'If in the streets you saw a man coming along with a particularly elastic step and a joyful frame of

[1] *Spectator*, June 13, 1885.
[2] *The Times*, June 10, 1885.   [3] Ibid.

countenance, 10 to 1 on coming closer you would find it was a member of the late cabinet.'[1] In short, this last dramatic dismissal of a Government by the House of Commons appears on closer inspection to have been very similar to the way in which Governments fell in the eighteenth century. The adverse votes or abstentions in the Commons represented the falling apart of the subsidiary factions which made up any party Government. It would be truer to say that leaders of different segments of a party, accompanied by their particular followers in the Commons, parted company from each other rather than to say that an independent-minded House rose up and dismissed the Government. What is true is that the party structure in the Commons was not yet as rigid as it was to become. The 'independence' was of political groupings rather than of individual Members acting as such.

If the Commons in the later nineteenth century were not as 'independent' as they may appear to hindsight, they were certainly not notably efficient. Indeed, then as now it was argued that the inefficiency of Parliament deterred able men from entering the Commons. Lord George Hamilton, one of the Tories who resigned from the Balfour Cabinet in support of Free Trade, looking back on the last ten years of his parliamentary life, could 'truly say' that a 'vast proportion of the hours which I spent inside the Chamber was a sheer waste of time'.[2] As for the quality of Members, 'the brazenfaced advertiser soon finds out that the House of Commons is the best advertising board in the world. Men "on the make" remorselessly make use of the opportunities this afforded them.' But men of ability, understanding and character would not become candidates because they knew that they would have 'little to do but to loaf and to vote'. A well-known Member had told Hamilton he did not know a single Member who, having achieved success elsewhere and then entering the Commons, did not regret so doing on account of 'the procedure and the intolerable waste of time under it'. Nor is there evidence that the general calibre of the membership was higher then than now, though it appears to our hindsight that the leading figures were cast in a bigger mould. Certainly the membership of the House remained almost as upper-class (in the somewhat loose English meaning of the term) as ever. The entry of the Labour MPs at the end of

[1] John Morley, *Life of Gladstone*, Vol. III, p. 202.
[2] Lord George Hamilton, *Parliamentary Reminiscences and Reflections* (John Murray, 1916), p. 210.

the century changed a fraction of the membership but for the most part (despite the popular franchise) the high cost of elections and the necessity for private means to sustain a life in the Commons enabled the landed and mercantile interests to keep their pre-eminence. In fact, the House in the early days of the expanding working-class vote was much less representative of the electors than it was in the eighteenth century, when gentlemen represented gentlemen, or in the mid twentieth when the working classes were represented by working classes—a trend now again being reversed with the increase in the number of middle-class Labour MPs.

It might be said that the private Member was more eager to scrutinise and control expenditure then than now and far more resistant to taxation. There was, for instance, the case of Joseph Hume, a private Member who was so dedicated to his self-appointed job of watching the Estimates that he kept an office and a clerk, at his own expense, to do his research for him. When Hume began his activities after the 1832 Reform Bill very little interest was taken in the Estimates and, with only a handful of bored MPs in the House, he kept at his task of prodding the government into economy for nearly forty years. He did much to reduce expenditure and also to induce principles of economy into public administration. But, of course, he had a much more limited field in which to work than the scrutineers of public spending do today and, indeed, the Victorian insistence on economy and low taxation was essentially a symptom of the class of men in Parliament and of the difference between their interest and that of the Government. Governments were increasingly having to spend in the name of electors of *all* classes, but the burden of taxation fell primarily on the class represented by the Membership of the House of Commons. Naturally it was resisted.

Nor was the House of Commons at this time the main channel through which outside interests approached the Government. Then, as now, pressure groups dealt direct with the government, often to the fury of the by-passed MPs.[1] MPs as such had little direct part in the 'formulation' of policy (to use mid-twentieth-century terminology) except insofar as they contributed to the climate of opinion in their parties. If private Members then produced a bigger, and the Government a smaller, share of legislation than now, the backbencher promoting a Bill usually reflected a particular interest, with which he

[1] For example, see Philip Williams, 'Public Opinion and the Railway Rates Question in 1886', *English Historical Review* (January, 1952).

94

identified himself, or had taken over some idea in the general currency. MPs in any age seldom invent ideas; they take them over. Thus imperial preference was a current idea (though it was regarded as eccentric) well before Joseph Chamberlain took it over. But his championship made it a real issue and gave it political credibility.

Yet there is one way in which the late nineteenth-century House of Commons was more 'independent' and perhaps superior to our own —but this has nothing to do with the machinery of Parliament. Politicians then were much more willing (aided by their independent financial and social standing) to break with their parties and take real political risks than they are now. For the most part, of course, political leaders were forced into policies by circumstances, not by careful design; short-term considerations were as dominant in the nineteenth as in the twentieth century. Gladstone's conversion to Home Rule—which was perhaps encouraged by the Irish threat to Parliament and the Constitution and by the dangerous dependence of the other parties on Irish votes—was an obvious example. Imperial preference was another. Nevertheless, however improvised was the policy-making of this period, parties would break and re-form on a more logical basis more freely then than now. The great issues which divided the Commons at the end of the nineteenth century and the beginning of the twentieth—home rule, free trade, taxation and the House of Lords—were deeply felt and passionately argued. Whatever the discipline of the Whips and the bonds of party organisation, the questions argued out in the House were those argued out, and along the same dividing lines—in the country. All this was possible because, even before the break-up of the Liberals over Home Rule, the two big parties of Disraeli and Gladstone were recognised as coalitions in a way foreign to the twentieth century. Thus it was perfectly normal to talk of the Whigs as an independent entity in the Liberal Party until the end of the century—and it was, of course, primarily the Whigs who seceded over Home Rule. The Radicals were no less a clear-cut entity. The willingness of sections of a party to hive off (for all the tense bitterness created in the drawing-rooms of London) both gave a reality to politics and, indeed, *helped to create stable parliamentary majorities*. The Conservative hegemony at the end of the century was due to the accretion of strength the party received by the attachment of the Liberal Unionists. Similarly, the damage the Conservatives subsequently did themselves over free trade ensured the Liberals of their great victory of 1906.

It was in the responsiveness of the political parties to the basic issues and arguments in the country, and in the prestige of the House as the forum in which these national issues were debated that the late nineteenth-century House of Commons was superior to the House of the mid-twentieth—not as a repository of independent-mindedness or as a maker and destroyer of ministries. One Prime Minister, it is true, was to fall as the 'golden age' came to an end—but Lloyd George's replacement of Asquith in the midst of war was a palace revolution compared with Churchill's replacement of Chamberlain in 1940. It was in no real sense a revolt in Parliament.

Chapter Three

Parliament and Democracy 1918–1931

Immediately after the First World War, Parliament met with attacks and demands for systematic reform which reduced any of the criticisms directed at it during the nineteenth century to comparative insignificance. It may seem ironical that scepticism about Parliament as an effective instrument in government should have become intense just when it was becoming responsible and responsive to a mass democracy encompassing three-quarters of the adult population —but it was not a coincidence. There was a clear connection between the new duties being performed by the central government on behalf of the community and the feeling that the House of Commons was no longer able to exercise adequate influence over the Executive. Government departments now had so enhanced a rôle in the management of the social and economic affairs of the new democracy that the ability of the House of Commons to scrutinise the conduct of the bureaucrats was called into question. Propped up on the one hand by their departments and on the other by powerful party organisations, Cabinet Ministers also seemed to be virtually free of House of Commons control. Moreover, the additional legislative and other work now before the House made it seem impossible for Members to do their job efficiently. Their control over parliamentary time had been steadily reduced and the status of the Member of Parliament as an individual seemed to be further diminished by the influence of the party machine in the battle for the democratic vote. These were the first causes of the new wave of criticism directed at Parliament: later in the twenties, there was to be a much graver motive for discontent— the apparent inability of parliamentary government to solve a dangerous national problem.

Though the franchise extensions of 1867 and 1884, together with the introduction of the secret ballot, had already created a limited democracy, the electorate still covered only a minority of the population until the end of the war. The Representation of the People Act, 1918, however, more than doubled the electorate, and all men over twenty-one except peers, lunatics, felons and conscientious objectors (who were disqualified for five years), could now vote if they had residential qualifications. So could women over thirty if they or their husbands were local government electors. The new electorate to which the politicians were responsible was one covering every conceivable limitation, as well as attainment, of intellect, education, and understanding. The politicians must henceforth produce, through the party organisations, policy-packages designed to appeal to mass segments of the population aligned in large political party allegiances. In turn, each of the sections of the population identifying themselves with one or the other of the political parties, included people representing a wide range of social conditions and interests.

Moreover, for the first time since the seventeenth century a large element in the House of Commons consisted of MPs—those of the Labour Party—nominated by an outside interest which had organised them and sent them to Westminster with prescribed objectives involving a fundamental change in the social and political basis of society. Unlike the Whigs and the Tories, the Liberals and the Conservatives, the Labour Party's roots were not in Parliament itself and the party in Parliament remained responsible, though diminishingly so, to an external organisation. (It might be argued that the nineteenth-century Radicals had been sent, or had sent themselves, to Parliament with clear intention to work for prescribed changes but they quickly grafted themselves on to the parties they found already at Westminster; they were certainly not answerable to an external organisation to the extent that the Labour Party continued, in some degree, to be throughout the first half of the twentieth century.)

The existence in the House of Commons of a major party which directly represented the working classes had its effect on the older political parties, on their organisations, inside and outside Parliament, and therefore on the atmosphere of the House of Commons. If they were to retain a sufficient share of the working-class vote to stay in business, the Conservatives and the Liberals had to bid more directly for it. In fact, the Conservatives were successful enough to ensure that, between the wars, the Labour Party never succeeded in getting on equal terms with them, either in proportion of seats in the House or votes in the country. Although Baldwin sought to bring Labour into the system of government and to make it a responsible alternative ruling party, it was not until after 1945 that Labour was finally accepted as a governing party in the fullest sense. Nevertheless, for all the limitations of its position after 1918, the new political status of Labour at Westminster was an important influence in changing the relationship of the political parties represented in Parliament with the electorate. Besides, the First World War had done much to break down the sense of social–political hierarchy which had been the cement of Victorian class-relationships. This process was not completed until the Second World War; nevertheless, the previously implicit right of the upper and middle classes to govern the country was undermined after 1918, even though—being armed with the weapons of money, education and self-confidence— they did not cease to wield the lion's share of influence. One important result of the 'democratisation' of Parliament and of society was the new relationship of Members to the mass electorate through the party organisations, which were generally the only effective avenue to the House of Commons and the essential means of keeping a seat there. Party organisation was not new but it was more important than ever before and this seemed to detract from the traditional position of the House of Commons as an 'independent' assembly of amateurs. The discipline of the Whips now seemed more obtrusive while parliamentary politics became more professional.

Outside the House of Commons, Members were subjected to the growing scrutiny of a popular, as distinct from a select, press. Inside the House, the atmosphere slowly changed from one of an exclusive club to that of a more businesslike assembly. An observer who began to serve Parliament in the Clerk's department just after the First World War has recalled that, in the 1918 Parliament, 'on a summer's evening, the Harcourt Room (then the only room in which Members could entertain lady guests) and the Terrace were like the foyer of the Opera on a gala night. Women in full dress (tiaras and all) dining at the "House" as a prelude to a ball or reception provided a picturesque spectacle during the "Season". The entertaining now is much more of the working lunch or dinner type, or for constituents, while permission to sponsor bodies of "strangers" entertaining in the private rooms on the Terrace is a post-1945 development springing from the desire of the Kitchen Committee to balance their budget.'[1]

[1] Sir Edward Fellowes, 'Changes in Parliamentary Life, 1918–1961', *Political Quarterly*, July–September 1965, pp. 256–65. The author was Clerk of the House of Commons from 1954–61, having served in the House since 1919.

The House also became much more professional and assiduous in its methods of working. Soon after 1918, both the Conservative and the Labour Parties established private parliamentary backbench committees to study particular subjects. The Conservatives had operated an Agricultural Committee before the war but it was not until 1922 that the practice of backbench committees was extended. After the break-up of the Coalition, the Tory Members who had been elected for the first time that year set up what was to become known as the 1922 Committee: its purpose was to keep the frontbench in touch with backbench opinion. Following the Conservative defeat of 1923, a deputation sent by the 1922 Committee to the party's leaders asked for regular meetings under the chairmanship of the leader, or his deputy, at which party policy could be explained and discussed. It is not clear that the expression of backbench feeling would have been as free as it later became had a Minister normally been present at the meetings but, at all events, the leaders rejected the suggestion in their own interest. However, they agreed to the presence of a Whip who could report the gist of the meeting's discussions to the leaders —and, more important, the 1922 Committee was enlarged to include all Conservative backbenchers. This body, formally known as the Conservative Members' Committee, though in practice always called the 1922 Committee, has played an important part ever since in making the party's leaders responsive to backbench opinion. When the Conservatives are in power, Ministers attend only by invitation; in Opposition, the leaders of the party take part in its proceedings, though the chairman is always a backbencher.

After the formation of the 1922 Committee a number of other committees was formed by Conservative backbenchers to study finance, trade and industry, foreign affairs and the armed services. Over the years the network of backbench committees has proliferated and all Conservative backbenchers may attend all of them if they wish. A comparable network of backbench committees exists on the Labour side. The Labour Party used backbench advisory committees before the war, though the present Labour system of subject committees dates only from 1945.[1] This general growth of backbench committees on all sides was one reason for the emptying of the

---

[1] Lists of both Conservative and Labour subject committees are given in Peter G. Richards, *Honourable Members, a Study of the British Backbencher* (Faber & Faber, 1959), which contains a useful short account of the work of such committees, pp. 97–107.

benches in the House itself when the more important of the private Members' party committees were meeting. Thus a product of the modern Member's wish to study special subjects in greater depth and to impress his views about them on his leaders has helped to give substance to the criticism that he has become a poor attender of debates.

The Parliamentary Labour Party has always had a more formal structure and constitution than the Conservatives. The Leader, Deputy Leader and Chief Whip have always been elected annually (and usually the men in possession have been re-elected) by the entire party in the House. When the party is in office, the leader elected while it was in Opposition becomes the Prime Minister. (The Conservatives did not adopt a comparable system of leader-election by MPs until 1965.) Labour MPs also elect twelve of their number who, with the elected officers, and four Labour peers, constitute the Parliamentary Committee, or 'Shadow Cabinet' when the party is in Opposition. When the party is in power, a Labour Prime Minister's choice of his Cabinet is now as free as a Conservative Prime Minister's would be—though in earlier years, the leaders of the Labour Party had to fight for the traditional right of Ministers of the Crown to be free from party dictates. On the other hand, the field from which a Labour Prime Minister picks his team when in power is to a certain degree pre-selected in Opposition by the rank and file's election of the 'Shadow Cabinet'. The elected 'Shadow Cabinet' has some influence over the evolution of policy in Opposition, which in turn is a preparation for policy-making in power.

In contemporary practice, the relationship between the front and backbenches of the Conservative Party differs little from the corresponding relationship within the Labour Party. Although the Conservative Leader, when in Opposition, may pick his own Leader's Committee at choice, he must pay almost as much regard to opinion in the party in making his selection as if his colleagues had been formally elected. It would certainly be wrong (as later chapters will show) to suppose that the Conservative rank and file have had less influence with their leaders in this century than their Labour counterparts have enjoyed. One of the most remarkable aspects of the Labour Party's arrival at Westminster was the speed with which it adopted parliamentary attitudes and was itself absorbed into the psychological fabric of the House of Commons. What one may reasonably suppose is that the arrival of Labour Members with new ideas of responsible channels between front and backbenchers may have helped to encourage similar notions on the opposite benches. At all events, 1922 was both the year in which the Conservative back-benchers set up their committees and the year in which a particularly potent intake of new Labour Members arrived at Westminster. On both sides, there seemed to be a determination to disprove the post-war allegations that the private Member had been rendered impotent by the Executive.

The early Labour Members arrived at Westminster anxious to change the social structure of the nation and with it some of the characteristics of existing institutions. Not least of the institutions which seemed to them ripe for reform was Parliament itself, with its ancient ceremonies and procedures which were part of the order of things that they wished to end. The 1922 General Election brought to Westminster an influx of new Labour Members, prominent among whom were those sponsored by the ILP and, in particular, the Clydesiders. To these men the revolution had come, even though the established parties remained in the majority. In their enthusiasm, they nearly all made their maiden speeches within a fortnight of arriving at Westminster and essentially these were repeat per-formances of their factory-gate election speeches.[1] No attempt was made to produce the usual, more or less discreet and not too partisan maiden speech. The new Labour men, contemptuous of parlia-mentary procedure, made no attempt to follow it and only a few tried to adapt themselves to the rules of debate. Scenes occurred frequently (on one occasion James Maxton and other Clydeside Members were forcibly ejected from the House) and Speaker Whitley had the greatest difficulty in keeping order. Emanuel Shinwell, himself one of this intake and a man who in his old age was to be a figure of the Labour establishment in the post-1964 period, has recorded the feeling of the new Labour Members: 'Some of my colleagues sought to tear away the thousand-year ritual and routine of Parliament with ill-tempered remarks and brash criticism. Kirkwood was the first to assert himself, on that first day of the new Parliament, as we stared at what was to us an incongruous ana-chronism of the pomp of the State opening, when he said in a loud aside to John Wheatley: "John, we'll soon change all this." The remark did not shock those who heard it. It was merely brushed aside as an infantile annoyance of no consequence.'[2]

[1] Emanuel Shinwell, *The Labour Story* (Macdonald, 1963), pp. 114 et seq.
[2] Emanuel Shinwell, *Conflict Without Malice* (Odhams, 1955), p. 85.

Shinwell, who later became a Minister, records his own very different view: 'We had still to learn that Parliament was all-powerful, that through its machinery we could achieve everything that was in our hearts and hopes; without its aid we were useless. I am myself sensitive to atmosphere and I caught a sense of this power of the House as I sat in there for the first time listening to the Address.' Shinwell observed how flat the maiden speeches of the new men fell because they were an appeal to the emotions instead of the mind: 'The machinery of government was ready to obey if it was told how to act rather than what to do.' The new men were, however, in due course absorbed in the parliamentary tradition and achieved power through it. Some of them were given lessons in procedure by one of the new Labour Members who had been a Liberal, H. B. Lees-Smith.[1]

The first reaction of most new Members of Parliament who have (whatever party they belong to) radical instincts and who wish to see social change, is one of impatience, and inevitably Labour Members have been most prone to discontent. Aneurin Bevan, who was to make the House of Commons the arena for some of the most ruthless and persuasive oratory in this century, recorded his own impression of a young Member's view of Parliament, looking back to his own entry to Westminster in 1929. 'His first impression is that he is in church. The vaulted roofs and stained-glass windows, the rows of statues of great statesmen of the past, the echoing halls, the soft-footed attendants and the whispered conversation, contrast depressingly with the crowded meetings and the clang and clash of hot opinions he has just left behind in his election campaign. Here he is, a tribune of the people, coming to make his voice heard in the seats of power. Instead, it seems he is expected to worship; and the most conservative of all religions—ancestor worship.'[2] In fact, the most purposefully radical Members—Bevan among them—have always learned how to work through the House of Commons and from 1922 onwards the new party was getting its feel of the House in which it was slowly but steadily replacing the Liberals as the alternative party of government.

In future, the House of Commons was to be representative of the social class-structure of the nation as it never had been before.

[1] Lord Williams of Barnburgh, *Digging for Britain* (Hutchinson, 1965) p. 57.
[2] Aneurin Bevan, *In Place of Fear* (MacGibbon & Kee, 1961), p. 6.

Between the wars its proportion of working-class Members rose steadily, and in the 'democratised' Parliament, the Members of the House were to become divided (after the final decline of the Liberals) into two main parties each orientated towards separate classes in the nation and yet each seeking the favour of a majority of the electorate. The new professionalism of politics began to have its effect on the composition of the Conservative Party: there was a decline in the proportion of country gentlemen among its Members who were not particularly interested in office and who had simply regarded membership of the parliamentary club (in defence of interest and fulfilment of duty) as part of the natural order of their lives. Members were now obliged to work harder, both in Parliament and in their constituencies. Owing to the increase in the work before the House, in the 1918 Parliament the practice of sending Bills (except Finance and Consolidated Fund Bills) to Standing Committees instead of Committee of the Whole House was started. This meant morning work (on Tuesdays and Thursdays) for many Members—and since those who have worked in the mornings may be less inclined to sit religiously on the benches of the House itself in the afternoon, it also no doubt contributed to the allegedly thinner attendance of debates.

In the new conditions of professional democratic politics, a tightening of party bonds, whether they were drawn through the Whips' offices or through the external organisations of party head-quarters and constituencies, was inevitable. Of course, party organisa-tion was no new development and it would be quite wrong to envisage the post-1918 MP as powerless before his Whips. As we have seen, Members on both sides of the House were organising themselves to ensure that their leaders had regard to their followers' opinions and individual groups of Members often conducted their own campaigns in favour of particular policies or attitudes. For instance, in the 1918 Parliament, a group of Conservative backbenchers who were mostly themselves to become office-holders later (they included Edward Wood, subsequently Lord Halifax, and Samuel Hoare) worked as a sort of internal 'opposition' from the backbenches of the Conserva-tive Party and were styled the 'Mountain'.[1] What did give the activities of the party organisations a fresh significance was the start of a tendency for the House of Commons to divide into two main contesting parties after 1918—though this was far from the im-pression that it gave at the time. On the face of it, the House of

[1] Lord Halifax, *Fullness of Days* (Collins, 1957), pp. 85–9.

104

Commons just after the First World War showed a greater fragmentation of parties than at any time since the 1850s. There were the Unionists and Liberals of the Coalition and, on the Opposition side, the Labour Party, the Asquithian Liberals, the Irish Unionists, the Irish Sinn Fein (who did not take their seats), the remnants of the old Irish nationalists and a small group of Independents. But this fragmentation did not represent the underlying political realities. After 1922, the Irish Members, one of the biggest threats ever faced by the House of Commons as an institution, disappeared with the establishment of the Irish Free State. The Coalition broke up and the Liberals, whether followers of Lloyd George or Asquith, went into decline. The future lay with the Conservatives and the Labour Party. As these two parties, each motivated by a social and political ethos wholly antagonistic to the other, fought to determine the shape of society, it was inevitable that the idea of the independent Member (though not the independent-mindedness of some Members) should be squeezed to the bone.

Yet the most important reason for the new criticism of Parliament was the enlarged activity of the Executive in the affairs of the community. The flood of new government business with which Members of Parliament were required to cope: the increased influence of the Cabinet and the bureaucracy: the sheer complexity of government activities—these were the new facts of political life which, after the First World War, raised the question whether Parliament was still adequate to exercise control over the Executive and to guard the rights of the citizen.

(ii)

The First World War was scarcely over, when Members of both Houses of Parliament turned their attention to the problem of parliamentary reform. The great legislative programme of the 1906 Liberal government had inaugurated a period of vastly quickened parliamentary activity. As we have seen, since the closing decades of the nineteenth century, there had been a steady adaptation of parliamentary procedure to give the Government more, and private Members less, control over the time of the House of Commons. The need to harness the total energies of the nation for the purpose of waging war on an unprecedented scale had led to a great rise in government activity of every kind. Government departments had increased in number and the supremacy of the small War Cabinet seemed to diminish the status of Ministers who were not in it to such a degree that traditional notions of Cabinet responsibility appeared to be in jeopardy. Ground between the powerful bureaucratic machine which was his department on the one hand and the demands of the small inner Cabinet on the other, the position of the ordinary departmental Minister already seemed to be gravely diminished— nearly as much so as the status of the ordinary Member of Parliament who was beginning to feel that, in the conditions of contemporary government, Ministers inevitably had far too little time for the House of Commons. But above all there was the complaint that the House of Commons was overworked and that Members could not conceivably digest all that was put in front of them.

The fashionable remedy was that there should be some form of parliamentary devolution, based on a federal structure of some kind, which would enable the Imperial Parliament at Westminster to hive off some of its more local activities affecting the United Kingdom. On June 3 and 4, 1919, the Commons debated, and in a small House overwhelmingly passed, a motion favouring 'the creation of subordinate legislatures within the United Kingdom' and calling for the appointment of a 'Parliamentary body to consider ways and means'.[1] The mover of the motion, Major Wood, later Lord Halifax, expressed the current concern with the failings of the machinery of government, in terms that would commend themselves to the critics of the 1960s. 'I do not want to exaggerate in any way the case that I wish to make, but I think it is safe to say that there is no department either of our executive, our administrative or our legislative life that is not showing signs of what I may call wear and depreciation', he

[1] The motion, as passed, read: 'That, with a view to enabling the Imperial Parliament to devote more attention to the general interests of the United Kingdom and, in collaboration with the other Governments of the Empire, to matters of common Imperial concern, this House is of opinion that the time has come for the creation of subordinate Legislatures within the United Kingdom, and that to this end the Government, without prejudice to any proposals it may have to make with regard to Ireland, should forthwith appoint a Parliamentary body to consider and report—
(1) upon a measure of Federal Devolution applicable to England, Scotland, and Ireland, defined in its general outlines by existing differences in law and administration between the three countries;
(2) upon the extent to which these differences are applicable to Welsh conditions and requirements;
(3) upon the financial aspects and requirements of the measure.'
The motion was passed by 187 votes to 34 against.

said.[1] Drawing attention to the increase in the number of government departments, and to the effect on departmental Ministers of a War Cabinet, Wood summed up his view as follows: 'Instead of the collective co-operation and responsibility of a Cabinet, we have now got to a great extent Government by semi-independent Departments, with an appeal to a Committee of Ministers to settle their differences, or, if not to a Committee of Ministers, to some outstanding personality such as the Prime Minister. That is a revolution in our system of government.'[2] But Wood saw no remedy in a reversion to the old method of Cabinet government. For he thought it was almost impossible for a departmental chief to form an intelligent opinion upon half the subjects coming before him in his capacity as a Cabinet Minister. Nor did he think that the use of Grand Committees was an answer. 'I have no doubt that the Grand Committees are turning out legislation. So does a sausage machine turn out minced meat. But the point is whether that is not being done by withdrawing Members and by withdrawing subjects from this House and committing them to a handful of Members upstairs, and whether that is not a cost absolutely out of proportion to the results obtained. I believe that it must produce results which are disastrous in this House', he said.[3] Since tinkering about with the existing system would not produce an answer, the question he raised was whether they could delegate part of their business to subordinate assemblies, perhaps in different parts of the country.

Much of the debate turned on issues and ideas which, within a few years, were totally irrelevant. The question of Ireland—for which a form of devolution had long been advocated as an alternative to Home Rule—continually crept into the debate. The notion of delegating internal United Kingdom affairs to subordinate Parliaments in order to provide more time for the Federal Parliament to discharge its Imperial obligations has a perverse ring to it at a time when Britain is in the process of discharging its final Imperial duties. But in other respects, those who advocated devolution were arguing upon lines more relevant to the discussion of the sixties. The congestion of the business of Parliament was mainly ascribed to the growth of legislative work and, as the seconder of the motion, Murray MacDonald, saw it, this was a natural and inevitable result of the growth of the franchise. 'As each new body of electors was

[1] H.C. Deb., Vol. 116, col. 1874, June 3, 1919.
[2] Ibid., col. 1875, June 3, 1919.   [3] Ibid., col. 1877, June 3, 1919.

brought within the framework of the Constitution new demands for changing conditions of our life arose, and the inability of Parliament to cope with these demands became every year more and more obvious,' he said. This it was, he considered, that marked the difference between the Parliament of 1919 and the Parliaments of the eighteenth century with their almost complete lack of any major legislative demands. He reminded the House that formal complaints of this congestion and of its injurious effects dated back as far as 1837, when the first of the long series of Select Committees had been appointed to consider the subject and report on methods by which the transaction of business could be expedited.[1]

Those who opposed the principle of devolution outright were in a minority. But some, who did not object to the notion of devolution in principle, emphasised the practical difficulties. Edward Carson, who had a Northern Irish axe to grind, was one of them. Were there to be different labour laws in the different provincial Parliaments, he asked? Were the railways to be an Imperial and national affair, or were they to be local?[2] But Carson at least saw merits in the idea of devolution: a Member who saw none was Sir Henry Craik, who made one of the most forthright and interesting speeches opposing the motion. He reminded the Commons that the idea that the House was receding in popular estimation had been heard in every generation 'and will be heard in every succeeding generation'. As for the plea of overwork, that might be so. 'But was there ever a time in the history of this House and Kingdom when the matters to be dealt with by the Grand Inquest of the Nation were not beyond the powers of individual Members?'[3] What would be the relationship of an English sub-Parliament to the Federal Parliament? Would the sub-Parliament, crystallising English opinion, seek to dominate the Federal Parliament? Should England itself be divided? Should the 'Dominions' be represented at Westminster? And what of the differences of franchise and the difficulty of allocating functions as between the Federal Parliament and the Imperial Parliament?

The essence of the argument for devolution was expressed by Captain Ormsby-Gore when he said: 'We shall never be an Imperial Parliament until we cease to be a gas and water Parliament. Until we have got rid of gas and water we are never going to get proper consideration of the big questions which this Parliament ought to deal

[1] H.C. Deb., Vol. 116, col. 1884, June 3, 1919.
[2] Ibid., col. 1898, June 3, 1919.   [3] Ibid., col. 1900, June 3, 1919.

with.'[1] Making due allowance for changed circumstances, and for the dissipation of Britain's Imperial rôle, one may suggest that Ormsby-Gore was touching on one of the fundamentals of the later argument about Parliament in the 1960s. Is it to be constantly distracted from the great political subjects by bread-and-butter work? And which subjects, so far as the lives of the governed are concerned, are 'great' and which are bread-and-butter? Is Parliament at its best, or at its least decisive, when discussing such major, but generalised issues, as foreign policy and the state of the economy? Whatever the answer may be to these questions, and whether it does or does not lie in some extension of the Committee system, it is instructive to note that there was a very wide consensus of opinion among Members in 1919, expressed in the Devolution Debate, that the Grand Committee system was a menace to the proper functioning of the House and also that, though Committees could get through much work, they could not give legislation enough detailed attention.

Perhaps the best case put up against separating the high functions of Parliament from more pedestrian duties was expressed in some words of Sir Henry Craik which seem relevant to any discussion of the character of Parliament. He pointed out that the comparative interest in Imperial (in modern terms, we may assume, he would have said 'foreign') and domestic policies varied from time to time. There were whole Sessions of Parliament when the central interest of the House rested upon some domestic question of great importance: he cited the occupation of the Session of 1906 with the Education Bill. But at another time the interest shifted and Parliament was occupied with some great foreign question. 'That is what enables our House to suit itself to the various interests and experiences, and to get hold of the hearts of the people it represents. Do not let us fancy that we will make ourselves a greater body if we try to wash our hands of what we call domestic questions and if we say to our constituents, "You must not trouble us with these local matters of yours, we leave them to others; we can only meet as a great Imperial concern; we can only have full-dress Debates which all the world will listen to." That is not what the Parliament of this country has been,' said Craik.[2]

The Conference on Devolution met under the chairmanship of Mr Speaker Lowther. It consisted of thirty-two Members chosen by the Prime Minister, Lloyd George, from the two Houses of Parliament.

[1] H.C. Deb., Vol. 116, cols. 1955–6, June 3, 1919.
[2] Ibid., col. 1904, June 3, 1919.

The Speaker reported to Lloyd George on April 27, 1920. His report and his letter to the Prime Minister, together with certain appendices dealing with different proposals for devolution, were published as a White Paper.[1] The Conference had less difficulty in forming an opinion about the powers which should be devolved than it did about the constitution of the subordinate bodies which should be the recipient of the powers hived off by the senior Parliament. The powers which it was agreed should be devolved were: the regulation of internal commercial undertakings, professions and societies (this category included advertisements, amusement places and theatres, building societies and loan societies, and liquor licensing); Order and Good Government (this category covered cruelty to animals, betting and gaming, inebriates, police, other than Metropolitan Police, and prisons); Ecclesiastical Matters; Agriculture and Land (including land drainage and improvements); Judiciary and Minor Legal Matters (including coroners, county courts, criminal law, minor offences, etc); Education, covering primary, secondary and university (except Oxford, Cambridge and London); Local Government and Municipal Undertakings; Public Health, including hospitals, housing, and National Health Insurance.

The significance of these proposals is twofold. First, they were produced not by academic critics of Parliament but by a group of practising politicians who were sufficiently impressed by the over-working of the existing parliamentary system, even in 1920, to be prepared to shed many of the existing powers of Parliament, despite the fact that most bodies find it easier to acquire new duties than to abandon influence they already have. Secondly, the proposals of 1920 are important because, despite the effort devoted to their formulation and the manifest willingness of Members of Parliament to make radical changes provided the essential functions of Parliament were not damaged, nothing was done. To all intents and purposes, the fundamental practices of Parliament in 1966 remained what they were forty-six years earlier. The retention of the *status quo*, in face of the repeated discussions on the subject in the intervening years, suggests that the failure to change has more to do with the intractability of the problem than with the conservative instincts of Members of Parliament. The greatest difficulty that the Conference of 1919–20 encountered was in deciding the composition of the subordinate legislative bodies which it was willing to see established. As

[1] Cmnd. 692, 1920.

the Speaker reported to the Prime Minister, 'for some time the discussion was carried on as a duel between those, on the one side, who supported the proposals, associated with the names of the late Lord Brassey and Mr Murray MacDonald, for setting up subordinate legislative bodies with separate election, and, on the other side, those who were so impressed by the disadvantages which appeared to them inherent in such a scheme, that, in the absence of an alternative, they felt themselves driven towards the necessity of opposing the principle of devolution itself'. In order to bridge this divergence of view, Speaker Lowther produced an alternative scheme. Whereas Murray MacDonald's scheme proposed that each subordinate legislature should have a directly elected chamber and that the members of each chamber should be elected for the same constituencies, and by the same electors as now returned Members to the UK Parliament, the Speaker's proposal was that the conference itself should not try to draw up new Constitutions for the component parts of Great Britain. Instead it was proposed that the method of composing the subordinate legislative bodies should be decided by each component part through its parliamentary representatives, without interference from any other part, but subject to the approval of the UK Parliament. One of the points of agreement, however, was that the areas to have local legislatures should be England, Scotland and Wales. The question of subdividing England itself was left open.

Parliamentary devolution, whether along the regional lines advocated in 1919–20, or on a functional basis, remained an issue for recurrent discussion in subsequent years. In 1920, the Socialist Webbs produced their plan for dividing the functions of Parliament and setting up a 'social' Parliament alongside the existing political Parliament.[1] In 1931, Beatrice Webb again outlined the plan for the devolution of business from the Cabinet and Parliament to a new 'National Assembly' which would have procedure based on local authorities and perform administrative duties by committees which would enable all members of the National Assembly to participate in government.[2] The model of local government, of which many Socialists had experience before arriving at Westminster, remained

[1] Beatrice and Sidney Webb, *A Constitution for a Socialist Commonwealth of Great Britain* (Longmans, 1920).

[2] Mrs Sidney Webb, *A New Reform Bill* (Fabian Tract No. 236, 1931). See also Mrs Sidney Webb, 'A Reform Bill for 1932', *Political Quarterly*, Vol. 11, 1931, pp. 1–22.

attractive to them: in the 1960s, however, local government itself came under criticism precisely on account of its lack of central direction on 'Cabinet' lines. Devolution of a sort—but to meet the specific problem of the national economy—was also to be advocated by Winston Churchill at the end of the decade: this will be discussed in the following sections. Although functional devolution became the more fashionable version after the early twenties, more recent proposals for regional planning advocated by the Conservative Government under Douglas-Home in 1963–4 and by the Labour Government under Harold Wilson that followed it, perhaps echo more closely the instincts which had prompted consideration of regional devolution just after the 1914–18 War.[1]

At the end of the twenties, the constitutional position of the House of Commons again came under scrutiny as a result of the politicians' failure to solve the fundamental problem of contemporary politics. Before that, however, Members of Parliament became involved in a new struggle for parliamentary power which was to produce some evidence that the backbenchers, for good or ill, had not lost ultimate control over the actions of their leaders.

(iii)

After 1918, discontent with Lloyd George's administration rose rapidly among the Conservatives in Parliament who were both the Prime Minister's main support and his captors. The Irish anarchy remained a running sore: many Conservatives were disconcerted by the apparent influence of trade-union threats in dissuading the Government from giving strong support to Poland in its struggle against Soviet Russia: there was a deepening industrial slump at home, bringing poverty and unemployment. Increasingly, the coalition after the outbreak of peace looked like a one-man show— and the one man was the Prime Minister. He was a leader without a party: the Conservatives, wielding the power of numbers, constituted a party without an effective leader. Lloyd George had been under pressure from the Conservatives for what they regarded as his softness in dealing with Germany in the Versailles peace negotiations—

---

[1] The appointment of Edward Heath as Secretary of State for Industry, Trade and Regional Development, in 1963 was a manifestation of this approach. The subsequent Labour Government's 'national planning' had a strong regional element.

though from the Left, Lloyd George was criticised as too harsh. Increasingly also, the Conservatives' old personal dislike of the Prime Minister was reviving. Yet it seemed questionable whether the Conservative Party could get rid of Lloyd George unless their revolt was led by one of their own prominent figures. Nevertheless, they brought him down, and the significance of the fall of Lloyd George, in terms of parliamentary history, was that it was achieved by the sentiment and the determination of backbench Members of Parliament, despite the frequent assumption that backbenchers are impotent against their leaders. In 1922, the Conservative leaders, Austen Chamberlain, Balfour and Birkenhead, supported Lloyd George. Against him were the backbenchers, most Junior Ministers and the apparently insignificant President of the Board of Trade, Stanley Baldwin.

The coalition headed by Lloyd George was destroyed at a meeting of Conservative Members of Parliament held at the Carlton Club on October 19, 1922. The particular issue which led to the break was the Government's attitude to the war which had broken out between Greece and Turkey. Lloyd George was pursuing a pro-Greek policy. Bonar Law, the former Conservative Leader who had gone into retirement owing to ill-health, had already given an intimation of his different attitude in a letter to *The Times* pointing out that the British Empire, with its large body of Mohammedans, ought not to show hostility or unfairness to the Turks. He argued that Britain's financial position did not enable it to act as the policeman of the world.[1] It was probably Bonar Law's intervention at the Carlton Club meeting which made certain of a majority vote that day against continuing in the Coalition. When called on to speak, Bonar Law came out strongly in favour of withdrawing from the Coalition on the ground that feeling in the party so strongly favoured doing so that to resist it would break the Conservative ranks. The result was a victory for withdrawal by 187 votes to 87. Yet for all the importance of Bonar Law's intervention it was, as he himself implicitly acknowledged, the feeling of the rank and file which fundamentally dictated the result. Bonar Law's intervention was potent not so much because it expressed his own view but because it was a statement, from an elder politician of the party, of what the Conservative Party itself wanted. The Carlton Club meeting is an important corrective for those who believe that the rank and file of a party will always

[1] *The Times*, October 7, 1922.

come to heel if told strongly enough by their leaders what they must do. This was what Austen Chamberlain and his friends also thought at the time and they were wrong. Chamberlain wanted the Conservative MPs' meeting to take place because he believed that by confronting the malcontents openly he and the other supporters of the Coalition were certain to be able to suppress the revolt. Instead, backbench feeling and Stanley Baldwin, whose speech on this occasion marked him as the party's future leader, brought Chamberlain and the leaders to heel. The Conservative Members of the Coalition immediately intimated that they must withdraw from it and Lloyd George resigned as Prime Minister the same day—not waiting either for a defeat in Parliament or for the result of the general election which must inevitably follow.[1] Bonar Law, though invited by the king to take office, would not do so until he had been elected Conservative Leader, which he was four days later.

Bonar Law proceeded to form a Government of what Winston Churchill called the 'second eleven'. The most prominent Conservatives, Austen Chamberlain, Birkenhead and Balfour included, felt bound to abstain from membership of an administration which had been formed as a result of the Conservative Party's rejection of their advice. For want of anyone more prominent, Bonar Law was obliged to appoint Baldwin Chancellor of the Exchequer: another recruit was Neville Chamberlain, who became Postmaster-General.

This was the first time the Conservative Party had appealed, without allies, to the people since 1910: it was the first Conservative administration to do so since 1900—and even then it had still contained Liberal Unionists, as it had since 1885. As it happened, the Conservative Party was at the start of an inter-war hegemony which,

---

[1] A. J. P. Taylor, *English History, 1914–1945* (O.U.P.), pp. 191–3, points out that Lloyd George was the first Prime Minister since Lord North to resign because of a decision taken at a private meeting of MPs and not as a result of an adverse vote in Parliament or at a general election. 'Thus he maintained to the end his disregard for the established constitutional machinery', is Mr Taylor's comment on Lloyd George's instantaneous recognition of the fact that the parliamentary support on which he had secured power had been withdrawn.

For accounts of the Carlton Club episode of 1922 see (*inter alia*) Robert Blake, *The Unknown Prime Minister* (Eyre & Spottiswoode, 1955); L. S. Amery, *My Political Life*, Vol. 2 (Hutchinson, 1953); Lord Beaverbrook, *The Decline and Fall of Lloyd George* (Collins, 1963); Sir Ivor Jennings, *Party Politics*, Vol. 11.

like its twenty year dominance at the end of the nineteenth century, was built on splits in the ranks of its opponents. The break between the Lloyd George and Asquith Liberals was the first stage in the process and Lloyd George's 'coupon' victory of 1918 was really a victory for the Tory Party. Henceforth the Liberals were to be split and declining and, less than a decade ahead, the rising Labour Party was also to break up—leading to the Conservative-dominated 'National' Government which endured until 1940. But, in the meantime, politics in 1922 seemed exceptionally confused. The Liberals' split was, though only temporarily, mirrored by an emotional division on the Tory side between the bulk of the Party and the former 'coalitionists'. Bonar Law, moreover, was reluctant for Conservative candidates to oppose even the Liberal Members of Lloyd George's former administration, let alone the former Coalition Tories. In return, he hoped that, in other constituencies, the Conservative candidates might be supported against the Asquith Liberals by those Liberals who favoured Lloyd George's Coalition. On the other hand, Lord Beaverbrook was sponsoring independent Conservative candidates in such constituencies. Finally, there was the growing importance of the Labour Party, which was seeking to become the second great party in the nation. Yet, despite its handicaps, the Bonar Law Government was returned to power with a clear majority of seventy-nine seats in the House of Commons over all other parties. Labour, with 142 MPs, doubled its numbers in the House and became the second largest party. The official Liberals were reduced to a mere sixty seats: Lloyd George's followers, the 'National Liberals', now numbered only fifty-seven.

In spite of the apparent security of the Conservative position, the state of politics in Parliament and in the country remained essentially fluid for much of this decade and this fluidity was one of the causes of discontent with the House of Commons as an institution. In 1922, the Conservatives might have seemed established for a full term of parliamentary power. But Baldwin, who had succeeded Bonar Law, adopted a protectionist policy within a few months of becoming Prime Minister and, in view of his predecessor's commitment of the party to free trade, felt obliged to appeal for a protectionist mandate. He failed to get it and in January 1924, a minority Labour Government was installed on sufferance of the Liberals, now uneasily united behind Lloyd George on free trade. This first Labour administration, headed by Ramsay MacDonald, quickly proved its impeccable adherence to the letter and spirit of the British Constitution, though it could only be a weak government. Obliged, through dependence on the Liberals, to compromise its socialist principles, it faced repeated attacks from its own left wing over domestic policy and quickly fell over the handling of the case of a Communist editor, J. R. Campbell, who had been charged with incitement to mutiny and whose prosecution had been stopped by the Labour Attorney-General. The General Election of October 1924 brought the Conservatives back to power with 419 seats against the Labour Party's 151.

The new Conservative Government formed by Baldwin was a strong one. Austen Chamberlain and Birkenhead were back in the Cabinet. Winston Churchill, not even officially a Conservative, became Chancellor of the Exchequer. Until 1929, the Conservatives provided an island of firm single-party administration in an unstable decade of three-party politics. Yet the traumatic event of the 1926 General Strike, for all Baldwin's success in dealing with it, was itself a dangerous symptom of the grave and chronic disease of economic depression which persisted throughout the twenties and continued into the thirties. This disease did not reach crisis point until Baldwin had gone out of office, after running the 1924-9 Parliament for nearly its full term. But well before the General Election of 1929, which again brought in a minority Labour Government, there was widespread discontent at the failure of the politicians to deal with the problem of unemployment and economic depression. Inevitably, this failure rubbed off on Parliament as an institution: to the argument that the House of Commons could not cope with the weight of work put before it, and that its Members were subservient to the Cabinet and the bureaucracy, were added two further interlinked criticisms. First, parliamentary government appeared to be unstable government; secondly, it proved incapable of solving the most pressing problem of the nation.

(iv)

Anyone interested in the problems of Parliament in the second half of the twentieth century, who did not possess some specialist knowledge of its recent political history, could be forgiven for assuming that the criticism which has flowed so freely in the fifties and sixties has represented an entirely new response to a new situation. For few of the more recent critics have made more than cursory acknowledgement, if that, to the discussions of the functions and shortcomings of Parliament that took place between thirty and forty years ago.[1] Some, indeed, have written as though the decline of Parliament was essentially a recent development.[2]

Yet a comparison of the more recent criticisms of the House of Commons with those made at the end of the 1920s and in the 1930s is highly instructive—and for reasons that are wholly practical. For the fundamental cause of the criticism was the same in both periods. Each produced a comparably intractable problem and there is overwhelming evidence that the criticisms of Parliament in both periods were symptomatic of a desperate urge to break through an enervating and apparently insoluble crisis of national politics. Of course, the economic problems of the two periods were different in character. In the fifties and sixties, Britain has failed to reconcile her internal prices and cost structure with the need to pay her way overseas. Endemic inflation is linked with responsibilities inherited from days when Britain had a greater world rôle than she has had since the Second World War—responsibilities which can neither be sustained by current resources nor too hastily rejected. Full employment has brought its own difficulties: it has enabled wage rates to be pushed up to an extent not justified by productivity and it has not been accompanied by an appropriate modernisation of industrial relations. The problem thirty-five years ago was very different: the chronic economic malady then was depression and unemployment. Successive British Governments, untaught as yet by Keynesian economics or by the habits of close government control over the economy, which were acquired in the Second World War, were defeated by the opposite

[1] In his *The Reform of Parliament*, p. 10, however, Professor Bernard Crick has acknowledged that 'Root and branch schemes for reform, such as were canvassed in the 1930s, are no longer the fashion and, indeed, no longer relevant'. Similarly Professor A. H. Hanson, in his article, 'The Purpose of Parliament', *Parliamentary Affairs*, Vol. XVII, No. 3, Summer 1964, pp. 279 et seq., suspected that recent books with such apocalyptic titles as *The Passing of Parliament*, *Parliament in Danger*, and *Can Parliament Survive?* would in twenty or thirty years' time seem as old-hat as Lord Hewart's *New Despotism* or C. K. Allen's *Bureaucracy Triumphant* seem today.

[2] Andrew Hill and Anthony Whichelow in *What's Wrong with Parliament?*, p. 9, specifically make their allegation of a fall in the status of Parliament by comparison with the year 1945, when 'the reputation of the British Parliament stood as high as ever before in its long history'.

117

problem—mass unemployment and depression. The social reper- cussions in the twenties and thirties were enormous. The apparent intractability of the problem naturally bred a widespread urge to question the efficiency of the institutions of government which failed to solve it. It was natural to ask whether these institutions remained competent to secure the greatness of Britain at a time when it seemed that this country's rightful place was still in the front rank of world powers.

It was no coincidence that a high tide of criticism of the existing parliamentary system occurred in 1929-31—the years when the chronic economic illness of the nation reached crisis point. By then (as in more recent years) the national self-confidence had been sapped by political failure and there was a widespread sense of de- cline. The mood of national introspection was expressed by Winston Churchill (among many others), himself an advocate of major changes in the parliamentary structure to enable it to deal with the country's economic problem outside the context of the conventional and apparently inappropriate party conflict. 'We see our race doubt- ful of its mission and no longer confident about its principles, infirm of purpose, drifting to and fro with the tides and currents of a deeply disturbed ocean. The compass has been damaged. The charts are out of date.'[1] The mode of expression was idiosyncratic: the sentiments were uncannily like those common in more recent years—as, indeed, was the thought behind Churchill's suggested remedy. Parliament, he argued, was fully capable, as no other body was, of dealing with practical politics. But he very much doubted whether the economic problems of the country could be settled by the same means as were appropriate for determining political questions. 'One may even be pardoned in doubting whether institutions based on adult suffrage could possibly arrive at the right decisions upon the intricate propositions of modern business and finance', he said in his Romanes Lecture. Churchill, it is plain, thought that the technical complexity of contemporary economic problems was so great that the 'right' answer could not be sought in the normal processes by which one political interest is allowed to clash in Parliament with another— perhaps, in the process, making clear-cut radical decisions impossible. Like many men of action, Churchill, great parliamentarian though he

[1] The Rt. Hon. Winston L. Spencer-Churchill, CH, Hon. DCL, MP. 'Parliamentary Government and the Economic Problem', The Romanes Lecture delivered in the Sheldonian Theatre, Oxford, June 19, 1930.

was, saw the intrinsic difficulty of reconciling parliamentary government with decisive action. In the circumstances of 1930, therefore, some sort of body which was not bedevilled by party-political motives seemed to be demanded. Churchill's own answer was an economic sub-Parliament composed of 'persons of high technical and business qualifications'. This urge to take a chronic economic problem out of politics in the 1930s was remarkably similar in character to that which led to the creation of the National Economic Development Council in 1962 and subsequently to the activities of the Department of Economic Affairs and the Prices and Incomes Board which were set up by the Labour Government of 1964. At both times there was a feeling that there must be a 'right' answer to the national difficulties and that this was being obscured by restricting debate to ordinary parliamentary processes. In fact, the economy quickly came back 'into politics' after 1964. Similarly, the crisis of 1930 showed that the economic problem of the inter-war period was too closely interlinked with conflicting political interests to be susceptible to political, expert solutions. To men of goodwill at the time, however, this was not so apparent. There must, it seemed to them, be an answer if only the squabbles of the politicians could be by-passed.

To many students of politics, the activities of Parliament seemed wholly contemptible as the crisis of 1930 drew near. 'An election at present, considered as a means of selecting the best qualified rulers, is so absurd that if the last dozen parliaments had consisted of candidates who were at the foot of the poll instead of those who were at the head of it, there is no reason to suppose that we should have been a step more or less advanced than we are today. In neither case would the electorate have any real choice of representatives.' So wrote Bernard Shaw in 1929.[1] In that year, an indecisive election result again put a Labour minority Government into office. It had been an election without a cause except for the statutory requirement to end the 1924 Parliament. 'For once, the election turned, as some modern theorists think all elections should turn, solely on the question: who should be the next prime minister?', observed A. J. P. Taylor.[2] The outcome of this first general election based on universal suffrage (all women over twenty-one had been enfranchised in 1928) was 288 seats for Labour, 260 for the Conservatives and fifty-nine for the Liberals. This result might well have been regarded as confirming the view

[1] Bernard Shaw, Preface to *The Applecart*.
[2] A. J. P. Taylor, *English History, 1914–1945*, p. 270.

expressed by the *Economist* before the verdict of the electors was passed: 'The fact which we have to face, and which the country has not yet faced, is that the two-party system has gone, and gone for ever. The three-party system has come to stay and we have got to learn how to work it.'[1]

Attacks on the current political practices of politics were not only directed at the procedures of Parliament and the means by which MPs were selected by the party organisations. Equally criticised was the electoral system of 'one man, one vote'. The logical absurdity of a system which allocates seats in the House of Commons in proportions that bear no relationship to the comparative size of a party's support in the country has long been apparent and in 1929, when it did not even have the merit, normally assigned to it, of providing Britain with strong, one-party governments based on secure majorities, it seemed particularly hard to justify. A Speaker's Conference on electoral reform in 1916–17 had proposed proportional representation by the single transferable vote for elections in all boroughs returning three or more Members each, including London outside the City, and the adoption of the alternative vote for elections in single-Member constituencies contested by two or more candidates. Nothing had come of these proposals. Now, after taking office in 1929, Ramsay MacDonald, under pressure from the Liberals whose support he needed and who suffered most from the existing system, set up a new all-party conference to discuss electoral reform, with Lord Ullswater presiding over it.

The Conference ended in total failure after ten sittings which achieved no agreement and only demonstrated that no agreement could be achieved. The *Economist* commented: 'Although by general consent the present system is unjust and liable, through its misrepresentation of the electorate, to lead to a position that might well jeopardise our democratic institutions, this important constitutional issue seems to have been considered, not on its merits, but from the point of view of tactical party interests of the moment.' This explanation may have seemed a statement of the obvious but, much more significantly, the *Economist* used the occasion to refer to the general and deeper discontent with parliamentary efficacy. 'The fire of criticism to which parliamentary government has been subjected in many countries of the world, the feeling of dissatisfaction with which grave economic questions have been handled in our own

[1] *Economist*, May 25, 1928.

country, and the disintegration which appears to have been occurring within our party system, are all indications that the nation will not indefinitely submit to the domination of the party machine.'[1]

The wish to break away from the confines of stereotyped political argument was not restricted to commentators. Lloyd George, who since Asquith's retirement had been officially the leader of the Liberal Party, was one who wished to find new solutions. While the Conservatives were arguing that it was unrealistic to hope for any spectacular cure for unemployment, and the Labour Party seemed unable to escape from hopeful generalisation into precise analysis, Lloyd George came forward before the 1929 General Election with proposals which foreshadowed the principles of Keynesian and New Deal economics. Having used his political fund to finance enquiries by economists into specific industrial problems, he produced a programme repudiating *laissez faire* and advocating deficit financing of large public works as a cure for unemployment and as a generator of economic activity. Lloyd George's programme went so far as promising to reduce 'the terrible figures of the workless in the course of a single year to normal proportions' without adding a single penny to national and local taxation. However, the electorate did not give the still distrusted Lloyd George the chance to test his schemes. The nation's grave problem remained in the usual political channels.

After the election, though there persisted as much fear of dangerous experiments as of inaction, there seemed to be enough general agreement about the ends for even a minority government to find some means of restoring economic prosperity. But goodwill was not enough. Subsequent events quickly confirmed the anxieties of those who believed that the politicians were letting the affairs of the nation drift. Each political party was insecure, self-centred and troubled by internal tensions. The Conservatives, preoccupied with fending off Beaverbrook's Empire Free Trade campaign against Baldwin, had nothing constructive to contribute towards a solution of the economic disease; the Liberals remained a small party dedicated to *laissez faire* and free trade who were more than ever distrustful of their leader now that he had become an economic interventionist. The Labour Party was much more timid and less socialistic than Lloyd George in dealing with the problem. Indeed, it was itself sufficiently attached to *laissez faire* to reject the programme of

[1] *Economist*, August 2, 1930.

economic planning put before it by Oswald Mosley, then a member of the Labour Government. In protest, Mosley resigned in May 1930.

By the middle of 1930, it was realised that there had been a change in the gravity of the problem: no longer could it be hoped that the British difficulties might be dealt with without regard to the depression that was now spread all over the world. MacDonald himself recognised this when he invited the leaders of the Opposition parties to take part in a non-party conference (Lloyd George accepted but Baldwin refused) and created a special Civil Service body to become a focus and a liaison for action to deal with unemployment. This was the background against which Winston Churchill delivered his Romanes Lecture, and I refer to it again to indicate how the problem seemed to a contemporary who sensed the gravity of the situation and saw the need for a new constructive approach to it. As Churchill saw it, the issues before Parliament were no longer political; they were economic. The nation was not interested in politics: it was interested in economics. 'It has in the main got the political system it wants; what it now asks for is more money, better times, regular employment, expanding comfort and material prosperity.' Further, in words that foreshadowed so many utterances of the 1950s and 1960s, he went on: 'It feels that it is not having its share in the development of the modern world, and that it is losing its relative position. It feels that science and machinery ought to procure a much more rapid progress. It complains that the phenomena of production, consumption, and employment are at this time in our country exceptionally ill-related. It turns to Parliament asking for guidance, and Parliament, though voluble in so many matters, is on this one paramount topic dumb.' Enumerating the economic principles of the Victorian textbooks (including 'absolute reliance upon private enterprise, unfettered and unfavoured by the State'), Churchill suggested that the party politicians simply picked out from the 'tables of economic law' the tenets most agreeable to the 'crowd that votes for them'. Yet public opinion instinctively rejected many features of the classical doctrines of economics. 'Few would agree that private enterprise is the sole agency by which fruitful economic undertakings can be launched or conducted', said Churchill. It was admitted that workers must be insured against external disturbance: that in one form or another the State must interfere in industry. 'We are in the presence of new forces not existing when the text-books were written', he said, but he thought that it was not a matter of simply

122

breaking up the old established foundations: the task was rather to build another storey upon them. Such new principles which required 'high, cold, technical and dispassionate or disinterested decision' were unlikely to be discovered by parliamentary institutions. Churchill made it clear that he regarded the problem as a technical one which had defeated all attempts to solve it, including the extremes of capitalism in the US and Communism in Russia. It would not be solved by parliamentary government or even by a general election. 'Are we, or are we not, capable of a higher and more complex economic, fiscal, and financial policy? Are we not capable of evolving a united body of doctrine adapted to our actual conditions and requirements? Could not such a system of policy be presented and accepted upon a national and not a party basis? Could it not when devised be taken out of the political brawling and given a fair trial by overwhelming national consent? Here then is the crux for Parliament.' Despite the threats to parliamentary government from both the Left and the Right, the British parliamentary system would not be overthrown by political agitation. 'It will pass only when it has shown itself incapable of dealing with some fundamental and imperative economic need; and such a challenge is now open', Churchill asserted. The economic problem must be examined by a non-political body, free from party pressures and consisting of people with special economic qualifications. Parliament should create such a body subordinate to itself. 'The spectacle of an Economic Sub-Parliament debating day after day with fearless detachment from public opinion all the most disputed questions of Finance and Trade, and reaching conclusions by voting, would be an innovation, but an innovation easily to be embraced by our flexible constitutional system.' He suggested that the political Parliament should choose a subordinate Economic Parliament of, say, one-fifth of its numbers in proportion to its party groupings. Parliament was on trial and if Parliament and the Ministries dependent upon it could not proclaim a new policy, the question was whether they should create a new instrument specially adapted to do so and delegate to it all the necessary powers and facilities.

Churchill was not alone in believing that the economic and unemployment problems should be taken out of conventional political argument. But if there was growing support for a non-party approach, Churchill had little backing for what the *Economist* reasonably enough called his 'rather vague suggestions' for an Economic

Sub-Parliament. The obvious objection was that a body one-fifth the size of the existing House of Commons and consisting of politicians in proportion to the different parties' membership of the political Parliament was hardly likely to shed partisan attitudes in coming to grips with the problem. The *Economist* commented: 'In order to create this non-partisan atmosphere it would seem essential to substitute for, or at least combine with the plan of Mr. Churchill some non-party method of selection. The suggestion raises constitutional issues of far-reaching importance.'[1] But the economic situation continued to deteriorate and, as it did so, disillusion with the working of Parliament and the behaviour of politicians spread. In August, the *Economist* observed that 'the "man in the street" viewed the past session with complete lack of interest, as one might watch indifferently a pointless and boring theatrical show. Now there are few who would dissent from the proposition that if indifference and inattention on the part of a theoretically sovereign electorate is an inherent characteristic of democracy, then democracy is a form of government ineffective, dangerous and doomed to supersession.'[2] These observations were made in the course of a review of a book by Ramsay Muir, which had just appeared, analysing the defects of Parliament and proposing remedies.[3]

Muir's approach and analysis was in many respects a model for the criticisms of Parliament, and for the remedies, which have regularly been produced since then. The Cabinet, Muir considered, was over-mighty and weighed down by administrative detail while the House of Commons, handicapped by overwork and by out-of-date procedure, was oppressed by the authority of the Cabinet. The result was that Parliament had no control over the Whitehall bureaucracy. Muir advocated as solutions a smaller Cabinet and a thorough-going reorganisation of House of Commons procedure which would hinge on the establishment of Standing Committees to enable the Commons to exert greater control over legislation and also finance. He advocated devolution along both functional and regional lines, and also a reformed Second Chamber, so as to relieve Parliament of some of its burden of business. Muir also proposed that the electoral law

---

[1] *Economist*, June 21, 1930.   [2] Ibid., August 23, 1930.

[3] Ramsay Muir, *How Britain is Governed: A Critical Analysis of Modern Developments in the British System of Government* (Constable, 1930). See also Muir's evidence to the Select Committee on Procedure, 1931–2 (below, pp. 136–8).

should be reformed by the introduction of proportional representation.

In one obvious respect at least, Muir's analysis hardly fitted the facts of the moment. However valid his other complaints might be, it hardly seemed true, as 1930 drew to an end, that the Cabinet was all-powerful. Speculation about the date of the fall of the Government were incessant and the indecisive position of the parties in the House of Commons made it impossible for the MacDonald Cabinet to pursue the policies it wished. The truth was that the state of the 'three-party system' at this time vitiated the ability of the Government to take effective decisions. If Parliament in the fifties and sixties could be accused of being supine before Governments rendered impregnable by huge majorities, during much of the twenties both Cabinet and the House were weakened for the opposite reason.

By the end of the year, two and a half million people were out of work compared with the 1·1 million who were unemployed when Labour took office in June 1929. In February 1931, the Labour Chancellor of the Exchequer, Philip Snowden, appointed a committee under the chairmanship of Sir George May, formerly the Secretary of the Prudential Insurance Company, to produce a scheme for the economy and the reduction of expenditure. The May Report, which appeared in July, just after Parliament rose for the summer recess, advocated the most stringent economies and was to provide the justification for Snowden's harsh Budget. But events were now moving too fast for the Government to control them. In August there developed a run on the pound which was largely a chain effect of bank failures in Europe. The City of London demanded a balanced Budget and blamed the Labour Government for the lack of confidence abroad. The solution was to be a drastic cut in unemployment benefit and it was this proposal that split the Government. At first it seemed that the Labour Government would resign: instead, the chain of events started which led to the formation of a National Government on August 24, with MacDonald as Prime Minister and composed mainly of Conservatives and Liberals. Apart from the fragment which followed the Prime Minister, the bulk of the now broken Labour Party went into Opposition. MacDonald and his supporters were regarded as traitors by their former colleagues. An autumn Budget introduced drastic economies but though these temporarily stopped the run on the pound it quickly started again. In September the gold standard was abandoned.

The National Government (which had been intended only as a crisis administration) appealed to the people in a general election in October 1931 and was rewarded by an overwhelming victory with 521 seats, of which the Conservatives held 473. The Independent Liberals were reduced to thirty-three: Lloyd George, now again outside the official Liberal fold, held, with his family, four seats. In giving this overwhelming support to the National Government, many electors hoped that they were escaping from the much-criticised party politics: in fact, they were voting for Conservative rule which endured until 1940. The period of complacent, and in many respects disastrous, government based on a huge parliamentary majority, which now began, was the price the nation paid for escape from the instability of the 1920s when, once again, the House of Commons had made, and unmade, governments, and had, with a broader spectrum of political parties, represented more precisely the shades of opinion among the electorate.

Whatever else may be said of politics in the years before 1931, it cannot be said that the House of Commons was unrepresentative of the arguments and changing moods of the nation or that the parties themselves were rigid to the point of allowing their leaders to ride rough-shod over them. The split in the Liberal Party; the division on the Tory benches between the mass of the Baldwinites and the former Coalition Tories; the independent position of Winston Churchill over free trade; the break-up of the Labour Party; the resignation of Mosley and the formation of his New Party—all these were signs of a considerable independence of mind among Members of the Commons. It was also the last period in which the personal rivalries and antipathies of individual politicians had a really profound effect on the course of political action.[1]

The failures caused by fragmented politics in these years might superficially be taken as a justification for the wish of Churchill, and others who thought like him, to take the economic problem of the period out of politics. Yet had this been done, it is questionable whether any better result would have been achieved. The 'expert'

[1] Probably the only period in which personalities played a much bigger part in the formation of governments and the shape of political groupings was that of Disraeli, the Peelites, Russell and Palmerston after 1846—though they were important at other times, including the period of the Liberal Unionists. In the 1920s distrust of Lloyd George was a basic factor in the behaviour of other politicians.

financial and economic opinion of the day had not yet grasped Keynesian economics and it was not the experts primarily, but two party politicians, Lloyd George and Mosley, who had put forward the only solutions which might have avoided disaster. Had some kind of impartial economic body been put in charge: had even an 'Economic Sub-Parliament' been established, it seems highly doubtful whether it would have escaped the limitations of contemporary thinking on financial and economic matters which would undoubtedly have dominated the formulation of any consensus in the years before 1931.

Chapter Four

The Problem of Parliament 1931

'Parliament is dying, and dying discreditably. Nobody, except the professional Parliamentarians, can sit through its languid and half-hearted proceedings and doubt it.' So wrote John Strachey, MP, and C. E. M. Joad in 1931 when they published an official statement of the plan of Sir Oswald Mosley's New Party for the reform of Parliament.[1] The remedy they proposed—that Parliament should cease to try itself to govern so as to be better able to place in office a ministry with real power for government—was based on a fallacious view of the historical functions of Parliament. Whatever may be said for or against the influence that Parliament has exerted on the processes of government, it has manifested few pretensions (taking one century with another) to executive power. Strachey and Joad were lured into their constitutional fallacy by the chronic economic difficulties of their period and by their belief that legislation could provide a cure for them. One of their proposals was the formal transfer of the initiation of legislation to the Executive, though Parliament would still have the right of dismissing the Government, by vote of censure, and of obliging it to hold a general election. The New Party also proposed that Parliament should be able to interrogate ministers more extensively and pass admonitory resolutions designed to inform the Government (but without dismissing it) of strong trends of feeling in the country. Today few would regard Parliament's legislative rôle as any serious handicap to the Executive. The current complaint is rather that the House of Commons is impotent before the Cabinet.

However, although the proposals of the New Party are both dated and imbued with an ominous impatience with parliamentary democracy, they did contain a very useful indication of the reasons why so

[1] John Strachey and C. E. M. Joad, 'Parliamentary Reform: The New Party's Proposals', *Political Quarterly*, Vol. 2, 1931, pp. 319–36.

many people in the 1930s were discontented with Parliament. Unemployment had sapped the strength of Great Britain; it had 'hung as a terrifying menace above the head of every worker', wrote Strachey and Joad, and they commented: 'Every few weeks Parliament has debated Unemployment. The enemies of Britain could have no greater encouragement of their hopes than these debates; her friends no graver confirmation of their fears. Year after year, session after session, under Government after Government, these debates have gone on. The endless, futile speeches have all been made—and remade. To those who care for the future of Great Britain nothing is more horrible than to sit through these debates. In the ornate and hideous Chamber the nation's breath seems to grow fainter, speech by speech.'

In the 1930s Parliament was under suspicion because it failed to solve the great contemporary problem. But was Parliament really in a state of decline in 1930 compared with previous periods? Sir Herbert Samuel (later Lord Samuel), himself an advocate of reform along geographical devolutionary lines, was doubtful. In his view, there never was a time in the course of modern English history when Parliament's prestige was not said to be at a low ebb. Was its prestige lower by comparison with the period fifty years earlier, when Irish obstruction was at its height and the House's legislative action was almost paralysed? Was it at a low ebb compared with a hundred years earlier, when 'the unrepresentative character of the House of Commons had brought it into disrepute throughout the whole nation'? Or was the comparison to be made with one hundred and fifty years earlier when the House of Commons was filled with placemen? It was a pity, in Samuel's view, that Winston Churchill and others should have raised the question whether the House of Commons stood as high in public estimation as it used to stand. The real point was whether it was fulfilling the tasks it ought to fulfil—and Samuel went on to prescribe his own remedies for procedural reform.[1]

In 1931 and 1932, a Select Committee of the House enquired into the conduct of Public Business and suggested improvements that might be made. But although it refrained from pronouncing on constitutional questions, it freely enquired into the broader and deeper issue of the function of Parliament and also into the question whether the institution had declined by comparison with former days.

[1] Sir Herbert Samuel: 'Defects and Reforms of Parliament', *Political Quarterly*, Vol. 2, 1931, pp. 305–18.

In doing so, it took evidence from Members who themselves formed a bridge with Victorian Parliaments and some of whom were men of notable stature. The Committee recognised, in its report, that 'one of the chief reasons for their appointment was the existence of a large body of criticism of Parliament, both by Members and by representative citizens, and they have interpreted their terms of reference in the broadest sense'.[1] It realised that the problems were neither new nor confined to the House of Commons. 'They present themselves in almost every elected assembly in all countries where modern views as to the powers and duties of the State are finding expression, and where the vastly complicated social, industrial, commercial and economic questions of our time are demanding parliamentary attention and solution.' Recording that these problems had been felt in the House of Commons since soon after the passing of the Reform Act of 1832, the Committee observed that numerous committees had considered the practice and procedure of the House since then and that alterations had been made to the rules of Parliament, nearly all of which had reduced the opportunities of the private Member and increased the powers of the Executive, so that the House might be able to deal with the ever-increasing volume of official business which confronted it.[2]

In 1931, as in the 1960s, there was no unanimity among parliamentarians on the nature of the problem nor of the best remedy. The Select Committee reported a cleavage between witnesses who wanted the machinery of the House to be altered in favour of the majority— that is to say, to expedite government business—and those who were worried that the increasing power of the government of the day made the position of a private Member 'less attractive than it used to be to many who would be useful Members of this House'.[3] The Prime Minister, Ramsay MacDonald, left no doubt that his chief concern was to expedite the business of government. MacDonald explained where he thought the fundamental weakness of Parliament lay. 'There is a doctrine that it is the function of the Opposition to oppose. I have always regarded that as a crime against the State', he said. 'It is not the function of the Opposition to oppose; it is the function of the Opposition to oppose Second Readings. . . . ' Thereafter, MacDonald asserted, 'the only function of the Opposition is to improve [a Bill] in its own direction within the scope of the Vote that has been

[1] *Report from the Select Committee on Procedure* (November 1932), p. iii.
[2] Ibid., pp. iii–iv.   [3] Ibid., p. v.

131

registered'. It had no right to obstruct 'in the sense of making Parliament barren or unproductive'.[1] MacDonald emphasised: 'I do want to get the House of Commons to understand that the guillotine is a legitimate and a normal method of getting business done.' But he proposed that the framing of guillotine resolutions should be settled only after consultation with a panel or consultative committee. As things were, he thought that 'on the whole' the existing procedure unduly handicapped the Government in getting its business through.

MacDonald's evidence was a splendid example of the way in which a politician's views change with his political rôle. Later during the hearing, a Conservative, Captain Crookshank took the opportunity to remind the Committee that in evidence before the Select Committee of 1914 'a private Member named Mr Ramsay MacDonald put the case in better words than I can: "It is the result of my experience in the House of Commons that at the present the procedure limits far too much the opportunities of private Members for getting Bills passed. It also limits their opportunities for really effective criticism of the Government. It does not safeguard either individual Members or groups of Members in their freedom of action as representatives." ' Crookshank went on to remind the Committee that the same Mr Ramsay MacDonald had at that former time held the view that there should be far greater freedom of voting on government measures in Committee, whether upstairs or of the whole House.[2] (But circumstances presumably changed Crookshank's views too. In 1931 he argued—as many parliamentary critics still argue—that the government should not so often insist that non-acceptance of Bills by its own backbenchers means 'disloyalty' or that a defeat was necessarily a matter of confidence. I have found no evidence that Crookshank argued in this way when he was a senior Minister in later years.)

MacDonald paid a warm tribute to what are called 'the usual channels'—by which euphemism he meant the contacts between the two frontbenches by means of the weekly discussions between the Leader of the House and the Government Chief Whip on the one side and the Opposition Leader and Chief Whip on the other. The 'usual channels', thought MacDonald, were 'simply admirable. Whenever a reasonable arrangement can be made it is made.'[3] By this

---

[1] *Evidence taken before the Select Committee on Procedure* (February 1931), p. 5.

[2] Ibid. (May 1931), p. 284.   [3] Ibid. (February 1931), p. 8.

he meant that the two frontbenches apportion time and arrange debates to accommodate each other, which is often bitterly resented by backbenchers on both sides. It is not surprising that MacDonald felt such warm admiration for the 'usual channels' since they led straight to Stanley Baldwin, the Conservative leader with whom MacDonald had had so friendly an understanding for many years, even before they joined in coalition.

Baldwin also gave evidence to the Select Committee. It showed, as might have been expected, a pragmatic acceptance of the existing processes of Parliament and of political realities. Baldwin did not go so far in dismissing the academic proposals for reform as his opposite number had done. MacDonald had informed the Select Committee: 'I have not come across a single, what I call fireside construction, that will bear practical examination; not one.'[1] However, Baldwin was not far behind in stripping the subject of illusions. In particular, he gave short shrift to pretensions that the House of Commons was able to control government finance. The bulk of the expenditure was outside the control of Parliament, Baldwin considered—agreeing that discussion of estimates was always confined to questions of broad policy and that there was no detailed consideration of the money which it was proposed should be spent. But committee after committee had looked for a remedy and had found none. 'The responsibility, of course, rests on the Executive, broadly speaking, and the remedy is to throw your Executive out, if you consider, or if the country considers, that they have squandered the finances of the country', Baldwin said.[2] He could see no way in which Parliament could do the work for which Ministers were responsible. In short, he agreed with Hore-Belisha, a member of the Select Committee, that it was impossible in practice for any parliamentary assembly to control finance in detail, unless this function were delegated to an expert committee.[3] He delicately avoided committing himself to approving the idea of a system of committees to watch the finances of different departments. But he put the matter in perspective by the way in which he answered the question whether he thought there was any remedy which would enable the House to recover control of finance, without having to throw the government out to do it. 'I quite see what you mean, but all the economies you

[1] *Evidence taken before the Select Committee on Procedure* (February 1931), p. 1.
[2] Ibid., p. 27.   [3] Ibid., p. 29.

are talking about, and all the economies that can be obtained, or that you could hope to obtain, by what you call control of Parliament, are a mere bagatelle compared with the power that the House of Commons had itself of spending money', Baldwin stated. It was 'broad policy' that meant 'expenditure' and 'over that the House of Commons has complete control, but, of course, that control is whether or no it accepts certain Bills'. Baldwin, in other words, was putting his finger on the essential point, that the House of Commons, through the election pledges of the majority party, is, in the twentieth century, essentially a spending body. For the rest, Baldwin had little to say except to regret the amount of legislation. As for the questions put to him (and to other witnesses), whether public criticism of Parliament was justified on the grounds of (*a*) being out of date; (*b*) dilatoriness; (*c*) ineffectiveness in controlling the Executive; (*d*) suppression of criticism or initiative on the part of private Members— Baldwin could only observe: 'I have been far too busily concerned in the last ten years in trying to run the machine to have ever attempted the reform of Parliament. Broadly speaking, I have, I am afraid, no suggestions to make.'[1] The style of Baldwin's evidence to the Select Committee is revealing both of his personal and his political character.

Opinions about whether parliamentary processes were unduly handicapping the Government or the private Member seemed mainly to depend on the position of each individual Member who gave evidence. But the evidence did produce some significant views of the essential function of Parliament. The Government Chief Whip, Thomas Kennedy, thought that Parliament should be less of a debating society than a legislative machine.[2] He considered legislation to be its primary function, with control of finance and the oversight of the Executive following in that order. But a former Conservative Chief Whip, Sir Bolton Eyres Monsell, put the legislative function of the House last. It was, he thought, a fallacy to suppose that the country wanted more legislation—and it was this fallacy that gave rise to the belief that it should be made easier for the House to turn out legislation more plentifully. He thought that the House of Commons 'should administer first, and more particularly it should most carefully administer the finances of this country'.[3]

Lord Eustace Percy, a former Minister, took yet another view of

[1] *Evidence taken before the Select Committee on Procedure* (February 1931), p. 22.

[2] Ibid. (March 1931), p. 69.   [3] Ibid. (March 1931), pp. 119–20.

the functions of Parliament.[1] The proper business of the House of Commons, he considered, was 'to focus public attention on the important issues of the day, to grant taxation limited to the immediate needs of the Executive, to appropriate the public revenues to particular services, to press the Executive (in return for the taxes granted) for the redress of popular grievances, and to grant the Executive such additional legal powers as may be necessary for the efficient conduct of public administration'. He defended himself in advance against the criticism that this definition was old-fashioned, by asserting that the House had never succeeded in extending its effective action much beyond the field where it had established itself 200 years ago against the Crown. 'It does not, and cannot, itself govern the country.' Many of its present defects arose from 'the recent "democratic" tendency to convert it into a sovereign parliamentary assembly on the Continental model, governing the country through a Committee of Ministers'. Although Ministers were responsible to Parliament, they were responsible for the discharge of duties which Parliament was 'radically unfitted to discharge for itself'. Percy argued that it was not even the business of the House to 'control' the king's Ministers if that meant controlling the details of their administration or even their expenditure. 'It controls Ministers most effectively by forming a broad general opinion as to their personal reliability and treating them accordingly, but it never has been, and never will be, able to offer them authoritative guidance in the efficient and economic management of their departments.' The greatest failure of the House of Commons, he thought, was its failure to focus public attention on important issues. In Percy's words, the old-fashioned definition of Parliament's functions took on an essentially modern significance. 'Its hopeless inefficiency as a publicity agent is mainly due to the fact that, during a generation when journalistic technique has been steadily tending in the direction of picturesque compression, parliamentary debates have been no less steadily tending in the direction of disjointed discursiveness.' Percy's diagnosis is retrospectively more interesting that the remedies he suggested. Two remedies he proposed were the abolition of all Questions and the utilisation of the hour given to them for short debates, and a proposal for linking Supply with the redress of grievances. (He suggested that when the estimates were debated, the

[1] See also Lord Eustace Percy, *Government in Transition* (Methuen, 1934).

Opposition should be able to move a motion on any subject connected with the Estimate and that, if the motion were passed, the government should be obliged to introduce a Bill along similar lines.)

Lord Winterton, another Conservative ex-Minister, conceded frankly that every Member's view of the function of the House must be coloured by his political views—a left-winger regarding the public interest as best secured by a House of Commons control of the financial and economic activities of the nation; a right-winger wishing to keep Parliament within its historic limits. The most radical criticisms of Parliament were voiced, in fact, by a former Labour Minister who had failed to achieve the executive action he wanted when in government, Sir Oswald Mosley. Mosley argued that the economic situation constituted a crisis which demanded a complete revision of the structure of Parliament. He wanted the Government to be given wide powers of action under a General Powers Bill, thus reconciling 'the requirements of the modern world and of the present crisis with the preservation of popular liberty and the original and proper functions of Parliament'. Mosley informed the Committee: 'The original, and as we conceive it, the proper function of Parliament was to preserve liberty and to prevent the abuse of power by the control of an elected Parliament over the Executive. That essential function we propose to retain.'[1]

Opinions were no less conflicting over the question whether, and by how much, Parliament had declined, and if it had, by comparison with what. Professor Ramsay Muir[2] had no doubt that a decline had taken place which was 'not a matter of popular prejudice, but of demonstrable fact'. He asserted: 'There is no country in North-western Europe in which the control exercised by Parliament over the Government—over legislation, taxation, and administration—is more shadowy or unreal than it is in Britain. Parliament is no longer, in any real sense, the sovereign power in the State. The reality of sovereignty is divided between the bureaucracy on the one hand and on the other the caucus of that political party which has had the luck of the gamble in the most recent parliamentary election. Parliament has sunk to be little more than (*a*) an electoral machine, whereby it is decided which of the party caucuses is to wield dictatorship for the

[1] *Evidence taken before the Select Committee on Procedure* (June 1931), p. 311.

[2] See also Ramsay Muir, *How Britain is Governed*, to which he referred in the Committee.

next period, but this function is normally exhausted at the moment of election; (*b*) a registering machine to give formal validity to the edicts of the ruling dictatorship, sometimes with minor modifications; and (*c*) an advertising medium for the eternal and often barren recriminations of parties.'[1] In these few sentences, Professor Muir epitomised much of the criticisms of Parliament that have been repeated again and again since the 1930s and which have appeared with fresh force and under a thin disguise of originality in recent years. Some increased scope for private Members' legislation, and reference of all Bills to a small committee, were among the remedies proposed by Professor Muir. But the essence of his proposals was the establishment of a series of Standing Committees, one for each big department, or group of departments, which would investigate in detail the work of the departments and present a report annually to the Committee of Supply. For all practical purposes, Professor Muir was arguing in 1930 and 1931 along lines which have become very familiar in more recent years. He referred to the American committee system but agreed that it could not be transplanted here, and that a distinction must be drawn between the broad lines of policy, for which only the Cabinet could be responsible, and 'the multifarious detail of expenditure and administration which the Cabinet cannot possibly control, and which is therefore left to the unchecked control of bureaucracy'.[2] Only the establishment of such a series of committees would give Parliament the power of exercising real control over finance and the detail of bureaucratic administration. The House of Commons should preserve its general sessions for discussions of principle (for example, on the second reading, and third reading of Bills), and for general surveys of the financial situation and national policy.

But Professor Muir believed that procedural reform was not enough to arrest the decline of Parliament. He also advocated electoral reform and proposed that 'Cabinet dictatorship' should be dealt with by taking from the Prime Minister the present 'unsound constitutional doctrine' of dissolution. Parliament should only be dissolved before the end of its legal term when either a major new issue had arisen upon which the country should be consulted, or when the government could not carry on without a dissolution.

[1] *Evidence taken before the Select Committee on Procedure* (May 1931), p. 256.
[2] Ibid., p. 259.

Failing legislation to establish fixed-term Parliaments, the House should, Professor Muir suggested, adopt a Humble Address to the Crown indicating its view that a ministry should accept the judgment of the House on all but major issues and ought not to resign on anything short of a formal vote of no confidence or a defeat on an issue of major principle. A resignation ought not to carry with it a claim to a dissolution unless it could be proved that government could not be carried on without a dissolution.

Professor Muir (who, as one of his interrogators on the Committee acidly pointed out, had himself only had one year's experience as an MP) was not the only witness to advocate an extended and altered committee system. A rather different version of the idea was suggested by the former Labour Minister, F. W. Jowett, who wanted to translate to Westminster something like the committee system which existed in local government and which gave Labour Members a sense of participation in positive government which they felt lacking in Parliament. Jowett wanted the House to abandon altogether the practice of going into Committee of the Whole House and to pass all its work to Standing Committees. These should be specialised and permanent—each one both scrutinising the administration and examining the legislation of the government department it was shadowing. The Minister of that department, thought Jowett, should be its chairman. Jowett, who had also advocated the break-up of Cabinet government, was to be accused by Herbert Morrison of seeking a major change in the fundamentals of British Government by overthrowing ministerial and collective Cabinet responsibility, though it is not clear that this would result if in the recommended Committees the parties were divided in the same proportions as in the House as a whole.[1] What would presumably result would be a degree of atomisation which would absorb Members in their own specialised field, in which they had quasi-administrative as well as critical functions, to the detriment of parliamentary functioning as a whole. Central direction both of Executive action and parliamentary criticism of that action might be weakened—as it is in local government where the Cabinet system is lacking.

Winston Churchill's blueprint for parliamentary reform was

[1] See Herbert Morrison, *Government and Parliament: A Survey from the Inside* (Geoffrey Cumberledge, Oxford University Press, 1954), p. 156, for criticisms of Jowett's and other views on committees.

substantially an elaboration of the outline he had given in his Romanes Lecture in the previous year. He suggested the establishment by statute of an Economic Sub-Parliament, which should consist of 120 Members, of whom forty would be Members of the House of Commons experienced in economic matters, and eighty businessmen, trade union representatives or 'economic authorities'. The total membership of 120 should be chosen in proportion to the strength of the parties in the House of Commons by the leaders of the parties: the Economic Sub-Parliament should have a term of three years without regard to the date of general elections, and all Bills dealing with trade and industry which had been given a Second Reading should be referred to the Sub-Parliament unless the House where the Bill originated determined otherwise. The Sub-Parliament itself might initiate inquiries or discussions on any economic, commercial or financial subject and report to both Houses of Parliament. As for its recommendations on Bills referred to it, it would be a matter for the Houses of Parliament to decide whether they were or were not accepted: thus the supremacy of Parliament would be preserved. Churchill was closely examined on the implications of his proposals, which contained more than one inconsistency—not the least of which was the idea that such a Sub-Parliament could be both nonpartisan and chosen by the party leaders. And could it in any real sense be a Parliament? 'It is rather euphemistic, is not it, to call this an Economic Sub-Parliament? It has not so much power as a Parliament, has it?' Sir Hugh O'Neill asked Churchill. 'Well, I was trying to make the most of it and build it up,' Churchill replied. 'It might develop more powers later on. As long as we had the assemblage I should not quarrel about the name.'[1] Another member of the Select Committee commented: 'Your proposal is really an enlargement on a more statutory basis of the existing Economic Advisory Council?'[2] Looking back from the 1960s, one is inclined to comment that Churchill had come near to proposing a prototype for the National Economic Development Council ('Neddy') which was set up by a Conservative Chancellor, Selwyn Lloyd, in 1961, though without including backbench MPs.

[1] *Evidence taken before the Select Committee on Procedure* (June 1931), p. 357.
[2] Ibid., p. 361. The Economic Advisory Council consisted of four businessmen, three economists and two trade union leaders. It had been established by MacDonald in 1930.

Churchill's advice to the Committee, however, extended beyond an explanation of his own pet idea for parliamentary reform. He gave the Committee his view of the primary function of the House of Commons which was, he thought, 'to be the grand forum of debate'. Churchill added: 'I never knew there was any difficulty in passing Bills.'[1] He favoured lightening the routine work of the House of Commons and giving the House more power to debate general topics when it wished. 'I should like to restore some of the old flexibility which has disappeared in the twentieth century and at the end of the nineteenth century,' he said. He dismissed the advocates of more stringent control over financial details summarily, 'I consider the debates on Supplementary Estimates are the most worthless of any that I have known in my career. They deal with comparatively small sums of money, that is to say small compared to the annual Budget, and yet very often five or six days are consumed in those debates.'[2] By economising on time, Parliament could cut the length of its session. 'If you wish to say what is wrong with Parliament (and that I suppose is within the scope of your enquiry) it is that it sits far too long in the year.'[3] He advocated that, except in times of war or great national emergency, Parliament should not sit for more than five months.

Churchill told the Committee that he thought the decline of the power of the House of Commons to command national interest had been in progress all the time he had been a Member and had been accelerated after the First World War. There had certainly been a 'complete falling off in the reporting of the Debates in the public press; that has almost come to an end as far as the generality of newspapers are concerned'.[4] The reason was that the electorate took far less interest in politics, because politics were less interesting, and Churchill wanted to resuscitate 'the fierce and tense threshing out of great public questions which is not going on now to any great extent'.[5] At the end of Churchill's first attendance at the Select Committee, the chairman, Ernest Brown, let him depart with the compliment, 'May I say that if Parliament has declined in the public interest it is no fault of yours, sir.'[6]

Most of the witnesses were prepared to agree that the performance

[1] *Evidence taken before the Select Committee on Procedure* (March 1931), p. 140.
[2] Ibid., p. 141.   [3] Ibid., p. 141.   [4] Ibid., p. 144.
[5] Ibid., p. 144.   [6] Ibid., p. 153.

of the House of Commons had declined in some sense—or at least that the public were taking less interest in it. Where they differed was in their views of why this should be so. One of the most thoughtful explanations was provided by Sir Austen Chamberlain. He felt that parliamentary debates in 1931 excited less attention in the country than they did when he first became a Member towards the end of the Parliament of 1886–92 simply because parliamentary debates created far less interest among Members themselves. He was painfully and increasingly impressed by the absence of interest shown by Members in the ordinary run of debates. But he dismissed any idea that this was due to obstruction. There was much less obstruction than in the days of the Irish Members. Nor did the fault lie with longer speeches. Some of the most interesting speeches were long ones. One reason for the lessened interest in debate was the character of the questions which the House now had to discuss. 'When I first came into the House we were still largely discussing great political issues of a very broad and simple kind, such as Home Rule, which dominated all other issues at the moment.' The broad issues were 'simply and easily put, and the questions were far less technical and far less complicated than the kind of economic questions which are now occupying a larger and larger share of our attention'.[1] Chamberlain considered that there was not the same dramatic clash of personalities in the House of Commons of the 1930s as there had been in the days of Gladstone and Balfour. Not only were the discussions in the earlier period 'profoundly interesting' but 'there was a kind of dramatic conflict of temperament with temperament, of mind with mind, which had been illustrated for many years before I came into the House by that clash of temperament between Gladstone and Disraeli'.[2] He thought the manners of the House had declined and the number of deliberately destructive interruptions had increased. The press was uninterested unless it could give a coloured account of 'some stunt issue'. Members were under much greater strain as a result of longer sessions and more business. Committee work was encroaching badly on the House. It was not simply a matter of Committees of the House but of Party Committees. Chamberlain stated that whenever he asked why there were so few people on his Party's benches, he was told because some Party Committee or other was meeting. Members were being called upon to do more than was possible in a working day.[3]

[1] *Evidence taken before the Select Committee on Procedure* (April 1931), p. 222.　　　　[2] Ibid., p. 223.　　　　[3] Ibid., p. 224.

Chamberlain also voiced another idea which has since gained widespread agreement. 'When it comes to the Party Committee, that which in olden days would have been decided on the floor of the House, and perhaps affected by the trend of the discussion in the House, is now sometimes decided upstairs in a Party meeting or a committee meeting of the Party, which really takes all the life out of the debate, and you merely come down to the House of Commons to register a decision which has been taken upstairs, which is a work of supererogation almost.'[1] He agreed with the words of the chairman, Mr Ernest Brown, that it amounted to 'what soldiers call going through the motions'.[2] As for the reference of Bills to committees— Chamberlain was convinced that if Grand Committees were increased too much, the work of the House itself, which was already suffering as a forum for debate, would be destroyed.[3]

The opinion that the general level of debate had declined, was not, however, universal. Lord Winterton, who, in 1931, had been a Member of the House for twenty-seven years, told the Committee there were fewer 'scenes' and less eloquence, debating power and wit —both changes being due to the departure of the Irish Members. There were probably fewer Members who could fill the House than there had been in 1904, but the general level of discussion was higher. Winterton believed that the decline in the prestige and efficiency of the House (both of which he conceded) was part of a general loss of belief in the efficacy of democratically elected bodies which had become apparent in every country. There was a natural feeling in a period of economic and other difficulties that a man (that is, a dictator) was better able to act than a committee (that is, Parliament).[4] Winterton, like Chamberlain, believed that the multiplication of committees, both official and unofficial, had had a bad effect on the Chamber by reducing the attendance of Members. 'The House of Commons is a deliberative assembly and if, so to speak, it is not interested in its own proceedings, it can hardly expect to interest the press and the public in them.' Winterton did not believe that the decline of the prestige of Parliament had anything to do with the growth of party discipline. 'I should doubt, for example, whether in the course of the twenty-five years of Parliament with which I am

[1] *Evidence taken before the Select Committee on Procedure* (April 1931), p. 224.
[2] Ibid., p. 224.   [3] Ibid., p. 235.
[4] Ibid. (June 1931), pp. 328–9.

142

familiar, party discipline has grown. I think it was as tight, so to speak, or as tightly bound, twenty-five years ago as it is today.'[1]

This account of the views of the men of 1931-2 may fittingly conclude with those of Lloyd George—himself one of the surviving 'giants' of a former political age, a man who was widely distrusted politically, and who had been squeezed out of any hope of power by the parliamentary and party 'system'. He was, moreover, essentially a politician of action—one who had devoted his efforts, and his money, to an investigation of the economic disease of the period, and who had, he believed, produced remedies to which no one would listen. He had no doubt at all of the 'very great and growing disappointment with Parliament' which was felt to be 'not coping with its task and not altogether discharging the trust which the nation has reposed in it'.[2] There was a feeling that the House had not devoted itself, as it should, to the problems of the condition of trade, industry and employment and of taxation and expenditure. The only real attempt to secure economy had been the result of pressure from outside on the Government, which had produced the Geddes Committee. There was no real examination by the Commons of the Estimates. Control of the Executive by the Commons was confined to 'rather perfunctory discussions, which do not excite any real interest, apart from an element of censure, which is conducive to excitement, but does not achieve the real purpose of establishing control over the Executive'.[3] Lloyd George put the attendance of the House, except for censure debates, at between 5 and 10 per cent of Members. This gave the impression that the House of Commons was only concerned with the political game and not with the real business of the nation. The heart of the matter was that the House of Commons had no real effective and continuous control over the actions of the Executive. Lloyd George was convinced that such control could only be achieved by referring more work to committees for examination. Control of a department, he considered, must still rest with the Minister, but the use of committees, which could summon both Ministers and civil servants, would enable the House of Commons to supervise and keep itself informed. The reports of such committees should be presented to Parliament.[4]

[1] *Evidence taken before the Select Committee on Procedure* (June 1931), p. 332.   [2] Ibid. (February 1931), pp. 41-2.
[3] Ibid. (February 1931), pp. 41-3.
[4] Ibid. (February 1931), p. 44.

Detailed consideration of the improvements in procedure recommended by the Select Committee of 1931–2, as a result of the evidence it had taken, are outside the scope of this study. It is enough to note that its most important recommendation was that the Estimates Committee should be enlarged; that it should have a close working arrangement with the Public Accounts Committee; that it should be enabled to consider policy, as well as matters of detail; and that the Estimates Committee ought to be provided with an official adviser analogous to the Comptroller and Auditor-General, who advises the Public Accounts Committee. It did not accept proposals for a number of Standing Committees to deal with the work of particular departments or group of departments.[1] Nevertheless, although the Select Committee regarded itself as unequipped, by its limited terms of reference, to make proposals for constitutional changes, the wide-ranging evidence that it took is invaluable as a means of gauging the fundamental nature of the problem of Parliament in the twentieth century. This evidence enables us to compare the problem of Parliament in the 1960s with that of the 1930s and, again, to compare both with the Victorian Parliaments which some of the witnesses of 1931 remembered.

Despite the conflicting evidence, certain common strands do appear, and the view of the fundamental nature of the problem which was held by Lloyd George, and others, who wanted the Commons to do more detailed committee work, were not wholly incompatible with the views of those who opposed this on the grounds that it would diminish the ability of the House to function as a great deliberative assembly discussing the most vital contemporary issues. For it appeared from the evidence of men of both schools of thought, that the fundamental problem of the House of Commons

[1] Eustace Percy castigated the Report of the Select Committee for its 'hopeless lack of originality'. 'That Report, in effect, recommends that Parliament should set its house in order by transferring the antimacassar from the sofa to the arm-chair', *Government in Transition*, p. 99. However, the main recommendations of the Select Committee, conservative though they might seem, were rejected by the National Government. Announcing the Government's decisions on the most important recommendations of the Report (paragraph 10), Neville Chamberlain told the House on May 2, 1933, that they would represent a 'major departure from present constitutional practice'. He saw no advantage in enlarging the Estimates Committee which 'could not deal with major matters of policy without encroaching on the powers of the Executive'. H.C. Deb., Vol. 277, cols. 669–70.

was over-loading. An assembly which had sufficed in the nineteenth century to debate great, and for the most part easily comprehensible, issues was now torn between this function and the need to exercise some sort of 'watch-dog' rôle over the administrative, spending and bureaucratic activities of an Executive whose field of action was widening every day. To some it seemed that the use of committees would enable the House both to perform this second task more efficiently and, at the same time, free the floor of the House for great debates. To others, it appeared that the counter-attractions of committee work, or the exhaustion of working in committee, would further diminish the attendance of Members in the Chamber. It also appeared that because the electorate had failed to place in power a Government able to solve the economic difficulties of the nation, the Commons were increasingly prone to blame themselves for failing to cure the crisis. Thus they judged themselves by a criterion which would have had no validity to their Victorian forebears, and found themselves wanting. The failure of the House of Commons to solve a *technical* problem was one reason why the House of Commons had fallen in the estimation of the public, or at any rate, the vocal public. It also explained why the public was less gripped, or entertained, by the performances of the House of Commons than it had been in the Victorian period. For the technological problems of government, which are the salient feature of twentieth-century society, cannot be comprehended to the same extent as the great issues of 'political principle' which divided the parties in the nineteenth century could be. And the more that ordinary MPs (whose counterparts in a previous generation would have been silent) sought to address themselves in their pedestrian way to these problems, the more boring the proceedings of the House appeared to be. In other words, the more the backbencher heeded the demands of his constituents and responded to the detailed problems of politics, the less attention he was liable to get. Similarly this sort of subject did not enable Ministers to scintillate in debate or to command the same reverence among their supporters, or distaste in the opposite benches. Gladstone and Disraeli, Asquith and Lloyd George, were perhaps giants among their fellows. But the evidence of 1931 seemed to suggest, on balance, that the backbenchers of the earlier period were more like pygmies by comparison with their leaders than the backbenchers of the twentieth century have been. They may have enjoyed more command over the time of the House but they were more silent, less active and—when it came to big issues—not much freer of party discipline. And if the quality of frontbench speaking had deteriorated in style, we can hardly regard the shortening of speeches as a loss in twentieth-century conditions. At any time in the twentieth century a three-hour speech of the sort that Gladstone could make in the House would have been entirely unacceptable both to Members and to the public. In the twentieth century Parliament has not done things so well because it has had so many more things to do. That was essentially the problem to which the men of the 1930s were addressing themselves and it remains the problem today.

Chapter Five

Low and High Tide in Parliamentary Government 1931–1945

In the years between the formation of the National Government and the end of the Second World War, parliamentary government first fell to its most inept level and then revived to attain what was in many respects the apogee of the House of Commons in this century. The extraordinary transformation in the effectiveness of Parliament which began just before the outbreak of war suggests that it was not the institution but the politicians and parties operating within it who were primarily to blame for the shortcomings of the 1930s and who equally deserve credit for making parliamentary government a reality in the emergency of war. It may be that the shortcomings of the politicians in the thirties reflected the nation's failure of will: that the political revival of the forties was a reflection of a revival in the nation. Yet a different quality of leadership in the years immediately after 1931 would probably have evoked some response in the country and certainly a poorer leadership after 1940 might well have vitiated the national will for victory. But however one assesses the relationship between the nation and the politicians: whether or not a people generally gets the government it deserves, the point to be made for the purposes of this study is that these years demonstrated the heights which Parliament can reach if the political climate is healthy and the depths of inadequacy to which it is condemned if the politicians and public opinion behind them are inadequate. This period also shows that, even at the most depressing moments of its history, Parliament is fertile ground for unorthodox voices and retains a reserve capacity to take charge of events itself in an emergency when a majority of its Members finally come to believe that the Government is no longer capable of doing so.

During the thirties the widespread disenchantment with Parliament which had taken root with the failure of party politics to solve the economic crisis continued even when the worst of the crisis was over. The formation of the National Government itself had been, in part, a symptom of the contemporary urge to relegate party politics to the background. It also reflected the power of a myth which has had some influence over British voting habits in this century: this is that Conservative politics are, in an emergency, less partisan than other politics. In the 1931 crisis, the British people, including Ramsay MacDonald and his friends, assumed that the flag to which it was proper to rally was the flag to which the Conservative Party was willing to rally. In 1931 it was also believed that a non-partisan national attitude could be built upon the willingness of individual political leaders to co-operate, regardless of differences of policy and objectives between the different parties they represented. It was this conviction which led to the appeal for a 'doctor's mandate' at the General Election of that year—or, in another metaphor, for a blank cheque. It is arguable that the blurring of the political argument by the coalition in its attempt at consensus government during the following years, together with the temporary destruction of the Labour Party as an effective vehicle for opposition, contributed largely to the political failures of the immediate pre-war years.

In deference to the urge to rise above party politics (or to sweep under the carpet all political differences except those which divided the National Government from the rump of the Labour Party) the most important immediate issue which confronted the Government had been glossed over for the duration of the election campaign. This was the question of whether a policy of economic protection should be adopted at the behest of the Conservative majority or rejected as both Liberals and Labour would wish. The impression was therefore given that a decision would only be taken after a searching inquiry. But the overwhelming majority of the Conservatives made protection inevitable and early in 1932 a Cabinet Committee accepted it. In one sense, this was the plainest example of straight pressure by the majority party—but the solution adopted to prevent the break-up of the National Government on this issue also showed how far politicians were prepared to depart from traditional attitudes of Ministers' relationship with their followers in the Commons in order to rise above party politics. To enable the free-traders to stay in office, they were made free by their colleagues in the Government to oppose tariff proposals in the House, which they did when Neville

Chamberlain introduced his Import Duties Bill. So much for collective Cabinet responsibility on that occasion—and for the normal assumption that Ministers should only participate in a Cabinet pursuing the broad policies of their party in the Commons. Not until 1932 did the Liberals led by Sir Herbert (later Lord) Samuel resign from the Government, and even thereafter they supported the National Government on most issues until the question of disarmament drove them into full opposition at the end of 1933.

In the early thirties, the economic situation gradually began to improve, perhaps despite the Government's measures (which included cuts in expenditure) rather than because of them. World trade began to recover, the terms of trade moved in favour of Britain and home production went up. From a peak of nearly three million at the beginning of 1933, the number of unemployed fell by half a million in a year and to below two million in 1936. Until war broke out in 1939 the unemployment figure fluctuated around one and a half million but it could not be reduced further. Although wages and prices were up and although a new prosperity came to stay for the middle classes, the hard core of unemployed, especially in the depressed areas, became steadily more bitter. In one sense, the prolonged economic crisis of the previous decade was over and it might have been thought that discontent with Parliament, which had largely arisen from the earlier failure to deal with this problem, would have died out. But there were now other reasons for it.

First, the embittered Labour Party now became steadily more Socialistic. It still wanted to achieve Socialism by constitutional means. But to many in the Labour Party, the events of 1931 seemed proof that, while capitalism was prepared to pay higher wages and introduce better social services so long as its own position was secure, once it appeared that capitalism itself was threatened by a slump, priority would be given to preserving the system at whatever social cost. The formation of the National Government was itself taken as a clear demonstration of the power of capitalism to overthrow an elected Government and many in the Labour Party began to prepare to take avoiding action against any similar menace when they came to power.

The Labour Party, as A. J. P. Taylor[1] has pointed out, derived some benefits from the defeat which reduced it to the smallest Opposition since the days of Charles James Fox and the war against

[1] A. J. P. Taylor, *English History, 1914–1945*, p. 327.

revolutionary France. Many of the senior union officials had lost their seats at the general election and from now on it became the exception, rather than the rule, for important union leaders to sit on the Labour benches in Parliament. (The importation of the General Secretary of the Transport and General Workers Union, Frank Cousins, into the 1964 Parliament was an exceptional and short-lived step and Mr Cousins was a reluctant parliamentarian.) After 1931, union leaders preferred to pursue their own policies with employers, without reference to the Labour Party. From this loosening of its trade union ties, the party in Parliament benefited. Freed to some extent from direct trade-union pressures in the day-to-day management of its politics, the Parliamentary Labour Party became more like a normal political party—although the Party Conference periodically tried (as it did over defence policy in 1960) to dominate the party in Parliament. The growing care for its independence exercised by the party in Parliament was a step in rebuilding the Labour Party as one which would eventually again be regarded as capable of providing a credible alternative government. To this extent, some advantages accrued to Labour from the 1931 defeat to offset the tendency of this shattered and bitter party to become more extremist.

Nevertheless, when all allowance is made for such accidental benefits from the 1931 defeat, it is also true that, throughout the thirties, Labour politicians remained disenchanted with the way in which Parliament was operating. Outside the Parliamentary Labour Party, the number of middle-class intellectuals who became extreme left-wing Socialists, and who were impatient with parliamentary processes, increased in response to a sense of guilt arising from the unsolved unemployment problem at home and from right-wing aggression against working-class movements abroad. Labour politicians in Parliament generally remained loyal adherents to normal parliamentary traditions. Nevertheless, in 1933, in a symposium entitled *Problems of a Socialist Government*, to which the future Labour leader Clement Attlee was a contributor, Stafford Cripps devoted a chapter to the question 'Can Socialism Come by Constitutional Methods?' He considered that it could and should, but he made no bones about the need to adapt Parliament to enable a Socialist Government to do its work. It was, he thought, unlikely that a Socialist Party could 'maintain its position of control without adopting some exceptional means, such as the prolongation of the life of Parliament for a further term without an election'.[1] An Emergency Powers Bill would be needed on the first day of a Socialist Parliament to allow 'all that will be immediately necessary to be done by ministerial orders. These orders must be incapable of challenge in the Courts or in any way except in the House of Commons.'[2] Cripps, like other Socialist writers, was also concerned to ensure that the large legislative programme which a Labour Government would introduce should not be congested by existing parliamentary processes. These processes would therefore have to be adapted.

The Cripps plan had an aspect uncomfortably near totalitarianism. Yet even the Labour Leader, George Lansbury, promised that Labour (following the examples set by Baldwin, as he put it) would take care that 'the House of Commons when necessary shall function as a House of Action, and not as a decaying institution'.[3] (A small Cabinet, a Committee system, and a House sitting less frequently and at an earlier hour of the day were among the Labour stock-in-trade for parliamentary reform.) On the other hand, Lansbury, instinctively a lover of freedom, tried to have it both ways. 'In my Socialist State, however, power will at all times remain with Parliament.'[4] By abandoning the 'absurd doctrine' that a Government must resign when defeated in the House, Members would be free of the 'dishonest' practice of having to vote against their convictions. This would ensure the free and unfettered control of Parliament and 'the present quite intolerable power of the Cabinet over the House of Commons would cease'. Lansbury stated categorically that 'no Member of Parliament has been a Member for a day before he realises that it is the Cabinet which controls Parliament and not Parliament the Cabinet'.[5]

However, a powerless decade lay before Labour after its defeat in 1931. In these years of hunger marches and Left Book Club politics, Labour had a smaller influence on the conduct of the nation's affairs than most Oppositions have. This was partly the result of the 'national' label tied to the Government; partly the effect of Labour's small numbers in the House of Commons and its discredited performance as a government in 1930. Although it appealed increasingly

[1] Stafford Cripps, 'Can Socialism Come by Constitutional Methods?', *Problems of a Socialist Government* (Socialist League, Forum Lectures, 1933), p. 39.　　　　[2] Ibid., p. 43.
[3] George Lansbury, *My England* (Selwyn & Blount, 1934), p. 135.
[4] Ibid., p. 132.　　　　[5] Ibid., p. 126.

to intellectuals, Labour was also handicapped by its own divisions, not least between the pacifists and the advocates of collective security in foreign affairs. Besides, as the nation rebuilt a new, if unevenly spread, prosperity, which was attributed to the National Government, Labour seemed unlikely to storm the MacDonald–Baldwin–Chamberlain fortress of broadening middle-class prosperity which existed alongside working-class unemployment. It was the Government's handling of foreign, rather than domestic policy that was, in the end, to prove vulnerable.

Prosperity and political tranquillity did not, however, diminish the flow of recipes for the reform of Parliament.[1] In 1934, for instance, after the economic recovery was well on its way, two books were written which proposed reforms from very different standpoints. One, *Parliamentary Reform*, by Ivor Jennings, regarded the appeal to public opinion as the fundamental aspect of parliamentary action[2] and he wanted the procedure of Parliament adapted to make that appeal more effective. He argued that Parliament had insufficient time for passing the Bills which a Government would wish it to pass (though he admitted that this was not provable); that Parliament was not equipped to discuss modern technical legislation; that insufficient scope was given for non-governmental legislation; and that the system provided no opportunity for the government to keep in touch with changing ideas. Like so many other parliamentary reformers before and after him, Jennings regarded an extension of the House of Commons committee system as the key to reform.

Jennings was a supporter of the Labour Party as well as being a constitutional lawyer. Another relevant book, however, was the work of a former Conservative Minister, Lord Eustace Percy, who believed that a state of national political apoplexy was near because the legislature had become physically incapable of legislating and the Executive was impeded in administration. He was, for instance, appalled by the way in which discussions on unemployment policy, both inside and outside the House of Commons, were restricted within 'the exasperating limits of a comparison between the merits of public works and all-round economy'.[3] He regarded the 'legal

---

[1] An admirably comprehensive summary of suggestions for making Parliament more effective in one way or another, is available in *Parliamentary Reform, 1933–1960* (Cassell, 1961), published for the Hansard Society.
[2] Like Professor Crick in the 1960s.
[3] Lord Eustace Percy, *Government in Transition*, p. 10.

fiction' that the people should govern as an idea now completely dead. The motive power of government must be, not popular desires, but administration initiative which would arise from the conviction of the 'governor' that he had a mission and an authority to govern. On the other hand, Percy wanted to get away from the sterile argument between Socialism and Capitalism. He asserted that since the General Election of 1931, the British political parties had shown a real tendency to abandon previous compromises of 'reformism' and to take their stand once more on the logical implications of their party principles, but whereas earlier feeble compromises had merely produced a form of political incoherence, the return to more clear-cut issues was equally incapable of clarifying politics because 'it is precisely these fundamental articles of Party creeds which have become irrelevant to the real issues of today'.[1] Percy's impatience with party politics was very similar in mood to the tendency in more recent years to despise the party battle in Parliament as unconstructive and to prefer the constructive decisions of experts placed in administrative or quasi-governmental positions. However, Percy also insisted that both nineteenth-century Capitalism and pure Socialism were out of the question and that the future lay with what we might call a mixed economy and the wider distribution of private property. But he considered that big political changes only came about through the work of the propagandists outside politics, and the trouble in the 1930s, he argued, was that the machinery of Parliament was generally considered so inefficient that the propagandists no longer felt it was worth while trying to convert the politician to his views by means of his constituents. So the 'gospel' had to be toned down to fit parliamentary habits. Percy's remedies were substantially those he proposed to the Select Committee on Procedure. His object was to free the House to focus more clearly upon the great issues of the day, to give the Commons more opportunity to ventilate the grievances of the subject, to avoid congestion by sending some Bills to Committees, and by the strict planning of parliamentary time. He advocated also the establishment of parliamentary committees charged with watching the operation of particular classes of legislation, rather than the *ad hoc* bombardment of Ministers with questions about individual grievances.

Pressure for the reform of Parliament, however, did not only appear in books. In 1934, for instance, a young Conservative,

[1] Lord Eustace Percy, *Government in Transition*, p. 91.

Duncan Sandys (who was later to be a Cabinet Minister under Macmillan and Douglas-Home) founded the 'British Movement' to combat 'Socialism, defeatism, and apathy'.[1] The aims of the British Movement were to strengthen the Empire and the Constitution. It asserted that Parliament was losing touch with the people and was in danger of being replaced by a dictatorship. The Constitution must be strengthened and brought up to date—but on British lines. Thus right-wingers were beginning to react in their own way to the assaults on Parliament which had been coming from the left and also to the consensus politics of the National Government. Cripps and his friends were virtually, it seemed, advocating the abolition both of Parliament and the Cabinet. Parliament seemed to be a sitting duck for an assault of this kind if a Labour Government should come to power.

But, of course, there was an even greater menace directed at Parliament from the extreme right. The mid-thirties saw the advance of the British Fascist Movement, the clashes between the extremists of the right and of the left and even an elaborate flirtation by elements in the Conservative Party with the Fascists as though to counterbalance the flirtation of some in the Labour Party with European Communism. (One London evening newspaper offered prizes to its readers for the best letters on the theme: 'Why I like Oswald Mosley.') In European countries, democracy was growing out of fashion and dictatorship was in the ascendant. It was not surprising that in Britain Parliament seemed, to some, to be inadequate, to others even to be in danger. Yet as the problems of international policy grew ever more pressing after 1934, discussion of the mechanics of government institutions naturally fell into the background.

(ii)

As the Government timorously retreated step by step before the advance of the dictators, Parliament lay impotent through the fear of war which paralysed the majority of all parties. The Labour Party, which included a vocal minority of pacifists, officially preached adherence to collective security but would not face the logic of rearmament. The National Government, slow to rearm and sceptical at heart about the League of Nations, was anxious to give no provocation that might unleash the terrors of war. Uneasily, the

[1] *Morning Post*, April 12, 1934.

Government (in which Baldwin succeeded MacDonald as Prime Minister in 1935) tried to reconcile the demand for rearmament, which was coming from a section of the Conservative Party, with what it took to be the pacifist spirit of the nation as demonstrated by the defeat of the Conservative candidate at the East Fulham by-election in 1933 and the nation-wide Peace Ballot in 1935. The Conservative rearmers were themselves divided into several groups: one, headed by L. S. Amery, favoured strong defence and no involvement with the League, another, in which Winston Churchill may generally be included, supported collective security as well as rearmament. But the influence of Churchill was at a low ebb as a result of his resistance to the India Bill which had dominated British politics until 1935.

Yet though the bulk of parliamentary opinion, probably following majority opinion in the nation, was pusillanimous, it would be wrong to suppose that parliamentary opinion exerted no influence over the Government. The reshuffle of the Government in 1935 when Baldwin took over as Prime Minister from MacDonald undoubtedly owed much to pressures from the Conservative backbenches. Henceforth it was to be an unmistakably Conservative Government. One of the chief changes was the replacement as Foreign Secretary of Sir John Simon by Sir Samuel Hoare. At a meeting of the back-bench Conservative Foreign Affairs Committee in June 1935 a strong attack on Simon had been made directly by two influential Conservative backbenchers and, by inference, by the veteran Sir Austen Chamberlain also. As it happened, this appointment led to one of the most notable examples of instant parliamentary influence over a government in this century.

In November 1935, a General Election returned the National Government to power, with 432 supporters in the House, though Labour increased its membership to 154. The first problem that fell to the new Foreign Secretary, Hoare, was the Italian invasion of Abyssinia, which had begun that autumn and which had been followed by ineffective League of Nations sanctions against Italy. Hoare quickly became convinced that sanctions would not stop the conflict. After promising 'steady and collective resistance to all acts of aggression', he joined with Pierre Laval in the production of a peace plan to end the war in Abyssinia. It involved the surrender of almost two-thirds of Abyssinian territory to Italy. The leakage of the proposed Hoare–Laval pact into the newspapers created political uproar in Britain. The Foreign Secretary himself was now on holiday in Switzerland and the Government carried out a holding operation in the House of Commons. At one point, Baldwin, declaring that his lips were not as yet unsealed, suggested that if the truth of the matter were known nobody would go into the Lobby against the Government. But a wholesale revolt of the Government's own supporters quickly gathered force and the press was no less critical. Conservative backbenchers of all views condemned the sudden reversal of Hoare's policy. On Wednesday, December 18, the Foreign Secretary resigned and there can be no doubt that it was primarily opinion in the House of Commons, and especially inside the Conservative Party, which forced Baldwin to abandon him. The Government might have surmounted the press campaign and could certainly have ridden over the inevitable attacks of the Labour opposition, had the Conservative Party been united. But it was not, and the crucial event in the fall of Hoare was a meeting of the backbench Conservative Foreign Affairs Committee on December 17. Recalling this meeting, Harold Macmillan has written that 'the final blow was struck, as is so often the case, by the most respected Conservative backbench Member— Austen Chamberlain, himself, a former Foreign Secretary'. Chamberlain expressed the general view when he said that 'gentlemen do not behave in such a way'. In Macmillan's words:

> That settled it. Hoare was forced to resign, and a few days later Eden was appointed in his place. . . . [Chamberlain] settled the fate of Hoare, and by his intervention convinced the Chief Whip that the game was up. Up to the day before the debate it was expected that Hoare would defend himself from the box as Foreign Secretary. Late on the night of Wednesday the 18th, his resignation was formally announced. Rightly or wrongly, the democratic processes in Parliament and outside had asserted themselves. . . .

Macmillan himself has little doubt that had the Government persisted in standing by Hoare

> . . . they would have been faced with a degree of opposition in their own ranks which would have threatened their survival. . . . With so large a majority, many risks can be taken. If the danger of abstention or a hostile vote had been confined to a few cranks like myself and some of my friends, [the Conservative Chief Whip] would have accepted it. But when anxiety and even anger spreads

to the central body of the party, then there is nothing for it but to give in. The names on the various amendments, all demanding in one form or another the abandonment of the Hoare–Laval agreement, were conclusive in the Chief Whip's mind. Right, Centre and Left of the Party were equally disturbed.[1]

Though the Government had survived, this episode did the Conservative Party, and Baldwin in particular, considerable harm with the public. It also virtually marked the end of confidence in sanctions and the League of Nations. By June 1936, the Chancellor of the Exchequer, Neville Chamberlain (without consulting Eden because he knew Eden would not agree), could speak of sanctions as 'the very mid-summer of madness'. From now on the Government suffered bitter attacks in the House of Commons from its critics, and none more overwhelming than the onslaught of Lloyd George after the defeat of Abyssinia. (A few days later Macmillan voted against the Government on a vote of censure and resigned the Whip.) Yet despite the outspoken speeches of its critics in the House of Commons, the Government Whips never failed to maintain a big majority during these difficult years. It was, perhaps, helped by the appearance of disarray and inadequacy presented by the Labour Opposition. Who was going to destroy the National Government to put Labour in its place when the Government was at least trying to offer the attraction of consensus politics? Besides, at the end of 1936, the nation and the Government became absorbed in the Abdication crisis. From his handling of this Baldwin drew great credit and immediately after the coronation of George VI, he resigned and handed over the Prime Ministership to Chamberlain.

Throughout the years of Chamberlain's appeasement policy the critics of the Government remained vocal and in due course attempts were made to build bridges between backbenchers on both sides of the House who wanted a firmer policy against the dictators. Despite this, however, and despite Eden's resignation as Foreign Secretary in 1937, the Government was never seriously shaken. Chamberlain's return from the surrender of the Czechs to Hitler at Munich, with his promise of 'peace for our time', evoked a wave of relief throughout the country that war with Germany which had seemed imminent had been averted. When the inadequacy of the politicians in these years is

[1] Harold Macmillan, *Winds of Change, 1914–1939* (Macmillan, 1966), pp. 446 et seq.

recalled, it is only fair to remember also the considerable extent to which the majority of Parliament still reflected a public opinion anxious to avoid war by any means that could be presented as reasonable. The minority of parliamentary opinion which opposed appeasement was in advance of public sentiment.

Nevertheless, what the critics regarded as the betrayal of Munich gave them a great stimulus to combine in their efforts to change the Government's policy. Duff Cooper resigned from the Cabinet and nearly forty Conservatives abstained from supporting the Government when the Munich 'settlement' was debated. Although Chamberlain still secured a majority of 366, with only 144 votes against him, the prevailing mood of complacency and fear, which had dulled the politicians' reactions to Hitler's earlier thrusts, from the occupation of the Rhineland onwards, was now largely dispelled. The Conservative Party was unhappy and divided: the critics of Government policy were heard with more respect. It was now accepted even by those most hopeful of peace that rearmament must be pursued more vigorously. Pressure groups on the Conservative backbenches designed to force the Government into a change of policy had existed long before Munich. In the early months of 1936 a group advocating accelerated rearmament, and including Austen Chamberlain and Churchill, had met regularly.[1] Subsequently Churchill had tried to unite all believers in collective resistance, whether Conservatives, trade unionists or Liberals. But after Munich much more serious attempts were made to combine the forces of opposition to appeasement. Before the debate on Munich, contacts were established, with Macmillan as an intermediary, between the Churchill group and Hugh Dalton, an advocate of rearmament on the Labour side. The Conservative dissidents feared that Chamberlain was about to exploit Munich by calling a general election and that dissidents in the forthcoming House of Commons vote might be proscribed as candidates. With this in mind, and in order to muster Conservative abstentions without giving hostages to Chamberlain, Churchill, Eden and Macmillan invited Dalton to Brendan Bracken's house for a talk.[2] The motion of censure tabled by the Labour Party enabled about thirty Conservatives to abstain.

[1] Earl Winterton, *Orders of the Day* (Cassell, 1955), p. 216.

[2] Hugh Dalton, *The Fateful Years: Memoirs, 1931–1945* (Frederick Muller, 1957), pp. 199 et seq. Harold Macmillan, *Winds of Change, 1914–1939*, pp. 568 et seq.

Looking back on these years, Macmillan, in his memoirs, remarked that many people

... may find it incredible that the British House of Commons remained apparently impervious to the steadily deteriorating position. The Government of the day neglected their duty. The Opposition encouraged them in that neglect; they even spent most of their time in blaming Ministers for the very small efforts that they belatedly made to remedy a rapidly worsening situation. ...
There is no precedent in history for a Parliament allowing the country to concede one diplomatic defeat after another; suffering staggering strategic set-backs; and finally undergoing military defeats with so little protest. The only parallel is to be found in the Parliaments that supported Lord North's administration from 1776 to 1783 during the American Revolution. Yet Members were not corrupt; they were bemused.[1]

This judgment is a fair one. Parliament as a whole cannot easily rise above the contemporary political climate though individual Members and groups of Members may try to change the prevailing opinions. Gradually the case that the critics had to make against Chamberlain's policies now gained wider acceptance. In the months before the war, the House of Commons, slowly and painfully, learned to give a lead to the Government and to the nation. Contacts between Conservative backbenchers and responsible members of the Opposition were maintained and the Labour Party accepted the need for rearmament even though it could not refrain from voting against conscription when Chamberlain at last presented national service legislation to the Commons. Yet the spirit of appeasement did not finally die in Parliament, or even in the country, until March 1939 when Czechoslovakia was dismembered by Germany and other predatory neighbours. Now it became obvious to most politically conscious people in Britain that war, whether sooner or later, was inevitable. Yet the Government itself, which for practical purposes meant Chamberlain and his immediate colleagues, was still reluctant to face this fact. It was Parliament rather than the Cabinet which in the last resort provided the will to resist. It is hardly asserting too much to say that, in reality if not in form, it was the House of Commons which decided on war in 1939.

[1] Harold Macmillan *Winds of Change, 1914–1939*, pp. 580–1.

(iii)

Before turning to consider the way in which Parliament rose to the needs of the nation in 1939–40, the question must be asked how far mechanical defects of Parliament, as distinct from the shortcomings of the politicians of the period, were responsible for the gross failures in economic and foreign policy during the decade before the war. Schemes for the reform of the House of Commons had been as abundant in the twenties and thirties as they were to be in the fifties and sixties. Would the adoption of any of them have made any substantial difference to the hard facts of politics? Would they have prevented or cured the tragedy of unemployment; or might they have stopped the ignominious drift to war?

Since these reforms were, after all, largely advocated because of discontent with the political handling of the nation's *major* problems, they must be judged in accordance with whether it now seems that they might have changed for the better the approach to these major problems. Almost certainly the answer is that, given the existing divisions between the main political parties, and within these parties, no mechanistic reform would have made much difference, short of changing the system so drastically that democratic processes were at least suspended. Policies which, with the advantage of hindsight, are now generally regarded as vindicated, were being advocated by minority voices in Parliament—and advocated both freely and loudly. But they were not acceptable to the majority (in either party) of the House of Commons and even if they had been deployed in, say, a developed committee system it seems unlikely that they would have converted much more speedily either the majority of Members, or the politicians in power. It was not fluency of argument by the minority but strength of will in the majority which was lacking. What might have made some difference would have been a willingness on the part of some of the dissidents to stand against their leaders on the great issues of the day, whatever the cost to party unity, instead of continuing to work within their parties. But the experience of the Labour Party in 1930–1, and its aftermath, was hardly an encouragement to discontented Tories to break ranks—and it was on the Conservative backbenchers that the main burden of influencing the Government rested in these years of so huge a Government minority. It is hardly surprising that Churchill and the other Conservative rebels against the Government's foreign policy chose to work within their own party. What other political home existed for them: what chance had they to retain their seats in Parliament standing as independents against the official Conservative Party? Their numbers were too small; their policies too unpopular for them to hope for success by outright rebellion.

Similarly, what effective future would there have been for the minority of Conservative backbenchers who were beginning in these years to preach the gospel of public works and national economic planning had they decided to leave their party behind? As it was, some of them, including Harold Macmillan as a young backbencher, were able to work through what was called the Northern Group of some forty Conservative Members of Parliament representing the constituencies in the north of England where the industrial depression was deepest. Later, left-wing Conservatives, again including Macmillan, were numbered among the Next Five Years Group, which in 1935 produced a scheme—supported by a large number of prominent people from all parties and no party—for economic planning by the Government. This early design for running a mixed economy, based on the belief that the old capitalist system could not be allowed to continue without drastic amendment, fell on unreceptive ears so far as the majority of Conservatives were concerned. It represented a compromise with Socialism for which Conservative opinion was not yet ready. Any close examination of pre-war politics shows that there existed a ferment of new ideas on both the right and the left of politics and a willingness, among a minority of politicians, to think out or adopt new ideas. This was a period far from sterile in political thinking: its sterility was in the actions of the politicians who had the ear of a majority of the nation.

The more enlightened proposals for foreign and economic policy made in these years failed to achieve translation into practical politics because even the longest list of distinguished names is unlikely to command enough consent to affect policies unless they are backed by a major political interest. The most they can do is to condition, however slowly, the climate of opinion and this much, at least, the discussion of new solutions in the pre-war years achieved. In a democracy there is no place for even the most enlightened policy if it has to be forcibly thrust down the throats of the majority.

Since the failures of these years resulted from the nature and views of the political parties, it is not surprising that many people should have looked to the possibility of non-party solutions. But the ultimate logic of this was the abandonment of parties for dictatorship, as had happened in some other countries. The only other alternative to the rigid party system of Britain appeared to be the fragmentation of parties and interests which paralysed the parliamentary institutions of the Third and Fourth French Republics, where governments were little more than ill-assorted party groups driving unsatisfactory and non-durable bargains with each other. In Britain, the periods when government had been based on a multi-party House of Commons had not been happy. For all the disadvantages of the huge Conservative majority of the thirties, few would have preferred a return to the parliamentary instability experienced during the twenties.

Thus for good or ill the British party system persisted, and it is at the door of the parties that the blame for wrong policies before the war must be laid. More drastic rebellions by the protesters would almost certainly have proved ineffective. As it was, their propaganda had a marginal effect on Government policy at home and abroad which gradually built up into something more substantial.

Moreover, for all the major policy failures of these years, the House of Commons did not cease to be vigilant in protecting the liberties of the subject and it sought to keep a watch on the encroachment of bureaucracy as the arm of government intervention into the lives of ordinary citizens stretched out ever farther. Inevitably, as the Government had more administrative functions to perform, it had to establish more bodies empowered to act for the Executive. For instance, new Marketing Boards were established and the Unemployment Assistance Board had powers which were very largely independent of Parliament.

Following an attack by the Lord Chief Justice on abuses arising from 'administrative law', Parliament had become increasingly sensitive about the growth of delegated legislation.[1] In 1929, therefore, the Government appointed a Committee on Ministers' Powers under the chairmanship of Lord Donoughmore. When this Committee reported in 1932, it found that delegated legislation was necessary and desirable in certain circumstances but recommended safeguards. Nothing was done to implement these recommendations until the war, when the Select Committee on Statutory Instruments was set up. In these pre-war years, there was an inevitable conflict, which still persists, between the rights of the individual and of

[1] Lord Hewart, *The New Despotism: An Essay on Bureaucracy* (Ernest Benn, 1929).

Parliament on the one hand and on the other the need for new, efficient administrative bodies to act in matters affecting the community without constant recourse to the legislature. Yet it is going too far to construe these pre-war developments as an indication of dictatorial instincts on the part of the National Government, as Professor Laski did in his otherwise brilliant and understanding *Reflections on the Constitution*. The growth of new administrative bodies and the increase in delegated legislation was inevitable in a modern society, and not a symptom of any deliberate wish to evade discussion in the House of Commons or a sign of quasi-totalitarian instincts, though one may indeed agree that British political life in these years was enfeebled by the Government's huge majority and the impotence of the Opposition.[1]

The concern of the House of Commons for the liberties of the subject was effectively shown when the Government brought in an Incitement to Disaffection Bill following the Invergordon naval mutiny. This Bill produced an immediate storm in the House. The King's Speech had already announced a forthcoming Bill to deal with disaffection and it had been thought that this would provide wider powers to control the activities of the Fascist Blackshirts, and also to prevent the incitement of serving forces. In fact, the Bill proposed to extend the existing law so far that it was described by the jurist, Sir William Holdsworth, as 'the most daring encroachment upon the liberty of the subject which the executive government has yet attempted at a time which is not a time of emergency'. The Bill was also regarded as a threat to muzzle extreme left-wing opinion and even the trade unions feared that it might be directed at them.[2] The Bill went to a Standing Committee consisting of forty-two Government supporters and eight Opposition Members. Although one

---

[1] Professor Laski was on safer ground in citing the interpretation of the Official Secrets Act to try to stop Mr Duncan Sandys, a young MP and a Territorial officer, from asking questions about the Government's preparedness to meet air attacks. On the other hand, the essential point was that Sandys was under inhibition as a serving officer rather than as an MP, though it was as an MP that he was asking questions in 1938. As a result of this affair the House established a Select Committee to look into it and consider the impact of the Official Secrets Acts upon Members in the discharge of their parliamentary duties.

[2] For an account of the provisions and effects of the Bill, see Harry Street, *Freedom, the Individual and the Law* (Pelican, 1963). The incident is also discussed in W. Ivor Jennings, *Parliament* (Cambridge University Press, 1939), p. 129.

Conservative voted once with the small Opposition group, which fought the Bill line by line, the Government supporters did not break ranks. They showed their disapproval in a different way. Government support was never higher than twenty-eight and went as low as fifteen, while sometimes the Government even failed to find a quorum. Yet, even though the Government could be sure of its majority, it bowed to the obvious opinion of the Commons, and to the campaign against the Bill outside, by removing the crucial clauses which would have curtailed the liberty of the subject. If much of the pressure against the original Bill was fuelled from outside Parliament, the House of Commons, acting through a protracted and arduous Committee stage, gave expression to these objections and preserved its rôle as the guardian of liberty. The Incitement to Disaffection Act, as finally passed in 1934, was only a shadow of the Bill originally put before Parliament.

A similar outcry came from all sides of the House when Neville Chamberlain, as Chancellor of the Exchequer, introduced a complex proposal for a National Defence Contribution on the profits from arms manufacture in his Budget of 1937. Shortly afterwards, Chamberlain became Prime Minister and for several weeks he persisted with the proposal. But eventually he withdrew it before the division on the Second Reading of the Bill and later substituted a straight percentage tax on profits. This incident showed that even a Finance Bill produced by a Government with a massive majority can be amended on a point of substance. Still more important, it showed that even a coalition Government with an impregnable majority felt it wise to bow to the overwhelming opinion of the House of Commons when that opinion was unmistakably expressed.

(iv)

Unfortunately, no such clarity of guidance had been given to the Government by the House on the great issues of foreign policy until the last minute. Though, after Munich, Chamberlain spoke of resisting any attempt to dominate the world by force; though the British guarantee to Poland was given after the rape of Czechoslovakia, the Prime Minister was still reluctant to face the truth about Hitler and to believe that appeasement had failed. On both sides of the House also there were deep-rooted inhibitions about accepting what had to be done. The Parliamentary Labour Party could not overcome its instinctive dislike of conscription; many Conservatives, in and out of Parliament, could not finally throw aside their feeling that Nazi Germany might be a counterweight against Communist Russia and international revolution. Such Conservative views were reflected in the British reluctance to contemplate a whole-hearted alliance with the Soviet Union.

Yet more and more heed was being paid to the Conservative dissidents who were now making the pace in demanding rearmament and a genuinely national government. The Chamberlain administration's acceptance of conscription was a response to these demands. It was not until the Nazi–Soviet Pact in August 1939 that a mood of resistance finally took hold of both sides of the House of Commons.

It is important to note that it was essentially a parliamentary mood.

> The stir was mainly confined to parliament. There were no great public meetings in the week before the outbreak of war, no mass marches demanding 'Stand by Poland'. It is impossible to tell whether members of parliament represented the British people. At any rate, the MPs were resolute and the Government tailed regretfully after the House of Commons.[1]

Even when the Anglo–Polish Defence Treaty was signed, a clause covering Danzig was kept secret so as not to annoy Hitler. Then, when Hitler invaded Poland on September 1, the Cabinet decided that if Germany would suspend hostilities war might still be avoided. That day the Cabinet decided to send a warning—which was not to be considered an ultimatum—to this effect. On September 2, the Cabinet decided that it was an ultimatum which should expire at midnight—but still no ultimatum was sent and Halifax, the Foreign Secretary, continued to seek a conference. The same night Chamberlain appeared in the House of Commons, and instead of announcing the ultimatum that Members expected, he spoke of what prospects there might be for a resumption of diplomacy, and what conditions might be necessary. The Prime Minister received no cheers when he sat down and, as Arthur Greenwood, the Acting Leader of the Labour Party, rose to speak, L. S. Amery shouted from the Conservative benches: 'Speak for England, Arthur.' Greenwood spoke of

[1] A. J. P. Taylor, *English History, 1914–1945*, p. 450.

the danger to life, national honour and interests if there were further delay. Hugh Dalton commented in his diary afterwards:

> In the Lobbies afterwards there was a terrific buzz. It almost seemed that, on a free vote, Chamberlain and Simon would have been overthrown.[1]

Immediately, Greenwood followed Chamberlain to his room and told him that unless a decision for war were taken before the House met the next day, he would find it impossible to hold the Commons.[2] That night, Chamberlain informed the French Prime Minister on the telephone that the parliamentary situation was grave and could not be held if they insisted in their suggested time limit to the ultimatum of forty-eight hours. The next morning, Halifax told the French Foreign Secretary that he understood why the French could not send their ultimatum before noon (Paris had been trying to enlist Italian mediation and had promised a forty-eight hours delay) but the British Government was obliged to send their ultimatum the same morning. If they did not, the Prime Minister that day might be over-thrown in the House of Commons by a unanimous movement of opinion.

Recording his memories of Chamberlain's announcement of war in the Commons—which even then contained no reference to the Poles but much about his own policies—Dalton recorded:

> I had not a shadow of doubt but that the House of Commons, and especially the Labour Party, had forced the British Government to force the French Government to take the plunge.[3]

Dalton still believed that some in high office in both Paris and London were planning on delay until a new *fait accompli* by Hitler provided the basis for another settlement. The special reference to the Labour Party's influence was perhaps rather more than the truth. Labour pressures could have done nothing had the Tories been united behind Chamberlain. It was the identity of views across the House of Commons which gave validity to Dalton's general point. But once again it had been shown that the decisive influence on a Government is its assessment of its ability to hold together its own party. When Members believe that a Government has betrayed the fundamental

---

[1] Hugh Dalton, *The Fateful Years: Memoirs, 1931–1945*, p. 265.
[2] L. S. Amery, *My Political Life*, Vol. 3, p. 324.
[3] Hugh Dalton, *The Fateful Years: Memoirs, 1931–1945*, p. 270.

tenets of their party, they are likely to turn against their leaders. When they apprehend, however belatedly, a divergence between party loyalty and national need, they are almost certain to do so.

In the period of the phoney war which followed, the Chamberlain Government's aim was victory without tears. Economic collapse would, it believed, break Germany without great bloodshed. Britain, meanwhile, could build up her strength slowly for the eventual show-down. Hitler, so Chamberlain considered by April 1940, had 'missed the bus'. Once again, Parliament had been reduced to comparative ineffectiveness because the Labour Party had been separated from the former Tory dissidents now that Churchill and Eden were in the Cabinet. By taking in these two critics, Chamberlain temporarily reunited his own ranks: by refusing to serve under Chamberlain, the Labour Party had temporarily made themselves powerless to affect the conduct of the war but had preserved their independence for the day when the overthrow of Chamberlain was achieved by the drawing together, once more, of the Labour Opposition with Tory protesters.

The failure of the Norwegian campaign in 1940 brought the final dismissal of Chamberlain by the House of Commons, and his replacement by Churchill. This change was the result of a spontaneous eruption in the House. When Chamberlain opened the two-day debate on the Norwegian campaign on May 7, he had not the slightest anticipation that he would be forced, by the vote at the end of it, to resign. Moreover, although many of the strongest criticisms came from the Conservative side; although Chamberlain, by the tone of his speech, showed some loss of self-confidence and a failure to rise to the occasion, even now the majority of the Conservative Party was reluctant to part with their leader. As one observer noted on the first day of this debate:

> To all appearances it had been just another debate, with the Tories rather more dutifully than spontaneously cheering the Prime Minister and resenting criticism of him. . . .

The cheers were still coming from the

> . . . embattled 'Yes men'; it lies with them to say whether Mr. Chamberlain retains their confidence and they have not done any-thing today to show that he does not.[1]

[1] Harry Boardman, *The Glory of Parliament* (Allen & Unwin, 1960), p. 68.

167

In the debate, Chamberlain had to face a strong opposition attack; a dramatic intervention by Admiral Sir Roger Keyes, in full uniform, denouncing the Government's leadership on behalf of the fighting men; and a bitter attack from the persistent critic Amery which concluded by redirecting Cromwell's scornful dismissal of the Long Parliament to the Chamberlain Government:

> You have sat too long here for any good you have been doing. Depart, I say, and let us have done with you. In the name of God, go.

Yet even now, who could be sure of the outcome? For once, it was clear, the decision of the House would be taken on the floor of the House. The Speaker had not called Amery until the dinner hour—deliberately as Amery thought, because he was expected to make trouble. Members had steadily dribbled out of the Chamber till 'barely a dozen were left'.[1] Amery nearly decided to leave his full effort against the Government to another day on the grounds that it depended on 'the response of a live House and not on those who might care to read my speech in *Hansard*'. But he persisted and the Liberal Member, Clement Davies, went off to round up an audience from the Smoking Room and Library. By the time he had made some opening remarks, Amery at least had, as he put it, 'the makings of a House' and throughout his speech, numbers increased and so did the murmur of approval from Conservative Members. Amery records that when he sat down he knew that he had done what he had set out to do and the look on the faces of Ministers showed that they also knew it. He was sure that he had carried with him far more Conservatives than the score who were normally associated with him in the campaign for a more dynamic war effort. Yet even so,

> Mr Amery's Phillipic was delivered, as usual, to half-empty benches on his own side, but there was a goodly muster of the Opposition to hear him,[2]

it was observed from the Press Gallery. Would the Conservatives rise to the occasion? And would the Labour Party give them a chance by forcing a division?

What course would our history have taken if the Labour Party had decided against dividing the House at the end of the debate and had

[1] L. S. Amery, *My Political Life*, Vol. 3, p. 360.
[2] Harry Boardman, *The Glory of Parliament*, p. 72.

therefore refrained from challenging the dissidents among the Conservative majority to vote above Party? On the first day of the debate, the Labour Party had not intended to call a vote of confidence (strictly it was a vote on the adjournment of the House, amounting to the same thing) for fear of unifying the Conservative backbenchers in obedience to the Whips, thus preserving the life of the Chamberlain Government. When Clement Davies, who had agreed with Amery that this debate must be made a trial of strength in the Commons itself, had sought to persuade Attlee to make it a direct vote of confidence, Attlee hesitated for these reasons. This hesitation may have been wise. It gave time for discontent to foment on the Conservative side with no unifying force being provided by the forewarning of an Opposition attack. The next day, however, the Labour decision to divide the House was announced by Herbert Morrison and this produced the response from Neville Chamberlain which did him so much harm with his own followers. Pale and angry, the Prime Minister rose to the Despatch Box in the righteous indignation of a party leader to say that Labour's challenge made the debate much graver: he appealed to 'my friends—and I have friends in this House'. Despite the unhappy overtones of this remark, Chamberlain still sat down to loud cheers from his own side. During the course of the day, however, he faced further attacks, two of the most effective being from Lloyd George and Duff Cooper. The outcome was that forty-one Members from the Government benches voted with the Opposition and about sixty more abstained. The Government's majority, usually around 240, fell to 81.[1]

The more or less consistent position of the Labour Party throughout had been that they would not enter a coalition under Chamberlain. Most thought that they should consider joining a National Coalition if Chamberlain were overthrown. Now, after the drop in the Conservative vote, it was obvious even to Chamberlain himself that the Government must be reconstructed on a national basis, taking in the Labour Party. It was not yet clear to him that he could not be its Leader but in the course of the next two days this painful truth was made known to the Prime Minister, even by some (including Kingsley Wood) who had been closest to him. Amery's group of dissident Tories, now risen to sixty at a meeting on the day after the crucial vote, unanimously decided that they would neither

---

[1] I have used the figures given by A. J. P. Taylor, *English History, 1914–1945*, p. 473.

support nor join a Government which did not contain Labour and Liberal representatives, though they would serve under any Prime Minister. Since Labour would not serve under Chamberlain, this meant that he must go. The double invasion of Holland and Belgium the next day: a message from the Labour Conference that Labour would serve under another Prime Minister than Chamberlain, brought the matter to a conclusion. After a last-minute attempt by Chamberlain to pass the succession to Halifax, the inevitable was accepted. Churchill was appointed Prime Minister at the head of a coalition of war—not by the will of a party but by the wish of the House of Commons.

(v)

With all three parties represented in the Government, the War Cabinet was furnished with a mandate which gave it immense power. Now, if ever, the influence of the House of Commons over the Executive might be held to be, if not diminished, at least surrendered for the duration. Yet during the war years, the House of Commons remained a living and an important institution and it kept alive a spontaneous critical 'opposition' to the Government. For this, Churchill's own punctilious regard for the tradition of consulting the House and his decision to base his Government on the party structure (he himself became Conservative Leader in October 1940) were in part responsible. But even had he wished to do otherwise, the House of Commons would not have let him. There were parliamentarians anxious to keep alive the critical traditions of the House of Commons. Outside Parliament, the tradition of independent political comment also persisted. Although a political truce existed under which none of the parties to the coalition contested parliamentary by-elections, an increasing proportion of by-elections were contested as the war progressed. In 1942, a year of exceptional difficulty for the Government and for Churchill personally, Sir Richard Acland, the Liberal Member for Barnstaple, founded the new Common Wealth Party. This quickly died after the war but during the war years it attracted to itself frustrated opposition opinion and in particular the support of discontented Labour voters who (as represented by the minority Party) suffered most from the electoral truce. In the five months of 1945, before the breakup of the coalition, six out of seven by-elections were contested and the Government candidates were defeated in three of them by a Common Wealth, an Independent, and a Scottish Nationalist candidate. Despite the dominance of Churchill, party political life had remained very much alive. As a result of the protest votes during the war period, the number of independent and minor party members in the Commons rose from nine at the opening of Parliament in 1935 to thirty-three at its dissolution. This, indeed, was a 'golden age' of the independent Member in Parliament during this century—a golden age that ended abruptly with the Labour landslide of 1945. But it was not merely a golden age reckoned in terms of the number of independent Members in the House. It was, more significantly, a golden age of independence in the ranks of the established parties. The formality of an 'Opposition' was provided by the device of having a group of senior Labour Members sitting on the Opposition frontbench and putting questions to the Government. (The job of Opposition spokesman was held first by a former Minister, H. B. Lees-Smith, and then, after 1942, by Arthur Greenwood who had just left the Government.) The real criticisms however were provided by independent-minded Members within the major political parties.

There was, to start with, the combined activity of the veteran Conservative backbencher, Lord Winterton, with Mr Emanuel Shinwell on the Labour side. In the winter of 1940, these two met and agreed on the need for critical comment on defence and foreign policy. Their relationship was dubbed 'arsenic and old lace' by Kingsley Martin of the *New Statesman* and the name stuck.[1] The immediate cause of the alliance was a debate on manpower in which Shinwell had called upon the Government to accept universal organisation and compulsion where necessary, with which Winterton, Hore-Belisha and others agreed. (This policy was eventually adopted.) It would be wrong to regard the activities of Shinwell and Lord Winterton as the most effective opposition to the war-time Government. Nevertheless, when Lord Winterton argued, in a debate on January 21, 1941, on the co-ordination of national production efforts, that while he and his friends did not form an organised group, they did represent a movement of public opinion 'which has been on a much more rapid scale than that of the Government during the last few weeks', he had a point.[2] The fact was that the House did provide a focus of public opinion during the war and it was important that even Churchill, for all his authority, regularly had to answer to it. Nor was his doing so a mere formality. To the mass of the people,

[1] Earl Winterton, *Orders of the Day*, p. 261.   [2] Ibid., p. 265.

Churchill's personal position seemed—and, indeed, in the last analysis almost certainly was—politically impregnable. Yet it was impregnable precisely because of the general understanding that he was not, even temporarily, a dictator; that his authority rested on maintaining the broad goodwill, whatever the criticism of particular policies, of all political parties. For this reason, the difficulties he faced within the House of Commons were genuinely serious. The impregnability of Churchill's position did not imply that the House of Commons no longer mattered but rather that nobody else could have commanded such general support in the House. But this support was far from unconditional.

Churchill's strongest weapon was that whatever his mistakes, whatever the setbacks, there was nobody who had a comparable standing with the public. Yet the latter part of 1941 and most of 1942 brought a series of military and naval reverses, including the forced retreat in North Africa and the loss of Singapore, which caused widespread discontent with Churchill's leadership. Much of this came from the left of the political spectrum. From 1941, Churchill had been under bitter attack from Aneurin Bevan who, from the left of the Labour Party, was advocating a Second Front to help Russia. Bevan also attacked the Prime Minister for one-man government and criticised the general competence of his direction of the war.[1] At the height of adversity, Churchill, who had just returned from the United States, demanded a vote of confidence in the House of Commons in January 1942, saying that any Member who thought the Government ought to be broken up should 'have the manhood to testify his convictions in the Lobby'. With only three ILP Members against him, Churchill got the overwhelming vote of confidence he wanted. But discontent did not die down. Shortly afterwards, as the agitation for a Second Front mounted, Sir Stafford Cripps returned from his mission to Moscow with a greatly enhanced prestige which brought him an 'extraordinary hero's welcome'.[2] Cripps might have been some embarrassment to Churchill since, though he was still cold-shouldered by the official Labour Party, which had expelled him before the war, his standing might have made him a focal point for left-wing rebellion. Thus the Labour Party might have been split and the position of its members who were in the Government affected.

[1] Michael Foot, *Aneurin Bevan*, Vol. 1 (MacGibbon & Kee, 1962), pp. 335 et seq.
[2] Ibid., p. 352.

Churchill thereupon embarked upon a reshuffle of his Government. He did so, as he admitted, in response to 'external pressure'. The main attack against him was as Defence Minister: what the critics, including Bevan, wanted was an independent Defence Minister and a Minister of Production under Churchill as Prime Minister. Although Churchill would not relinquish his rôle as Minister of Defence, he did now appoint a Minister of Production, Oliver Lyttelton, and Cripps was made Leader of the House of Commons with a place in the War Cabinet. Once again it had to be recognised, even by Churchill, that the composition of his Government must have regard to feeling in the House of Commons. As so often happens, a rebellious episode in Parliament had ended in a compromise between the Government and its critics.

Even these concessions, however, did not bring Churchill's parliamentary tribulations to an end. The fall of Tobruk in June 1942, when Churchill was in Washington, brought the Government under such criticism that to some it even seemed that Churchill's future might be in question. Churchill reassured the Americans that the voluble critics in Parliament did not represent the House of Commons: he saw the agitation as press chatter and the work of would-be profiteers of disaster in Parliament. Commenting on this incident in his life of Bevan, Michael Foot observed that Churchill and the Government, in treating the criticism in this way, might be pardoned

> ... for not stopping to consider what sinister developments might have occurred if the deep anxieties of the people had found no expression in the House of Commons or the press. One glory and one strength of the British people throughout the war was that they were not prepared to put all their democratic habits in pawn for the duration.[1]

On his return from Washington, Churchill was told by Cripps of a 'very grave disturbance of opinion both in the House of Commons and in the country'. The debate in the House of Commons which followed was the most critical since the overthrow of Chamberlain and it took place on a motion of 'no confidence in the central direction of the war' which was sponsored by a respected and responsible Conservative backbencher, Sir John Wardlaw-Milne, Sir Roger Keyes and the former Minister, Leslie Hore-Belisha. The ill-assorted

[1] Michael Foot, *Aneurin Bevan*, Vol. 1, pp. 370–1.

combination of Wardlaw-Milne (who ruined his case by recommending the Duke of Gloucester as British Commander-in-Chief), Roger Keyes and Aneurin Bevan caused the attack to founder. Nevertheless twenty-five Members voted against Churchill and some forty more abstained. Once more the Prime Minister was given a reminder, if he needed it, of his ultimate responsibility to the House of Commons.

The influence of backbenchers during the war was, however, also exerted in more mundane ways. If Bevan and his friends thought that the coalition paid too little attention to Labour feelings and policy, the Tories for their part began to have misgivings about the Socialist tendencies of the Government. On one occasion, they achieved a major victory: in 1942, the 1922 Committee was instrumental in forcing the Government to abandon a plan for coal rationing, based on a report by Sir William Beveridge, after a Cabinet Committee had approved the adoption of a fuel-rationing scheme.[1] The press joined the Conservative backbenchers in supporting the campaign against fuel rationing and at one point it looked as though forty or fifty Conservatives might vote against the scheme. During the course of this argument, Dalton, who was as President of the Board of Trade responsible for the scheme, addressed the Conservative 1922 Committee but afterwards the Committee unanimously decided that, although coal consumption must be reduced, a simpler scheme was necessary. A Conservative Member told Dalton later that the 1922 Committee had never before passed a resolution on a matter of policy and they did so now because they felt the Labour Party in the Government was getting too much of its own way. And, indeed, the Labour Party under the coalition was extremely active in forwarding social change and preparing itself for presenting the electorate with its design for a planned, welfare state when the war ended.

Political discussion was far from moribund during the war: indeed, it was seldom more lively. In February 1943 the Parliamentary Labour Party (except for Ministers) voted against the Government's luke-warm reception of the Beveridge Report on social insurance. On two other occasions Labour backbenchers abstained from supporting the Government—once on consideration of the Town and Country Planning Bill, and again over the Government's policy on Greece.

[1] Hugh Dalton, *The Fateful Years: Memoirs, 1931–1945*, pp. 385 et seq. See also Earl Winterton, *Orders of the Day*, p. 280.

Aside from party politics, the House of Commons did its best to preserve its normal function of overseeing Government expenditure with a view to looking for economies. The National Expenditure Committee (whose Chairman was Sir John Wardlaw-Milne, Churchill's challenger in the censure debate) instituted investigations into a wide field of war expenditure, looking for possible savings. In the course of its investigations its members visited factories and interviewed large numbers of witnesses; the Committee performed, broadly, the functions of the later Estimates Committee.

Faced with an even sharper increase in delegated legislation, particularly under the Emergency Powers (Defence) Acts, the House decided that it must at last take some action to ensure that the citizen was protected against encroachments by the bureaucracy. In 1944, a Select Committee on Statutory Instruments was established to scrutinise all Instruments made by a Minister which are laid before the House and on which the House may, or must, pass a resolution. This Committee was to draw the attention of the House to any Instrument that seemed to make unusual or unexpected use of the power conferred by the original Statute. Thus, under the pressures of war, one of the recommendations of the Donoughmore Report of 1932 was implemented. Equally, throughout the war, the House remained eager to debate all cases where it suspected that the rights of individuals were being unnecessarily infringed by the demands of the emergency.

Yet the overriding function of Parliament during the war was to act as the Great Council of the nation in which the Executive could consult with and obtain the consent of the representatives of the governed. The authority of the Cabinet and of the Prime Minister was exceptionally strong and yet, even more than in peacetime, the Government needed to be sure of the support of the House. In normal circumstances, a Government, though it must take account of the feelings of the House as a whole, must respond particularly to the majority party on which it relies. During the war, however, the Churchill Government relied on a majority of the whole House which, beside giving it great authority, also obliged it to respond to all sections of the Commons. The participation in the Cabinet of Labour Ministers depended on the assent of their followers and for this reason the views of Labour Members as well as of Conservative backbenchers had to be taken into account. Although freedom from the normal confines of inter-party rivalry enabled backbenchers of both parties to combine on occasions against the Government, both the Conservatives and the Labour Party were jealously guarding their particular attitudes and interests in preparation for the resumption of peace. Despite the obsessive demands of war, political argument remained exceptionally vigorous during these years largely owing to the preservation of political dialectic within the House of Commons.

Part II: The House of Commons since 1945

Chapter Six

The Influence of the Backbench Member 1945–1951

Since the Second World War, and particularly during the fifties and sixties, the efficacy of Parliament has been called into question as vehemently as it was thirty years earlier. The basic contemporary questions have been summarised in the introduction and the first part of this study has shown how little they are new. In the final chapter, I shall discuss the underlying causes of the contemporary discontent and the agitation for reform. The chapters which follow, however, seek to express the function of the House of Commons in the practice of post-war politics and to test, by reference to actual cases, the allegation that the Commons, whether collectively or individually, are now subordinate to the Executive to a degree that renders Parliament incapable of doing a worthwhile job.

Is it true that the backbench Member is a pawn in the hands of his leaders and the party Whips: that he exerts negligible influence over the formulation of government policy and the conduct of administration? Practical men, as well as intellectuals, who are concerned to find the 'right' answer to pressing contemporary problems are increasingly impatient with the conventional joustings in the Commons. They know that the official Opposition is fore-ordained to lose every battle, if victory is to be measured in Division figures or in terms of a government retreat from some major policy decision as a result of an adverse vote in the House. They are no less sceptical about the reality of the influence now exerted on a Government by its own followers. Supporters of modern Governments are seen to vote pliantly for policies in which they do not believe. Much-publicised backbench revolts collapse when the Members who sponsor them have to face the test of the Division lobby—especially when their party is in power, which is the only time a backbench revolt can normally have an impact on current policy. Everyone knows that the solidarity of party interest frequently ignores, if it cannot conceal, deep internal party divisions when votes are taken in the House. Voting figures for the House as a whole seldom reflect with much accuracy the opinion of the House on the merits of a case; how can they when Members are simply required to answer 'yes' or 'no' to Government policies when it comes to counting heads? To the extent that critics concede the influence of Members on their leaders privately, in backbench party meetings or less formal discussions, this is regarded as a poor substitute for influence exerted on the floor of the House or in open all-party specialist committees.

The impotence of the Opposition against a Government with a large majority; the alleged inability of Government supporters to influence their leaders who have the power of patronage and discipline; the response of Ministers to the external pressures of party organisations and other interested groups in the country; the discretion given to the bureaucracy—all these persuade many people that the House of Commons is in decline. It may be that the earlier chapters of this study will be taken as demonstrating that there has been little real decline in the position of the House of Commons since there has been little essential change in its political rôle. Even the allegation that decisions are now taken more often off the floor of the House than they used to be may be questioned. Whether in the private Puritan synods of the sixteenth century; the secret deliberations of the Providence Island Company in the seventeenth; or in the great private houses and clubs of the eighteenth and nineteenth centuries, political groupings in Parliament have always sought to determine their policies and to marshal support for them before final decisions were registered on the floor of the House. The modern private meetings of backbenchers and the efforts made behind the scenes by party leaders to 'sew up' their followers behind agreed party policies are no more than the contemporary counterparts of the more informal gatherings of former centuries. Certainly since party organisation began to take on its modern form during the last century, voting decisions have seldom been determined by what is said in the House itself—though it is true that Members who dissented seriously from their party on some major issue of principle or policy were formerly more willing to vote against their leaders—or even, occasionally, to break altogether from their party—than they appear to be today. Such breaks as those which took place over the

Corn Laws and Irish Home Rule were, of course, exceptional. It would be foolish to suppose that they could in no circumstances be repeated, if there were a big enough issue, in the second half of the twentieth century.

Yet even if it is accepted that the House of Commons has not greatly declined in influence, the questions still remain: what form does this influence take in the conditions of contemporary politics and how relevant is it to the essential political decisions required in the second half of the twentieth century? The influence of the Opposition and of the Member in his independent capacity will be dealt with in later chapters: so will the House of Commons' control over the administration of policy. The next five chapters, however, deal exclusively with the influence of backbenchers, mainly on the Government side, over policy-making in the period between 1945 and 1966. These chapters include one devoted entirely to the examination in greater detail of a specimen case of backbench influence—that exerted by Conservative backbenchers over 'resale price maintenance' policy—as an example of how the mechanics of backbench pressures function.

Opinions among MPs themselves about the effectiveness of back-bench influence vary according to an individual's seniority—whether this is measured in terms of office-holding or of years of service in the House. Most Ministers, of whatever party, insist that any Government must, and does, heed the views of its backbenchers in forming policies and making decisions. The newest MPs, on the other hand, are almost invariably disappointed by what they find to be their position and status once they arrive at Westminster—especially if they are men and women who feel they have entered politics to 'get things done'. A man who may well have been in command of his own day, and who may have been used to holding executive authority, suddenly finds himself at the disposal of his Whips. He must hang about for Divisions on subjects that do not interest him; amenities are inadequate; Westminster is exhaustingly conducive to time-wasting and sterile political talk. The new Member finds that he is normally obliged to wait for something to happen so that he can react to it; only rarely, by taking up some external 'happening', can he feel that he has made any impact on affairs. One who arrives with burning zeal for some particular reform finds himself faced with the inertia of his fellow politicians on *his* particular issue and by the Government's control over the parliamentary timetable. It is true that every Member, if only in his political gossip, is a part of the important opinion-forming process of Westminster to which the leaders of all political parties listen; but he is only a fraction of it. If his party is in power, the new Member finds that his Government's policy is fashioned by the prior commitments of the last general election manifesto and, even worse perhaps, by responses to the demands of unexpected emergencies which may require a Government to take action that harmonises poorly with what the Member took to be the general ethos of his party.

Discontent on the part of the new Member is commonplace. Such symptoms are recalled by most long-standing MPs who look back to the reactions of earlier intakes. Nevertheless, disillusion of this kind was particularly bitter among the new intakes of the 1964 and 1966 Parliaments. Young Members who had been big fish in smaller ponds—whether in their constituencies or in party research groups— found themselves to be small fry at Westminster. Their sense of impotence was exacerbated, in the 1964 Parliament, by the need for their constant presence at Westminster imposed by the small majority of the Labour Government. Their frustration was inflamed by the discussion that had been so persistent in the previous half-dozen years of the need to reform Parliament. In 1966, many of the new Members came from academic jobs where such discussion was an occupational habit: naturally, those who were so conditioned found more or less what they expected to find. Their first impression convinced them that there was an urgent need to reform not only Parliament but the machinery of government generally. The indisputably maddening lack of decent professional auxiliary services at Westminster seemed to confirm the belief that Parliament was a thoroughly inefficient body.

Such frustration was evident in private conversations with Members of both the Conservative and Labour Parties. But the urge for reform was naturally stronger on the Labour side—partly because the Labour Party is, by its nature, more critical of institutions but principally, perhaps, because supporting a Government is a tamer and less interesting way of passing the time than trying to demoralise one. Learning to attack the Government of the day and seeking new policies in Opposition provided a more satisfying occupation for Conservatives on the backbenches as well as on the frontbench. To coincide with the 700th anniversary of Parliament, therefore, and partly stimulated by the frustration of all-night sittings on the Finance Bill, a group of new Labour MPs tabled a long and detailed motion setting out their proposals for reform of parliamentary procedure and gave a press conference to launch it. Morning sittings; the dispatch of all major Bills to Standing Committees; specialist committees on administration and legislation; modern methods of voting procedure to enable the sick to be spared the summons to the Division lobbies; a time-limit on speeches and better facilities—all these were among their proposals.[1]

More significant than the motion itself, however, was a remark made by one of the sponsors, Dr Kerr, who said that the group had rejected the idea of associating one of the older Labour MPs with their activities. 'We take the view that new Members bring in new ideas and we have noted the tendency that the longer people stay here in Parliament the more they regard the system as perfect and not needing improvement. Having been Members for eight months, our experience leaves us in no doubt that, if we are to carry out Harold Wilson's promise that the country would have a greater say in Parliament, we have to get rid of a procedure which is designed to do exactly the opposite. With the bubbling up, the ferment of ideas among the new MPs—of whom we think ourselves symbolic—there has got to be a better channel for the communication of ideas between the backbenches and the Government. The present divorce of government policy-making institutions from the MPs is something we want to reverse.' Another MP in the group, Mr Park, said that backbenchers, by taking part in specialist committees, would have the opportunity to share in the formulation of policy instead of being kept in the position of having to say 'yea' or 'nay' at the end of the process.

The implication of Dr Kerr's observations was plainly that older MPs had been seduced by participation in the parliamentary 'club' or had grown complacent with the years. There is, indeed, an inevitable tendency for men who know an institution well to defend it: on the other hand, it is equally true that men who have not yet learned to know an institution often do not fully understand its merits and its potency. At all events, the general function of Parliament has always been to say 'yea' or 'nay' at the end of a process of policy rather than to be associated formally in its production. A reversal of this situation would not be to restore Parliament to some ancient glory: it would be fundamentally to change its nature. On the other hand, the 'divorce

[1] *The Times*, June 22, 1965.

of government policy-making institutions from the MPs' (by which was presumably meant the separation of Members from Ministers and their departments) has never meant that the views of Members and particularly of the government backbenchers have been excluded from policy-making. The following chapters will show that backbenchers' impact on current policy has been very far from negligible in the post-war years. But before moving on to this more detailed discussion, two more general points may be made.

The first, which I draw from personal discussions with MPs of recent intakes, is that the enthusiasm for parliamentary reform tended to die down as Members have found appropriate niches of activity and interest at Westminster. Some (I do not refer to any of the group mentioned above) admitted within a matter of months that they had revised their initial view and had found Parliament a more useful base from which to influence political opinion than they had supposed. Others found their natural outlet in the traditional parliamentary activity of harrying their own government from a more extremist position than it was prepared to adopt: many of the group who sponsored the motion of June 21, 1965 became quickly identifiable as Members whose energies went mainly into promoting left-wing attitudes on foreign and domestic policy against the line adopted by their own leaders. Not a great deal more was heard about the 'ferment of ideas among the new MPs': it is not quite clear what these new ideas were and most of the new Members (apart from giving enthusiastic support to certain fairly fashionable attitudes on social 'morality') quickly and understandably fell back on promoting the traditional attitudes of their own party.

The second general point to be made is that Ministers and former Ministers of all parties have testified convincingly to the attention Governments pay to backbench opinion. Their argument is not necessarily to be rejected because they have held ministerial office. Lord Morrison of Lambeth, who had held senior Cabinet office in the wartime coalition and post-war Labour administrations, analysed the influence exerted by backbenchers on the framing of legislation as follows: 'This may be described as the process of concession in advance of parliamentary proceedings, though sometimes Ministers may prefer to save up concessions until Parliament is dealing with the matter. To the extent that the Government in shaping its policy has anticipated backbench and Opposition criticisms, Ministers are entitled to the credit.'[1] The leaders of both main political parties, whether they are in Government or Opposition, pursue this technique of anticipating the reactions of their followers and, so far as possible, avoiding hostile reactions either by adapting their own conduct accordingly, or by a process of softening up the critics in their own party by advance persuasion. Sometimes a combination of concession and persuasion is used.

Morrison, who had never been a Minister to suffer backbench revolts gladly, conceded that they were not always to be deplored: sometimes they gave reality to parliamentary life and stimulated public interest in the House of Commons. The Labour Government of 1945–51, in which Morrison had continuously been a senior Minister (among his offices had been that of Leader of the House) had to contend with a full share of backbench pressures and revolts. How the Attlee Government set about responding to the feelings of its backbenchers in these years has been described by Herbert Bowden, himself subsequently Leader of the House from 1964–6, in a television broadcast made when he was Opposition Chief Whip. When the Government discussed business coming before Parliament, the Chief Whip would be called in and would be asked, probably with the Leader of the House, what would be the views of backbenchers on particular parts of the legislation in question: could he take soundings; did he already know the views of backbenchers? The Chief Whip would then give his advice to the Cabinet on these points —and Bowden commented: 'If the Chief Whip were to say to the Cabinet: if you do this, there is likely to be a great deal of opposition from our own backbenchers, I am pretty sure that that influence of the backbenchers would be felt in the Cabinet and they would think twice about introducing a clause in legislation which would be likely to cause trouble for them on the floor of the House.'[2] Bowden, it will be noted, only said 'think twice'. He also spoke of objections to a clause of a Bill rather than to a Bill itself. But objections in principle to a Bill are normally taken into account at an earlier stage. It may be that a Government will feel that the balance of political advantage or sheer necessity will drive them to go ahead with a Bill which they

---

[1] Herbert Morrison, *Government and Parliament: A Survey from the Inside*, pp. 166–7. See Morrison also for an account of the various consultative mechanisms that have been employed between the Labour front and backbenches over the years.

[2] *Power and Parliament*, June 20, 1963: BBC transcript.

know will raise a storm among their supporters. The Labour Government's introduction of 'wage-freeze' clauses into their Prices and Incomes Bill in 1966 was a case in point: sheer economic crisis obliged them to ride over the objections they anticipated and to bank on the majority of backbenchers rallying to them in the crisis since the alternative could only be to unseat the Government. Yet no Government damages the morale of its followers in this way without very strong reasons.

In the broadcast already referred to, the former Conservative Chief Whip, Martin Redmayne, agreed with Bowden about the extent to which policy is swayed by privately expressed backbench opinion and pointed out that the Chief Whip sees the Prime Minister at least once every day, often more than that, and has 'absolute right of access to him'. The Chief Whip also attends other ministerial meetings, though not a Cabinet Minister himself, and frequently gives advice on the parliamentary consequences of proposed action. On the same occasion, the then Leader of the House, Iain Macleod, also testified to the value of private party meetings as a means of keeping Ministers in touch with backbench, and sometimes specialist opinion. Macleod also pointed out that the committee stage of almost any Bill produced a considerable number of amendments which represented the Government's second thoughts—though they were admittedly in normal circumstances minor ones.

So much for the assertions of a fairly representative selection of frontbenchers about the influence of backbenchers. It may be, however, that frontbenchers will be suspected of overstressing, for reasons of political tact, the attention they pay to their supporters. I now turn, therefore, to an account of the form backbench influence has taken in post-war politics.

(ii)

Since 1945, the leaders of both major political parties, whether in or out of power, have had to contend with a series of more or less rebellious pressures exerted by groups of their own backbenchers who have wished to bring about a reversal of official policies. In a study primarily concerned with the influence of the House of Commons over the Government, the pressures of backbenchers against their leaders are mainly of interest when their party is in office. Rebellions within a party which is out of power have a different significance:

186

their chief effect is likely to be either on the policies offered by that party at the next general election or on the public's opinion of the internal cohesion of the Opposition, which is generally taken as one measurement of its fitness to govern. Though the rebellions of a party in Opposition may have considerable political significance, the effect is usually delayed so far as the Government of the country is concerned. Therefore, although brief reference will be made to the pressures exerted by Opposition backbenchers on *their* leaders, the main concern of the following chapters will be with government backbenchers—leaving Opposition influence on the Executive for separate consideration.

It is logical as well as chronologically convenient to discuss separately the influence of Labour and Conservative backbenchers over their leaders. For backbench pressures within the two parties since the war have generally focussed on different kinds of policy and the backbenchers on the two sides have employed dissimilar techniques. Moreover, the effect that backbench revolts and pressure groupings have had has been very different in the two parties. The activities of Labour backbenchers in trying to change official party policies have been both more ferociously insubordinate and, at the same time, less effective than the comparable activities on the Conservative side, taking the post-war period as a whole.

Throughout their period of power, the Labour Government of 1945–51 had to contend with open rebellions by their own backbenchers which were frequently carried into the Division lobbies and which were designed to force the Government to change its foreign and defence policies. The very size of the Labour majority at the 1945 General Election was an encouragement to malcontents to carry their activities to the point of rebellion since they could feel confident that they could do so without jeopardising Labour's hold on power. The contrast between the rebellious mood of the Labour Party under Mr Attlee's Prime Ministership, when the Government enjoyed the overwhelming majority of 146, and the quiescent reaction of the Labour rank and file under the Wilson Government of 1964, with its tenuous majority of three to four in the House, needs no elaboration. Yet the Wilson Government was asking its followers to accept policies which departed radically from traditional Labour attitudes.

So, of course, was the Attlee Government on a number of issues: defence, policy towards Russia, conscription and Palestine in particular. The result was a series of major rebellions in the years after 1945. Yet despite the frequency and numerical strength of these revolts, the Attlee Government was not permanently deflected from any of its chosen policies as a result of them. For the rebellions related almost entirely to foreign and defence issues—the one aspect of the Government's activities in which it could be confident that it had the support of the Conservative Opposition. In contrast, there were no comparable backbench rebellions against the Governments' domestic policies which were bitterly opposed by the Conservatives. There was no reason why there should be. During the immediate post-war years, the Labour Government (again, there is a clear distinction between the Attlee Government and the Wilson Government up to 1966) did pursue a 'socialist' domestic policy with which the bulk of the party could find little fault. It nationalised a number of important industries; it maintained a controlled economy; it established an entirely new welfare state on socialist principles. With all this, there was no disagreement on the Labour backbenches: indeed, the Government's supporters were unified by the unceasing and bitter attack which the Conservative Party, supported by the bulk of the press, maintained against the Government's legislative programme. The unremitting Conservative propaganda, in and out of the House, for an end to nationalisation, the restoration of free markets and the dismantling of controls, which the Conservatives alleged unnecessarily hampered the freedom of the individual as a consumer, was a great force for unity on the Labour benches.

No such unity was possible for the Labour Party on foreign affairs, however, for the simple reason that a substantial element of the party believed that the policy pursued by the Foreign Secretary, Ernest Bevin, represented a fundamental departure from socialist principles. From the start, the left-wing Labour Members of Parliament sought to deflect the Government from its policy of close association with the United States and the alignment of the British, with the Americans, in a defensive alliance against Stalinist Russia. Resistance on the Labour backbenches to the American loan negotiated by the Government in December 1945 was the first major manifestation of this form of protest. To some extent, this revolt anticipated the later Bevanite movement but it cut right across the normal Left–Right distinctions in the Labour Party. An examination of the Division lists shows that there was a roughly equal balance between Left and Right Labour MPs among those who voted against the loan. Some of Bevan's closest associates, including his wife, Jennie Lee, and Michael Foot, were among those who voted against the American loan on the grounds that it would make British policy subservient to Washington. The Left were particularly resentful against the close Anglo–American bonds which, they felt, broke away from traditional Labour attitudes of friendliness towards the Soviet Union. On the other hand, there were important MPs from the Right and Centre of the Labour Party who voted against the loan and some who might normally be called Left-inclined who voted for it. Richard Stokes, a Right-wing Labour MP, was one of those who sponsored an amendment (which was not called) to the motion approving the loan agreement. This amendment sought to have the loan rejected on the grounds that it committed Britain to an international monetary system which was likely to frustrate the effective planning of British industry and trade. Stokes was one of those who voted against the loan. Another young Labour MP resigned as a Parliamentary Private Secretary in order to be able to oppose the loan; he was the future Chancellor of the Exchequer, James Callaghan.[1]

Indeed, hostility to the loan existed on both sides of the House: the argument cut right across party. Although the Attlee Government suffered the embarrassment of having twenty-three Labour Members voting against the loan and forty-four Members abstaining, there was at least the comfort that the Conservative Opposition was no less divided. Though counselled by Churchill to abstain (as 118 Conservatives did on a free vote) seventy-two Conservatives voted against the loan and nine actually voted for it. The impact of the American loan on the psychology of both parties was significant: it marked the beginning of a resentment of the American post-war dominance and of Britain's new dependence on American money. This resentment has pervaded sections of both parties intermittently since then and has been particularly marked on the right of the Conservative Party and in Labour's Left-wing.[2]

Indeed, so far as the Labour Party was concerned, the revolt against the US loan, though not confined to the Left, was the start of the long drawn-out attempt of the party's extremists to detach Britain from its close association with the United States. Henceforth, however, the attempt was to manifest itself mainly in defence and

[1] For the Division list, see H.C. Deb., Vol. 417, cols. 735–9.

[2] For the effects of the loan on British political sentiment, see Francis Boyd, *British Politics in Transition, 1945–1963* (Pall Mall, 1964), pp. 127 et seq.

foreign, rather than in economic policy, and it was to produce its most dramatic eruption in the movement for unilateral disarmament which threatened the leadership of Hugh Gaitskell in 1960–1. For more than fifteen years, variations on the same basic defence theme were hurled against the official policies of the party by a group which, with remarkable consistency over the years, continued to number between fifty and sixty MPs. Of these, a small handful might be described as Communist sympathisers, but the majority were either pacifist-inclined or radical-leftists who wanted to create for Britain an independent mediating rôle between the US and the USSR and could not accept that all the virtue in the East–West cold war was with the West.

One of the main rebellions against the Attlee Government's foreign policy occurred a year after the American loan. In November 1946, an amendment was moved to the Address in reply to the Queen's Speech by Richard Crossman (then a Labour backbench Member), demanding the Government to 'recast its conduct of international affairs' so as to provide a '. . . democratic and constructive Socialist alternative to an otherwise inevitable conflict between American Capitalism and Soviet Communism in which all hope of World Government would be destroyed'.[1] The amendment was not forced to a division by the sponsors. But two Independent Labour Party Members forced a vote with the result that seventy Labour MPs abstained. The Conservative Opposition voted with the Government, which obtained a majority of 353 against none (the two ILP Members acted as tellers). The rebels had made their point and they continued to make it on innumerable occasions in subsequent years. The foreign affairs group of the Labour Party was the main instrument employed by the Leftists in their campaign against Ernest Bevin.[2] Several strands of internal Labour 'opposition' were woven together in these years. Anti-Bevinism was also fuelled by the dislike of the Zionists (for whom Crossman was also a spokesman) of Bevin's policy for Palestine. This, in 1948, also led to a revolt of Labour backbenchers against their Government when thirty of them voted against the Palestine Bill in 1948.[3] More important, however, was the revolt of Labour backbenchers against the Government's conscription policy.

[1] H.C. Deb., Vol. 430, col. 526.
[2] Ivor Bulmer-Thomas, *The Growth of the British Political Party System* Vol. 2, 1924–64 (John Baker, 1965), p. 164. [3] Ibid., p. 165.

This began in 1946 when the Left was in general rebellion against the Attlee Government's foreign policy but it attracted far wider support in the Labour Party than the normal Left-wing outcry against the American connection ever did. Dislike, even fear, of conscription was felt in all sections of the Party. Instinctively, many of those bred in the pre-war Labour movement regarded conscription as politically immoral. They not only disliked compulsion; whether they were pacifist or not, they particularly resented compulsory recruitment into the armed forces to defend (as they saw it) the capitalist order they existed to destroy. To understand the instinctive feelings of Labour men and women on this issue one must remember the form that much Labour anti-war propaganda took in the years before the Labour Party itself was totally involved in the struggle against Hitler. In Labour pre-war mythology, wars were created largely by profiteering armament-kings who looked on with equanimity while working-class boys were conscripted to die in defence of capitalism and profits made out of munitions. These are heavily dated sentiments in the second half of the twentieth century but they were once real enough. Labour was strongly pacifist in tradition. Though conscription, which at least had the merit of egalitarianism, had been accepted as a necessity in the war against Hitler, old feelings die hard and in 1946 they could easily be revived—especially when conscription seemed to be directed at Soviet Russia, the state which, for all its faults, had set a Socialist example to the world. Besides, the trade unions had always feared that military conscription might pave the way for industrial conscription. For all these reasons, the revolt against conscription was successful enough to show how potent backbench feeling can be when it spreads right across a party and is not confined to a single wing which can be separated from the rest.

At a meeting of the Parliamentary Labour Party on November 6, 1946, the Prime Minister, Clement Attlee, indicated that the Government intended to bring in a Bill to retain conscription on the grounds that voluntary recruitment would be inadequate for Britain's man-power needs. The question was debated by the Parliamentary Party and the Government secured a favourable vote in the proportion of about five to two.[1] This was one of the rare occasions when the Labour Party has not only discussed, but has also voted on a major issue of Labour Government policy after the Prime Minister

[1] R. T. McKenzie, *British Political Parties*, 2nd Edn. (Heinemann, 1963), p. 451.

191

had virtually made it a vote of confidence. A similar occasion was the vote taken on the Wilson Government's East of Suez policy in 1966— again after a speech by the Prime Minister. For a Prime Minister to take part in a debate inside his own party logically runs counter to the assertion by Labour Prime Ministers that, on policy matters, they are answerable to the House, not their own party, and that if discontented Labour MPs wish to take punitive action they must do it on the floor of the House. What a Labour Prime Minister would do if, after making such a private speech to his followers, he were defeated by a vote of the party meeting is probably beside any practical point: a political leader can usually assess the outcome in advance and if he expected defeat, he probably would not speak. But on such occasions, certainly in 1946 and 1966, the Prime Minister of the day considered the morale and the assent of party feeling sufficiently important to take some risk with his personal reputation in making a personal appeal to his followers in the House.

In 1946, Attlee got the majority he wanted but discontent was so widespread in the Labour Party that the campaign against conscription was carried from the comparative privacy of the Parliamentary Labour Party's Committee to the floor of the House of Commons. In November 1946, forty-five dissident Labour MPs voted for an amendment to the Address on the King's Speech to register their disapproval of conscription and as many as 132 abstained on the Division. The Government, however, was rescued by the Conservatives. After the introduction of the Bill itself, which imposed national service of eighteen months on all youths, the protest campaign among Labour MPs continued with mounting force, inside and outside the Chamber. Once again the Prime Minister had to defend the Bill at a meeting of the Parliamentary Labour Party but in spite of his efforts, seventy-two Labour MPs voted against it and as many more abstained on Second Reading of the Bill.

As a result, the Government made a partial concession and reduced the conscription period from eighteen to twelve months, on which the Bill was passed with only seventeen Labour MPs voting against it. This time the Conservatives forced a Division because of the reduction in the conscription period. The Government's concession to its followers, however, endured for little more than a year. In 1948, an Amending Bill was introduced to raise the period of service to eighteen months on account of the deteriorating international situation and the Russian blockade of Berlin. Even now, forty-five Labour MPs voted against the Bill on second reading and many more abstained. The Government again carried the day with the Conservative support. In the end, therefore, it could be said that the conscription rebels had been defeated—and even the original concession did not destroy the principle of the Bill, though it was to the *principle* of conscription that the Labour Party objected. Nevertheless, this was the most successful backbench Labour revolt against its own Government's policy in the immediate post-war years and only the developing gravity of the international situation enabled the Government to have all its own way in the end.[1] Why, then, did this revolt fail when it had such widespread support on the Labour backbenches? It did so because no group of backbenchers, however strong, can force their views upon a Government of their own party if the general climate of opinion in the country is against them. In 1946–8, despite the potency of the conscription revolt in internal Labour Party terms, and even though the rebels were too strong to be disciplined by their leaders, the revolt could not be followed through because conscription was generally accepted by the public as a necessity. In such circumstances, the Attlee Government could obtain sustenance from public opinion, from press support, and from the knowledge that the Conservatives, on such an issue, could not play politics and must support them. The anti-conscription Socialists of the 1940s were an ineffective minority in the House of Commons because they represented so small a minority in the country. The majority of the House—Conservatives and Government pro-conscriptionists—represented the consensus of the nation on a major issue and, therefore, the Government's defeat of its rebels was no symptom of backbench powerlessness before an arrogant Executive but a sign that parliamentary government can, despite party barriers, adequately represent feeling in the nation.

The Government knew that, in the last resort, it was safe on this issue. But the question therefore arises whether the opponents of conscription, and of the Government's foreign policy generally in these years, only pressed their rebellions as far as they did because

[1] 'The original revolt on the national service issue is perhaps the most striking single illustration of the effectiveness of back-bench opposition to Government policy during the lifetime of the 1945 and 1950 Governments.' R. T. McKenzie, *British Political Parties*, pp. 451–2. For a general account of the revolt see McKenzie, ibid., and also Ivor Bulmer-Thomas, *The Growth of the British Political Party System*, Vol. 2, pp. 166–7.

they understood that their activities would not bring their Government down. The contrast between the rebelliousness of Labour backbenchers in these years and their quiescence when Labour was in power with very small majorities in the 1950 and 1964 Parliaments proves that the risk, or otherwise, of bringing a Government down as a result of a backbench revolt in the Division lobby is carefully calculated by the rebels. Labour discontent with the Attlee Government's foreign policy was not less strong in 1950–1 than it had been earlier—but they were not going to dethrone Attlee to make Churchill Prime Minister.

Yet it would be quite wrong to assume from this backbench caution that, in a duel between a Government and its backbenchers, all the advantages are on the side of the Government or that the backbenchers are deprived of effective influence because they dare not risk bringing their own Government down. For one thing, a Government will always do what it can to meet its backbenchers half-way because it needs to avoid the damaging publicity of such episodes. Equally, political leaders know that their power is ultimately dependent on their active followers in all sections of a Party: inside almost any Cabinet most sections of party opinion have one or two representatives. So far as possible, therefore, the conclusions of a Cabinet do normally represent something like a compromise between different shades of opinion in the parliamentary rank and file.

But on certain great issues—foreign and defence policy are the obvious examples—a Cabinet must have regard to a wider consensus than that of its own party. It must look to what it apprehends to be national feeling and national interest. (The two may not be identical but the Government must make the best approximation it can.) The greater the issue in national terms, the less a Government which has exercised competent judgment needs to give way to a strong minority group in its own party for the sake of party unity, and the less chance the rebels have of securing concessions—which is not to say that any Government would willingly choose this sort of dangerous victory over a substantial section of its own followers. Conversely, when backbench pressure groupings are concerned with less vital issues, they stand a better chance of influencing government policy.

Although the Labour Left was rather less actively antipathetic to the United States in the final years of the 1945–50 Parliament, foreign policy remained the chief focus of backbench discontent. In these years, the Government wholly failed to silence or manage the critics of its foreign policy on its own benches. The 'Keep Left' group of Labour Members produced pamphlets, propagandised the press and kept up a constant attempt to deflect the Government from its bi-partisan foreign policy. This group played an important part in the conscription episode and its members were to be the nucleus of the 'Bevanite' group which was formed after the resignation of Aneurin Bevan from the Cabinet in 1951.

Among the embarrassments suffered by the Attlee Government in the declining years of the 1945 Parliament was the affair of the 'Nenni telegram' which had been sent by extreme Left-wingers to Nenni, the leader of the Italian Socialists allied to the Communists—despite the Labour Party's official support for the Italian Free Socialist Party. This led to the expulsion of the Left- wing organiser of the Nenni telegram, J. Platt-Mills. In 1948 and 1949, other Left-wingers, Konni Zilliacus, L. J. Solley and Lester Hutchinson, were expelled for extreme Left-wing views. These isolated incidents of Government reprisals against their backbenchers indicate the nature and the limitations of party leaders' disciplinary control over troublesome supporters. A Government can discipline a small, unrepresentative group—and especially one which is widely regarded as striking at a fundamental party position, as these Left-wingers, in their praise of Communist Governments, seemed to strike at the basis of post-war Labour attitudes. They were expelled because the views they expressed were regarded as fundamentally subversive to the party—and yet, despite the danger they might represent, they could only be expelled because they were themselves insignificant and isolated from the main stream of the party's thinking. The far more potent rebellion against conscription had not been susceptible to discipline: nor in the final stages of the 1945–50 Parliament could the Government take reprisals against either the fairly formidable rebellion of Labour backbenchers against the Ireland Bill—on the ground that it perpetuated partition—or against the Zionists in the party, who also resisted the Government's Palestine Bill.[1] None of these events put the life of the Government at risk, despite adverse votes and abstentions by backbenchers, because they took place only when the Government was assured of Conservative support, or neutrality, or of adequate support from its own side. For this reason, they had no influence on policy. On the other hand, they were worrying and

[1] For a short description of these episodes: Ivor Bulmer-Thomas, *The Growth of the British Political Party System*, Vol. 2, p. 165.

damaging for the Government—yet, because so many Members were involved, it was impossible to take action against them. The bigger and graver the revolt, the safer the rebels are from punishment.

The 1950 General Election, however, transformed the situation by reducing the Labour Government's majority to six. Warnings by Ministers that backbench rebellions would not be tolerated in future hardly seemed necessary. In June 1950, the Korean War broke out and, bringing as it did a wholesale commitment of the British Government to the anti-Communist camp and a major rearmament programme, it might have been expected that an even bigger series of backbench rebellions would have begun. Indeed, Labour backbench criticism of the Government's actions was intense. Every effort was made to put pressure on the Government in private, and discontented Left-wingers found an outlet in signing protesting Early Day Motions on the Order Paper of the House. As it happened, the Korean War was partly responsible for the most traumatic blow inflicted on the Government during the short life of this Parliament—a blow far more damaging than any of the other backbench revolts had been to the Labour Party's standing in the country. In April 1951, Aneurin Bevan resigned as Minister of Health (accompanied by Harold Wilson, President of the Board of Trade, and John Freeman, Parliamentary Secretary to the Ministry of Supply) on the grounds that Hugh Gaitskell's Budget had imposed National Health Service charges. The cost of the Korean War was the major reason for these charges, although it is also probably true that Bevan was partly influenced by chagrin at having failed to obtain a more senior Cabinet office when Ernest Bevin gave up the Foreign Office shortly before his death.

Yet neither the Korean War nor Bevan's resignation shook the Government in the House of Commons. The resigning Ministers did nothing in the House which might enable the Conservatives to defeat the Government. In fact, the only major issues on which Labour backbenchers were prepared to vote against the Government were the Seretse Khama affair in 1950[1] and the Reserve and Auxiliary Forces Bill of 1951 on account of the latter's conscription requirements. Yet again, these rebellions took place only when it was obvious that, as in the 1945 Parliament, the Attlee administration would be saved by the Conservative Party.

[1] Seretse Khama, a tribal chief of the Bechuanaland Protectorate, had created trouble in his tribe by marrying an English girl and, to avoid a rebellion, the British Government withdrew recognition from him.

The contrast between the temerity of the Labour Left-wingers in the Division lobbies during the 1945 Parliament and their timidity after 1950 might superficially appear to provide evidence supporting the view that the activities of backbenchers are no more than a charade which is shown up as such once it is put to the test. Yet there are some indications from officials who have been able to watch the comparative performances of post-war Governments from behind the scenes which suggest that, to their eyes, the 1950 Government was more conciliatory than most Governments are to minor pressure groups: the accuracy of this statement, however, can only be tested when the official papers are available for a detailed history of Labour government in this short Parliament. This apart, however, the contrast between the rebellious backbenchers of 1945–50 and the unrebellious backbenchers of 1950–1 is proof of nothing more than that open revolts in the Division lobbies are a poor indicator of the influence exerted on a Government by its followers. Indeed, one might almost go so far as to say that rebellions such as those mounted by sections of the Labour Party after 1945 are a sign that the normal channels of influence have broken down: a symptom of the *failure* of the group in question and therefore doomed in advance to fail. On the other hand, such rebellions, though themselves almost a recognition by their authors of the failure to change Government policy, may have a profound impact on public opinion—and therefore on subsequent voting behaviour by the electorate.

The Labour Government of 1950 was a tired and dispirited administration. Harassed by the Conservative Opposition through the night as well as by day, it was forced to subject its backbenchers to an intolerable strain, requiring even invalids to come to the House to register their votes. Ministers were tired—in many cases as a result of continuous years of Government service since 1940. Deep divisions existed in the party and these communicated themselves, through the House of Commons and through the press, to the public. As one member of the Government, Hugh Dalton, was to put it: 'From 1950 onwards the Labour Party lost its unity. The drive and self-confidence, the will to power and to compromise rather than to split, which had carried us through the shining years, were gone. Factions fought and slanged each other in public, seeming to think that public opinion, which sways voters, neither saw nor heard them.'[1]

In fact, public opinion saw and noted the disarray in the Labour

[1] Hugh Dalton, *High Tide and After*, p. 353.

197

Party all too well. The long tale of rebellions and disunity over foreign and defence policy, culminating in the late forties and in 1950–1, was a major factor contributing to the change in public sentiment which turned Labour out of office in 1951 even if a less potent one than a sense of disillusion and resentment of austerity. Moreover, it is reasonable to suppose that the subsequent period of Labour Opposition was prolonged to thirteen years partly as a result of this same disunity, mainly over foreign and defence policy, which continued to handicap the party's leaders. The period 1951–57 saw the rise of the Bevanite faction when, for the first time, the Left-wing of the party had a really able leader. The Labour Party was rent over German rearmament and the Bevanites were now prepared to take their hostility to official Labour Opposition policy into the Division lobby. They took it also to the Party Conference where they commanded the support of a majority of Labour constituency delegates and where the official leadership of the party had to depend for support on the votes of the trade unions. So too, the Bevanites rebelled against the broad support given by their leaders at this time to the Conservative Government's policy of dependence on a nuclear defence 'deterrent'. For a short period, indeed, the Whip was withdrawn from Bevan.

It was after this exercise in Labour disunity that the Conservatives, under the Prime Ministership of Anthony Eden, appealed to the country in the General Election of May 1955 and were rewarded by a new period of power and an increased majority. For a brief time after 1956, when the Conservative Government plunged into the disastrous Suez adventure, the Labour Party in Parliament achieved a temporary renewal of harmony through its detestation of the courses pursued by the Eden Government—though in the country, Labour voters were far from equally united in disapproving of the action against Egypt. The Labour Leader, Hugh Gaitskell, and Bevan submerged their temperamental and political antipathy to each other in order to hound their political opponents. It was now the Conservatives' political unity which seemed at risk but, after the resignation of Eden, the danger quickly passed.

Labour, however, was less fortunate. A new rift was developing. Although Gaitskell and Bevan, reconciled to each other at the 1957 Party Conference, were now allied against the former 'Bevanites' of the Left-wing, a new movement for the unilateral renunciation of nuclear weapons was gathering pace inside the Labour Party. In

1959, the third successive Conservative general election victory, again with an increased majority, plunged Labour into a frenzy of self-criticism not merely over defence policy—but over domestic policy as well. Gaitskell and the moderate reformist elements of the party wished to keep Labour firmly in line with the defence policies of the nuclear-armed Western alliance and also to modify some of the traditional Socialist attitudes of the party towards domestic policy—notably, to remove the Labour Party's uncompromising formal commitment to complete public ownership by traditional forms of nationalisation. On both issues Gaitskell was bitterly opposed by traditional Socialists and also by the unions, now no longer the bulwark of the Right. At the annual Party Conference of 1960 the official Labour defence policy was overturned and Gaitskell's leadership threatened. During the following year, he fought back, using as his base the Parliamentary Labour Party for his counter-attack, and the official defence policy was accepted at the Party Conference of 1961. By the time of his death in 1963 Gaitskell had restored a large degree of unity to the Labour Party and had secured the acceptance of moderate policies which played a part in helping the party to power, though by so small a majority, in 1964. The significance of this episode in the present context is in Gaitskell's use of the parliamentary party to re-establish his control over the Party Conference, the dissident unions and the hostile constituency parties. This rebellion, occurring at a time when it was fashionable to regard parliamentary parties as subordinate to the pressures of party organisations, re-established Labour as a parliamentary party in the traditional sense.

Detailed attention to backbench Labour pressures against official policies of their leaders in Opposition has no place in a discussion mainly concerned with parliamentary influence over the Executive. Obviously, the internal Labour 'opposition' could have even less effect on the Conservative Government's policies than it had on those of the Labour administration—though the Government had to watch carefully and reply to the campaign for nuclear disarmament which at times looked like reaching dangerous proportions. Yet the disharmony in the Labour Party during these years was highly significant in parliamentary politics. First, the very fact of its disunity (whether over defence or nationalisation) made Labour an ineffective Opposition in Parliament. Repeatedly the Conservatives could make play in the House of Commons with the divisions within the

Opposition—and the electorate took note. Secondly, the defence controversy as such helped to dissipate confidence in Labour's capacity to govern strongly. During the troubled years of Labour Opposition, a former Cabinet Minister of the 1945 Government expressed to the author his view that the impression of Labour as an 'unpatriotic party' after it left office in 1951 had done it profound damage with the electorate. Even official attitudes of the Opposition contributed to this: the obvious sympathy for the Egyptians at the time of Suez and for the rebels in Cyprus when British troops and their families were being murdered there were obvious examples. But in particular, the defence controversy may have helped to revive memories of Labour's hostility to rearmament in the years before the war. This impression of 'unsoundness' probably contributed to the meagre size of the majority given to Labour in 1964 even though there had been clear indications beforehand that the electorate wished to turn the Conservatives out. Why, at the last minute, did so many voters hesitate to do so: why, when the day came, were the Liberals given a much larger, and the Labour Party a much smaller share of the national vote than had been expected? It may be that, at the moment of decision, many electors who on other grounds wished to put the Conservatives out, hesitated to entrust power to a Labour Party which had incurred suspicion because of its foreign and defence attitudes in Opposition. It may be that the Conservative Leader, Sir Alec Douglas-Home, did wisely for his Party in stressing foreign policy, though at the time he was criticised for doing so on the grounds that the electorate is normally more influenced by domestic policy issues.

At all events, there is enough circumstantial evidence that even rebellions of backbenchers in Opposition have a considerable longer-term impact on politics though they influence, not the Government itself, but the electors. But when a party is in power, backbench pressure can have a considerable direct effect on policy-making. That it did not do so during the period of Labour administration from 1945–51 can be explained on three counts. First, the mass of the party was content with the Government's domestic performance and its social and economic 'revolution'. The backbenchers had no quarrel with their leaders and therefore the question of exerting contradictory pressures in this field hardly arose. Secondly, the rebellions that occurred were almost entirely over fundamentals of foreign and defence policy and they were rooted in a particular segment of the party so that it would be inaccurate to equate the 'rebels' of these years with the Labour rank and file as a whole. When a rebellion was more widespread, as in the case of conscription, it came much nearer success. The failure of the conscription rebellion is to be explained on the third count—which applied also to the other immediate post-war Labour backbench rebellions: the Government had the support of the Conservatives.

Despite their defeat, these rebellions were an integral and important part of the nation's political debate and though the argument was carried on in the press and at party conferences, there is no doubt that its most regular and potent forum was the House of Commons. The Labour Left-wing failed to have its way in these controversies not because an all-powerful Executive exercised dominance over the House of Commons but because the rebels failed to achieve any substantial following in the electorate, whose views were reflected by the majority of the House.

Chapter Seven

The Influence of the Backbench Member 1951–1957

The relationship between the Conservative leadership and its followers during the post-war period has assumed a pattern which differs in many important respects from that displayed on the Labour side. In Opposition after 1945, the Conservatives were remarkably free from dissension, whereas some of the worst outbreaks of Labour strife took place when the party was out of office. On the other hand, when the Conservative Party was in power, its backbenchers showed a greater tendency to exert rebellious pressures on their Government over a wider range of issues than Labour backbenchers had done when their leaders were in office. But though they were more numerous, Conservative backbench rebellions were in a different style from those on the Labour side and, more important, they were generally over a different sort of issue. Finally, Conservative backbench pressures on a Conservative Government have tended to be more effective in influencing policy than Labour pressures on a Labour Government.

The reasons for the internal harmony of the Conservative Opposition after 1945 are clear. Although there were differences of emphasis about methods and although the public appearance of the post-war generation of Conservatives—notably those who called themselves the One Nation Group—was very different from that of the older type of Tory, a basic unity of purpose cemented all segments of the Party after its defeat by Labour. Conservatives of all dispositions were united in their determination to restore, unfettered, the freedom of private enterprise and of the market-place, though in a fashion which would fit the context of the post-war social and economic climate. These were the years in which the Conservatives produced their Industrial and Agricultural Charters—designed, as Lord

Woolton, the Party Chairman, said in his memoirs, to stop the nation from believing that the Conservativism being expounded in the late forties was no different from that of the thirties.[1] The Industrial Charter emphasised that, while the Conservative Party was determined to restore private enterprise, it would not abandon all control over the economy nor countenance any risk of a return to unemployment. Moreover, while attacking restrictive practices by managements and employees, the document accepted the nationalisation of some industries (but not including road transport or steel) and embodied a Workers' Charter which was to provide for the status and security of workers.

Yet the Industrial Charter and other manifestations of the Party's policy-shaping after 1945 represented not a revolution in policy but rather a reformulation of traditional Conservative attitudes. The work of R. A. Butler and his colleagues at the Research Department of the Conservative Party in these years was designed, as a study of the Party during this period has expressed it,

> . . . to retrieve the Conservative Party from the image, which the 1945 election campaign had helped to foster, of a party relatively indifferent to social reform; to rationalise its response to Labour's innovations; and, by establishing the limits beyond which Conservative acquiescence would not go, to delineate the distinctively Conservative manner in which the party proposed to take over, administer, and improve upon the newly developed social and economic structure of society.[2]

Harold Macmillan, one of the Conservatives responsible for producing the Industrial Charter, made the same point unambiguously. Referring to accusations by Lord Beaverbrook that he had seduced the Conservative Party into a progressive statement of policy, Macmillan said:

> I would gladly accept the blame for this, if it were blame. But in fact there has been no seduction. The *Industrial Charter* is merely a restatement in the light of modern conditions of the fundamental and lasting principles of our party.[3]

[1] *The Memoirs of the Rt. Hon. The Earl of Woolton, CH, PC, DL, LL.D.* (Cassell, 1959), p. 347.

[2] J. D. Hoffman, *The Conservative Party in Opposition, 1945–51* (MacGibbon & Kee, 1964), p. 208.

[3] Quoted in J. D. Hoffman, *The Conservative Party in Opposition, 1945–51*, p. 158.

The very fact that the Industrial Charter attracted no serious resistance except from a handful of Conservatives on the extreme right, who were dismayed at its acceptance of many Socialist measures,[1] may be taken as evidence that it offended no basic tenets of the Conservative creed which, since Peel's leadership of the party, has always included bowing to accomplished political facts.

Although the Conservative leadership during this period suffered from little open rebelliousness in its rank and file, there were occasions of confusion over policy. But these arose largely from the unusual situation that the Conservative and Labour Parties had so recently been locked together in coalition. There was, inevitably, a distinction between the opposition-mindedness of many Conservative backbenchers and the sense of responsibility felt by Churchill, and other Conservative leaders who had so recently left office, so far as the main strands of economic and defence policy were concerned. Thus, Churchill indicated to his party that he would wish it to abstain on the vote to approve the American loan in 1945 and would deprecate any large number of Conservative votes against it. In the event, as already noted, the party split three ways—much as it was to do, momentarily, in 1965 over the then Labour Government's Rhodesia policy.

The steadfast support given to the foreign and defence policy of the 1945 Labour Government by the Conservative Opposition was based on their assessment of the merits of the case, but it was undoubtedly made easier for the Conservatives to give it by their admiration for the personal qualities of the Foreign Secretary, Ernest Bevin. Indeed, the hangover from the war-time alliance between the two major parties was evident in a verbal slip by Bevin in his opening words after Churchill had sat down during the House of Commons debate on the US Loan:

> I never thought that I should meet my Right Honourable *Friend* in the capacity of an abstainer.[2]

Conservative confusion on this and other issues during the immediate post-war period was partly the result of a lack of clear

[1] J. D. Hoffman, *The Conservative Party in Opposition, 1945–51*, pp. 154–66.
[2] My italics; Churchill was no longer Bevin's Rt. Hon. Friend in the parliamentary sense of the word. H.C. Deb., Vol. 417, col. 725.

leadership[1] and partly a symptom of the party's unfamiliarity with the techniques of Opposition, after so long a spell in office. It was certainly not caused by backbench revolts against any clear line of policy advocated by the party's leaders but unacceptable to the rank and file.

Detestation of Socialist domestic policies, and a determination to refit the Tory shop-window so as to recapture the allegiance of voters who had defected in 1945, provided common ground for all Conservatives during their years in the political wilderness. But once back in office after 1951, the Conservatives began to experience a two-way pull between the party leaders, who were concerned to rebuild their party's popularity with the electorate by pursuing 'consensus' policies, and the Conservative rank and file in Parliament who were anxious to push the Government into accepting more distinctively Tory policies. A study of Conservative backbench relations with their Governments after 1951 suggests that rank-and-file MPs had a positive and discernible influence on policy-making.

If Labour Governments must adopt some right-of-centre policies (to the distress of their own activists) in order to command the middle ground of politics, Conservative administrations must pursue left-of-centre policies and play the rôle of a 'national' rather than a party government. The 1951 and the 1955 General Elections were both won by the Conservatives largely on their claim to be a party of competent administration; on the personality of their leading figures; and on discontent with Socialist Government. They were not won because the electorate was positively in love with Conservative policies in any doctrinaire sense. Moreover, Winston Churchill was more inclined by disposition to head a Ministry of All the Talents than to be a Conservative Party Leader of the traditional sort. Faced, therefore, with a Prime Minister with longings for a leadership above the narrow confines of party interest and with tacticians in the Government whose main concern was with the electorate as a whole, Conservative backbenchers inevitably sought to drag their Cabinet back into purer Tory practices. For example, disturbed by Churchill's lack of interest in the idea of denationalising steel and road haulage, thirty-nine Conservative Members signed an Early Day Motion in April 1952, criticising the Government for its delay.

[1] For this lack, the age and health of Churchill may have been in part responsible; see Lord Moran, *Winston Churchill, the Struggle for Survival, 1940–65* (Constable, 1966).

Within a week, Churchill had announced that both steel and road haulage would be denationalised as quickly as possible. It would be saying too much to suggest a simple cause-and-effect process from this episode; on the other hand, there can be little doubt that the denationalisation of steel and road haulage was a necessary response by the Government to the feeling of the majority of Tory Members.[1]

Throughout the earlier years of Conservative Government after 1951, the party's backbenchers exerted pressure on their leaders to act more enthusiastically in the interest of private enterprise and, where it was not possible to abolish nationalisation, to subject the nationalised industries to more commercial considerations. The eventual establishment by the Government of a Select Committee of the House of Commons on Nationalised Industries in 1955 was the direct result of backbench pressure exerted mainly by the Tory Members of the House.[2] This had been a slow process. In 1949, Hugh Molson (later Lord Molson), a Conservative backbencher, had advocated such a committee in a letter to *The Times*.[3] Once the Conservatives were in power, pressure mounted, mainly though not exclusively from the Government's own backbenches, for the establishment of a committee through which the state-owned industries could be made accountable to a Minister in Parliament. As a result, the Government set up a Select Committee to consider this problem and this proposed a Nationalised Industries Committee. But it was not until 1955 that the Government provided for this Committee to be established and then only with terms of reference so circumscribed as to make any thorough examination of the state-owned industries impossible. When it met, the new Committee itself decided that its terms of reference were inadequate and the support it received from the Conservative backbenches was so strong that the Government capitulated and agreed to expand its terms of reference.

It may be argued that this episode illustrates not so much the

[1] Lord Woolton's *Memoirs*, p. 378. Reports in the *Daily Telegraph* and *Manchester Guardian*, April 10, 1952.

[2] A short account of the establishment of the Nationalised Industries Committee is given in Bernard Crick, *The Reform of Parliament*, pp. 90 et seq. A full account of the work of the Committee is in David Coombes, *The Member of Parliament and the Administration, The Case of the Select Committee on Nationalised Industries* (Allen & Unwin, 1966).

[3] *The Times*, September 8, 1949.

power of backbenchers to influence *policy* as such, as the extent to which MPs collectively can, when they have a mind to do so, make the Government see sense on a more or less technical matter. It is certainly true that, once established, the Nationalised Industries Committee operated in a non-party way and changed the whole level of parliamentary discussion of the industries concerned, and their organisation. Equally, many Labour as well as Tory Members favoured the establishment of the Committee. Nevertheless, bringing the Nationalised Industries Committee into being was a highly political act which primarily reflected the determination of Conservative backbenchers to bring the state-owned industries under parliamentary control. But for Tory suspicions of these industries, the House of Commons as a whole would probably not have mustered the strength to put pressure on the Government successfully. Moreover, it is likely though unprovable that the same result would not have been achieved had Labour been in power—certainly so long as Herbert Morrison was Leader of the House.

During the years of post-war Conservative power, a determined group of Government backbenchers persistently subjected the nationalised industries to more or less hostile criticism. They opposed increases in the price of coal; they objected to the protection of the nationalised coal industry to which both frontbenches were committed—the Labour Party on grounds of sentiment, the Conservative Government from motives of expediency. Prominent among this group of Conservatives was Gerald Nabarro who, in 1955, resigned as Joint Secretary of the Conservative Fuel and Power Committee because he objected to an increase in the price of coal. Nabarro was a persistent critic of the Government in other respects too. He later subjected Chancellors of the Exchequer to an annual bombardment of questions designed to remove anomalies in the purchase tax structure and obtain reform. He campaigned successfully for clean air legislation and was frequently an embarrassment to the Government by the frankness with which he interrogated Ministers at Question Time.

Until the late 1950s, Conservative backbenchers kept up a constant pressure on the Government through their weekly private committee meetings, and in the House, to secure the subjection of the nationalised industries to a stricter financial discipline. Thus, in May 1956, a group of Conservative backbenchers voted against the Government's Bill to increase the Exchequer loan to the National

Coal Board. Throughout these years, the attitude of Conservative backbenchers reflected a certain ambiguity of instinct. On the one hand, they wished to make state-owned industries more efficient in the interest of the taxpayer. On the other hand, their doctrine suggested to them that, so long as industries were owned by the state, real efficiency was hardly attainable. There is no doubt, however, that the general approach of the Conservative backbenchers during the fifties had a considerable impact in speeding denationalisation and changing the terms of references for industries that remained in state ownership. The denationalisation of the instrument-making company, S. & G. Brown, by the Macmillan Government was owing to Conservative pressure. On the other hand, Conservative backbench pressure failed to secure the denationalisation of the remaining state-owned steel company, Richard Thomas and Baldwin during the thirteen years of Conservative power.

Similarly, the support and prodding given to the Conservative Government under Harold Macmillan was a considerable help in strengthening the determination of Ministers to reform the organisation and finances of the railways to deal with the cumulative deficit of the British Transport Commission. It was a report by the Nationalised Industries Committee in 1960 on the British Railways which set off the train of events which led to the Government's decision to appoint Dr Beeching (formerly of Imperial Chemical Industries) as head of British Railways with a mandate to produce a plan to overcome the chronic financial difficulties of the state-owned transport system. But by the late fifties and early sixties, the Conservatives had, in the Cabinet of Harold Macmillan, one far more responsive to their view of a private enterprise economy than the Tory rank and file had in the early years of their power after 1951. Under Churchill, the departure from some of the attitudes of the post-war Labour Government was still tentative—not least because of the small majority the Tory Party then still had in Parliament.

Even so, the Conservative backbenchers achieved one major victory soon after their return to power in securing the break-up of the British Broadcasting Corporation's television monopoly and the establishment of commercial television. This was the work of a group of Conservative MPs, many of whom were associated in one way or another with the radio or advertising industries. They were backed by interested parties outside the House of Commons and advocates of commercial television were strongly entrenched inside the Conservative Central Office. This victory was achieved despite the opposition to commercial television of a number of senior Conservatives, as well as probably the majority of committed Tories in the country. (On the other hand, the bulk of non-political public opinion was either indifferent or favourable to the idea of a new dimension for television.)

The successful 'pressuring' of the Conservative Government by a comparatively small group of Conservative MPs over commercial television represented the victory of the younger, more commercially-minded Conservatives—many of whom were leaders of the One Nation Group—over an older generation of Tories. It might seem tempting to dismiss this backbench triumph as a demonstration, not of the independence of backbench Members of the House of Commons, but rather of their vulnerability to external pressure groups. But this would be to misunderstand the traditional relationship of parties and of MPs to the various interests which traditionally support them. The Conservative Party is closely bound up with the world of business and private enterprise—and, by its nature, responds to them. The older Members of the Churchill Government, including the Prime Minister himself, were out of touch with the new commercial modes of thought which were making themselves felt among the younger members of the party. If the backbench Tory group which secured this victory needed outside aid, the external pressure groups who were their allies could not have achieved their objective had they not been talking the kind of language which was beginning to appeal to the rising generation of Conservative leaders. The age of Conservative affluence and of the consumer-dominated society, which reached its zenith in the prime years of the Macmillan Government, received an appropriate send-off with the victory of the backbenchers who persuaded their leaders to adopt commercial television. In his detailed study of this episode, H. H. Wilson observes:

> This study would seem to establish the fact that a small number of M.P.s, well organised, with good connections among both party officials and outside interests, and pushing a definite, limited programme, may exert considerable influence and even overwhelm an unorganised majority in their own party.[1]

[1] H. H. Wilson, *Pressure Group: The Campaign for Commercial Television* (Secker & Warburg, 1961), p. 208.

It would be wrong to conclude that this represents anything very new in British politics. Many of the most substantial changes in the social and political order have, in former periods, been achieved, for good or ill, by the ability of a dedicated minority to manipulate the more passive bulk of their fellow party members.

The years of Churchill's second Prime Ministership from 1951–5 saw the emergence of a new style of Conservativism and the determination of the 'new men' to present the old private enterprise motivations of their party in a new guise, despite the absorption of their aged leader with the broad canvas of foreign affairs. During these years, the party's backbenchers made themselves felt in a number of ways apart from the nationalisation issue. In 1954, for instance, despite a free vote of the House accepting an increase in MPs' pay, Conservative backbench objections were strong enough to force Churchill to compromise with them by granting a higher allowance in place of a straight increase in salary.

The successes of backbenchers in these years are no proof that backbenchers are better able to influence their leaders when their party has a small majority. (As we have seen, the 1950 Labour Government offers some proof that the opposite is sometimes true.) The 1951–5 period does suggest, however, that a Government which is seeking to consolidate its hold on the centre ground of politics must also compromise all the time with the desires of their immediate followers and of the interest groups which mainly support them. Equally, though the Government's backbenchers will not succeed in their objects by mounting big offensives against their leaders in the Division lobbies, they can oblige their leaders to compromise with them provided they concentrate on issues over which the Government, without being forced into wholesale retreat, can come to meet them.

(ii)

On Churchill's retirement, the new Prime Minister, Sir Anthony Eden, increased the Conservative majority in the 1955 General Election to one of fifty-eight in the House of Commons. During the election campaign, the Conservatives kept the political temperature down and the new Prime Minister presented himself as a tried national leader of international standing and experience rather than as a political partisan. Although the Conservatives had not neglected to give the electorate a sweetener in the shape of income tax concession in the pre-election Budget, the cruder sort of politics were ostensibly ignored by Eden during the campaign. The Conservative victory was largely owing to four reasons. First, there was the satisfaction experienced in the first flush of freedom from post-war restrictions which were associated with the Labour Government. Secondly, there was the tendency of the post-war British electorate to give the benefit of the doubt to the Government of the day. Thirdly, there was the personal stature of the Conservative Leader in the eyes of ordinary people at this time. Finally, there was the contrast between the unity of the Conservative Party and the divisions within the Labour Opposition which had developed during the Churchill Government's tenure of office.

This unity was quickly to be shattered by the embarkation of the Eden Government on the Suez adventure. Yet though the divisions in the Conservative Party over Suez were among the most acute faced by any Conservative Government since the war, their impact on the course of events once the Suez affair had started was limited: the pressures that Conservative backbenchers exerted on a number of domestic issues certainly had a greater influence on policy. Therefore, since this general study is concerned with the effective influence of backbenchers on government policy, rather than with MPs' rebelliousness as such, however dramatic, I shall not dwell on the numerous revolts over Suez policy after the invasion. The ultimate failure of the adventure lay in its nature and in foreign reactions to it rather than in the House of Commons. But Conservative pressures on the Government's Suez policy before the adventure itself are, perhaps, more relevant to my general theme. The existence of a Conservative right-wing pressure-group which was nagging the Government, and Eden in particular, for strong action to preserve British interests in Egypt in the years before the 1956 affair, may have been at least a factor in pushing the Prime Minister towards the disastrous course of action which he eventually undertook.

In 1954, when he was Foreign Secretary, Eden had made a treaty with Egypt under which the United Kingdom agreed to give up its military base in the Canal Zone. It was this action which led to the formation of the Tory Suez Group, which numbered between twenty-five to forty discontented Government backbenchers. Because of the Churchill Government's small majority, only one of the Suez Group, Major Legge-Bourke, actually went so far as giving up the

Conservative Whip. But, by the time President Nasser decided to nationalise the Suez Canal in the autumn of 1956, Conservative dislike of the new revolutionary government in Egypt had hardened so much and spread so far beyond the bounds of the Suez Group that there was probably hardly any Conservative who did not believe that firm action should be taken to keep Suez an international waterway. When Eden took his largely personal decision to join the French in an invasion of Egypt, he was no doubt motivated by his memory of the consequences of pre-war appeasement; stimulated by pique at Egypt's dishonouring of the spirit of the agreement he had negotiated in 1954; and confused in his assessment of the situation by the handicap of ill-health. But it is also difficult to doubt that he was buttressed in his decision by the knowledge that instinctively the bulk of the Conservative backbenchers would sympathise with strong action. A political party is most happy, however, when it has a leader who can coolly counteract, if necessary, its collective kinks. Unhappily for the Conservatives, they had in Eden a Prime Minister who did not counteract but rather gave expression to the Conservative 'kink' about Egypt.

There was, of course, a small 'liberal' wing of the Conservative Party which instinctively disliked Eden's strong-arm policy. Their views were expressed by the resignation from the government of Sir Edward Boyle, Economic Secretary to the Treasury, and Anthony Nutting, Minister of State for Foreign Affairs.[1] In subsequent debates, it became clear that a significant group of Conservatives objected for one reason or another to the Government's action and they certainly numbered more than the eight who, even though by then hostilities had been stopped, abstained in the crucial division of confidence on November 8, 1956. According to one account, the Government's decision to end the Suez operation was partly influenced by a threat of a group of forty Conservatives to vote against the Government in the Commons if hostilities were not ended.[2] In fact, Conservative 'liberal' backbench influence played at most a small part in the decision to abandon the Suez enterprise. The effect of the affair on the balance of payments and on sterling, together

---

[1] Anthony Nutting, *No End of a Lesson* (Constable, 1967), and Hugh Thomas, *The Suez Affair* (Weidenfeld & Nicolson, 1967) have thrown further light on this episode.

[2] Merry and Serge Bromberger, *The Secrets of Suez* (Pan Books, 1957), p. 159.

with American and Commonwealth opinion, were undoubtedly the main reasons for the decision to withdraw the British forces.

Yet it is a fact that there were meetings of left-wing Conservative critics at the House.[1] The Government was confronted both by a hard core of objectors in principle, and by many more who were critical of the Eden policy because they knew it could not succeed and was likely to wreck both the Government's foreign relations and the nation's economy. If backbench (and constituency) Conservative pressure was partly responsible for Eden's action in the first place, the difficulty of holding together different sectors of backbench opinion was probably a factor contributing to the Government's decision to withdraw. The critics of the Conservative Left alone would have been impotent: what gave them some influence was the fact that the Government was now assailed from all sides and the confidence of its followers collectively was almost entirely destroyed. If Eden had not been obliged by ill-health to resign, there would have been pressures on him to do so and conceivably (no more than that) they might have succeeded.

The most vociferous group of critics, of course, was on the right wing of the party. The rebellious tactics of the Suez Group itself were continued after Eden had been replaced by Harold Macmillan in January 1957 but the new Prime Minister, undaunted by their gestures and unabashed by his personal involvement in the original action, steadily reversed the policy of his predecessor while publicly continuing to defend it. On May 16, 1957, the House of Commons was asked to approve the Government's decision to advise British shipowners to use the Suez Canal on terms laid down by Egypt. Outraged by this retreat, fourteen of the Suez Group abstained and eight renounced the Government Whip. Of the eight extreme rebels, five remained as an independent Conservative group, led by Lord Hinchingbrooke, until 1958. None of these met with such heavy criticism from their local Conservative association as the left-wing Conservatives who had opposed Eden's action did. Three of these, Nigel Nicolson, Sir Frank Medlicott and Cyril Banks were disowned by their constituency associations.

In this early period of his Prime Ministership, Harold Macmillan proved adroit at pulling his Party out of the morass into which it had fallen. He set about rebuilding the damaged Anglo–American

[1] Nigel Nicolson, *People and Parliament* (Weidenfeld & Nicolson, 1958), p. 133.

relationship and restoring the economy. He also devoted himself to restoring the Conservative Party's self-confidence and building its trust in his leadership. He was able to retreat from the Suez policy partly because he had not, under Eden, been one of those Ministers who was suspected of disagreeing with it and partly because most rational Conservatives could now see that it had been a failure.

In fact, probably the most concrete result of backbench feeling over the Suez affair was the selection of Macmillan instead of Butler as Leader of the Conservative Party. Against Butler's seniority in the party hierarchy, Macmillan was chosen not so much because a numerically powerful section of the party had positively wanted him, as because a significant minority, extending well beyond the Suez die-hards, would not accept Butler, who was suspected of being opposed to the Suez policy. Although the selection of Macmillan has been depicted as largely the work of the Cabinet itself, and of influential top layers of the Conservative Party, there is no doubt that the decision they took was largely influenced by their view of feeling in the rank and file. It is in the author's personal recollection that several Conservative backbenchers told him on the night before Macmillan was chosen that they would never serve under Butler. The fact that they were men who were unlikely to be invited to serve under anyone did not mean that their views, and those of like-minded backbenchers, were of no account to the seniors in the Party whose main objective was to select a leader who could heal all divisions.

So far as changing policy was concerned, the Conservative rebellions over Suez were hardly more influential than Labour rebellions against Bevin's foreign policy had been. Like the Labour rebels, the Conservatives who went into the Division lobbies against their leaders could be confident that they were not risking the life of the Government. Yet, as in the case of Labour foreign policy rebellions, the Tory revolts over Suez were extremely damaging, for a time, to the Conservative standing with the electorate.

(iii)

The exit from politics of Anthony Eden in January 1957, and his replacement as Prime Minister by Harold Macmillan, took place at a time when there were tensions between the Conservative leadership and its followers other than those created by the Suez crisis. Two of these conflicts are especially worth a little detailed scrutiny since both resulted in major concessions by the government to its backbenchers. The measures concerned were the Shops Bill and the Rent Act. Of course, there had been a number of other issues over which the Eden government had given ground to its discontented followers— especially when they were speaking for strong local constituency feeling: thus in 1955, Heathcoat-Amory, the Minister of Agriculture and Fisheries, had felt obliged to appease a threatened rebellion by Conservative MPs representing fishing areas, by agreeing to a modification of the subsidy cut he was proposing in the White Fish Bill. But it was under the Macmillan Government—which during most of its seven years' existence was extremely sensitive to back-bench parliamentary opinion—that these two major instances of Conservative retreat before backbench pressure occurred. In one case, the Shops Bill, the Government capitulated altogether and abandoned the measure it had been proposing. In the other, the Rent Act, the Government was obliged to make substantial concessions to delay the impact of the Act, the essence of which was the decontrol of the rent of 800,000 hitherto protected tenants.

Few proposed measures were received with more mixed feelings by Conservative Members during the post-war years than the Rent Bill introduced by Duncan Sandys, when he was Minister of Housing, in November 1956. Conservative free enterprise instincts warmed towards a Bill which was designed to restore, partially, the free market in houses. They welcomed a Bill which was designed to make more economic use of available and under-used housing premises. On the other hand, many Conservative Members, particularly those representing constituencies where a large number of tenants would be hit by decontrol—notably in inner London and some seaside areas— were also extremely anxious as they contemplated the impact of the measure on their constituents.

The crucial Clause in the Bill (Clause 9) provided that the rents of some 800,000 tenants would be decontrolled within six months. While the Labour Opposition resented the general approach of the Bill (Labour would have preferred some other means of fixing a 'fair' rent) Conservative misgivings were directed less against the principle of the Bill than against the short period of notice that affected tenants would have. Conservative opinion generally accepted that, under rent-control, many landlords were suffering hardship as a result of their responsibility for property for which they often received a derisory rent in contemporary money values. On the other hand, the

216

minority of Conservative Members who were acquainted with the housing conditions in the affected areas had vivid mental pictures of elderly people turned hastily into the street as the proposed measure took effect.

The idea of a short, sharp Bill which would get the dislocation over quickly was, however, favoured both by Sandys and by important civil servants in his Ministry (including its Permanent Secretary, Dame Evelyn Sharp) though opinion in the department was far from unanimous in approval of the precise terms of the Bill. It was this Bill that was inherited by Henry Brooke, when Macmillan appointed him to succeed Sandys as Minister of Housing and Local Government on January 13, 1957. Brooke, who as Home Secretary as well as Housing Minister was to have a number of extremely unpleasant political nettles to grasp, was often depicted as a less than humane politician because of his rigorously scrupulous and unimaginative adherence to literal duty. Yet on this occasion he was far from easy about the terms of the Rent Bill he had inherited and was not indifferent to the hardship that it seemed likely to cause. On the other hand, no new Minister can immediately change the policy of a predecessor who is of the same party.

When the Rent Bill reached the Committee stage in 1957, Brooke found it not merely strenuously opposed by the Labour Opposition but also under constant criticism from Conservative backbenchers who had tabled a large number of amendments. By January 31, there had been eleven sittings of the Standing Committee on the Bill and yet only Clause 2 had been reached. At this rate of progress, it seemed that the controversial Clause 9 would not be reached for at least a further three weeks. The Government therefore decided to 'guillotine' the Bill—that is to say, to put before the Commons a time-table motion which would allocate the amount of time to be allotted to the remaining stages of the Bill.

The terms of the time-table motion, published on February 1, required the Standing Committee which was considering the Bill to complete its work by March 13. This meant that the Committee would have eighteen more sittings in which to deal with the remaining sixteen Clauses of the Bill, after which the later stages of the Bill would have to be completed in three allotted days. The Government's intention was to get the Bill through the Commons by Easter and through the Lords and on to the Statute Book by Whitsun. In addition, the debate of February 4 on the 'guillotine' motion

217

itself—which was bitterly opposed by the Labour Opposition as stifling discussions on the proposed measure—was itself an occasion for the House to discuss, with full publicity, the crucial principles of the Bill.

But the Government's response to backbench, Opposition and external discontent was not simply to impose the 'guillotine'. Before this less pleasant parliamentary decision was announced, the Minister, Henry Brooke, had second thoughts about the crucial Clause 9. Brooke and his department quickly decided (and let their decision be known) that there could be no compromise over the number of houses decontrolled since the more houses that came on the market, the more likelihood (they believed) there was that rents would be kept down to reasonable levels. On the other hand, the Government could lengthen the period of time before tenants would be evicted, giving them longer security of tenure than six months. This was what many Conservative Members wanted. One backbench motion, tabled by Anthony Marlowe, the Member for Hove, wanted the period lengthened to three years. Another group of Conservatives tabled an amendment later which would have given tenants five years' security: this would have virtually wrecked the Bill. Among a number of exchanges between Conservative Members and the Minister during this period, was one meeting between this particular group of backbenchers and Brooke, on February 13, which lasted for about an hour and a half. Their lack of satisfaction was indicated by their decision not to withdraw the amendment.

It would be impossible to show precisely how far Brooke was moved by his backbenchers' pressure and how far by press criticism. At all events his own earlier misgivings, press attitudes and the backbench campaign—not to mention the play being made by the Opposition with the Rent Bill—combined to produce from him in February the concession that tenants would have security of tenure for fifteen months, instead of six, before decontrol took effect.[1] But this did not satisfy the strongest Conservative critics. When the Bill reached the Report stage in the House, two of them, William Rees-Davies and Robert Jenkins, moved an amendment to safeguard tenants against excessive rents by prescribing for three years a rent ceiling. The Government imposed only a two-line whip and eleven Conservatives openly abstained.

After the Bill became law, discontent in the Conservative Party did

[1] S. E. Finer, *Anonymous Empire* (Pall Mall Press, 1958), p. 70.

not die down, but rather increased. Rents were debated after the Queen's Speech opening the next Session of Parliament and early in 1958, Conservative backbenchers began to put pressure on Brooke to soften the effects of rent decontrol. On February 26, a group of Conservative MPs wrote to the Prime Minister asking him to receive a deputation about the working of the Act. The letter, which was signed by Robert Jenkins, the Member for Dulwich, Dame Irene Ward (Tynemouth), Sir Albert Braithwaite (Harrow W.) and Anthony Marlowe (Hove), was said by its signatories to have the backing of at least twenty-five Conservative backbenchers and to have the moral support of three junior Ministers who sat for London constituencies. It was not so much that the agitated Conservative backbenchers had specific remedies to propose: they wanted to discover whether the Government itself was going to deal with landlords who had abused the Rent Act by raising their rents exorbitantly. The group contended that threats of eviction were running at the rate of about 200 notices-to-quit on average in each of their constituencies. At the same time Mr Brooke was asked to come to the backbench Conservative Housing Committee.

Brooke, however, had already made a public week-end speech warning landlords not to abuse the Act and rebuking those who, without justification, 'use eviction notices as a prelude to negotiation'. It was now plain that Brooke had modified his previous view that the Rent Act should stand unamended and that he had become suddenly convinced that the Government was taking a real risk with public opinion. On this occasion, it seems to have been press criticism— and in particular comment from some of the Conservative newspapers —that was mainly responsible for the modified Government view. Brooke began to see that he faced a possible press campaign built upon the personal stories of dispossessed elderly tenants. Besides, the Government had just suffered a defeat in the Rochdale by-election and the Prime Minister was alive to the electoral unpopularity of the Rent Act. There was now fear of large-scale evictions when the Act took full effect in October 1958.

In his public speech warning the landlords not to abuse the Act, Brooke said: 'There is still plenty of time for my words to take effect and those who do not heed them may regret it.' Further than this he was not prepared to go when he met the backbenchers in their Committee. His Ministry's view was that it would not be possible to make any valid assessment of the extent of the eviction-threat problem until April, when landlords who aimed at turning their tenants out by the autumn would have had to give notice. When April came, Brooke announced in the Commons that his warning had failed and that he proposed to amend the Act. The Government then proceeded to pass through Parliament a Bill temporarily enabling county courts to delay the eviction of tenants threatened with hardship. Almost certainly, in this final phase of the Rent Act controversy, feeling in the press and the election looming in 1959 together exerted a bigger influence than backbench Conservative pressure in forcing the Minister to amend his Bill. Nevertheless, taking as a whole the Rent Act campaign, which lasted for the best part of eighteen months, the pressure of backbenchers was not negligible as a focus for public opinion. The backbenchers were, after all, themselves feeding the press with stories of their concern and with the dimensions of the problem. If it is the business of Members to represent the views of their constituents to the Government, however inconveniently for prevailing policies, those MPs sitting for the constituencies most affected did their duty on this occasion.

(iv)

The Shops Bill was a classic instance of a piece of proposed legislation which was the product of interaction between a Whitehall department and external pressure groups and which was dropped at the insistence of the Government's own backbenchers. Chiefly because there was no great public row in Parliament (where the Suez crisis was the chief focus of attention at the time) and also, no doubt, because a controversy over shop assistants' hours hardly provides the most enlivening material for political analysis, the issue has so far received little written attention.

Yet the affair of the Shops Bill is of considerable relevance to one of the main theses of this book which admits the weighty influence of external pressure groups exerted directly upon government departments and of the views of civil servants, but suggests that, in the final analysis, the feelings and impulses of backbenchers can exercise a powerful checking effect, even a veto, upon government policy.

The Shops Bill brought in by the Conservative Government in 1956 was the direct result of the report of a Committee of Inquiry into the closing hours of shops and other related matters which had been set up by the Labour Home Secretary in 1946. One of the main recommendations of this Committee, which had been under the chairmanship of Sir Ernest Gowers, was a general closing hour of 7 p.m. instead of 8 p.m. Owing to other preoccupations in its declining years, the Labour Government had not produced legislation to implement the Gowers Report.

But by the mid-fifties, a campaign to establish a five-day week in the retail trade and to limit working hours was well advanced, and on November 15, 1956 the Conservative Government introduced its Shops Bill, based on the recommendations of the Gowers Report, to enforce earlier closing hours. The Bill proposed that the hour of night closing on a weekday should be 7 p.m. instead of 8 p.m. and with late closing one day a week at 8 p.m. instead of 9 p.m. The Bill also prohibited Sunday trading in England and Wales, with certain specified exceptions, such as fruits, sweets, flowers, ice-cream and so on. It contained various other proposals for regulating the working conditions of shop-workers. The Bill was a perfect example of a piece of almost neutral (in the party-political sense) and 'departmental' legislation. Between the publication of the Gowers Report and the production of the Bill, the Home Office, which was the department concerned, continued to work on the question in direct discussion with the interest affected. Later, Mr R. A. Butler was to tell the House of Commons that sixty-six associations had been consulted in drafting the terms of the Bill. Essentially, then, the Bill was an inherited one: the seeds had been sown by the Labour Government, they were nurtured inside the Home Office for several years and the fruit was reaped by the Conservative Government. It was a Bill which, in its preparation, had almost entirely by-passed the House of Commons. At this stage it could be taken as a perfect example of the way in which Whitehall works with pressure groups, almost ignoring the parliamentary process. The Bill was basically supported by most of the bigger established organs of retail trade and by the unions concerned. If the influence of Parliament were as small as it is often held to be, there was small chance that this measure would fail to reach the Statute Book. Yet it did fail to do so.

The Bill was introduced into the House of Lords, where it was given a second reading, on November 29, after a good many hostile speeches. It was attacked by Conservatives and Liberals with a wide variety of arguments, ranging from the contention that Parliament should not legislate for the 'so-called protection of adults' to the assertion that the closing hours proposed were far too early. But criticism in the Lords was not the half of it. No sooner was the Bill published than there was something like a spontaneous eruption of distaste which seemed to engulf the bulk of the Conservative back-bench Members and made itself felt by the Government. Conservative Members made their dislike of the Bill known verbally to Ministers and the Home Office was bombarded with protesting letters from them. Yet it is fair to say that organised retail opinion generally favoured the Bill and so did the unions. The pressure groups opposing it—representing small independent shopkeepers, especially confectioners and tobacconists—were what one might call minority opinion. They represented the point of view which had been 'beaten' during the preparatory work on the production of the Bill.

For these reasons, it can hardly be maintained that, in reacting against the Bill, Conservative Members were responding to organised outside pressures. The explanation of the Conservative backbench attitude was rather to be found in the sensitivity of the party in Parliament to its position as the guardian of the 'small man' who is one of the chief supports of Conservatism in the constituencies. Further, the Bill seemed to Conservative instincts to be an infringement of the principle that *competition* should be encouraged wherever possible. This Bill was seen as inhibiting the 'small man's' urge to competition since small retailers, being often without employed staff, wanted freedom to keep their businesses open beyond the stipulated hours. It is true that the enthusiasm for competition of many (but not all) Conservative backbench Members died down rapidly when it came to ending resale price maintenance, however brightly it burned over shop hours. The paradox is mainly to be explained by the fact that the 'small man' was against the Shops Bill but was in favour of keeping R.P.M. which, he argued, was essential if he were to survive in competition with the price-cutting supermarkets. Besides, support for R.P.M. united not merely the one-man and the bigger conventional retailers: it also had the support of some manufacturers. Conservatives could persuade themselves that R.P.M., though it might keep some prices up, encouraged competition by preserving the existence of independent retailers and by maintaining standards of quality. On the other hand, the Shops Bill was seen as damaging to these interests: it was regarded as a restrictionist hangover from a period of Labour Government and as inimical to the spirit of free enterprise which the Conservatives were trying to foster in the fifties.

Immediately the Shops Bill was published, Conservative MPs were bombarded with protests—to which they listened with great sympathy —from small shopkeepers on the general grounds that the Bill would damage their trade, and by traders in seaside resorts who insisted that their seasonal business would be adversely affected. While the shopworkers' union announced its full support for the Bill, and opposed any suggestion that a shopkeeper not employing others should be exempt from its provision, the National Union of Retail Confectioners opposed it—particularly on the ground that 7 o'clock closing would hit their members just at the hour when the sweet trade was starting up in the evening. (As things stood before the Bill, they could sell sweets and chocolates for one and a half hours after general evening closing.)

By January there were signs at Westminster that the Government was having second thoughts about the Bill: that the measure might be heavily amended or even shelved. By 'signs' I mean that Conservative backbenchers who were actively putting pressure on the Government believed that one or the other of these things might happen and the replies given by Ministers to inquiring political journalists did not rule out the possibility.

The tone of Government response to critics of the Bill changed abruptly precisely when Mr R. A. Butler became Home Secretary and Leader of the House. On January 14, Butler accepted these offices at the invitation of the new Prime Minister, Harold Macmillan, who had succeeded to this office despite Butler's expectation of doing so himself. Despite the failure of his own personal relationship with the Conservative Party as a whole at this time, Butler always had the acutest ear for disaffection in the Conservative Party and he believed that, where possible, a Government should heed its followers' instincts and feelings. So strong were the rumours of the Government's intention to abandon the Bill, that when the Committee stage began in the Lords on February 12, Viscount Alexander of Hillsborough from the Labour frontbench asked Lord Hailsham whether there was any truth in them. 'No,' replied Lord Hailsham, 'We intend to go on with it.' And go on with it they did through a long and protracted Committee stage in the Upper House which dragged on until the summer. The Government purported to be impressed by the growing support for the Bill in the trade itself and, indeed, in March 1957 the National Chamber of Trade said in its journal that (despite Tory Opposition) it was vital that MPs of all

Parties should know that the organised retailers were anxious that the measure should be adopted and with it the amended closing hours: the Government was aware of the need for clarification over certain points.

Nevertheless, the Government found itself faced with a shoal of amendments and Tory complaints about the resentment that would be caused by depriving shoppers of their liberty to shop when they wanted to.[1] Answering a Liberal peer, Lord Grantchester, who wanted the early closing hours clause deleted entirely, Lord Hailsham suggested that Grantchester should attack Moses for the Fourth Commandment which recognised that if it was socially desirable to have periods of rest, one had to organise them socially, by legislation. Nevertheless, in response to the pressures exerted on them, the Government indicated, through Lord Hailsham, that it would be prepared to make concessions for retailers of confectionery and tobacco, as it later did. Hailsham also said the Cabinet would consider the amendment which would enable car sale-rooms to stay open longer on early closing days, although the Government 'had had no pressure so far from the owners of car showrooms'. But the Government was now also facing heavy criticism in the non-Labour press for its persistence with the Bill—a criticism which plainly reflected the feeling within the ranks of the Tory Party. *The Times* joined in the attack and, in a leading article on March 11, 1957, the *Financial Times* criticised this 'preposterous Bill' on the grounds that it would reduce the competitive power of the small man. Pointing out that the origin of the Bill was the 'restrictionist report of the Gowers Committee', this leading article asserted: 'The Government by now know that its own supporters consider the Bill ridiculous, as indeed do many members of the Government itself.' This article, emphasising some of the absurdities which would result from the different arrangements made in the Bill for the sale of different categories of goods, was far from being the only press attack of its kind which the Government had to face.

On March 14, 1957, political journalists at Westminster were given off-the-record hints that the Government would review the Bill. This first delicate step at back-tracking took the form of guidance from the Minister who was both most qualified to give it and most adept at conveying the nuances of such a situation without involving the

[1] In fact, there was nothing new about legislating for shop hours.

Government in any premature commitment. The essence of the guidance given (distilled between the lines of carefully chosen words) was conveyed in *The Times* (among other newspapers) the next day which reported that the legislative programme was becoming so overcrowded that 'there is at least a possibility that the Shops Bill will eventually be abandoned—at least for the present Session'.[1] Yet the Government was still not prepared to make up its mind finally to jettison the Bill entirely. It was still taking the temperature of backbench feeling in the Conservative Party, and in the meantime, the Lords had to persist with its unrewarding slog through the Committee stage. On March 26, Hailsham told the Lords that, as he had stated on February 12, 'the Government intended to go on with their business'.

On April 17, the Government itself introduced amendments which would make major changes in the Bill. Although the new statutory closing hour of 7 p.m. was not to be altered, the power for local authorities to fix earlier closing by order was removed. In seaside resorts, local authorities would be given the power to dispense with statutory closing hours in the summer. Yet, despite these concessions to the critics, the Tory hostility to the Bill did not diminish, and on May 23, the usual channels between the Government and the press were giving clear guidance that the Bill might be dropped from its programme that Session. Reporting this, the *Manchester Guardian's* Political Correspondent noted that 'in the event the Government could only save this legislation by launching the Bill anew in the next Session' and he continued: 'Ministers are so unenthusiastic about it that if the Bill is dropped now it will probably be killed for good.' Commenting on Hailsham's hint that the Lords might be wasting their time on the Bill, the Political Correspondent of the *Manchester Guardian* noted: 'Perhaps Ministers allowed the Bill to go so far as it did in the Lords largely to provide an outlet for Lord Hailsham's energy and to give him so necessary training in Committee work.' (It was the first Bill Lord Hailsham had piloted through a Committee.)

So far, the Government had pursued a classic technique of political public relations which involves a gradual preparation of opinion for a possible *volte-face* while leaving the Government free to continue with the policy in question if it eventually concludes that to do so is wise. Not only is public opinion less outraged by a change of policy of which it has received some warning: such tactics also enable the

[1] *The Times*, March 15, 1957.

Government to procrastinate long enough to be able to pretend that no change has, in fact, occurred. Instead it can be claimed that the policy has been overwhelmed, not by parliamentary opinion (as in this case) but by the exigencies of the parliamentary time-table. Everyone knows what has really happened—not least the Opposition of the day—but politicians of all parties use these conventions which, they believe, save face for them. The same sort of technique was used by the Labour Government of 1964 with the steel nationalisation Bill when it was plain that there was no hope of passing it through Parliament in view of Labour's narrow majority and of the opposition of a few Labour Members.

On May 30, Mr R. A. Butler, speaking in his dual capacity as Home Secretary and Leader of the House, announced to the Commons that the Government would not proceed with the Bill. At that time of the Session, Mr Butler reminded the House, the first claim in its time was for financial legislation and for the concluding stages of legislation—including urgent Bills which had recently been introduced. Clearly the Shops Bill would need prolonged time in Committee in the Commons. 'The Government have concluded that it would not be practical to proceed with it in the Commons.' The Conservative cheers which greeted the announcement showed the enthusiasm with which the Government's own backbenchers viewed the abandonment of the Bill, and a Conservative backbencher, Mr Nabarro, said that it would be greeted with enthusiasm by the shopping public. But the Labour Opposition was naturally of a different opinion and its Leader, Hugh Gaitskell, immediately made the point that Butler's statement was completely at variance with the Government's previous undertaking. Was it still the Government's intention to carry out the Gowers Report, he wanted to know?

Butler replied that he had made the position perfectly clear—as indeed he had, despite his careful avoidance of a straightforward statement that the Bill was jettisoned for good. It had, he said, no hope of getting through the House in the Session. As for the future, he could give no undertaking and he could not anticipate the next Queen's Speech. Nor could he enlarge his statement, which had been made 'after careful study'.

The following conclusions may be drawn from this episode. First, the Shops Bill was a good example of legislation whose genesis is departmental: it was essentially a non-Conservative Bill introduced by a Home Secretary, Mr Gwylm Lloyd George, who was a 'Liberal and Conservative' and whose finger was not upon the Tory pulse.[1] Secondly, though it showed how far proposed legislation may get without party-political support, the Bill was in fact overthrown by the weight of Conservative backbench opinion against it. This Conservative reaction was less a response to group pressures in the ordinary sense of the term than an instinctive backbench feeling that the Bill went contrary to one of their main supporting 'interests' in the constituencies and to the free-enterprise theme which was so important to them as a party. Thirdly, the Government's retreat was assisted by the appointment to the Home Office of a particular Minister, R. A. Butler, who not only had the most sensitive antennae for backbench feeling, but who also had a strong personal interest in establishing himself with the rank and file of the party which had by-passed him once for the Leadership. In future years, Mr Butler was to show himself no less sensitive to the feeling of hostility inside the Conservative Party over the British attempt to join the Common Market in 1962 and to the issue of R.P.M. This is not to say that Butler conceived it to be the invariable function of a Government to adapt itself to policies and attitudes favoured by the rank and file. Where he saw a broader consensus in favour of a policy (such as those he adopted over crime and punishment) which was opposed in a substantial section of his party, he was prepared to stand against this internal Conservative Party opposition. But where there was no such crossbench consensus, where a policy was offensive to his own party and was attractive merely to the Opposition, as in the case of the Shops Bill, he could see no reason to fight for it.

Addressing a meeting of the 1922 Committee in March, Butler said that he saw a case for some sort of consultative committee for future liaison between the government and the Conservative rank and file on matters of legislative policy: the committee might include both Conservative Members and representatives of constituencies. Such a committee, he suggested, could keep Ministers informed of opinion among Conservative supporters in the country, as well as among MPs, when the legislative programme was being prepared. This, in turn, should prevent Conservative MPs from being faced with legislation they were reluctant to support and which aroused constituency unrest. Butler was speaking with the much-criticised Shops Bill in mind: indeed, he hinted on this occasion that the

[1] Though it is worth noting that some Liberal spokesmen in the Lords were even more opposed to the Bill than were Conservatives.

Government would propose substantial amendments to it in the Lords—as indeed the Government did, before it decided to drop the proposed measure entirely.[1]

If Butler had been in charge of the Home Office in 1956, the Shops Bill would never have seen the light of day. Nobody can say what would have happened within the Conservative Party in the Commons if, in 1957 (which was a very difficult year for the Conservatives anyway in the wake of Suez) Butler had insisted on going on with the Bill. But again one may guess that, though the measure would probably have reached the Statute Book, it would have precipitated a row which could have soured the whole relationship of the backbenches and the Government in the crucial first year of Harold Macmillan's Prime Ministership. What might have happened was a controversy on the scale of the crisis in the Conservative Party over resale price maintenance in 1964.

[1] *The Times*, March 29, 1957.

Chapter Eight

The Influence of the Backbench Member 1957–1964

When Harold Macmillan took office as Prime Minister in 1957, he had two main objectives in his national policy. The first was to restore the Anglo–American special relationship which had been severely damaged by the Suez affair and to find a new and viable place of influence for Britain in the Western community of nations, having regard to the realities of power. The second was to rebuild the British economy and the status of sterling which had also suffered badly from the strains of the Suez period. Arising from these two general objectives a third practical policy quickly emerged: this was the decision to switch the emphasis in defence policy from a conventional to a nuclear basis, partly in order to save money and partly to preserve a nuclear status for Britain internationally. From the same two initial general objectives, there also arose, but more gradually, the commitment to a European policy which was ultimately to lead to the attempt to join the Common Market. Domestically, Macmillan also needed to heal the wounds within the Conservative Party and, partly by restoring Conservative unity, to recreate public confidence in Tory administration.

Macmillan was ideally suited by temperament to perform this multiple operation. He was a realist who could accept the inevitability of Britain's reduced international status in the second half of the twentieth century, but who had the imagination to understand that national morale depended on finding some positive replacement for what had been lost. He had a sense of history and of proportion. He understood the need to restore something like a partnership with the United States and he enjoyed a personal friendship with President Eisenhower which was to be a help in rebuilding the broken Anglo–American bridges. Further, while his political instincts were judged by the right and centre of the Conservative Party (at this stage, anyway) as virtually impeccable he was also, unlike many right-wingers in his Party, an economic expansionist who understood that, if his Government could not secure the prosperity of the people, the Conservatives would lose the next general election. Thus, from the start, a policy of financial restraint which was essential to restore the standing of sterling was regarded as providing a spring-board from which a new period of expansion could be launched.

This is not the context in which to discuss the policy-making of the Macmillan Government nor how the various decisions were taken. But it is necessary to state Macmillan's general aims, because from them flowed several individual acts of policy which affected the Government's relationship with its own backbenchers. First, Macmillan's conception of Britain's future rôle in the world, and therefore of her defence and foreign policy, gave rise to a new nuclear policy which was to bring the Government into a state of tension with its supporters in the Commons. Secondly, foreign policy and economic considerations combined to bring about the decision in 1961 to apply for membership of the European Economic Community. This was a further source of strain between the Government and its supporters. A third major strain also arose indirectly from the Government's economic policies: the adoption (also in July 1961) of the 'pay pause' and incomes policy by the Chancellor of the Exchequer, Selwyn Lloyd, and the subsequent unpopularity of this policy in the country, led to the peremptory dismissal of Selwyn Lloyd by Macmillan in July 1962 in order to arrest the slump in the Government's popularity. The dismissal of Lloyd and six other Ministers put such a strain upon Conservative loyalty to Macmillan that when the Profumo scandal broke in 1963, its effect on the Conservative backbenchers was traumatic. As a result, Harold Macmillan came nearer to being turned out of office by an adverse opinion expressed in Parliament, than any Prime Minister had done since Neville Chamberlain had been forced to resign in deference to the wishes of the Commons in 1940.

During the first years of Macmillan's tenure of office, however, there was a steady revival of Conservative morale in Parliament. The Government was, of course, still confronted with the criticism of the group of Conservative 'Independents' who had resigned the Whip over Suez and who frequently joined forces with otherRight-wingers in the Party over economic policy. Throughout its life, the Macmillan

Government came under criticism from economic 'purists' on the right wing of its party on the grounds that its economic policy was insufficiently disciplined. Indeed, it was this sort of criticism within the Government itself which led to the resignation of the Chancellor of the Exchequer, Peter Thorneycroft and the other two Treasury Ministers, Nigel Birch and Enoch Powell, in January 1958 because they could not approve of the Government's Estimates for the next year projecting an increase in spending. During most years of the Macmillan Administration, similar criticisms of the Government's economic policy were voiced by the Conservative Right-wingers. Nevertheless, the Tory critics made no public impact because they formed a small group arguing along lines which wholly ruled out any co-operation with the Labour Opposition. Occasionally, there were open demonstrations of revolt, as when five Conservatives (of whom three were 'Independents') abstained from supporting the Government's economic policy in a Division in July 1957 on the grounds that it was leading to serious inflation.[1] But such protests commanded little support in the country where the Government's policies were generally popular. The Right-wing critics of the Government's economic policy were in as isolated a position as Lord Salisbury was when he resigned from the Government because he disagreed with its Cyprus policy. He had the support of the Conservative Right wing—but Right-wing protests, whether on economic or overseas policy, made little impression against the rising tide of affluence in the country. In 1959, the Conservatives obtained their third successive general election victory with a majority increased to 100. After achieving so remarkable a success in so short a time, Macmillan's position in his party seemed fundamentally unshakeable. Yet statistics have been compiled which show that Conservative backbenchers voted more often against Government policies and against the injunctions of the Whips between 1959 and 1964 than in any other Parliament since the war, taking major and minor rebellions together.[2] These rebellions plainly reflected the backbenchers' consciousness that the size of their majority gave them a safety-margin within which they could rebel without endangering their party's hold on power. However, it would be wholly wrong to infer

---

[1] *The Times*, July 26, 1957; H.C. Deb., Vol. 574, cols. 726–7.
[2] Robert J. Jackson, *Party Discipline in Britain since 1945* (Thesis, unpublished), submitted to the University of Oxford.

from this that backbench pressures on the Macmillan Government were superficial. Nor can an Administration's responsiveness to its own backbenchers be measured in terms of its reactions to their open rebellions. Immediately the Conservatives were returned in 1959, the Prime Minister realised (and said as much privately) that his back-benchers would have to be given more latitude. In particular, the Government sought, by meeting backbench wishes on comparatively minor points, to keep morale high and secure the assent of Conservative Members for the Cabinet's major policies. One of the most constant Conservative backbench complaints was of the burden of taxation on enterprise and particularly on the managerial and other middle classes. The imposition of surtax on earned income starting at £2,000 a year was regarded as wholly inappropriate in view of the decline in the value of money. In 1961, the Budget of Selwyn Lloyd, the Chancellor of the Exchequer, introduced tax changes designed to meet this situation. In rough terms, it was worth about £500 a year to the £5,000-a-year man and it gave a great boost temporarily to Conservative backbench morale. This was largely achieved by cuts of £83m. in the burden of surtax—an action with which the Opposition was able to make much play during the 'pay pause' period which followed shortly afterwards.

Yet despite Mr Macmillan's conscious attempt to keep his back-benchers happy, he was not able to prevent rebellions on a wide range of policies, domestic and foreign, during this Parliament. There was, for instance, widespread Conservative distrust of the policy being pursued in Rhodesia by the Colonial Secretary, Iain Macleod. Macleod was attacked, openly and privately, in the bitterest terms by Right-wing Conservatives for too enthusiastic pursuit of African advancement and for alleged indifference to the interests of the Europeans in Central Africa. Over 100 Conservative backbenchers signed a motion, tabled in the House of Commons on February 9, 1961, which criticised the Government's Central African policy: this episode did Macleod's subsequent ministerial career much harm. Yet it could not too seriously embarrass the Government since on this issue the Labour Opposition was certainly not critical of the Government's progressiveness but believed, instead, that the Government was not progressive enough. In much the same way, a big Conservative rebellion which aimed (against the Government's policy) at restoring corporal punishment failed to produce any serious effect even though sixty-nine Conservatives voted against their leaders.[1] Again, the reason was that the rebels had no support from across the gangway. Once again, as with the rebellions of Labour backbenchers against their Government's defence policies, it was shown that the open revolts of Government backbenchers cannot normally succeed unless they either reflect a consensus of opinion in the House or in the country. I shall not, therefore, dwell on such rebellions but rather turn to three more significant issues in the relationship between the Macmillan Government and its followers. The first of these was the Common Market: the second, the Government's nuclear defence policy: the third, the Profumo scandal.

(ii)

Britain's relationship with western Europe had been an issue in British politics from the earliest post-war years when the first steps were taken towards the formation of what was to become the European Economic Community. Neither the post-war Labour Government nor the succeeding Churchill administration considered, however, that political opinion in Britain would allow this country to associate itself with the steps being taken to build up an economic union which might eventually lead to some form of political integration. In 1957, the Treaty of Rome was signed by Belgium, France, Germany, Italy, Luxembourg and the Netherlands, establishing the European Economic Community, more generally known as the Common Market. It was the year in which Harold Macmillan became Prime Minister, and during the whole of his tenure of this office, Britain's relationship with Europe was a theme of mounting importance. From the outset of his administration, Macmillan understood that Britain could not stand wholly aside from Europe. Thus there first took place the abortive negotiations for the association of Britain with the Common Market in a wider free trade area. This would have allowed the building up of tariff-free trading between Britain and the members of the Common Market. But Britain would have been free of the Community's common tariff arrangement and would therefore be able to retain preferential trading with the other members of the Commonwealth. In addition, the proposed free trade area would have excluded agriculture.

The next phase in Britain's highly tentative approach to Europe was the establishment of the European Free Trade Association of

[1] H.C. Deb., Vol. 638, cols. 57 and 145.

Britain, the Scandinavian countries, Portugal, Switzerland and Austria. This was seen as a possible help towards bridge-building with the Common Market. But it was not until 1960 that the Government's European policy began to turn into a major issue affecting the relationship between the Government and its backbenchers in the House of Commons.

On July 27, 1960, Macmillan, in re-shaping his Cabinet, appointed Lord Home to be Foreign Secretary and Mr Edward Heath, as Lord Privy Seal, to be a second Foreign Office Cabinet Minister in the House of Commons. Mr Heath was to have special charge of European affairs. The Prime Minister had now become far more concerned about the political implications of Britain's separation from a united Europe than with the purely trade problem. Henceforth, therefore discussions with Europe were to be in the hands of a 'political' Minister rather than a Minister in charge of one of the economic or trade departments. A year of much more intense probing of the prospects for negotiations with Europe now began in Whitehall. Membership of the Common Market was seen by many Ministers, civil servants and Conservative Party officials as a solution for Britain's economic difficulties. It would also give Britain a more solid position in the changing world order. Successful negotiations to enter Europe *before the next general election* were also seen as the best hope for a Conservative victory. There had been no mention by the Conservatives of any plan to negotiate with Europe in the 1959 election manifesto and it was clear that the next election was more likely to be lost than won by the Conservatives if they went to the country proclaiming an as yet unfulfilled promise to join forces with the Common Market. For one thing, the Beaverbrook press was campaigning bitterly against British involvement in Europe: more important, considerable sections of the Conservative Party in Parliament and in the constituencies were hostile to a project which they felt, not without reason, was likely to loosen Commonwealth relations and would mean radical changes in the system of protection hitherto provided for domestic British agriculture. On the other hand, the accomplished fact of membership could be represented as a political triumph opening new vistas for Britain in the future. Foreign Office hostility under Eden and Conservative Party attitudes had kept Britain out of Europe hitherto. Now, as Edward Heath began probing the prospects for successful negotiations, an intensive re-education of Conservative backbench and constituency opinion was necessary.

At the end of July 1961 the Prime Minister announced in the House of Commons that the Government had reached the conclusion that Britain should seek membership of the European Economic Community and should sign the Treaty of Rome. But the Government also stipulated that such an agreement would be dependent upon finding 'satisfactory arrangements' for the special interests of Britain, the Commonwealth and the European Free Trade Area. These conditions were named in the motion approving the Government's decision which was passed by the Commons on August 3 by 313 votes to five. (The Labour Party, having been defeated on a 'reasoned' amendment of its own, abstained on the main Division.) From now on there was sustained pressure inside the Conservative Party by backbenchers from all its wings who feared that the Government's Common Market policy would both damage the Commonwealth and British agriculture and also eventually lead to an infringement of British national sovereignty.

On July 26, forty-nine Conservatives signed a motion which expressed fear that British sovereignty might be in danger. From now until the final collapse of the Common Market negotiations, a campaign designed to stop Britain from joining the Common Market was pursued in and out of Parliament. Its parliamentary leaders were two former Conservative Ministers, Sir Derek Walker-Smith and Robin Turton. They were aided by an able younger Member, Peter Walker, who, ironically, was to be one of Edward Heath's principal supporters for the Conservative leadership in 1965. The anti-Common Market campaign on the Conservative side included, of course, the essential core of the party's right wing: MPs like Lord Hinchingbrooke, Paul Williams and John Biggs-Davidson who had long been critical of the Government's policies on such subjects as colonial advancement and, of course, Suez. But what made the campaign a force to be reckoned with was the leadership given by essentially older men of moderate Conservative politics with considerable standing in the party and the constituencies. Broadly speaking, the division of opinion was (with, of course, a number of important exceptions) one of age. Younger Conservative Members were generally enthusiastic for joining the Common Market while the older ones could not easily overcome their suspicions.

Nevertheless, the Government won support for its policies at the 1961 Conservative Party Conference by emphasising that it would agree to entry into Europe only if special conditions for agriculture and Commonwealth trade were fulfilled. The anti-Common Market campaign inside the Conservative Party was, in fact, very circumspectly organised. In debates in the House, the campaigners avoided either voting against the Government or deliberately abstaining as a demonstration of hostility. Early in 1962, the author was made aware on several occasions of some Ministers' consciousness of the political struggle still before it inside the Conservative Party as Mr Heath approached the crucial phase of the negotiations, dealing with agriculture. Ministers whose fingers were always on the pulse of party feeling feared that if the negotiations dragged on without a clear issue until the autumn, the Government would not by any means be assured of the same easy victory at the next Party Conference as the one it had gained in 1961.

On March 21, 1962, another substantial demonstration of Conservative backbench anti-Common Market feeling took place. More than thirty Conservatives put down a motion in the House of Commons demanding that the Government should make 'completely clear' to the Common Market countries 'the assurances of the Secretary for Commonwealth Relations that if we cannot secure special arrangements to protect the vital interests in the countries of our own Commonwealth partnership, Britain will not join the Common Market'. This demand was made in an amendment tabled to a Liberal pro-Common Market motion. Its importance was that it was signed not merely by prominent campaigners against the Government's policy but also by a considerable number of moderates who had hitherto seemed uncommitted.

The crucial question was, of course, what 'special arrangements' would have been considered satisfactory by the critics. The question is hypothetical since, eventually, the negotiations foundered on the intransigence of President de Gaulle. Nevertheless, there is little doubt that the Government would have been satisfied with 'special arrangements' of a much weaker kind than those wanted by the critics. On this assessment, there can be equally little doubt that a minority of Conservative Members might well have abstained, or voted against the Government, had the negotiations been successful. But, of course, voting against the nearly accomplished fact (even though it may be overtly more dramatic than the exercise of more subtle pressures) is a lesser form of backbench influence than that which attempts to prevent the policies from getting off the ground. The latter sort of pressure was what Macmillan had to counter in the

236

early months of 1962 and he did so with skill. Suspicions in Commonwealth capitals of British policy increased Conservative misgivings and as the worries of the critics hardened, some of Mr Macmillan's public utterances seemed to harden also. Thus, speaking to the Parliamentary Press in March 1962 he observed:

> It would be a great error to believe that the decision rests with us alone. We are too apt to assume that. An equal responsibility lies on the member states of the Community.

Conservative suspicions were not allayed by the terms in which Mr Heath was now speaking to the Europeans. While the whole emphasis of Government statements in the Commons dwelt upon the minutiae of economic negotiations and emphasised the trade aspects, Heath was making it clear to the Economic Community that Britain supported political union and expected eventually to play a full part in it. Speaking to the Western European Union Ministerial meeting on April 10, he said:

> We are looking forward to joining you as soon as possible in constructing a Europe united politically as well as economically.

His emphasis was one which would have been unthinkable in the political climate of twelve months earlier and it marked the growing confidence of the Government both in the course of the negotiations in Brussels and in the process of 're-education' of Conservative backbench opinion. Nevertheless, some Members of the Government were in no way disposed to regard the political dangers at home as solved. About this time, one senior Cabinet Minister spoke of the Common Market issue to the author as potentially the most fundamental shake-up in the Conservative Party since Disraeli's break with Peel over the Corn Laws.

The Government had hoped that the Brussels negotiations would be completed by about July 1962. But before then it was clear that they were running well behind time. Early that month, the Prime Minister had to inform the Commons that a 'concluding picture' of the negotiations might not be known until after the adjournment of Parliament for the summer recess. As the Cabinet was considering whether to allow Edward Heath latitude to move from the existing British position, the Conservative anti-Common Market group on July 30 put down yet another motion on the House of Commons Order Paper exhorting the Government to

... stand firm and to insist on definite assurances for Commonwealth trade and for the continuance of the power of sovereign decision by the British Parliament and for our agricultural and horticultural policies.

Immediately, thirty-six Conservatives signed the motion and not all of them were Members hostile to British membership of the Community provided appropriate safeguards could be made. Realising that a motion of flat rejection would achieve nothing for their cause, the anti-Common Market campaigners had drafted their protest in terms designed to attract wider support. At this time there were between thirty and forty convinced opponents of the Common Market, of one brand or another. But there had also been a constant murmur of anxiety from at least a hundred Conservative MPs, notably from those who represented agricultural constituencies and who, though not opposed to entry on principle, would insistthat the safeguards for British agriculture must be adequate.

On October 11, despite some earlier misgivings, the Government secured an overwhelming and enthusiastic vote of confidence for its Common Market policy at the Conservative annual conference. The ground had been skilfully prepared and the Government had been helped by a speech attacking the Government's policy by Hugh Gaitskell at the Labour Conference in the previous week. This speech the Conservative leaders could represent as 'backward looking' and the atmosphere of the Conference at Llandudno that day was one of a forward-into-Europe rally. Yet if the Conservative Conference could be converted in this way (and quite apart from the skilful speeches of Cabinet Ministers, a great deal of propaganda work had been done by the party organisation) Members of Parliament could not be so easily persuaded. As the negotiations moved towards the final failure, forty-seven Conservative Members signed a motion on December 13 urging the Government to remain firm in its conduct of the Brussels negotiations—even if it meant breaking them off. Furthermore they urged the Government 'to formulate as soon as possible an alternative policy based on a major Commonwealth initiative'. This motion was tabled after the House of Commons had heard a progress report from Heath on the course of the negotiations, and it represented not only an open recognition on the part of a fairly representative sample of backbenchers that it might be better in certain circumstances to discontinue the negotiations but also voiced the first definite request that the Government should begin planning for the possibility of failure. Heath himself was still speaking as though the negotiations would end in success. But the signatures appended to the motion of December 13 made it absolutely clear that the Conservative Party would not stomach entry into the Common Market on any terms. One of the significant signatures was that of Sir Anthony Hurd, Chairman of the Conservative Party's Parliamentary Committee on Agriculture; his approval of the motion could be taken as reflecting the views of the large number of backbench Conservatives representing agricultural constituencies.

In the end, the essential will which aborted the negotiations was that of the French President. Nevertheless, the influence of the Conservative Members of the House of Commons on the course of events was not negligible. It is possible, for instance, that it was easier for de Gaulle to adopt the line he did because of the knowledge in Europe that the Conservative Party was divided and the Labour Party was generally hostile to British membership of the European Community. This was one instance in which the line taken by an Opposition was of considerable importance in political developments. European Governments could always ask whether a Labour Government in Britain might disown a treaty which the Conservatives had signed. But perhaps more important was the growing conviction in Europe that the Community would have to make real concessions, in view of the feelings of Conservative backbenchers, if a formula enabling Britain's admission to the Community were to be found. It cannot be doubted that Macmillan and Heath, and a very potent section of opinion-formers at the time, would have been prepared for British entry into Europe on virtually any terms, and leading ultimately to some form of political integration. It is equally incontrovertible that they were brought to understand that opinion in the parliamentary ranks of the Conservative Party would not stomach British membership of the Community on any terms and, indeed, that parliamentary opinion as a whole, if the Labour Party is also taken into account, would not assent.

The Government had undertaken a formidable re-education process inside the Conservative Party and it had achieved a great deal. New attitudes had been created which were to pave the way for the acceptance of the European ideal by the Party under Heath's leadership after 1965. Nevertheless, Conservative parliamentary feeling had imposed clear limits on the extent to which the Government could go. In naming terms, it had circumscribed the Government's action in negotiations. By circumscribing this action it had contributed towards the failure of the project. The failure of the project was, in turn, one cause of the gradual loosening of Macmillan's personal grip on the Conservative Party.

(iii)

On January 24, 1957, within a fortnight of taking office, Macmillan announced in the House of Commons that he had entrusted his new Minister of Defence, Duncan Sandys, with the task of formulating a defence policy which would secure a substantial reduction in expenditure and in manpower. This would involve reshaping and reorganising the armed forces and Sandys had been given new powers over the individual Service Ministries to enable him to fulfil this duty. Macmillan informed the House of Commons that although the first fruits of the new policy would be in the defence Estimates for the new financial year, the initial priority was to make a long term plan. At this stage, it was already clear that one result of the new policy was likely to be the ending of conscription. The day after Macmillan's announcement Sandys flew to Washington for his first discussions on defence policy with the United States Government. As a result of the reappraisal of defence policy thus begun, the annual Defence White Paper was postponed from the middle of February, the conventional moment for its appearance, until the end of March. But in the meantime it was revealed when special Navy, Army and Air Force votes on account were published (owing to the delay in the full defence Estimates) that the armed services were to be cut by 65,500 men in the coming financial year. Meanwhile, British Ministers were busy defending the changes in Britain's defence policy to governments of anxious Western European allies while Macmillan himself explained the new policy to his friend President Eisenhower when the two met in Bermuda just before the publication of the Defence White Paper.

When it appeared on April 5, the White Paper was officially described as marking the 'biggest change in defence policy made in normal times'. The essential motive for the change was probably the one indicated in the following observation: 'Britain's influence in the world depends first and foremost on the health of her internal economy and the success of her export trade. Without these, military power cannot in the long run be supported.' The essential points of the new policy were three: the progressive reduction of National Service, which was to end in 1960; the build-up of regular serving forces; high priority for the development of nuclear weapons for delivery by bombers, rockets and guided missiles. The result of this plan (so it was thought) would be an appreciable reduction in the burden on the national economy as well as the release of skilled men, including much-needed scientists and technicians, for employment in civilian industry. It was admitted that Britain had been bearing a disproportionate share of Western defence and it was hoped that this would be corrected by the new plan.

Such was the genesis of the new Conservative defence policy in which reliance on a national independent deterrent became the cornerstone of British international strategy while conventional forces were run down. The military credibility or otherwise of this policy is not a relevant question in the present context. It is enough to note that the credibility of nuclear independence for Britain came under serious question in 1960 when the Conservative Government found itself reluctantly obliged to cancel the development of the British missile 'Blue Streak'. Instead, Britain was to rely on the provision, at a future unspecified date, of the US missile Skybolt, which was then in an early stage of development.

When Macmillan negotiated the Skybolt agreement with the Americans at Camp David in 1960, technical doubts were already being raised about the suitability of Skybolt, though it appears that both the US Air Force and the British Air Ministry may have been reticent in expressing them for internal reasons. But there was another fact which was a potential cause of discord. American and British aims were not identical: the two governments cast Skybolt in a different rôle. The United States was working towards a guided missile: Britain, on the other hand, was simply concerned to have a missile that could be dropped by its own bomber force. One thing that is clear is that the British Government failed to understand the American attitude towards cost-effectiveness in defence policy and failed to appreciate the way in which the US would be prepared, if necessary, to cut its losses. Consequently, the Macmillan Government was thrown right out of its stride when the American Government decided at the end of 1962 to abandon the development of Skybolt.

Yet the UK Government ought not to have been surprised at the American decision not to go ahead with the air-launched Skybolt, in the development of which the UK was to have a subsidiary rôle. For instance, in June 1961 the US Defence Secretary, McNamara, said that development of Skybolt 'may or may not be successful' and reports appeared of doubts among defence experts in Washington about whether Skybolt could do precisely what was claimed for it. In March 1962, McNamara told a Congressional Committee that Skybolt was having development problems although it was unlikely to be cancelled. At home both Harold Wilson and George Brown, speaking for the Labour Opposition, cast doubts on the survival of Skybolt as a project. Later in the year, there were a number of test failures but as late as November the Air Minister, Hugh Fraser, could reply answering a Question in the Commons: 'Her Majesty's Government are quite resolved that this programme shall go through.'[1] However, it was the resolution of the American, not the British Government which counted. In December McNamara flew to London to discuss the future of Skybolt and it quickly became clear that the Americans had decided that strategically it was not worth its cost. On December 15 McGeorge Bundy, President Kennedy's special adviser on defence policy, said on American television that the US did not have a fixed commitment to provide Britain with an alternative nuclear weapon if the Skybolt project were cancelled. The main question would be the organising of the NATO missile forces. One thing that was now clear was that the US would be only too pleased if Britain would gracefully abandon all pretensions to being an independent nuclear power.

But this was what Macmillan neither would nor could do. The precise reasons for the strength of his own personal commitment to the policy of the independent nuclear deterrent are not yet clear. The economic argument, which had been one of the main reasons for the original emphasis on the nuclear defence policy, plainly no longer applied. Britain had been involved in mounting costs incurred through the attempts which had so far been unsuccessfully made to provide for the future.

American observers of the episode were inclined to believe that Macmillan was not the man to be misled into believing that Britain was ever likely to play a nuclear rôle independent of the US. On this analysis, the Prime Minister was moved, not primarily by belief in the credibility of a nuclear rôle for Britain (in strict military terms)

[1] H.C. Deb., Vol. 668, col. 378, November 28, 1962.

but by the exigencies of domestic politics. On the other hand, there was a strong school of thought among British defence experts at this time (as later) which argued that the only vital defence interest for Britain was the protection of the United Kingdom as such, which could only be achieved by nuclear weapons. The defence of other British interests by conventional weapons was held to be secondary. (Indeed, there developed an argument that Britain should save money spent on conventional defence East of Suez and elsewhere and devote it to the nuclear protection of the homeland.) These arguments no doubt influenced Macmillan and the Defence Minister, Peter Thorneycroft. Another part of the explanation for Macmillan's personal commitment to the nuclear policy may have been a belief that, by maintaining Britain's position as a nuclear power, the Government would keep its position at the 'top table' in international defence policy and would at least be provided with the knowledge and the language with which to talk internationally on nuclear affairs. Macmillan's own work towards the achievement of the Test Ban Treaty at the end of his term of office may itself be a partial justification of the policy.

Yet making due allowance for these considerations, it is difficult to escape the conclusion that Macmillan's negotiation of the Skybolt agreement in 1960 and his fight to find a substitute for it in 1962 resulted substantially from the need to respond to feeling on the Conservative backbenches in Parliament. Indeed, the formulation of the Conservative nuclear defence policy in 1957 may itself have been motivated by the need to restore the morale of the Tory Party after the Suez affair and to let both the Party and the country feel that Britain had a major rôle in the new era of her diminished world responsibilities. By 1962 the preservation of Britain's nuclear status had become a matter of fervent conviction among the majority of Conservative backbenchers and they were in no mood to let the Prime Minister reverse the Government's policy. When the Minister of Defence, Peter Thorneycroft, formally admitted in the Commons on December 17 that the future of Skybolt was 'in question', bitter Conservative criticism erupted on the benches behind him. Air Commodore Sir Arthur Vere Harvey, then Chairman of the Conservative Backbench Defence Committee, stated bluntly, to the accompaniment of many Government backbench cheers:

Some of us on this side of the House, who wish to see Britain retain a nuclear deterrent, are highly suspicious of some of the American motives.

This was the message that Vere Harvey wanted conveyed to the Prime Minister and hence to President Kennedy and he added that the British people were 'tired of being pushed around'. Conservative criticism from the backbenchers that day reached a point at which Mr Thorneycroft felt obliged to observe: 'I think I should say that we are speaking of perhaps our closest ally.'

It was against this background of party feeling at home that Macmillan's meeting with Kennedy at Nassau in the Bahamas must be assessed. Thorneycroft, less committed to Skybolt than Macmillan, was already prepared to accept Polaris and may even have been prepared to do without that if necessary. Macmillan, on the other hand, still wanted Skybolt. But on the way to the meeting, Kennedy, by speaking of Skybolt in the past tense, made it clear that the project was doomed and he put British aspirations in their place by pointing to the negligible contribution that Britain would have made to the project compared with the expenditure involved for the US. For Macmillan, the Nassau meeting was an uncomfortable one. Once he realised that the American decision to abandon Skybolt was irreversible, the Prime Minister is said[1] to have remarked at Nassau that Skybolt was the lady he wanted but she had been violated in public. Thereupon he set about persuading Kennedy of the moral obligation of the United States to provide an alternative which could only be Polaris.

One of his most insistent arguments was that he must have this alternative if he were to survive with his backbenchers at home. Did he overstate their influence in order to make his case? No doubt he was glad to be able to bolster his arguments by calling into evidence the feeling of his backbenchers. Yet this is no reason for supposing that the backbench pressures were unreal. At this stage, and with an election due in the next year or two, it would have been electorally extremely damaging, if not impossible, to ask the Conservative Party to contract out of Britain's nuclear status. Macmillan was under pressure both from the aviation 'lobby' and from the Conservative backbenches. The pressure exerted on Macmillan from the back-benches of the Conservative Party in Parliament to some extent represented the 'lobby' of the aviation industry which feared the effect

[1] This, at least, was what was being reported in American government circles at the time.

on itself if Britain lost the 'fall-out' of nuclear knowledge which it gained as a by-product of British nuclear defence. But far more important was the instinctive feeling among Conservatives of all shades of opinion, except for a negligible and unrepresentative handful of Tory MPs on the extreme left of the Party, that Britain must retain the ability to act, with nuclear weapons, in her own defence and alone, if the need arose. Conservative Members had long been restive at the increasing dependence of Britain upon the US. They wanted to ensure that Britain would be capable of acting alone, to protect her own vital interests, if the US were unwilling, when asked, to do so.

It was against this criterion that the backbenchers judged the Nassau Agreement between Macmillan and Kennedy under which Polaris was obtained in substitution for Skybolt. Although Polaris was to be made over in practice to the NATO alliance, it could be withdrawn for use by the British Government alone if 'supreme national interests' were at stake. On their return from Nassau the Prime Minister and Mr Thorneycroft had to persuade their doubting followers of the validity of this escape clause. On January 1, 1963, a meeting took place at the Ministry of Defence between Thorneycroft and thirteen Conservative MPs headed by Vere Harvey. It was not an easy meeting and it lasted for one and a half hours. One of the reassurances given to the backbenchers (and hence to the aviation industry) was that there would be further expenditure on the stand-off flying bomb Blue Steel, which would bridge the gap between the V-bombers (which *had* given Britain a credible independent nuclear weapon) and the availability of Polaris missiles (less warheads) for British submarines. This commitment to improve Blue Steel was clearly a concession to win the backbenchers' support for the Polaris deal. The Polaris agreement itself certainly cost Britain dear in economic terms, for it involved this country in paying for a weapon which was essentially a weapon of the Western Alliance and with which Britain could have been protected without payment. But the pressures from the backbenches of the Conservative Party were real and they had to be met by the Government. Vere Harvey himself had privately indicated to the Government that, if he were not satisfied, he would be prepared to resign the Conservative Whip and there seems little doubt that others would have joined him. The Nassau Agreement, which in American eyes at least had been a triumph of negotiation for Macmillan, was accepted with the greatest reluctance by the Conservatives in the House of Commons. Yet the Government might have been driven neither to the Skybolt nor the Polaris agreement had backbench feeling in the House of Commons been less strong.

(iv)

The nuclear defence issue and the failure of the attempt to enter the Common Market were themselves, perhaps, contributory to the slackening of Macmillan's hold over the allegiance of his followers in Parliament in 1962-3. But a far more damaging event was Macmillan's sudden dismissal of the Chancellor of the Exchequer, Selwyn Lloyd, and six other Ministers on July 13, 1962, to counteract the damage done to Conservative standing in the country (as measured in by-elections) by Selwyn Lloyd's handling of the Government's incomes policy and the 'pay pause'. Macmillan had decided that, if his party was to win the next election, it must present an entirely new front. But, to his backbenchers, the peremptory dismissal of the Chancellor seemed to be a sign of panic and, indeed, a failure of the proper relationship between a Prime Minister and his senior colleague. When the Conservative backbench Finance Committee met four days later, strong protests against Mr Lloyd's dismissal were voiced in private. Bitterly a number of Conservative Members asked what their position was supposed to be now that Selwyn Lloyd—the Minister whose policies they had been steadily peddling up and down the country on a Conservative Central Office brief—had been dismissed. Moreover, the Conservative Members took no trouble to hide their feelings when Macmillan first entered the House after the dismissals. A frozen and embarrassed reception was given to the Prime Minister, and his entry was received in complete silence by his own side, in the sharpest contrast to the warm and long cheer which greeted the entry of the dismissed Chancellor. Two days later the Prime Minister went privately to address a meeting of the 1922 Committee. After a reception which was afterwards described officially as 'cordial' (a less glowing word than was usually applied to the reception given to a Prime Minister by his followers) and was unofficially spoken of as frigid, the Prime Minister explained to his backbenchers the pain he had felt in parting with the ex-Chancellor of the Exchequer. He had done so in the country's and the Party's interest, he maintained. The Prime Minister's argument was that after eleven years in power, the Conservatives had to present a new image and if changes in the

Government were necessary it was best that they should be dealt with quickly. When Macmillan, a few weeks later, defended the Government's economic policy in the House he had a rather better reception but there was little warmth in it and Macmillan looked tired and dispirited. But throughout 1962, as the Common Market project moved towards failure and unemployment increased, Macmillan's reputation failed to recover. In November, a round of by-elections produced a pronounced anti-Government swing which further disillusioned Conservative backbenchers with their leadership.

Nevertheless, by the spring of 1963, it had become generally accepted among Conservatives that Macmillan would again lead the Party at the next election. On April 10, at the annual luncheon of the 1922 Committee, the Prime Minister himself made this quite clear. The truth was that there was no generally acceptable heir in sight. The Prime Minister and his colleagues now began to prepare for the election that was expected in the autumn of 1963 or the spring of 1964. Yet no sooner had this degree of assurance been given to Conservative Members, than they were precipitated into the midst of the Profumo scandal.

This affair nearly cost Macmillan the leadership of his Party. When it was revealed that Mr Profumo, who was Minister of War, had lied to the House of Commons in denying any improper relationship between himself and a Miss Keeler, the question was immediately asked whether the Prime Minister had been in a position to know anything from any other sources, notably the security services, which should have caused him to doubt Mr Profumo's earlier denial and to refuse to accept a colleague's word. Further, had Mr Macmillan taken positive steps before Profumo's earlier statements in the House to find out what facts were known to the Government in view of the persistent rumours? During the dramatic days of early June Macmillan rallied his Government colleagues to his support, but the basic question remained whether he could still command the loyalty of the Conservative backbenchers. It was not that there existed any doubt of Macmillan's good faith. The question was rather whether he was sufficiently in touch with his colleagues, whether he should have interviewed Profumo himself, and whether five Ministers who did question Profumo had done all they could to find the truth of the allegations against him. Although it was clear that the issue of Macmillan's leadership had again been opened, the party organisation still believed that he would do well enough in the censure debate in which the Labour Opposition challenged not his integrity, but his competence.

In the event, the Prime Minister did much worse than the Government had expected. At the end of the debate on June 17, the Conservative's overall majority dropped from ninety-three to sixty-nine and twenty-seven of the Government's backbenchers abstained. Even more significant was the cold reception given by the Conservative backbenchers as a whole to the Prime Minister's explanation of his handling of the affair. The next day, the one question being asked among Conservative backbenchers was who could succeed Mr Macmillan as Prime Minister and how quickly could the change be made? For the moment (and it was only a moment) Conservatives seemed almost unanimous that a change of some sort was needed. An important member of the Party said to the author at this time that the backbenchers had 'panicked'. Whether they had or not; whether the Conservative Members were justified in their critical attitude towards the Prime Minister, there was no doubt that they were not tamely following their leader. On the other hand, Macmillan was sustained by two important facts. First, there was still no agreement about a successor. Secondly, many of those who wanted him to go believed that he should not go so quickly as to give the impression that his departure was owing to any sort of guilt from the Profumo affair. For this would reflect not only on Macmillan himself, but on the Conservative Party of which he had been the leader. A long enough period had to elapse to make clear that Macmillan's departure was not connected with the scandal.

But, of course, a delay naturally worked on behalf of Macmillan as the incumbent. Besides, prominent Conservatives were now taking steps to silence the discussion about the leadership. When one attempt to raise it was anticipated in the 1922 Committee, preventive tactics were adopted to stop discussion. By June 28, Macmillan felt confident enough to say in a television interview that he hoped to lead the Conservative Party at the next general election. The difficulty of replacing him by some undetermined successor had now become apparent even to those in the Party who most wanted him to go. On July 15, the Prime Minister had a long meeting with the Executive of the 1922 Committee. At the end of this meeting, which had ranged widely over policy questions and the state of the Party's morale, the backbenchers had formed the distinct opinion that Macmillan had no intention of resigning in the near future. Immediately afterwards,

Macmillan met the full 1922 Committee and he predicted that the Conservative Party could and would win the election: the implication was that he would be leading it. Early in August, he claimed on television that he had the full support of Conservatives, though he did not answer precisely the question whether he would lead the Party at the election. This question was still in doubt when the Conservative Annual Conference was due to meet at Blackpool. On the eve of that Conference Mr Macmillan indicated to Cabinet colleagues that he intended to lead the Party at the election. But illness disposed otherwise. Mr Macmillan was suddenly struck down: he indicated his intention to resign and the processes were set in train which resulted in the selection of Lord Home as his successor.

What, then, does this episode tell us of the relationship between a Government and its backbenchers? First, of course, they did not manage to force Mr Macmillan into retirement that summer, though a majority of the Party plainly wanted to do so. On the other hand, had they been clear about a successor (how unclear they were was made evident by the proceedings at Blackpool when they unexpectedly found themselves without a leader) they might well have been able to do so. It is not quite true that a party cannot bring down a Leader. The retirement of Winston Churchill had finally been secured as a result of strong feeling in the Party on account of his age and indisposition, revered as he was. A few more abstentions in June 1963, a resignation or two from the Government, or an obvious successor, might well have made Macmillan's position impossible. As it was, he had to justify himself to his backbenchers and they repeatedly made their feelings clear. The attitude of the backbenchers to the Prime Minister during these months undoubtedly had a strong impact on the public's view of the Conservative leadership and was certainly a contributory cause to the defeat of the Party at the 1964 Election. The relationship between Macmillan and his followers during 1963 shows the immense strength a leader has *vis-à-vis* his party, however discontented it may be, if he lacks rivals and if he has the nerve. But it also shows the need he has to command their loyalty and the damage they can do his reputation if confidence between the two breaks down.

Chapter Nine

Resale Price Maintenance:
A study of Backbench Influence

No single parliamentary rebellion in the post-war years has thrown more light on the essential nature of the relationship between Ministers and their rank and file in the Commons than the fight of a significant section of Conservative backbenchers against the proposal of Sir Alec Douglas-Home's government in 1964 to abolish resale price maintenance. An analysis of this conflict—in which the possibility that the Minister concerned, Mr Edward Heath, might be obliged to resign was at least raised in the minds of some of the Conservative Members involved—demonstrated how far a Government needs to heed the sentiment of its backbenchers and to understand the art of parliamentary management. It shows both the reality and the limitations of the influence of the Government's own supporters over Ministers.

Yet the real political significance of resale price maintenance (R.P.M.) is to be found less in this single dramatic episode than in an examination of how successive Conservative Ministers dealt with the backbenchers over the issue for a decade before that. The open conflict between Mr Heath and the rebels of 1964 was merely the culmination of a long debate inside the Conservative Party, and it is arguable that the normal relationship of a Government and its backbenchers was better demonstrated during the years before 1964, when feeling inside the Conservative Parliamentary Party repeatedly and comparatively unobtrusively inhibited government action on R.P.M., than in the final eruption against the decision to abolish it.

Resale price maintenance—the practice by which manufacturers obliged retailers to sell their branded goods at stipulated prices—has been the subject of a number of inquiries during the past forty years: the question was examined in 1919 and again in 1931. But it first moved into the foreground of post-war politics in August 1947 when

Sir Stafford Cripps, for the Labour Government, announced the setting up of a committee to make a general inquiry into the practice by which manufacturers fixed minimum retail prices for their goods. The committee, whose chairman was Mr Lloyd Jacob, K.C., was required to examine the effect of R.P.M. on supply, distribution and consumption; and the committee took evidence from individuals, trade associations, economists and other interested parties. The goods chiefly involved were cars, cigarettes and a large variety of proprietary articles such as those sold in chemists' shops.

The Lloyd Jacob Committee reported to Harold Wilson, then President of the Board of Trade, in March 1949. The Committee found that R.P.M. was not necessarily bad and had considerable support among women. Its use by individual manufacturers was not to be censured but its collective use by Trade Associations might be a threat to eliminate price competition over a very large field of the goods sold in ordinary shops. It was found that Trade Associations had built up complicated 'police' systems to make R.P.M. rigidly enforceable by collective action which sometimes involved fines, stop-lists and secret codes. The two main conclusions of the report were that no action should be taken by the Government which would deprive an individual manufacturer of the right to prescribe and enforce R.P.M. for brand goods, provided the power was not used to obstruct the development of trading, to impede distribution by another manufacturer of competitive goods or to deprive the public of improvements in distribution. But the report recommended the abolition of 'collective' R.P.M. It advocated that steps should be taken to make illegal the application of sanctions which would extend beyond the remedies open to an individual producer to enforce R.P.M.

The Lloyd Jacob Report was considered in the Board of Trade, in a Cabinet Committee and finally by the Cabinet itself. A draft Cabinet paper and a parliamentary statement were produced inside the Board of Trade and it was determined that legislation could not be introduced before the Monopolies Commission had produced reports on certain current cases in which resale price maintenance was of importance. It was therefore decided that the Minister's notes for replying to Supplementary Questions after his statement in the House of Commons should include the observation that, if legislation were necessary, it could not be undertaken in that Parliament: in fact, when the statement was eventually produced no reference was made to the timing of possible legislation, presumably because no question was asked which provided a natural opening for this answer.

At a Cabinet meeting at the end of May, approval was given to the main lines of the paper which had been submitted (subject to some slight alterations) and to the draft statement which was made to the House of Commons by the President of the Board of Trade on June 2. The effect of this statement was to urge industry to take steps of its own volition, in the coming months, to free distributors from the many restrictions imposed by Trade Associations. In other words, the Government wanted to try to end collective enforcement of R.P.M. by co-operation with industry.

The Conservative Party, heir both to the traditions of nineteenth-century *laissez-faire* and to the paternalist Tory philosophy, has always had a split mind about protection. Certainly in the early post-war years the Conservative Party was far from sympathetic to the abolition of restrictive practices. The implicit support given to R.P.M. generally in the Conservative Party was demonstrated in a question put from the Conservative backbenches by Mr Frederick Erroll[1] (himself later to be a President of the Board of Trade who made an abortive attempt to secure acceptance of R.P.M. abolition) to the Labour President, at that time Harold Wilson. In July 1949, Mr Erroll asked Mr Harold Wilson to bear in mind, when considering the proposals of the Lloyd Jacob Committee, that some of its members had 'strong Left-wing bias'.[2] Again, in a parliamentary Question later the same month, Mr Erroll sought to link collective R.P.M. with 'collective systems for protecting the wages of employees in the retail trade' by asking if the Minister would take similar steps to see that the latter practice was ended also. 'Is it not an inevitable corollary of fixed wage agreements that there must be some fixing of prices too?' Erroll asked.[3] Again, another Conservative back-bencher, Sir Thomas Moore, defended collective R.P.M. when he asked Mr Wilson on July 26 whether 'in view of his appeal for efficiency and economy in the distributive trades, he will give further consideration to the loss of efficiency which will result to producers in enforcing the resale price maintenance of their goods if the system of collective enforcement is abolished'.[4]

---

[1] Later Lord Erroll of Hale.
[2] H.C. Deb., Vol. 466, col. 2306, July 7, 1949.
[3] H.C. Deb., Vol. 467, col. 2240, July 26, 1949.
[4] H.C. Deb., Vol. 467, col. 107, July 26, 1949.

The Labour Cabinet, being unable to contemplate legislation during that Parliament, had authorised the Ministers concerned to hold discussions with Trade Associations to see that in future individual enforcement of R.P.M. should be operated reasonably and flexibly. But it was very anxious not to commit itself to approval of R.P.M. in any form. The Cabinet had laid it down that nothing should be said either to imply that legislation would not eventually be required or to express unqualified acceptance of R.P.M. by individual producers.

This Government scepticism about the practicability of voluntary reform proved to be justified. A year later, Wilson, after his discussions with trade interests, asserted that there was no sign of traders making any changes in their arrangements in the light of the Committee's report. If this persisted, he suggested, the House of Commons would be forced to the conclusion that legislation, though it would not be easy to draft, would be necessary.

But in 1951, Labour went out of office and the prospect of immediate legislation faded. In any case, legislation might not have been wholly without embarrassment to Labour which, as the debates in 1964 showed, was less than united on the issue. Widespread counter-propaganda had been mounted in favour of R.P.M. and this, in turn, attracted propaganda in favour of its abolition. In particular, the mid-fifties produced agitation against the use of R.P.M. in particular cases, notably car accessories and television tubes. Early in 1955, the Labour Party set up a special Committee of its own on Monopolies, Price Fixing and Secret Trade Courts. Yet, despite misgivings among the interested Tory rank and file, it was the Conservative Government which, in 1956, passed the Restrictive Trade Practices Act, banning collective enforcement agreements. This measure did not, however, escape heavy criticism from the Conservative backbenches. It was argued that making collective enforcement of R.P.M. unlawful would hit the small shopkeeper and play into the hands of the combines. One of the more sophisticated arguments was that as a result, pharmaceutical prices might come down, and therefore cease to help finance the health service to which the answer of the President of the Board of Trade, Peter Thorneycroft, was that the problem was to get prices down.

Gradually, R.P.M. had been breaking down in certain sections of industry, notably the grocery trade. In 1959, the President of the Board of Trade, Sir David Eccles, began considering the possibility of abolishing R.P.M. altogether, as the one concrete step which would encourage the lower prices which Ministers increasingly regarded as the prerequisite for the achievement of economic stability in 1960. The basic question was whether the clause in the 1956 Act which still allowed the individual enforcement of R.P.M. by legal action should be amended or deleted. Was it any longer right to retain individual enforcement which had an arbitrary social incidence according to whether or not individual manufacturers were prepared to go to the courts to enforce their rights?

These were the questions which, after the General Election of 1959, confronted the new President of the Board of Trade, Mr Reginald Maudling. By January 1960 he was being asked from both sides of the House whether he would legislate against R.P.M. But by then he had become well aware that the idea was far from having general acceptance and he came to the conclusion that an inquiry might be the solution to his problem. This could provide further factual information which might bolster the argument (which in principle he accepted) for ending R.P.M. and it was also a convenient way of winning time in an embarrassing situation. Accordingly, Mr Maudling took up the position that the information available to his department was insufficient for him to reach firm conclusions about the extent and the effects of R.P.M. He therefore announced on March 12 that he had set up an internal fact-finding inquiry which would be confidential. It would be conducted by officials of the Board of Trade who were concerned with the subject and was to be different in character from previous investigations. In the past, inquiries had been concerned with the arguments for and against R.P.M. This time, the inquiry would find the facts about the practice. Eight thousand questionnaires to manufacturers, wholesalers and retailers were despatched to representatives of the interests concerned. When the time came for the Government to consider the findings of this inquiry, Mr Maudling was no longer at the Board of Trade.

In October 1961, Mr Frederick Erroll, who had previously been Minister of State at the Board of Trade, was appointed President, with a seat in the Cabinet. To him fell the task of deciding what to do about R.P.M. in the light of the facts made available by the inquiry established by his predecessor. This inquiry had been internal to the department and its report to the Minister was therefore never published. The Board of Trade report, based on facts which included a comparative study of the effects of R.P.M. and its abolition in other countries, maintained that these provided an overwhelming economic case for ending the practice. These findings reinforced a long-standing and clear-cut 'departmental view' that in the interest of trade competitiveness R.P.M. should be ended. It was now for Mr Erroll and the Cabinet, being in full possession of the economic arguments for abolition, to decide whether it was a political decision the Government should take.

Mr Erroll decided to advocate the abolition of R.P.M. to the Cabinet. After some consideration of various alternative methods, including the possibility of a gradual process, he opted for a simple act of abolition. A scheme which would mean the outlawry of the practice, with one or two named exceptions, was prepared inside the department and submitted to the Economic Policy Committee of the Cabinet, where Mr Erroll received a lukewarm sanction to take it to the Cabinet itself. Here he found himself up against the powerful influence of those senior Ministers, headed by Mr R. A. Butler (then, for all practical purposes, deputy Prime Minister), who regarded the abolition of R.P.M. as too dangerous to tackle because of the split it would provoke in the ranks of Conservative MPs and the resentment it would cause to their supporters in the constituencies. Mr Iain Macleod was another opponent of action. After a brief hearing, the plan for abolition was thrown out by the Cabinet.

At the time that the internal Board of Trade report was being considered in Cabinet, the backbenchers of the Conservative Party got to hear about it and the backbenchers' Trade and Industry Committee summoned Mr Erroll to meet them and give them his views. In the circumstances, Mr Erroll was carefully non-committal. This sensible restraint from commitment, however, was interpreted by some of the backbenchers who were fearful of R.P.M. abolition as a sign that the Government was going to legislate to end the practice. Accordingly, a shoal of representations against the expected Government action began to pour in, though in fact the Cabinet had by now decided against abolition. At this time, the Chief Whip, Mr Martin Redmayne, found more complaints against Mr Erroll than any other Minister. By now, Erroll himself was beginning to see the difficulties which action would have created.

In the argument over R.P.M. that could be heard among Conservatives at Westminster at this time there were two competing points of view. One (and this partly represented the composition of many Conservative constituency organisations) argued that since the

Conservatives enjoyed the support of the small shopkeeper and, indeed, had the emotional appeal of backing the 'small man', it would be highly impolitic to offend him. Other critics argued that Mr Erroll would do far better to attend to the bigger question of monopolies first. On the other side, it was argued that the most important problem facing the country was to get prices down and to induce industrial efficiency. Many younger Conservative MPs also argued that the Party's main rôle now should be to defend the consumer rather than the shopkeeper. This was the period in which the Conservative leadership was moving towards the ideas of planning at home and eventually joining the Common Market abroad. Those who advocated one or other of these policies inevitably found themselves moving in the direction of favouring the reorganisation of British industry into larger units with a view to achieving economies of scale in the belief that membership of the Common Market would provide the necessary stimulus of competition to these bigger units. This sort of attitude naturally involved some abandonment of the Conservative Party's traditional rôle as protector of the 'small man'.

Between these two extreme attitudes was the more pragmatic position of those Conservatives who wanted to see an end to resale price maintenance but who were convinced that the time had not come when this could be legislated for without endangering Conservative unity. Those who were in this position believed, or persuaded themselves that they believed, that the practice of R.P.M. would gradually wither away, without causing internal trouble to their Party. These pragmatic opponents of action, together with the dogmatic supporters of R.P.M., probably constituted a majority on the Tory backbenches. On the other hand, probably a majority of the Cabinet would have been in favour of abolishing R.P.M. on *purely economic grounds*. But political problems were decisive, and when the Cabinet rejected Mr Erroll's original abolition proposal they were reacting to pressures from their backbenchers, who in turn were expressing pressures on them from their constituencies and from interested trade associations. At this point, the R.P.M. issue was a classic instance of Government and Whitehall policy-making being deflected by the influence of Government backbenchers.

Yet the issue was not closed. As it happened, it was the Prime Minister, Macmillan, who himself next raised the possibility of ending resale price maintenance. In 1962, he broached the possibility of wrapping up legislation to forbid R.P.M. in a package-deal covering a number of consumer-protection problems: in other words, a housewives' charter. But for the second time, the Cabinet could not bring itself to deal with R.P.M. and for the second time the proposal was dropped. On this occasion, by now very conscious of the strength of feeling he had discovered when the backbenchers had suspected him of planning an attack on R.P.M., Mr Erroll was one of those who felt obliged to warn the Prime Minister of the dangers of offending backbench opinion. But by the late summer of 1963 Erroll was again involved in considering the matter. This time he brought to the Economic Policy Committee of the Cabinet a plan for having R.P.M. referred case by case to a sub-division of the Monopolies Commission. In other words, goods would be referred one by one, and an established case law built up. This idea was still before the Economic Policy Committee when the Chancellor of the Exchequer, Reginald Maudling, suggested that he and Erroll should discuss the question with the Prime Minister before it was taken further. The International Monetary Fund Meeting intervened to make this discussion impossible before the Party Conference of that year and that Conference, in fact, saw the end of Mr Macmillan's Prime Ministership.

In October, 1963 Sir Alec Douglas-Home succeeded Macmillan as Prime Minister. How he came to be selected is now a familiar story and it is enough to recall here that he succeeded to a relatively weak position. The new Prime Minister's own Party was, at bottom, still divided about his Leadership and two prominent Conservatives, Mr Iain Macleod and Mr Enoch Powell, had refused to serve in his Cabinet. A general election at some time during the next twelve months was inevitable, and public opinion polls suggested that the Labour Party was heading strongly for victory. The Conservatives had been discredited by one political crisis after another. Economic difficulties, Macmillan's dismissal of Selwyn Lloyd and six other Cabinet Ministers, the Profumo scandal, and the Tory Leadership crisis had all badly weakened the Party. Finally, the Conservatives had chosen as their Leader a man who, despite his personal qualities, hardly seemed an embodiment of the modernisation theme with which the Conservatives had hoped to win the next election.

Sir Alec Douglas-Home, lately the 14th Earl of Home, had been made painfully aware of his shortcomings. In forming his new Government he was circumscribed by the need to make it as broad-based as possible, which meant he was in no position to exclude from it any member of the Macmillan administration, however weak, who was prepared to serve. But one thing he could do was to demonstrate that his would be a modernising and reforming Government which, despite the Prime Minister's own inexperience in economic matters, would tackle in a new spirit the pressing industrial, trade and social problems facing Britain. The most significant practical outcome of this intention was the appointment of Mr Edward Heath as Secretary of State for Industry, Trade and Regional Development and President of the Board of Trade. Mr Erroll was moved sideways and downwards to his last Ministerial appointment as Minister of Power. Douglas-Home thus upgraded the Board of Trade by enlarging its functions so that, in some degree, they anticipated the rôle which Wilson was to assign to the newly created Department of Economic Affairs in the Labour government of 1964. The Board of Trade, which, in recent years, had, it is fair to say, a diminished status in Whitehall, was now given new scope and prestige—and not simply by the gift of new functions. A government department's standing in Whitehall normally reflects the personal status and the personal calibre of its Minister. Erroll, for instance, had been a Cabinet Minister of comparatively junior status in the Conservative Party's hierarchy. During the Macmillan government, it had been the Treasury, with its new planning mechanism and an additional Senior Minister, which had achieved a new source of influence. Now the Board of Trade not merely had new functions: its President had the rank of Secretary of State and was a Minister who had earned much credit from his conduct of the negotiations for British entry into the Common Market, even though they had ended in failure. Indeed, Heath was a symbol of new attitudes in the Tory Party. He had enjoyed an extremely successful political career since the time he had kept the ranks of Tory backbenchers in order during the Suez crisis, he was eager for modernisation and he had a devoted personal following among younger Conservatives as well as in industry and the City.

From the moment that he entered the Board of Trade, Heath showed every sign of being a Minister who intended to ginger up and master his new Department. Above all, he wanted to find, before the general election, some clear-cut outlets for immediate action. Primarily, perhaps, his immediate focus was on regional planning. It was sometimes said, when he became embroiled in resale price maintenance, that he had deliberately chosen this issue, in preference to the more complex one of monopolies, as something that could be dealt with by a piece of short, sharp legislation before the election. Mr Heath, it is true, was instinctively sympathetic towards trade liberalisation. But the evidence I have been able to gather suggests that it was the accident of a backbench Bill which appeared in the Commons at this time to abolish R.P.M. that set Mr Heath on the path which produced the Government's Bill to do so.

Indeed, when Mr Heath first arrived at the Board of Trade he examined the file on resale price maintenance and turned away with some distaste. He was aware, as a former Chief Whip, of the sentiment on the backbenches. (Monopolies were also considered but it was clear that there would be no time for a Bill here before the election). The issue was therefore lying dormant, and the Board of Trade seemed as far away as ever from getting its Bill, until Mr Stonehouse, a Labour MP, obtained first place in the Private Members' Ballot and introduced a Bill in December to end R.P.M. This had the support of a number of Conservative MPs. Moreover, the second place in the ballot had been drawn by a Conservative, Mr John Osborne, who produced a Bill (which had Mr Stonehouse's support) to regulate trading stamps and make them exchangeable for cash. It was the almost mechanistic need a Minister and a Government Department have to define their own position when a Bill of this sort comes up in the Commons, that was to set Mr Heath on the road towards abolition of R.P.M.

If Heath's Bill was a reaction to these backbench initiatives, the backbenchers themselves were reacting to a new situation presented to politicians generally by the advent of trading stamps. In the autumn and winter of 1963, the trading stamps 'war' was at its height. Retailers were offering trading stamps (which could be redeemed for 'prizes' or cash) and in practice this meant that they were circumventing R.P.M. (by giving a discount on the brand price). The campaign against R.P.M. had never ceased and it had already driven those manufacturers who supported the practice onto the defensive. There had been some change of ground in arguments for the defence of R.P.M. The old contention that manufacturers had a duty to maintain prices to ensure that quality did not suffer was now perhaps less often heard than the argument that manufacturers needed R.P.M. to enable them to maintain the good-will of their network of conventional retail outlets against the aggression of the price-cutting supermarkets. The Government now found itself faced with a controversy about whether trading stamps (which made nonsense of

R.P.M.) should be abolished or at least subjected to legal regulation or whether R.P.M. itself should be made illegal. One argument was that, if R.P.M. were abolished, it would remove one of the main incentives for giving stamps as a form of discount to the public.

As the trading stamps 'war' reached its peak and some manufacturers (for instance Cadbury's, the confectionery-makers) decided to enforce resale price maintenance by extending their conditions of sale to prohibit shopkeepers from issuing trading stamps with their products, the political implications of the twin problems were considered both inside the Board of Trade and by Conservative backbenchers. One senior Conservative MP expressed his view to the author that trading stamps were the last nail in the coffin of R.P.M.— but that the Government should allow the situation to ride for several months. He suggested that any intervention now by the Government would be a political mistake. On the other hand, it was clear that the matter would not be allowed to rest. Individual backbenchers on both sides of the House were publicising their intention to bring in private members' legislation on the subject if they were successful in the ballot for Private Members' Bills. The Trade and Industry Committee also had separate meetings with industrial opponents and with representatives of trading stamp companies. On December 11 Heath himself went to discuss R.P.M. and trading stamps with the Trade and Industry Committee. On the same day the Private Members' Bill to abolish resale price maintenance had been introduced into the House by Mr Stonehouse and so had Mr Osborne's Bill to regulate trading stamps. From this moment, the decision to tackle R.P.M. had been virtually taken by Mr Heath. It was now obvious that the Government could not adopt a non-committal attitude to the Stonehouse Bill. Nor, however much Ministers might wish to see the Bill dead, could the Government oppose it without offering one of its own, since this would be to take up a definite stand in support of R.P.M. which was wholly against the general trend of its trade policy. It also seems clear that by now Heath was totally convinced, intellectually, of the case for abolishing R.P.M. as a result of his study of the information put before him by his department. If, as an ex-Whip, he anticipated trouble from the backbenches, he also expected (again drawing on his own experience) that the present Chief Whip would be able to quell it. For the time being, however, while he and his department were working out their tactics, Heath could make no pronouncement. Despite the pressures on him to state the government's view when he met the Trade and Industry Committee on December 11, he could only tell them that a Government decision on resale price maintenance might be expected in the New Year. The related issues of R.P.M., monopolies and mergers, were under renewed study by the Government, Heath told the Committee.

At the beginning of January, Heath took to the Cabinet his proposal to bring in legislation to abolish R.P.M. outright, with one or two clear-cut exemptions, including books. Like Erroll before him, Heath found himself opposed by a number of senior Cabinet Ministers. R. A. Butler, Hailsham and Selwyn Lloyd were among those who demanded that at least Heath must compromise. On Heath's side were Maudling, Sir Edward Boyle, Erroll and Sir Keith Joseph. The Cabinet discussions were long and heated. Heath could say that he had the support of the National Economic Development Council and that R.P.M. abolition was essential if he was to achieve the trade modernisation for which he had been given a brief by the new Prime Minister. His opponents, critical of the timing of the Bill rather than of its contents, were convinced that Heath would provoke trouble on the backbenches which the Conservative Party, so soon to face a general election, could ill afford. The outcome was a compromise. When Heath announced the Government's decision in the context of a general statement on monopolies and mergers on January 16, he told the House of Commons that the Government was to produce a Bill abolishing R.P.M. but providing the right for manufacturers to seek exemption before a judicial tribunal. Politically, the important point is that neither the Minister nor his department had got the Bill they wanted. Instead of outright prohibition, R.P.M. abolition was to be subjected to a judicial process of appeal which would inevitably delay its eventual disappearance. The trades which applied for exemption from abolition would be able to maintain R.P.M. until the case was decided; and one question now, therefore, was whether there would be a congestion of cases before the tribunal which was to decide on exemption.

Although the Government's Bill had been watered down to meet the objections on the Conservative backbenches, it was still violently resented. When Mr Heath met the Conservative Backbench Trade and Industry Committee after making his statement in the House, about a hundred MPs were present, and of those who spoke, about three out of four were said to have been against the Bill. But despite the angry criticisms of some of those who spoke, it still seemed possible at this stage that Heath might get his Bill through without too much difficulty. In fact, it was the beginning of the most bitter fight between a Minister and a section of his own party that the Conservatives had known in the post-war years. The matter was discussed at a weekly meeting of the 1922 Committee on January 17 and on the next day the Chief Whip, Martin Redmayne, reported the views of the backbenchers to the Cabinet. Anger was felt, not merely by the supporters of R.P.M.: many moderate Conservatives objected both to the timing of the decision and to the fact that they had not, as they considered, been adequately consulted. When Stonehouse's Bill for R.P.M. abolition came before the Commons (it failed to get a second reading and was talked out) a large contingent of Conservative backbenchers turned out in demonstration against it even though it was known that it would not go to a Division. Their presence, however, was rather a gesture of defiance to Heath than to Stonehouse's Bill.

The issue was now taken out into the country. The Prime Minister, the Chancellor of the Exchequer, Reginald Maudling and Edward Heath himself all defended the Government's decision. During the subsequent weeks, the opponents of the Bill maintained their campaign to try to get Heath to water it down. In particular they sought to persuade him to remove the onus of proof for making a case to the proposed judicial tribunal from manufacturers and instead to put it onto the consumer. In other words, they would have obliged consumers, or the government, to make a case for abolition in individual instances, instead of making the manufacturer prove his case for retention. This was one of the issues discussed at a further meeting between Heath and the 1922 Committee on January 23, which lasted for an hour and a half. Heath would concede nothing. By this time, the parliamentary advocates of R.P.M. were fully organised and had the help of an external pressure group called the Resale Price Maintenance Co-ordinating Committee: one of the deputations of this Committee to Heath, protesting against the ending of R.P.M., was led by a Conservative MP, Sir Richard Glyn.

Before the Bill itself was published, however, the activities of the Conservative backbenchers took a new direction. The officers of the Conservative Trade and Industry Committee led by Sir John Vaughan-Morgan, the Chairman of the Committee, put to Heath proposals which, though they did not oppose the abolition of R.P.M.

as such, would have had the effect of preventing the new measure from reaching the Statute Book before the general election. It was proposed that the R.P.M. Bill should be held back so that the coming White Paper on Monopolies and Mergers could deal with Resale Price Maintenance. It was also proposed that the Bill abolishing R.P.M., when it came, should provide a number of 'gateways' through which manufacturers could obtain exemption from the general abolition. The proposals were reasonable and reasoned and they came from responsible and senior Members of the Party. Their importance, however, lies not in their details but in the fact that this episode showed the extent to which Heath faced opposition to this particular measure at this time, even from those who were not committed advocates of R.P.M.

On February 16, 1964, the Bill to abolish R.P.M. was published and within an hour or so a group of Conservative backbenchers had tabled a motion for its rejection, using the parliamentary language of proposing that the Bill should be read a second time within six months. It was almost unheard of for Government supporters to propose the rejection of one of their own Ministerial Bills and this action demonstrated the strength of feeling in sections of the Party against the measure. In the Bill, Mr Heath had given little away to supporters of R.P.M. Manufacturers might seek exemption on the grounds that the abolition of R.P.M. in a particular case would be to the detriment of the public for three prescribed reasons. The Bill also included a provision designed to prevent the practice of 'loss-leading'[1] in the strictest sense of the term, though this provision was not enough to satisfy the critics.

Mr Heath met his critics again at a meeting of the Trade and Industry Committee on February 27. Once again the opponents of the Bill predominated. Advocates of ending R.P.M. were, with few exceptions, silent and the moderate senior men in the Party for the most part held their counsel. The grounds for exemption in the Bill were regarded as wholly unsatisfactory by the critics and the provisions against 'loss-leading' were said to give manufacturers virtually no protection against 'loss-leading' as it was actually practised. Heath defended himself but again he conceded nothing. He met some heckling and afterwards it was said that he had 'bludgeoned his way through the encounter'.

[1] Loss-leading is the practice of offering for sale goods below cost price in order to attract customers to other goods in the shop.

An examination of the names of those who signed the motion proposing that the Bill should be rejected is far from suggesting that they were all spokesmen of the interests directly concerned. Only two could probably be so described with any precision. Sir Stephen McAdden was Vice-President of the National Chamber of Trade, which was a force in the opposition outside the House, but his own business interests were not affected. Another, Sir Hugh Linstead, did speak directly for the Pharmaceutical Society, of which he had been Secretary all his working life. The rest felt themselves to be speaking not for the small shopkeeper organised into pressure groups, or for big business, but for traditional Tory attitudes towards the 'small man' and with regard to the feelings of many active Conservatives in the constituencies. The rebels, however, did include some who might be regarded as habitually rebellious and others who were not expecting to be in the next Parliament, either because they intended to retire or because they were defending seats with exceptionally small majorities. It remained to be seen what general support the hard core could muster when the Bill reached the floor of the House.

In the event, the Government did much worse in the Division of the second reading of the Bill than had been generally expected. Twenty-one Conservatives voted against the Government and about twenty-five others deliberately abstained. (In fact, fifty Conservatives were absent from the division, but the Whips calculated that about half were officially absent. It was not only the biggest demonstration against the Government by its followers during the thirteen years of post-war Conservative power; it was the biggest Conservative revolt since the defeat of the Chamberlain Government.) In evaluating this remarkable parliamentary protest, two countervailing points should be taken into consideration. On the one hand, the rebels were able to stage the revolt knowing that, since the Labour Party was abstaining in the debate, there was no risk of reducing the Government's majority so drastically that there would be any moral obligation on the Prime Minister to resign. On the other hand, the fact that this division was actually brought about by the Government's own supporters was itself of great significance. The rebellion was of such dimensions that it had to be taken seriously and some solution acceptable to both sides negotiated.

Strong efforts had, in fact, been made before the second reading debate to bring the rebels to heel. The Conservative Chief Whip, Redmayne, had called them to a meeting in order to persuade them to drop their attack on the Bill, but he completely failed to do so. The encounter was hardly made more impressive to the rebels by the knowledge that Redmayne himself was one of the opponents of R.P.M. abolition inside the Cabinet. On the eve of the second reading, fourteen of the Conservative dissidents had an interview with Heath which produced no satisfaction for them and no undertaking of their better behaviour for him. Immediately afterwards, the group met together and decided to vote against the Bill unless the onus of providing a case for exemption from the general ban on R.P.M. were removed from manufacturers and the Government were required instead to prove the case for ending R.P.M. in particular instances.

It was not surprising that the meeting between the rebels and Heath produced no results, for by this time the issue had, for many Conservatives, become one revolving round the personality of Heath and his method of handling his followers. There was a feeling in the Conservative Party, extending well beyond the hard core of R.P.M. supporters, that Heath had ignored the normal relationship between the Government and the backbenches and had failed to try to reach a compromise which would accommodate the different points of view. Feeling against Heath became extraordinarily bitter. In conversations with the author, senior backbenchers accused Mr Heath of being 'arrogant' and 'autocratic'. One contrasted the handling of the R.P.M. affair with that of the negotiations to enter the Common Market. This backbencher had disagreed with the Common Market venture but he had been prepared to support the Government on it because he regarded it as a carefully thought out policy by Macmillan. But R.P.M. abolition had not been carefully thought out: it had been rushed, 'Macmillan would never have sanctioned it', he said in implicit criticism of the new Prime Minister, Douglas-Home. The author was told also by a senior backbencher that he had written to the Prime Minister protesting against the treatment of the Party by Heath: after all, he said, 'this man might be our Leader one day.'[1] Heath's resignation was freely spoken about among Conservative Members. When the author suggested to one normally mild Conservative backbencher that pressure against the Bill would presumably not be such that Heath was forced to resign, he received the surprising reply, 'Who cares about that?' At one meeting which Heath had later with the backbench 'Steering Committee' which finally

[1] Heath became Leader of the Conservative Party in June 1965 in succession to Douglas-Home.

negotiated a solution, Mr Heath remarked, presumably with irony, 'Am I supposed to resign?', to which he received the answer that it had not come to that yet.

Heath had not done his case much good by the manner in which he replied to his critics in the second reading debate: it was the style of the lecture-hall rather than of the House of Commons. The question after the second reading was whether a compromise could be found or whether the Government might even be forced to the desperate expedient of applying the 'guillotine' to its own supporters in order to get the Bill through the Committee stage. Time was extremely important: it was now March and although the general election did not, in fact, take place until October, the Prime Minister at this stage still had an option on a June election, and it was important that the R.P.M. controversy should be settled before then. Amendments to the Bill had been put down by Conservatives and already seventy Members had signed them compared with the forty-five, or so, rebels in the second reading debate.

A way out of the apparent deadlock was in fact found by a 'Steering Committee' which was set up with Heath's approval, under the Chairmanship of Sir John Vaughan-Morgan, Chairman of the Trade and Industry Committee, to negotiate between Heath and the rebels. This Committee was an unprecedented device, for it excluded both the Chief Whip, Redmayne, and the Leader of the House, Selwyn Lloyd, through whom soundings between the front and the back-benchers normally take place. Apart from Vaughan-Morgan, the Members of the 'Steering Committee' were Mr John Hall, the Vice-Chairman of the Trade and Industry Committee, and its Secretary, Mr Leonard Cleaver. Representing the supporters of the Bill on the Committee were Mr Peter Emery and Mr Philip Goodhart. Opponents of the Bill on the Committee were Mr Roy Wise, Sir Hugh Linstead and Sir Richard Glyn. Heath was represented on the Committee through his Parliamentary Private Secretary, Mr Anthony Kershaw, and Selwyn Lloyd by Mr Peter Walker, his Parliamentary Private Secretary.

The first problem of the 'Steering Committee' was to reach a decision on which essential points should be the subject of some compromise, and both sides agreed that the essential issues were loss-leaders and the question of 'onus of proof'. Draft suggestions for dealing with these and other matters were put in front of the 'Steering Committee' by the officers of the Trade and Industry Committee

267

and it was quickly made clear to Heath that they expected a compromise to be reached. One of the officers of the Trade and Industry Committee told the author at the time that the Bill was 'not worth dying in the last ditch for' because it was a 'bad Bill'. While the Steering Committee was still at work, Selwyn Lloyd, who had been one of the strongest critics in Cabinet of the timing of the Bill, gave a public hint on March 16 of the way the wind was blowing. 'We intend to work out a fair solution, taking account of the interests of both the consumer and the shopkeeper,' he said in a speech at Fulham. Meanwhile, the amendments on the House of Commons Order Paper numbered nearly 150 and the technical arguments over the Bill had reached a point of extreme complexity. During the course of the week, the Prime Minister spoke to the annual luncheon of the 1922 Committee and appealed to the Party not to tear itself apart over R.P.M. The next day, Heath agreed to the amendment of the two crucial clauses—clause 5 of the Bill which dealt with 'onus of proof' and clause 3 which forbade the practice of 'loss-leaders'—along the lines suggested by the Steering Committee after he had been told that, if he did not, they would table two amendments anyway. The essence of the first amendment was that, instead of being presumed illegal but subject to appeal, all R.P.M. arrangements were to be 'registered' after which the Board of Trade would have the function of recommending cases to be brought forward to the Restrictive Practices Court.

This was, for all practical purposes, the end of the wider backbench revolt over R.P.M. On the same night, Heath himself announced to the 1922 Committee that compromise amendments were being tabled with the approval of the Government. His manner was said to have been conciliatory. But the question now was whether the amendments represented a substantial concession to the rebels or whether they amounted to no more than a form of words. There was more than a suspicion that the concession was more apparent than real. Yet by now there was a widespread wish inside the Conservative ranks to end the split which was doing the Party damage in the country through the extensive press publicity it was receiving.

The next day, March 21, the new compromise amendments were tabled by Sir John Vaughan-Morgan with the Government's approval and the gloss on them given to the press by the Board of Trade was emphatically that they did not impair the fundamental principles of the Bill. While the Board of Trade would have a permissive right to call certain cases if they thought them desirable, the crucial point was that all manufacturers who wished to keep R.P.M. would have to register, since if they did not do so R.P.M. would be automatically illegal. Indeed, in the coming weeks, Heath showed himself increasingly annoyed at any references in the press suggesting that there had been any weakening of the crucial elements of the Bill. On the other hand, the opponents of the Bill continued to press their case, and Heath did make other concessions: perhaps the most important of them was the provision to enable R.P.M. to continue in cases where 'the goods would be sold under conditions which would be likely to lead to their misuse by the public'. For some amendments, the hard-core rebels fought stoutly during the Committee stage and on an amendment dealing with the position of chemists they were defeated by only one vote. Mr Heath later admitted that, had he lost this Division, he would have had to consider his position in the Cabinet and the whole future of the Bill would have been in doubt.[1]

In the end, however, the concessions, most of them involving 'gateways' through which manufacturers might improve their chances of exemption from the general ban on R.P.M., might be counted a small achievement compared with the energy expended by the rebels in securing them.

Although some of the participants in the settlement still assert that the compromises negotiated were meaningful, on the grounds that they did impose some delay on the process of dismantling R.P.M., the weight of professional opinion is that they were little more than window-dressing. Questions which it is impossible to answer satisfactorily at this stage are how far the rebels were conscious that they were being asked to accept amendments (notably the provision for 'registration' of R.P.M. arrangements) which were essentially meaningless: and how far they connived, to get the Party out of its difficulties, at a face-saving formula which masked their own retreat. But almost certainly the officers of the Trade and Industry Committee, having failed in their original plan to get Heath to put off his abolition plan until after the election, realised that the ultimate solution must be essentially the one that the Minister wanted, merely decorated with gestures of appeasement to the rebels. The precise attitudes adopted by the parties to the compromise were difficult to disentangle with any precision at the time, and it is hardly easier to do so now that the people concerned, who are the only source of

[1] B.B.C. Television interview, Jan. 20, 1967.

evidence, have rationalised their position after the event. Nevertheless, the importance of the R.P.M. struggle is not dependent on certainty about the state of mind of the participants in the final stages of the rebellion, nor can it be assessed in terms of how administratively meaningful the compromises were. For the purposes of this study, the lessons of the controversy are clear.

First, although Heath and the Board of Trade got through the House of Commons substantially the same Bill they sent to it, despite the backbench rebellion, this original Bill was not the one they had wanted. The real struggle which forced Heath to compromise with the backbenchers took place behind the scenes in the Cabinet, where other Ministers fought successfully for a compromise with the backbenchers. The form in which the Bill appeared represented an anticipation by the Cabinet collectively of just how much the backbenchers would stand. Had Heath's manner been more tactful after the introduction, they might even have stood it without feeling driven to rebellion. On the other hand, though it was a weaker Bill than the department had wanted, it was seen a year or two later not to be doing badly. Apart from agreements not registered at all, it was clear that many were registered and were not likely to be fought in view of the cost of doing so. A pretty massive break-up and extensive price-cutting had occurred in a wide range of products.

Secondly, the impact of backbench opinion over the R.P.M. issue is to be gauged more by its effect in stopping Ministers from legislating on this trade practice for the previous decade than in the actual rebellion of the winter of 1963–4. For years, as I have shown, successive Ministers had tried to deal with the problem and had failed to persuade the Cabinet that it was safe to do so.

Third, of course, it was the initiative of two backbenchers in the other camp—Stonehouse and Osborne—which finally drove the government into action. One must not allow the rebellion of the defenders of R.P.M. to obscure the existence of those MPs of both Parties who were campaigning for the ending of R.P.M. and here the attitude of the Opposition was of importance. The Labour Party was, like the Tories, divided over R.P.M., and this trade practice had some surprising adherents on the Left of the Labour Party. Nevertheless, the existence of R.P.M. abolitionists on the Opposition benches and the fact that the Opposition officially was unlikely to oppose the Bill was something Heath could take into account.

At all three points I have mentioned it was the interaction of opinion inside the House of Commons which was important and it is arguable that the final synthesis of opinion was worked out, if not in Parliament, at least with regard to parliamentary opinion.

The R.P.M. episode as a whole seems to demonstrate once more that it is easier for backbenchers to influence domestic than foreign policy and that their success is not to be measured by the open fighting which, in this case, was less effective than their earlier pressures. The 1963–4 conflict also showed how much depends on the ability of backbenchers to get up a 'moral' head of steam when it comes to an open clash with their leaders. Resale price maintenance may seem an odd issue over which to work up moral enthusiasm. Nevertheless, it is characteristic of the Conservative Party that it should become emotional when it considers itself 'betraying' one of the 'interests' for which it considers itself to stand. For many Conservatives, R.P.M. 'repeal' had some of the characteristics that Corn Law repeal had for their forebears of 1846: indeed, Heath, in his cold and uncompromising conviction of the intellectual merits of the case might be regarded as having some resemblance to Peel in this matter.

Rebellions on this scale are most likely to break out when Party morale is low and personal relations poor. In 1963–4 morale in the Conservative Party was still low as a result of the leadership succession crisis of the previous autumn. Moreover, Heath's personal relations were bad because he had not managed to throw off the attitude he had adopted as a Whip when, for instance, he was able during the Suez crisis to demand loyalty in the collective interests of the Party. In 1964, by contrast, he seemed to be demanding loyalty for a *personal* policy and to be demonstrating (this, at least, was how many Conservative backbenchers saw it) contempt for their opinions and for their ability to exert any influence. Whereas Selwyn Lloyd, the Leader of the House of Commons, predicted from the moment the Bill was brought to Cabinet that it would cause serious trouble in the Conservative Party, Heath refused to believe that this trouble could not be overcome without danger to unity. He believed that the Party would quail when called to order by a strong Minister. This was essentially the same mistake that Austen Chamberlain had made in 1922 when he persuaded himself that if the Party were called together at the Carlton Club meeting, it would fall in behind its leaders. Heath believed, against advice, that once the Bill was published the malcontents would yield to the accomplished fact. At each of the early meetings with the rebels, he expected that his own determination would outface them. Only slowly did he come to accept that some gesture of compromise on his part was essential, since by now his attitude to the Party had become more important in the eyes of many of the Government's supporters than were the actual contents of the Bill.

Throughout this rough passage, Heath enjoyed the loyal support of Sir Alec Douglas-Home, whatever misgivings the Prime Minister may have come to have as the storm developed. Having given Heath the 'brief' of modernisation, it was not in the Prime Minister's nature to desert him when trouble came. Without the Prime Minister's support, it is certain that Heath would never have been able to steam-roller the Bill through the Cabinet.

His success in doing so, where Erroll had failed, illustrates how reliant any government department is on the standing in Cabinet of its Minister. Heath's position among his colleagues was much higher than that of either Erroll or Maudling had been when they were at the Board of Trade. Heath stood out, partly because of his personal strength and determination; partly because so many of his colleagues had been weakened in the 'succession' crisis after Macmillan's resignation, whereas he was strengthened by his support of Douglas-Home; partly because the new Prime Minister's own position, *vis-à-vis* his Cabinet, was much weaker than Macmillan's had been—though it must be remembered that if Douglas-Home had won the election his power would have been altogether changed. Though unprovable, it is probable that this crisis would never have occurred under Macmillan—and not simply because of the difference in personality between the two Prime Ministers. Douglas-Home was particularly dependent on Heath as his symbol of his Party's somewhat vulnerable modernisation theme. If loyalty explains why he stood by Heath after the storm broke, this dependence on his lieutenant for the modernisation theme is enough to explain why he let Heath have his head against his opponents in the original arguments in the Cabinet over the Bill.

The measure of the rebels' success is not in the amendments they secured, but rather in the psychological lengths that Heath had to go to in order to placate them. He had to accept meetings and negotiations of a character no other Minister had been obliged to enter with the 'other ranks' of the Parliamentary Party and the cold reception he got from his followers in the House at this time demonstrated a failure of parliamentary management that was damaging to the Party and to his own standing in it.

On the other hand, the limitations of backbench 'power' when a Minister is determined and his nerve holds are also demonstrated. If Heath's inflexibility and apparent contempt for his parliamentary followers first got him into trouble with his backbenchers, it was also his inflexibility which got him out of it again. Once it became clear that Heath would not be driven to submit and that the conflict was damaging the Conservative Party, the critics on the backbenches became anxious for an end to the strife.

The R.P.M. episode suggests that though it is not the normal function of the backbenchers to initiate policy, they can still put a brake upon the adoption of policies they dislike. The political history of R.P.M. during the decade before Heath's crisis with his back-benchers illustrates with some clarity the theory of anticipated reactions. The crisis of 1964 demonstrated what can happen when backbenchers' reactions cease to be anticipated.

The cost of this fracas to the Conservative Party was considerable. One senior member of the Douglas-Home Cabinet has expressed to the author his opinion that the R.P.M. affair lost the Conservative Party the 1964 Election which, against all expectations, the Labour Party only managed to win by a handful of seats. On this view, the importance of the Bill was its timing not its contents: it ought to have been brought in soon after the 1959 General Election but, since this had not been done, the Conservatives would have been better advised to leave it until after the 1964 Election. This Minister argued at the time that the Bill was likely to cause so much trouble that the Con-servatives would be prevented from holding the May/June Election which Douglas-Home originally favoured. Time would have to be allowed for the electorate to forget the disunity which had given the Party so much bad publicity (there was, of course, no immediate benefit from lower prices: these came later) and the interval before a May Election was not long enough. As it was, the Conservatives did recover quickly enough to be able nearly to rob their opponents of victory. The argument on this thesis is that a quiet run-up to a May/June Election, with no trouble over R.P.M., could well have enabled the Conservatives to win.

Some observers would doubt this: they would argue that (with or without the R.P.M. episode) the Conservatives needed to stay in office that summer and to wait for a loss of momentum by the Labour

Party in order to come as near as they did to a fourth successive general election victory. While there is room for argument here, there can be no doubt that the R.P.M. episode was harmful to the Conservatives whatever the general election date. Non-Conservative politicians sometimes dismiss the R.P.M. episode because the issue itself seems to them so small. But to the Conservatives it was not a trivial matter. There was nothing simulated about the clash; little was exaggerated in the public reports of it.

The temporary unpopularity this incident brought him did not prevent Heath from becoming Leader of the Conservative Party little more than a year later. The Conservative Party is always willing to overlook particular instances of nonconformity in a man whose basic attitudes they regard as sound. Even so, Heath might not have become Conservative Leader had the choice been a little wider. Anyone who followed backbenchers' attitudes closely in the election of 1965, when they had to choose between Maudling and Heath was aware that, apart from a small band of dedicated supporters on either side, the choice was exercised by probably most Conservative MPs with a marked lack of enthusiasm. If the lack of sufficient support for Maudling resulted in part from his alleged failure to keep down national spending while he was at the Treasury, the lack of enthusiasm for Heath was encouraged by the view that some backbenchers formed of his political judgment during the R.P.M. episode. On the other hand, Heath probably learned a useful lesson. The pains he took to achieve a Party consensus over Rhodesian seizure of independence in 1965 suggests that he had become much more aware of the importance of parliamentary management.[1]

[1] The main sources for this chapter are the author's study of the episode at the time and subsequent research and conversations with the participants. Since private information provides the theme of this chapter, it seems unnecessary (except for direct quotations) to document it with references to the public sources (*Hansard*, the Order Paper and press reports), which are in any case too voluminous to enumerate in a study of this length. The episode achieved very full coverage in the press and daily reports appeared in *The Financial Times*, *The Times*, and other newspapers. All statements (as distinct from judgments) in this chapter are based on definite information and not on speculative reconstruction though, since the official papers are not available, and the author is reliant on his witnesses, there may well be inaccuracies. It should be stressed that information gained at the time has sometimes been preferred to retrospective accounts by participants where there has been any clash, since time often blurs the memory and encourages a retrospective rationalisation of politicians' actions and opinions.

Chapter Ten

The Influence of the Backbench Member 1964–1967

It is too soon yet to make any satisfactory assessment of the relationship between the post-1964 Labour Government and its own supporters in the House; nevertheless, there are indications that Labour backbenchers will exert no less influence over their leaders than Government backbenchers have done over the Executive in the period since the war as a whole. Of course, the Labour rank and file in the House of Commons was quickly required to accept new attitudes in power and to assent to policies which it had found objectionable in Opposition. The narrow majority by which the Government held office in the first eighteen months after its election victory in October 1964 was itself an incentive to party solidarity and backbench obedience. Nevertheless, it is possible that, for reasons I shall discuss later, Labour backbench influence in the future may prove to be more effective than it was in the previous period of Labour rule between 1945 and 1951.

It was ironical that, just as criticism of the House of Commons as an organ of government reached a new crescendo, the Labour Party was returned to power with a tenuous majority of four, which was soon to be reduced to three in a lost by-election at Leyton. Thus, at a time when it was commonly argued that Parliament was impotent under the Whips of the Executive, the House of Commons was once more in a position when it seemed to have a chance of unmaking a Government—and in which Government policies had to be tempered with due consideration for parliamentary statistics. However accidental were the electoral mechanics which produced this result, it is undeniable that the near stalemate in the House of Commons reflected with notable aptness a political stalemate in the country. A majority of the electorate wished to be rid of the Conservatives

275

(whose vote dropped more heavily than either big party's vote had done since 1945) but they were hesitant yet about trusting Labour to rule. The result was a large increase in the Liberal vote since, even though in certain respects the Liberals were to the 'left' of Labour, this point was not generally taken by the new Liberal voters. For many of these, voting Liberal represented a tolerable compromise between disenchantment with the Conservatives and distrust of Labour.

The heavy Liberal vote was a sure indicator to Harold Wilson, the new Prime Minister, that he must try to capture the centre ground of politics and not alienate floating voters by any tendency towards extremism—supposing he had any temptation towards it, which is unlikely. For the eighteen months after October 1964, Wilson set himself to prove to the nation that a Labour Government could be trusted. Solidarity within the Western alliance was demonstrated up to the hilt. Against the gravest economic difficulties the Labour Government fought to maintain the parity of sterling and pursued an impeccably orthodox financial policy. Efforts were made to secure a national consensus for economic planning which would secure long-term growth and overcome inflation. The Prime Minister personally gained much respect through his handling of the crisis caused by Rhodesia's unilateral declaration of independence. In March 1966, at a further General Election, Labour was rewarded with a majority of ninety-seven.

Between these two elections, Mr Wilson was both helped and hindered by his exiguous majority. He was helped because the danger of defeat for the Government in the House of Commons, and the fear of loss of office for the Labour Party, kept rebellious impulses on the Government's backbenches well under control. Further, on a number of major issues, the Government received *de facto* support from the Liberals who, as a party claiming to be of the Left, dare not risk the odium of being held responsible for ejecting Labour from office over policies over which both they and the Government were more or less in agreement.

On the other hand, the Government had to modify some of its policies, including land nationalisation, to meet Liberal opinion. Most important, however, it was obliged throughout this Parliament to temporise over steel nationalisation, which the Labour Party was pledged to implement. The steel industry had been nationalised by the previous Labour Government and denationalised by the Conservatives. In Opposition, there had been dispute between the Labour traditionalists (the bulk of the party) and more pragmatic Socialists to whom the older form of nationalisation had become unattractive and who regarded it as an electoral liability. Nevertheless, to most Labour activists, nationalisation still represented what Mr Wilson himself liked to describe (at the time of Hugh Gaitskell's attempt, after the 1959 General Election, to secure the repeal of the party's official dedication of universal public ownership) as the Ark of the Covenant. In 1964, steel nationalisation, which had become something of a King Charles's head, was accepted as inevitable by common consent in the Labour Party. So, at his first Party Conference as Leader, Harold Wilson had given a strong off-the-record hint to the press that he would follow Lord Attlee's dictum and get the unpopular measures over in the first year. There was a clear implication that this referred, *inter alia*, to steel nationalisation, which was known to be unpopular with the public but required by the party. Had Labour secured an adequate majority in 1964, there is no doubt that steel would have been quickly renationalised. As it was, the Prime Minister had to reckon not only with his tiny majority (on this issue the Liberals were fervently opposed to him) but with the declared hostility to steel renationalisation of two of his own backbenchers, Mr Woodrow Wyatt and Mr Desmond Donnelly.[1] It was quickly plain that the Government could never be sure of passing steel nationalisation through the Commons and, if it brought in a Bill, would risk a defeat which would oblige it to appeal to the country on an issue and at a time not of Mr Wilson's choosing. If by any chance the Government had been able to secure a Second Reading for a steel nationalisation Bill, it would almost certainly have failed to take it through the Committee stage.

On the other hand, the Government could not lose face by capitulating to two rebellious and generally unrepresentative Labour right-wingers whose views were disliked by the bulk of the parliamentary party. Moreover, the essence of the Prime Minister's public attitude during the difficult year 1965 was to act as though he had an

[1] Some other Labour backbenchers were known to be hostile to steel re-nationalisation, including Mr G. R. Strauss, the former Labour Minister who had been responsible for nationalising the steel industry in 1949. But only Wyatt and Donnelly were expected to carry their hostility to the point of abstaining or even voting against the Government. One interesting procedural question raised at this time was whether the Speaker would cast his vote for the Government in the event of a tie.

adequate majority and to establish Labour in the minds of the electorate as the governing party which had the authority provided by a popular mandate. He needed time for his Ministers to make themselves known to the public and for former Conservative Ministers to fade from the popular mind's eye, as most of them did with notable speed. He must, therefore, neither risk a defeat in the House by pressing on with the Bill nor provoke his Centre and Left by giving them the impression that he was bending the Government's policies to the will of an unholy alliance between the Tory and Liberal Parties with Wyatt and Donnelly. A series of hints to the press, through the usual informal channels, were therefore given at the end of 1964 and the beginning of 1965 suggesting the date at which a steel nationalisation White Paper might appear in advance of legislation. Successively, however, these promised dates receded, though as late as March 18, 1965, the Prime Minister stated in the House that the nationalisation Bill would be introduced in the 1964–5 Session.

In April 1965, a White Paper[1] was published setting out the Government's nationalisation plan and its compensation terms. The nationalisation proposals as such were attacked by the Opposition: the compensation terms were regarded as far too generous by a number of Labour MPs. On May 6, the White Paper went for approval in the House of Commons and it seemed clear that Wyatt and Donnelly would be obliged by their previous statements either to abstain or to vote against the Government unless it made some concession to them. At the very end of his winding-up speech, the Secretary of State for Economic Affairs, George Brown, suddenly produced an offer to 'listen' to alternative proposals if the steel industry produced them. Both Wyatt and Donnelly therefore voted for the White Paper. There followed a series of ambivalent indications from Ministers about precisely what sort of alternative proposals the Government might be prepared to listen to but it quickly appeared that they must be based on full public ownership if they were to be acceptable. Brown's words did not, after all, carry a meaning that would satisfy Donnelly or Wyatt. However, the immediate parliamentary crisis was over and the long summer recess was only two months away. When Parliament re-assembled in the autumn any mention of steel nationalisation was omitted from the Queen's Speech. Ministers now virtually conceded that there would

[1] Cmnd. 2651.

be no steel nationalisation in that Parliament. On November 17, 1965, the Chancellor of the Exchequer, Mr James Callaghan, admitted to the House of Commons that steel would be nationalised 'when we have got a majority to do it'.

It is plain that in the Parliament of 1964, the Government was obliged to defer to parliamentary opinion and shelve this measure: in turn parliamentary opinion represented pretty accurately, on this issue, the balance of opinion in the country, which was for the most part hostile or indifferent to steel nationalisation. On the other hand, the Government had to deal warily with its own backbenchers and not give them the impression that it was lukewarm on the issue; hence the introduction of the White Paper. When Labour was returned with a large majority in 1966, it was despite, not because of, its pledge to nationalise steel. Electors who had cared little enough one way or the other in 1964 now seemed to care even less whether steel was nationalised or not. The Government was now free to pay more heed to the majority of its own backbenchers—and the result was that it promptly scaled down the proposed compensation terms for steel now that it was sure of its parliamentary majority. However, the narrow balance of the parties in the 1964 Parliament had at least obliged the Government to defer to the consensus of parliamentary opinion on the issue until the Wilson administration had, on general grounds, secured a full mandate to govern.

(ii)

The influence of parliamentary opinion on the Labour Government in the 1964 Parliament was also illustrated by the related issues of race relations and Commonwealth immigration. These were questions of conscience for many Members and also issues on which the two major parties were divided on party lines. Conservative opinion had overwhelmingly favoured some restriction on the number of Commonwealth immigrants into Britain and it was in response to this that the previous Conservative Government had put through Parliament the Commonwealth Immigrants Act of 1962, which laid down conditions of entry and enabled the Government to limit the number of immigrants. Conservatives were convinced that some such limitation was essential if the growth of race tension in Britain was to be stopped.

Labour sentiment, on the other hand, had been bitterly opposed to this Conservative Act on the grounds that it operated mainly against coloured immigrants and therefore amounted to a colour bar. Correspondingly, Labour opinion, for the most part, had consistently favoured legislation against race discrimination in Britain and one Left-wing Member, Fenner Brockway, had repeatedly sought and failed to obtain Commons' approval for a Bill of this sort. But the Conservative Party was generally opposed to such legislation in the belief that it would be ineffective and might operate against the freedom of the individual to decide, for instance, whom he would admit as a lodger to his house or other premises. The public (as several public opinion polls conclusively indicated) was overwhelmingly in favour of limiting Commonwealth—and for practical purposes this meant coloured—immigration.

When in opposition the Labour Party, under Gaitskell's leadership, had fought with uncompromising hostility the Conservative Commonwealth Immigrants Act. In power, Labour was morally bound to try to replace this Act with some voluntary agreement with the governments concerned to control the flow of immigrants 'exported' by Commonwealth countries. On the other hand, Labour had public opinion to take into account: race had figured in the 1964 Election campaign and, indeed, was the major factor in Labour's loss of the constituency of Smethwick.[1] It was also obvious, though unadmitted by Labour, that a voluntary quota scheme arranged with Commonwealth countries was impracticable. Finally, it must be noted that Labour came to power publicly committed by Wilson (in February 1964) to take over the Race Relations Bill for which Brockway had so often tried to gain parliamentary acceptance.

In the new Parliament, Wilson lost no time in registering the Government's moral fervour against the introduction of race into politics and its chagrin at the loss of Smethwick: he suggested in the debate on the Queen's Speech that the Conservative victor of Smethwick, Peter Griffiths, would be treated as a parliamentary leper. This remark created uproar in the House but within a matter of days it was apparent that both political parties were anxious that the race and immigration issues should not become the subject of fixed party positions which might create even more dangerous fissures in the country. When the House debated the renewal of the Common-

---

[1] See A. W. Singham, 'Immigration and the Election', Appendix 3 to D. E. Butler and Anthony King, *The British General Election of 1964* (Macmillan, 1965).

wealth Immigrants Act (ostensibly pending something better) there appeared to be general agreement that there must be some sort of control on the numbers of immigrants. But it was also widely felt that there must be more positive action to secure and quicken the integration of coloured immigrants into British life. The movement towards taking the race issue 'out of politics'—which for practical purposes meant out of party politics—had begun. Backbench opinion and initiative played a decisive part in it.

Within a few weeks, the Home Secretary, Sir Frank Soskice, had informed the House of Commons (February 4) that the Government would tighten up controls on immigration under the 1962 Act. Moreover, immigrants who still managed to evade the rules would be almost invariably deported. Labour backbenchers were inevitably much disturbed by this pronouncement. The Conservatives, on the other hand, did nothing to make public capital out of this apparent reversal of Labour attitudes but on March 11 a private meeting of the Conservative backbenchers' Home Affairs Committee rejected a proposal for a bipartisan policy on immigration. Immediately afterwards three Conservatives (Norman St. John Stevas, Humphry Berkeley and Richard Hornby) signed a statement with some Labour and Liberal Members favouring the removal of immigration from party politics. In the same month, an all-party group of liberal-minded backbenchers established itself for the purpose of studying the race problem as a whole and seeking to prevent it from becoming an issue of bitter controversy.

On the Labour side there was a number of younger Members, including Shirley Williams, Roy Hattersley, Ivor Richard and Brian Walden. Conservative Members in the group included Aubrey Jones, Norman St. John Stevas, Nigel Fisher, John Hunt and Sir Anthony Meyer. The Committee had, as its Secretary, a Labour backbencher, Donald Chapman, who had been a very active opponent of the Conservative Commonwealth Immigration Act, and its Chairman was a much respected older Conservative from a traditional mould, Sir Godfrey Nicolson. In general the view of the group was that some control was necessary temporarily but the integration must be assisted. Integration and limitation of immigrants were regarded as complementary to each other.

On March 9 the Prime Minister announced in the House of Commons a three-pronged attack on the immigration and race problem. First, a junior Minister, Mr Foley, was given a brief to look into the question of integration. Second, a Race Relations Bill was promised which would outlaw both racial discrimination and incitement to racial hatred. Third, a Mission (it was later announced that Earl Mountbatten would lead it) would be sent to Commonwealth countries to discuss voluntary control of immigration. It is primarily with the Race Bill in the present context that we are concerned.

What might be called the first edition of the Bill was published on April 7, 1965. This would have prohibited discrimination on racial grounds in public places, such as hotels, restaurants or inns, and would have prescribed a maximum fine of £50 for the first offence. The Bill also sought to create a second new offence—incitement to racial hatred at a public meeting or in a public place, whether by the spoken or the written word. Six months' imprisonment or a fine of £200 (or both) were the maximum penalties on summary conviction: on indictment, the penalties would be maximum imprisonment of two years, or a fine of £1,000, or both. Boarding houses and private hotels were excluded from the scope of the Bill.

This Bill was attacked from all sides. The chief objections to it were that it failed to introduce any conciliation element and instead introduced a wholly new concept of criminality into race relations. Another criticism was that race discrimination was made a crime where it seldom existed—in places of public resort—but that nothing was done to prohibit it in housing and employment, where it was most frequently found. It was on such grounds that the Bill was attacked by a pressure group called the Campaign Against Racial Discrimination and also by the Conservative Opposition. At a meeting of the backbench Conservative Home Affairs Committee, it was decided almost unanimously on April 12 that the Bill was inept and inefficient. The Society of Labour Lawyers was equally critical and joined in the pressure on the Government to change the Bill.

It was an open secret that the Home Secretary himself, Sir Frank Soskice, had been averse to legislating at all against racial discrimination but had been committed to do so by the Prime Minister. It is probable that the personal lack of sympathy on the part of the Home Secretary contributed to the production of a draft measure which was generally considered to be misbegotten. At the end of April the Cabinet agreed in principle that the Bill must be drastically amended. In the debate on the Second Reading of the Bill in the House of Commons on May 3, the Home Secretary promised to listen to criticisms and said that the Government had given thought to the Opposition criticism that a conciliation process would have been more appropriate. Further, the Home Secretary gave a strong hint that criminal sanctions might be dropped and made it clear that the Government would be sorry to see this become a major party issue. The Conservative Opposition nevertheless persisted in its attempt to defeat the Bill on the ground that it introduced criminal sanctions into a field appropriate for conciliation, and might endanger freedom of speech. This attack was overcome by a Government majority of twelve votes—obtained by the support of some Liberal Members.

Between the Second Reading of the Bill and the Committee stage, the Government was subjected to intense pressure to amend the Bill. On May 8, for instance, Chapman put down an amendment which proposed to set up a Race Relations Conciliation Commission in place of criminal procedure. He also wanted to widen the scope of the Bill to deal with the colour bar in shops, offices and clubs. At the end of May, the Home Secretary tabled amendments which virtually met the *first* of these points. The original proposal to make discrimination a criminal offence was dropped; instead, local conciliation committees would be set up to enquire into complaints. There can be little doubt that these amendments owed much to the pressure of Labour and Conservative backbenchers and also something to the attitude taken by the Opposition. In an article on April 30 in the *Guardian*, that newspaper's Legal Correspondent (who had himself been associated with non-parliamentary pressures to change the Bill) suggested that the amendments represented primarily a victory for the Campaign Against Racial Discrimination (CARD) whose views had been taken up by the British Caribbean Association, the Society of Labour Lawyers and the journal *Socialist Commentary*. Yet, giving full weight to the preparatory work of these pressure groups, it is also true that the Bill would never have been altered so smoothly if the agitation had not been given a focus in the House of Commons and if backbenchers on both sides had not seen the force of working together. The official Opposition, Government backbenchers and crossbench parliamentary opinion all played a part in working towards a synthesis which the Government could accept. The process by which this Bill was shaped, cumbersome and confused though it was, represents an argument against the view that parliamentarianism is dead. In the Committee on the Bill, the Home Secretary acknowledged on May 25 that it was owing to debates inside and outside Parliament that the Government had decided to replace the criminal procedures in the Bill.

However, the success of the Government's own backbenchers did not stop there, though they failed to secure further amendments to widen the scope of the Bill during the Committee stage. Chapman's amendment, which would have included shops under the provisions against racial discrimination, was defeated on June 23 by six votes to ten. During the Committee stage, there was a good deal of cross-voting and on some occasions the Home Secretary only secured the defeat of Labour backbench proposals to strengthen the Bill because he had the support of some Conservative Members on the Committee.[1]

But the Committee stage was not the end of the pressure exerted on the Government by its own backbenchers; more effective steps were, in fact, taken by them subsequently. Six Labour backbenchers (Mrs Shirley Williams, Messrs Hattersley, Ivor Richard, Chapman, Walden and Ennals) went privately to see the Leader of the House, Mr Herbert Bowden, and pressed for a Government commitment to extend, in due course, the Bill's provisions to housing and employment, where racial discrimination was mainly to be found. They left convinced that they had the undertaking they wanted and, in the Third Reading debate, the Home Secretary promised that if there was found to be discrimination in other fields, the Bill would be extended. The pressure groups concerned (notably CARD) thereupon set about collecting the relevant information and the group of MPs was convinced that the promised changes would probably become law sometime during the 1966 Parliament. This promise they considered their most significant achievement.

One other manifestation of successful backbench pressure on the Government over the race-immigration issue must be briefly mentioned. In August 1965, the Government published a White Paper on immigration policy in which the three main points were a drastic reduction to 8,500 a year (including 1,000 Maltese) in the number of Commonwealth immigrants, new restrictions on the entry of immigrants' dependants and an obligation on immigrants to produce health certificates. The White Paper, moreover, asserted that there must be 'speedy and effective powers to repatriate immigrants' who

[1] A useful account of cross-voting on the Committee stage is given by Keith Hindell, 'The Genesis of the Race Relations Bill', *Political Quarterly*, 1965, pp. 401–5.

evaded the stricter controls. The Government would seek 'for the Home Secretary a general power, in addition to his power to act on the recommendations of a court—to repatriate such Commonwealth citizens if he considers the public interest requires it'.

This White Paper provoked Labour backbench indignation, though it was regarded as a sensible measure by the Conservatives, who acknowledged that Labour in power had moved closer to their position. Once again, however, Labour backbenchers pressed their views upon the Government, and with success. After Sir Frank Soskice had been replaced as Home Secretary in 1966 by Mr Roy Jenkins, who sympathised with the views of the backbenchers, it became virtually certain that the idea of any new deportation powers had been dropped.

One Labour backbencher closely involved in these affairs who had arrived at Westminster feeling very conscious of the limitations upon backbench influence, told the author that he found, during this episode, that they had far more influence than he had thought possible. The race-immigration issue provided a good example of pressure being exerted discreetly and persistently by thirty or forty people from the backbenches of the governing party who, if they had been more publicly aggressive, might have failed in their purpose, not least because they were representing an attitude which was not popular. It is also perhaps significant that this younger group of Labour MPs (most of whom were Parliamentary Private Secretaries) also had influence because some of them enjoyed the ear and the friendship of some Members of the Government: indeed, one of their number, Mrs Williams, joined the Government after the 1966 General Election. Finally, not the least of the positive results secured by the parliamentary handling of the race issue was that, whereas it had played a major part in the 1964 Election, it was of almost no importance in the Election of 1966. Parliamentary attitudes had helped to secure a reduction in the temperature of popular feeling on this issue, had educated public opinion and had helped to secure its removal from the cruder sort of Party politics.

(iii)

The leaders of any major political Party have two main obligations to fulfil if they are to take and to keep power. First, they must have the confidence of a majority of voters—which means that they must hold the middle ground of politics. Second, they must satisfy their own active supporters on whose work they rely for victory in an election campaign. Moreover, a majority of the electorate will not be convinced of the stability of a party, or accept its fitness to govern, if they observe its activists constantly at loggerheads with each other.

For a number of reasons, including the traditional 'conservativism' of the British public, it is easier for a Conservative Government to reconcile satisfaction for its own followers with satisfaction of a national consensus. This is especially true over defence and foreign policy. Labour's difficulty in this respect had been repeatedly demonstrated under Gaitskell's leadership. When Wilson came to power, he set about capturing the centre ground of politics, and his Government's attitudes during the 1964–5 Parliament had little in common with those of the old Labour 'Left' with which he had once been associated. Wilson's Socialism had always been a little mysterious. As an undergraduate he had been a Liberal and, after he became Prime Minister, 'pragmatic' became, not inappropriately, a political vogue word. With this temperament he was well equipped to manage his party in power and to make it accept new attitudes designed to appeal to the more or less uncommitted voter. In his first year, he faced heavy but ineffective criticism of the Government's support for the US administration in the war in Vietnam. He also faced the charge from some on his own side that the Government should have acted more strongly against the illegal régime in Rhodesia. But Labour's narrow majority after 1964 helped Wilson lay the foundations of his national consensus policies since even his strongest Socialist critics had no wish to quarrel if the result was to put the Conservatives back in power. Besides, Mr Wilson had adroitly taken most of the leaders of the old 'Left' into the Government where they quickly found the joys and preoccupations of power and departmental administration to be a wholesome substitute for rebellion on issues of general and emotional principle. Even the leader of the Transport and General Workers Union, Mr Frank Cousins, was able to swallow his disagreement with the Government's Incomes Policy until 1966 when he resigned his post as Minister of Technology.

Sound government and consensus politics; insistence on preserving Britain's national position in the world; and the electorate's continuing disillusion with the Conservative Party, which now had its own internal leadership problem—all these brought Wilson victory, with a majority of ninety-seven, in the General Election of 1966. The question now was whether the Labour Government would have to be more responsive to its followers' feelings on both foreign and home policy. Three months after the General Election, the Prime Minister was faced with the most serious rebellion inside the Labour Party that had taken place since he first entered No. 10 Downing Street. A broad spectrum of Labour backbenchers, from both the Right and Left wings of the Party, joined together in attacking the Government's policy of maintaining Britain's position East of Suez. As the Prime Minister could correctly point out to them, they were united only under this negative banner and did not agree on any single issue of overseas policy.

Yet Wilson, sensitive to the feeling of his rank and file, thought it necessary to go to a meeting of the Parliamentary Labour Party and address them before a motion, exhorting the Government to change its policy, was put to the vote. The outcome was a roll-call of fifty-four declared critics voting against the Government, with probably as many sympathisers deliberately abstaining on these grounds, apart from which it was known that a large number of those present, including some Ministers, voted reluctantly for the official policy. Yet bearing in mind the essential non-cohesiveness of this internal Labour 'opposition', the extensive 'whipping-up' operation which the Government had deemed necessary before the meeting (the Whips covered, unusually, Ministers and Labour peers as well as backbenchers) and Wilson's decision to address it personally, the outcome was a good deal short of a triumph for the Prime Minister. There had been no comparable demonstration by the Parliamentary Labour Party against its leaders in *power* on a major issue of national policy (the rebellions against Gaitskell were not comparable because Labour was then out of office) since the conscription issue in 1947, which was the last major occasion on which there had been an internal vote by the Parliamentary Party against a Labour Government. Admittedly, the conscription issue had been more serious because the rebels in 1947 had actually carried their protest onto the floor of the House. But the two events had something else in common: on each occasion, the Prime Minister of the day had felt it necessary to appeal to his followers for their support.

In June 1966, Mr Wilson made his speech the occasion for a lesson in constitutional history to his followers. He asserted that, although there must be two-way consultation between the Government and the Parliamentary Party, the party meeting, 'however important, cannot become a government or a substitute for government'. Whether Mr Wilson was entirely wise to re-state this important constitutional point for the benefit of newer Labour Members of Parliament and yet at the same time to deliver a speech which virtually called for a vote of confidence within a private meeting of the Parliamentary Labour Party on a particular point of policy may be debatable. The position of the Parliamentary Labour Party had been settled in the 1930s and early forties, when attempts to make a Labour Government responsible to the Parliamentary Labour Party rather than to Parliament as a whole had been defeated. Certainly under Wilson's Prime Ministership there had never been the least question of raising the issue in these terms again despite the pressure on the Government to change its mind on certain issues. Indeed, the Wilson administration had been singularly free to pursue its empirical policies without interference. But now the Prime Minister himself was drawing attention to the old claims of Labour backbenchers by challenging his followers in the vote on the critical motion before them. Yet the conventional position of any Government is that if their supporters wish to challenge them in a vote they must do so on the floor of the House and risk the consequences, which might be withdrawal of the Whip from the rebels or, if the rebellion is successful, loss of power for their party.

Was the Prime Minister setting an unwise precedent for himself by speaking over a critical motion inside the Parliamentary Labour Party which was to be the subject of a vote? Would similar votes be demanded in future over other matters of foreign policy—or even over domestic issues, such as unemployment caused by the Government's deflationary policies? As it happened, the Prime Minister was again, within a month, having to face the Parliamentary Labour Party on a critical vote—and upbraiding them for forcing him to do so. The action of the US Government in bombing near Hanoi and Haiphong in N. Vietnam had unleashed the already barely controlled anger of a large number of Labour MPs over Government support for general US policy in Vietnam. Immediately, the Labour critics set about trying to force the Government to concede a debate in the House of Commons, which the Cabinet (through the Leader of the House, Herbert Bowden) stolidly resisted. For half an hour on June

288

30, Bowden was kept on his feet at the despatch box as Member after Member demanded a debate. Bowden was accused by the Conservatives of coldly ignoring the wishes of the House and was reminded by Michael Foot, from the Labour backbenches, that nothing brought the House more public discredit than its inability to debate fundamental issues of policy because of the Government's control of its procedures.

Baffled in the House by the Government's resistance, the Labour critics the same night tabled a motion calling on the Government to dissociate itself entirely from American policy in Vietnam. Almost 100 signatures were eventually appended to the motion which had the support, therefore, of nearly one-third of the Parliamentary Party and amounted to something much more powerful than the usual Left-wing mutiny. Inevitably, the Government had to concede a debate— but on the morning of the debate on July 6 the Prime Minister was again addressing the Parliamentary Labour Party and reminding them that the Government must govern, and that his Government would do so on the basis of the Party's Election Manifesto, sections of which he quoted. Bitterly Mr Wilson rebuked his followers for cheering the Conservative Leader's demand in the House for a debate. 'The cheers for Ted Heath came from behind me, and nobody here was elected to cheer Ted Heath against a Labour Prime Minister,' said Mr Wilson, according to reports afterwards.[1]

If taken literally, this novel doctrine would mean the end of the tradition that, in the last analysis (the dismissal of Chamberlain can be counted as such) the private Member is a responsible representative who has duties above his allegiance to party. But Mr Wilson had a more substantial rebuke to deliver; he also admonished the Labour Left for holding him to account at short intervals at party meetings. He reminded the meeting that between 1945–51 only eight motions challenging the Labour Government had been tabled. Mr Wilson achieved the vote of confidence he wanted. Only forty-six Members voted for the critical motion before this meeting of the Party, calling for the Government to dissociate Britain from US policy in Vietnam, as against 214 who voted for the Government. But there was still the House of Commons to face—and Mr Wilson even had to cut an important dinner with the visiting French Prime Minister to do so. At the end of the debate, there were thirty-two Labour abstentions from supporting the Government's policy and there might have been

[1] *The Times*, July 7, 1966.

more had the Prime Minister not taken the wind out of the Left- wing sails by announcing his imminent visit to Moscow to try to secure Russian support for a new initiative in Vietnam. When this episode is examined, it hardly supports the contemporary view of a pliable House of Commons. Though the Government won the day, the House of Commons was split three ways between the Conservatives, who advocated full support for the US, the Government, with its qualified support, and the Labour dissidents, who wished to withdraw support. Once again, it was probably a fair reflection of public opinion.

In the same July, the Labour Government faced the severest of the currency crises that had yet confronted it. Drastic restraints on the economy were imposed by the Cabinet, and by the autumn, when Wilson and his colleagues met their Annual Party Conference, there were signs of rising unemployment and depression. The Government had no difficulty in riding over its Conference and, where there were adverse votes, ignoring them. With the Parliamentary Labour Party, however, it was another matter. There is plainly a limit to which any Government—even that of Mr Wilson, who was seeking, as he put it, to convert Labour from 'a party of protest' into a 'party of power'— can wholly flout the attitudes for which the bulk of its Members have gone into politics. It can, of course, overcome a minority wing on a specific topic but between 1966 and 1967 the Labour Government faced revolts from wings other than its Left. In July 1966, about twenty-seven Labour MPs abstained on the Prices and Incomes Bill and the wages 'freeze' imposed by this measure caused widespread discontent. Nevertheless, new more 'gentle' tactics of persuasion were adopted and a milder code of conduct was laid down. This appeared to imply that MPs could abstain on matters of conscience other than the traditional ones of religion, pacifism and so on. In exchange, 'personal attacks' were prohibited and party groups were supposed to be 'registered' with the Chief Whip.

Nevertheless, the biggest revolt so far on defence broke out in March 1967, when the traditional Left were joined by Right-wing abstainers who believed, on grounds of cost-effectiveness, that Britain should withdraw from East of Suez, and also by loyalists who were abstaining in protest against the abstainers. The old fissures in the Labour ranks were showing again and, in consequence, Harold Wilson addressed a party meeting with a notorious speech (of which verbatim sections were made available to the press) telling them that every dog (MP) might have one bite, but if there was persistent biting, its 'licence' (party ticket) might be withdrawn. In this speech Wilson caused a furore by stating more strongly than ever before the doctrine that MPs were primarily at Westminster to support the Government and that without the party ticket, none of them would be in Parliament. In one sense, Wilson was making the claim for support that is made by all Prime Ministers and had he appealed to the minority to support the decisions of the majority (represented by the Cabinet) he would have created less trouble. As it was, at a time when parliamentarians were acutely sensitive about their lack of influence, they were (it seemed) being told that they were, not so much representatives, as licensed delegates.

The tone of Mr Wilson's speech was perhaps ill-advised. Although he subsequently asserted that the press accounts of this private meeting failed to appreciate the humour which had been apparent to those who were present, many of his followers saw him (as one report put it) as 'threatening, sarcastic, contemptuous and despotic.'[1] However carefully he had calculated his warning, these reactions to his style may not have been fully foreseen by the Prime Minister. Although the fuss died down quickly and the 'dog licence' metaphor turned into a joke, its amalgam of crude humour and uncertain taste did not enhance the Prime Minister's reputation and may have done some lasting, if concealed, damage to the political trust of the rank and file for their leader.

On the other hand, the Prime Minister could argue that the rebels were irresponsible and that (unlike the old Bevanites) they had no coherent position. He could also fairly maintain that he spoke for the mass of the party who were incensed that the rebels should indulge in the luxury of revolt while relying on the loyalty of the majority to maintain the Government in office. Indeed, so enraged were some of the 'loyalists' that they had argued with the Chief Whip that they should abstain in protest against the abstainers— as two of them did. This 'tomfoolery' was one of the main causes of Mr Wilson's anger.

Less justly, the Prime Minister argued afterwards that most of the rebels were simply looking for something new to oppose each week. For the fractiousness of Labour backbenchers did reflect genuine unhappiness about the policies they had been forced to accept. Many beyond the Left were distressed by the Government's support of the United States' policy in Vietnam. The party was also disturbed

[1] *The Times*, March 3, 1967.

by the Government's proposals at this time for statutory sanctions to reinforce the period of voluntary wage restraint which was to follow the unpopular statutory restraint. Many Labour backbenchers also disliked the Government's intention to seek British membership of the Common Market. Above all, there was bitter resentment at the unemployment produced by the Government's deflationary measures.

Despite his uncompromising mien in March 1967, Wilson was aware that he faced a real problem and in practice he began to be more responsive to Labour backbench opinion. At this time, he steered the Cabinet away from the more extreme proposals then before it for Government sanctions to reinforce future incomes restraint. He also took care to publicise knowledge of the Government's new review of defence expenditure which was designed to reduce commitments East of Suez. Although this review ante-dated the actual defence rebellion, general sentiment on the Labour backbenches over this issue, as well as the economic need to make savings, helped to stimulate the Government's decision. Further, to prevent further trouble with his backbenchers, Wilson announced a 'great debate' inside the Parliamentary Party on the Common Market. Information collected by the Prime Minister and Foreign Secretary on their European travels was to be specially available to the backbenchers .

Finally, in the summer of 1967, the first steps towards reflation were taken and Labour backbench feelings, as well as economic considerations, were a spur to action. Increased old age pensions were announced and so was the intention to improve family allowances to deal with child poverty, on which Labour backbenchers had been pressing hard.

By 1967, backbench influence seemed to have taken on the traditional pattern in which the main lines of policy are determined by the Government but with some shading at the edges to maintain a backbench consensus. The Government had not been deterred from its major policies; nevertheless, it had repeatedly had to fight hard to gain its followers' acceptance of them. Moreover, the formidable changes in the Labour Party's official attitudes during these years were not simply a symptom of Government dominance and backbench pliancy. With the influx of a younger generation holding new ideas, the character of the Labour Party was changing in a way helpful to the Government. In general, this Government seemed unlikely to find it easier than its predecessors had done to ignore the pressures of parliamentary opinion.

Chapter Eleven

The Use of the Opposition

Since an Opposition can only remove a Government from office in the most exceptional circumstances, and can rarely force it to change any major item of policy or legislation that has already been announced, it is often asserted that the battle between the two sides of the House of Commons is no more than an empty gladiatorial display. It is certainly indisputable that the backbenchers of the governing party normally have much more impact on the production of policy than the Opposition has, while the comparatively uncontentious work of the parliamentary committees on Estimates, Public Accounts and Nationalised Industries exercises greater influence over government administration. On the other hand, to the extent that Professor Crick is correct in regarding Parliament primarily as a forum of publicity whose 'real functions are those of alerting and informing the public on matters relevant to the decision which way (or whether) to vote' one might suppose that the conflict between the Government and the Opposition was the most important function of the House of Commons, not the most superficial. For only an Opposition can pursue a Government with sustained criticism and keep before the voters, between general elections, the options that will eventually confront them.

It is obvious that the formalised struggle between the Opposition and the Government in the House does have the character of a continuous election campaign and this fact alone is enough to refute the facile criticism that the battle of the two major parties is a charade. On the other hand, it would be wrong to infer from the general point made by Professor Crick that the waging of the continuous election campaign is the *main* 'real' function of Parliament, or even of the Opposition. The rival parties are doing more, in their parliamentary contests, than simply providing electors with material on which to make future voting decisions. Earlier chapters have shown that the Government's own backbenchers can exert an immediate influence over the evolution and shaping of Government policy. Equally, it can be shown that the influence of the Opposition over the formulation of Government policy is not negligible; though, of course, once a Government has firmly decided on a course of action, no Opposition is likely to be able to force a change unless with the aid of the governing party's own backbenchers.

One is also a little uneasy in accepting in its totality Professor Crick's assertion that the theory which fits the contemporary facts is that Parliament influences the electorate which controls the Government—not that the electorate influences Parliament which controls the Government.[1] There is, for one thing, two-way traffic of influence and MPs constantly bring to Westminster information about electoral and constituency party mood which conditions the acts and the public utterances of their leaders. Moreover, the pressures exerted by backbenchers of either major party (pressures to which the leaders sometimes find it advisable to yield) are not always motivated by vote-winning considerations but by party beliefs and interests which may even be vote-losers. For example, the Labour backbench pressures on foreign and domestic policy under Gaitskell were certainly not electorally popular, yet, although the party leaders managed to resist most of them, they did play a part in influencing the formulation of official policy which finally emerged as a compromise. Similarly, when the Conservatives reduced surtax under Selwyn Lloyd's tenure of the Exchequer, it was an expression of an essentially party viewpoint and this action, which Labour could contrast unfavourably with the 'pay pause' imposed on workers by the same Chancellor of the Exchequer, was, if anything, an electoral liability for the Tories. Though backbenchers give their leaders wide discretion in policy-making, parliamentary government involves a continuous and sometimes almost involuntary striking of bargains between a Cabinet and its backbenchers, in which vote-winning considerations are not always paramount. Equally, as discussed in the next chapter, a Government may have to respond favourably to crossbench feeling on matters involving the consciences of Members, even though the result may be actions which arouse no popular support. Similarly, the Opposition's policies and utterances are not always directed at vote-winning in the next election but sometimes at trying to influence a situation immediately, or simply voicing

[1] Bernard Crick, *The Reform of Parliament*, p. 28.

the reactions of its supporters. Above all, however important the composition of the next House of Commons may be, the first job of a Government is to keep its support in the existing one. That there is never much doubt that it will do so means, not that it can do as it likes, but simply that it understands what it can and cannot do— taking into account the views and influence of all sides.

The influence of the House of Commons is the aggregate price exacted from the Government by all sections of the House for the general support it enjoys. What part can the Opposition as the minority party have in this total influence? What exactly is the impact of the Opposition on politics apart from the 'continuous election campaign?' How irrelevant and empty is the party battle on the floor of the House in terms of a more immediate influence over policy decisions?

However long an Opposition is obliged to remain out of office and regardless of whether it achieves power at the next general election, it is of vital importance to the political health of the nation that there should at every moment be seen to be a credible alternative government ready and waiting to take over. It is not enough for an Opposition to work for power in the next Parliament by diminishing confidence in the present Government: it must work to persuade the public that it is a credible alternative in the present by behaving responsibly. For an Opposition to succeed in both is not easy. It must constantly criticise, but the more it criticises, the less responsible it seems. Moreover, in a competition to appear responsible, all the facts of political life in Britain are weighted in favour of the Government. For Governments can act but Oppositions can only offer opinions. The men holding office have the aura of authority; and they can at least give some appearance of motivating, as distinct from reacting to events— however illusory this impression may be. Even the best-argued Opposition case has little chance of seizing the headlines from a government announcement of some impending action, however flimsy. Parties in Opposition find it difficult to conceive that there is not a press plot to stifle them and the more recently they have enjoyed the privileges of office, the more difficulty they have in finding other than sinister reasons to account for their sudden plunge into comparative obscurity. It is not easy for them to understand that newspapers are more interested in news than views—which is why the press turns its attention to an Opposition party chiefly at times of quarrels and divisions, when such attention is least welcomed. When a party is in the process of splitting, or threatening to split, it is at least *doing* something as distinct from *saying* something.

The tendency for the public to give the benefit of the doubt to the party in power has been demonstrated throughout the politics of the post-war period. In 1951, despite a sharp swing of public mood against the austerities which had been continued by the post-war Labour Government, the electorate could only bring itself hesitantly to give a small majority to the Conservatives. But between 1951 and 1955, while the Opposition diminished public confidence in itself by the internal feuding to which parties are prone when they have been deprived of the cement of power, the Conservative Government built itself up as the party the country knew and therefore trusted. The result was the decisive Conservative victory in the 1955 General Election—and the same process was repeated in 1959. In neither of these elections did Labour look like a credible alternative. By the early 1960s, however, there was a pronounced swing of opinion against the Conservative Government. The public opinion polls showed that for nearly two and three-quarter years before the 1964 Election, the public was in a mind to turn the Conservative government out: during this period, Labour was consistently ahead to a greater or lesser extent, and Gaitskell and Wilson had at last managed to establish Labour as a credible alternative Government. Yet when the time came, the electorate could only bring itself hesitantly to give Labour a majority of four. When all allowances are made for the part played by the economic cycle in determining election results, there can be little doubt that public preference for the party in office (even one so badly dented as the Conservatives were after the Profumo affair and the succession crisis in which Douglas-Home succeeded Macmillan) played a part in nearly depriving Labour of its expected victory. Once in office, of course, Labour itself benefited from the same consideration. Former Conservative Ministers faded quickly from the public's awareness and in their place Labour Ministers enjoyed the initiatives of government and the authority of office. Within seventeen months, despite grave difficulties which prevented the new Government from fulfilling its election promises, it was rewarded by the decisive victory of 1966.

Thus an Opposition suffers, in the struggle to command the respect of the electorate, from being in Opposition regardless of the merits or demerits of its case. It is particularly difficult for it to reconcile the need to be both critical and responsible. For a time, the late Leader of the Labour Party, Gaitskell, was criticised for being too prone to speak as though he had the responsibility of office. To do this is to concede the Government's case too often: to concede the Government's case is to play into the Government's hands. What inducement is there for the electorate to change parties if the Opposition is not seen to differ?

Yet 'irresponsibility' is also a damaging charge against any Opposition and, in particular, its leading spokesmen must often speak with circumspection about the critical issues of foreign affairs and the economy. Thus, no Opposition Leader, Labour or Conservative, has dared to speak with bluntness about sterling devaluation. Since there is a rough-and-ready equation in the public's mind between the existing exchange rate for the pound and patriotism, neither party has been able to give hostages to the other on this issue, least of all when an election is looming. For this reason, though there has been a measure of support, on technical grounds, for devaluation among Members of both parties, it can find expression in private only because of the embarrassment open expression would bring to the party. As a result, one of the major economic talking points of the early sixties was virtually taken out of politics by mutual consent: every political leader felt obliged to preface criticisms of his opponents' economic policy by testifying his own whole-hearted support of the sterling rate.

In defence and foreign policy too, it is clear that there are really only limited options open to any party in power—unless there is to be virtually a policy revolution of a kind which would command no common support. Though there are strong differences of emphasis between the parties, and a bi-partisan policy in the immediate postwar sense is a thing of the past, the scope for the Opposition to strike out on a wholly new tack is small. This barely concealed lack of differentiation between the major parties on foreign and economic policy produces debates in the Commons which appear to many critics to by-pass the real issues. Debates are seen as too crudely partisan in point-scoring and yet tending to fudge the real issues. The Liberal Party, however, can bring the major issues less delicately into the open; it could, for instance, talk as though devaluation was not absolutely an indecency and could advocate unconditional British entry into the Common Market in a way which the interests supporting the main parties would make impossible for them. It is, indeed, understandable that the Liberals, as their former leader Jo

Grimond repeatedly said, should find the debates between the two frontbenches unreal and sterile. Yet to change the nature of the dialogue means a fundamental amendment of the two-party system rather than procedural reform of Parliament. The Liberal Party can bring delicate political issues into the open precisely because, being unlikely to hold office in the foreseeable future, it has been able to enjoy instead the luxury of opinion-forming. In the present context, however, it is enough to note that to the extent that there is a lack of clear differentiation between the two main parties it usually works to the advantage of the Government.

Moreover, the frustrations of Opposition frequently lead to a drain of talent from its ranks in the House of Commons.[1] Personal reasons, advancing years, the rigours of parliamentary life—all these partially account for it. But the heavy concentration of desertions to other jobs from the Labour frontbench after the 1959 Election, when it was freely predicted that the Party might have another ten years out of office, can only be explained by the natural urge of able men not to deprive themselves of all chances of executive activity before they are too old. Few Members of Parliament regard backbench life as an end in itself: those who appear to be congenital backbenchers did not necessarily covet the rôle in which they have come to shine in default of anything better. Certainly a Member who is prepared to persist indefinitely in a 'shadow' Ministry while his Party is in Opposition needs enormous staying power and confidence in his political star as he gambles on harnessing his ability to office one day. In the years of Labour Opposition, Harold Wilson at one time appeared condemned to apparently endless speeches as 'shadow' Chancellor of the Exchequer, or 'shadow' Foreign Secretary, with no life of a Labour government in office in the foreseeable future. Only the most dedicated persist against a background of such uncertain prospects.

Finally, one must remember the depression into which parties are invariably plunged when they are ejected from power. Electoral defeat immediately breeds recriminations and demands for panaceas which will speedily bring back power. Lord Chandos has vividly described the Conservative mood after the defeat of 1945: "'You can never get back as long as you stick to the name Conservative." "Winston's Gestapo broadcast cost us the election." "Our propaganda is puerile!" "Our organisation is obsolete!" "Our policy was never put over, it didn't reach the people." "They are there for twenty years,"

[1] See p. 438–9.

and so forth.'[1] The Conservative defeat of 1964 produced a less immediate reaction because it was so nearly a victory. But once it was seen that the Wilson government, even on so small a majority, was establishing itself in power, the reaction began which demanded a change of leadership and substituted Heath for Douglas-Home. Similarly, after the Labour defeat of 1959, the party's leader Gaitskell and others immediately plunged into an attempt to get the party to modify its total commitment to nationalisation in a belief that this was the reason for Labour's unpopularity—thus contributing to the disarray which did the party further harm at this time.

For all these reasons, it is not surprising that the doctrine has gained widespread acceptance that an Opposition cannot win an election: the Government has to lose it for a change to take place. Nevertheless, the Opposition is not as hamstrung as this might suggest. Even if a Government is grossly mishandling the nation's affairs, an Opposition stands no chance of taking over unless it looks like an attractive alternative, and it can only present that appearance inside the House of Commons. This is what the Conservatives succeeded in doing in the years before 1951 and the Labour Party just before 1964. By its promise to 'set the people free' and by the Industrial Charter, the Conservative Opposition gave expression to the public discontent during the years of Labour austerity after 1945 and presented itself as a natural and responsible alternative. Similarly, the work of Gaitskell and Wilson in reassuring the country that Labour was a responsible social-democratic party which could appeal to discontented middle-class, as well as working-class voters, was crucial in securing electoral victory in 1964. Indeed, this work was primarily focussed on Parliament. Gaitskell worked from his parliamentary base to repel the attempt of the left-wing to secure the dominance of the Party Conference over Labour's policy. Had the Parliamentary Labour Party been obliged to accept the policies that the Conference sought to foist on it, Labour would probably have lost the 1964 General Election.

I have shown some of the disadvantages of the Opposition and have so far discussed the conflict between the Government and its challengers in terms of its impact on the electorate. But there are other questions to be answered. How unreal and irrelevant to the real issues of politics is the battle waged between the parties in Parliament for the sake of achieving a future electoral victory? Does

[1] *The Memoirs of Lord Chandos* (The Bodley Head, 1962), p. 330.

its partisan crudity destroy its usefulness in terms of constructive, immediate policy decisions? There are several reasons for suggesting that it does not. In the mid-twentieth century, the essential battle between both parties is one to occupy the centre ground of politics: to achieve what is suggested by the vogue word of the sixties, 'consensus'. This means that any party in power tends to move away from the specifically partisan position of its followers and to adopt policies that will retain the allegiance of the floating voters. Secondly, any party in power is to a considerable extent fuelled by the fashionable views of the moment, by the opinion-formers and especially by advice from Whitehall. Indeed, a party in power can, as we have seen, move a long way from its traditional attitudes in response to such pressures, as the Conservative Government did when it adopted planning in 1960–1 and Labour did over defence and foreign policy after 1964. In view of this tendency for government decisions to be taken in the light of neutral or expert advice, it is as well that there should still be available crude and even unfashionable statements of party views. An Opposition is, in a limited way, alienated from the current political fashions and from this position it can provide criticisms of a kind which could be available in no other way.

The crude clash of Government and Opposition in Parliament expresses a kind of truth about both parties and it performs much the same function as the clash of counsel for the defence and for the prosecution does in a court of law. You do not have to believe the whole of the case: you simply understand that you are hearing from both sides an extreme case from which it is perhaps easier to make a choice between them than it would be from more circumspect and 'accurate' utterances. Each side's caricature of the other represents a kind of truth which it is useful for voters to apprehend. The underlying truths of politics are not always to be expressed in language suitable for a Civil Service brief.

(ii)

All this might still be seen in terms of '*the continuous election campaign* of the whole life of a Parliament',[1] but if it is that, it is also more. The Opposition itself participates in the process of governing because it helps to condition the contemporary climate of opinion through which the Government of the day is itself influenced

[1] Bernard Crick, *The Reform of Parliament*, p. 26.

in the production of its policies. The conversion of the Conservative Party to planning under Macmillan may have owed most to the example set by 'indicative planning' in France but it also owed something to the existence of a party in Britain which would naturally capitalise on the fashionable swing-back towards planning the economy. In the climate of opinion in the early sixties, the existence of a Labour Party with a plan to control the heights of the economy without wholesale reliance on nationalisation was an incentive to the Conservatives to produce a counterbalancing policy. Similarly, the plans for reform of education, transport, and hospitals produced at the end of the Macmillan Government's period of power were designed to meet what was clearly to be the main challenge of the Labour Party—that while the Conservatives had provided for consumer affluence, they had failed to plan for some important sections of the nation's social and economic life. Just as a Government must anticipate the reactions of its backbenchers and prepare to meet them, so it must do the same in relation to the Opposition. Of course, an Opposition attack is much less menacing than a widespread tide of rebellion within the governing party. Nevertheless, although a Cabinet, to satisfy a particular demand inside its own party, may be prepared to brave the Opposition storm, in many other cases it will modify its policies in the light of what it expects the Opposition case to be. If it suspects that the Opposition will have an attractive case, it will do its best, within broad limits, to make that case less attractive—or to steal and adapt the Opposition's clothes. In this broad sense, therefore, the voice of Opposition contributes to the policy-making of Government in any given Parliament and is not simply a factor in deciding what the composition of the *next* Parliament should be. For example, although Conservative Party opinion prompted the production of the Commonwealth Immigrants Act which became law in 1962, an assessment of Opposition feeling was an important factor in preventing the Government from going further.[1] As it was, the Bill was fought bitterly by the Labour Opposition. This was a generally popular measure but had the Government taken it so far as to have appeared to ordinary people to be unreasonable, or motivated by colour prejudice as distinct from trying to prevent a colour problem from arising, then many more people might have been swung against it and the Opposition would have been presented

[1] Lord Butler of Saffron Walden: interview in the *Listener*, July 28, 1966.

with a very much stronger case. To see this point, one has only to try to envisage what shape the measure might have taken had the Labour Opposition not expressed such uncompromising hostility, *in advance*. Indeed, leaving aside the question of the Opposition's part in determining the issues and outcome of any next election, one has only to try to imagine the silence of the Opposition during any Parliament to comprehend what difference it would make to the current conduct of politics.

Apart from the real if indirect effect it has on the evolution of Government policy, the Opposition can also, by a carefully fought and reasoned campaign, get the details of legislation amended. Many, perhaps most, crucial amendments to Bills are in the name of the Minister concerned, yet they may well have arisen from the activity of the Opposition. Thus the capital gains provisions of the 1964 Labour Government, notably in respect of the sale of gilt-edged securities, were heavily amended by the Chancellor. Yet the detailed pressure for amendment and the exposure of weak elements in the Government's original proposal came from the Conservative Opposition. The Government's acceptance of some of them cannot be explained in terms of its small majority but rather reflected the Chancellor's understanding that he had to meet a powerful Opposition case.

In British politics, everything depends on the convention that the power of the majority should not be used to steamroller into silence the protests of the minority. If numbers were all that counted, a Government majority could any day silence the minority Opposition, and it is owing less to the formal rules of Parliament than to an acceptance of the spirit of common procedures that it does not do so. Occasionally a Government breaks the spirit of common convention that the rights of opponents should be protected, and when it does, the importance of normal good behaviour in this respect becomes very clear. An example of a Government's breaking the spirit, rather than the letter, of House of Commons' conventions occurred in 1966 over the Labour Government's Prices and Incomes Bill. After the House of Commons had agreed to the principle of this hotly contested Bill by giving it a Second Reading, the Government appended drastic changes—including those which provided statutory authority for a wages and prices freeze—to a Bill which had originally been of a very different nature. This it did when the Bill was already in Standing Committee. Pressures to remove the Bill from Standing

Committee and to have these fundamental changes examined in Committee of the Whole House were resisted by the Government but, as it happened, the Opposition had a free Supply day available. Abandoning their planned business, therefore, the Conservatives put before the House a Motion that the Committee stage of the Prices and Incomes Bill should be taken on the floor of the House, in view of the major changes in principle. Although the Opposition was defeated in numerical terms, theirs was the moral victory. Discontent about the Bill was widespread in the Labour Party and, as a result of the abstention of many of its backbenchers, the Government's majority dropped from ninety-seven to fifty-two, more because Labour dissidents disliked the terms of the Bill than because they objected on the procedural point. In this affair, the Opposition used its time well and ensured that fundamental amendments which would otherwise never have come before the whole House were discussed in the full blaze of publicity.

This episode also illustrated incidentally the way in which Members who feel themselves unjustly treated can have their revenge on the Government by causing a loss of the precious commodity, parliamentary time. In a long sequence of exchanges between Members and the Speaker, after the Liberal Leader, Jo Grimond, had tried unsuccessfully to secure the adjournment of the House under Standing Order No. 9 to discuss the matter, the Leader of the House, Herbert Bowden, remained rigidly silent. (There is reason to suppose that he was discomfited by the Government's decision to add crucial new clauses to the Bill and there is some doubt about whether he had been fully informed in advance.) Immediately after the exchanges with the Speaker, therefore, more than twenty Members (the stipulated minimum) rose to object to the reference to Second Reading Committee of an uncontentious measure, the Family Provision Bill—thus threatening, by bringing this unnecessarily on to the floor of the House, to disrupt an already choked Government time-table.[1] Childish though this sort of retaliation might seem, it represents a warning to the Government that if it rides roughshod over the wishes of private Members they still have means of imposing some return pressures. The episode was a reminder also that the observance of the spirit of parliamentary procedures on all sides is essential to the smooth running of the House of Commons—and, therefore, of Government business.

[1] H.C. Deb., Vol. 733, cols. 38–44, August 1, 1966.

Yet the most profound impact an Opposition can make on parliamentary politics may be when it provides a focus for great national debates on matters which deeply divide or disturb the community. The outstanding post-war example was the Suez affair of 1956. Never was the atmosphere of the House more embittered than then; never did the two big parties, locked for once in genuine mutual hatred, find it more difficult to subject themselves to the discipline of procedure. Yet they did so and their arguments not only led, but to a great extent created, the debate in the nation. In all this, the crucial element was the decision of the Labour Opposition to withdraw the conditional support it had earlier given to the Government's general policy and to launch a wholehearted attack on the Suez invasion *while it was in progress*. These events had a profound and lasting effect on the character of the Conservative and Labour Parties and probably influenced the political allegiance of many electors.

One result of the Opposition attack was that it became almost a hallmark of 'liberal' opinion to regard the invasion of Egypt as a jingoistic act of aggression committed by a Conservative Party still pervaded by imperialistic instincts. Moreover, while the Labour Party was briefly united in this episode, the Conservatives themselves were for a time divided. Yet the Conservatives recovered with remarkable speed and won the next general election, while Labour quickly relapsed into disunity. This seeming paradox is not inexplicable. The Suez invasion had a good deal of support among working-class people and the attempt of the Labour Opposition to undermine it—which appeared to sabotage the efforts of British forces in the field—certainly solidified the Tory working-class vote and perhaps attached to the Conservatives other working-class votes which might have gone to Labour at the next general election. There is no doubt that many Labour voters were by no means sympathetic to their leaders' policy in this matter. For the Labour Party, the episode was probably damaging for the next few years because it alienated some of their supporters.

Yet in one important respect the Conservatives eventually suffered and the Labour Party gained from the Suez affair. The Opposition's attack on the Eden Government's Suez policy began the alienation of 'liberal–progressive' middle-class people from the Tory camp and this was to bear fruit in the years leading up to the 1964 General Election. After 1945, some 'liberal' opinion had swung back to progressive post-war Toryism, and Eden, in particular, was highly

304

regarded because of his pre-war record as Foreign Secretary. This regard was shattered in 1956 and the Suez affair marked the beginning of a more intense dislike of the Tory Party in the section of the community which might impressionistically be described as the *'Guardian-Observer'* readership belt. Over subsequent years, anti-Conservative feeling, which had its origins in the Suez episode so far as a vocal minority were concerned, began to pervade opinion-formers generally. Despite this adverse minority opinion, the Conservatives won the 1959 General Election because of the general prosperity of the Macmillan period—but once the success of Macmillan's expansionism began to falter, the anti-Conservative attitudes of so many opinion-formers began to fall on more fertile ground. The anti-Tory middle class vote (whether for Labour or the Liberals) was an important factor in Labour's narrow 1964 election victory.

Moreover, the attack to which the Conservatives had been subjected over their Suez policy was the start of a new uncertainty in the party about what it stood for in the mid-twentieth century. The Suez affair had exposed to the Conservative Party and to the nation Britain's reduced position in the world. What was to be the Conservative attitude to prestige politics in future? What new rôle could be found for Britain, to solace the nation for its lost world power? For good or ill, all these questions arose from the battle in the House of Commons over Suez. The schism in the nation was largely created by the schism in Parliament. Had the Labour leaders not turned so savagely on the Government, had they not reversed so absolutely the conditional support they had given to the Government earlier, the nation might not have been so bitterly divided and the effects of the affair on party politics might have been less sharp. But the Opposition's assault on the Government in Parliament may well have had another more immediate effect on politics, though this can never be more than a matter of inference. The main reason for the final withdrawal from Egypt was, of course, the hostility of world opinion and the effect on the British balance of payments. But would the Government have yielded to adverse criticism from abroad quite so easily if Parliament had been united? Indeed, it is possible that world—and especially American—opinion would have been less starkly hostile if Parliament had not advertised to the world that Britain itself was bitterly divided over the Suez action. The Opposition announced to the world that Britain was split and did not wholeheartedly believe in the policy being followed—in much the same way as Congressional opposition came near to convincing the world that American opinion was split over the Vietnam War in 1966. Seeing that Britain's own self-confidence was broken, the Americans found it easier in 1956 to press their view uncompromisingly—and the British Government had to toe the line. In this great debate in the Commons, spread out over several months, the Opposition played a major part in deciding that the outcome of the Eden Government's Suez policy should be a failure.

Apart from the influence of Opposition on the evolution of Government policy, the constructive amendment of legislation, and the defence of rights of minorities and citizens, an Opposition will also on occasions be able to frustrate a decision of the Government. Thus in 1952 an outcry of resentment from the Opposition stopped the appointment of Lord Waverley as chairman of the Royal Commission on the Taxation of Incomes and Profits. Waverley, previously Sir John Anderson, was a former Chancellor of the Exchequer and although nominally an Independent was by now generally associated with the Conservative Party. The Labour Opposition attacked his appointment after it had been announced, on the grounds that he had strong partisan views on tax matters, and Waverley immediately resigned. Answering further questions in the House, the Prime Minister, Winston Churchill, sourly observed that no doubt the Government would find it difficult to find anyone of the right distinction to stand up to the insults of the Socialist Party—to which Gaitskell replied with the question whether Churchill considered it an insult to say that a man had views on taxation.

The influence of the Opposition is particularly strong when the Government is vulnerable to attack over a matter of public concern and when it might be accused of either dragging its feet or failing to face up to a problem. An instance of this was the scandal over abuses in rented property which received much publicity in the summer of 1963 and which was summarised as Rachmanism, after the name of the property dealer who was accused of such practices. Rachmanism was described in the House of Commons by Wilson, the Leader of the Opposition, as 'buying properties at low prices and using every means, legal and illegal, blackmail or physical violence, to bring about evictions which, under the 1957 Rent Act, have the effect of decontrolling the property'. At this time, the Government was particularly vulnerable on this issue, not simply because of the scandal caused by the abuses themselves, but because Rachman himself was connected in the public mind with some of the persons associated with the Profumo scandal, which was still very much in the public's mind. Moreover, the Opposition was able to relate this sort of abuse to the 1957 Rent Act, which it had consistently attacked. It was on this basis that the Labour Leaders put down a motion of censure against the Government which was debated in the House of Commons on July 22, 1963. The motion demanded that the Government should take 'immediate and drastic action to restore security to threatened tenants'.

The Opposition plainly had a good case and it received much publicity. Impressive speeches were made both by Harold Wilson and the Labour frontbench spokesman for housing, Michael Stewart. Before the debate it was plain to the Government that a definite plan of action had to be produced there and then—and so it was. The Minister of Housing, Sir Keith Joseph, had for some months been contemplating an independent inquiry into abuses of rented property and he had indicated as much in a White Paper on Housing issued a few months earlier. But nothing firm had yet been decided about when such a committee would start work. The Opposition forced the Government to make up its mind quickly so as to meet the attack in the House of Commons. As a result, Sir Keith Joseph announced during the censure debate both an inquiry into housing abuses under the chairmanship of Sir Milner Holland, Q.C., and also that the Minister himself would start urgent consultations with local authorities to see what further powers they needed, if any, to prevent such abuses. Furthermore, the debate produced a promise from the Minister that if legislation to strengthen such powers was needed, it would be brought forward. Before the debate, the Minister was already making extensive inquiries into the problem and was reacting to the pressure of public opinion. Nevertheless, the Opposition attack in the House obliged him to produce a firm commitment to act and it prompted him to hurry forward two inquiries.

Plainly much depends on whether an Opposition has public opinion on its side and, in an emergency when serious attempts have to be made to shake the Government, on whether it can enlist some sympathy on the Government's own backbenches. But whether or not it succeeds in hastening Government action or forcing a Government to amend or abandon detailed items of policy, it performs a vital function in focussing public attention upon issues which

Ministers might be glad to leave unemphasised. The Opposition forces the Government to answer publicly the case for the prosecution against their handling of an affair. The Opposition is equipped to do this as no extra-parliamentary process—neither press nor television—is. In the first place, despite the Government's take-over of so much parliamentary time at the expense of the backbencher (who obviously, in an age of concentrated state activity, can no longer be allowed to disrupt the parliamentary time-table by forcing attention on whatever happens to interest him personally), the organised Opposition still has a generous share of parliamentary time. This may be put at between 25 per cent and 30 per cent of the total.[1]

The Opposition has at its disposal twenty-six Supply days annually and three Consolidated Fund debates, each of two days, making thirty-two days in total. It is true that on a handful of these days the Opposition must discuss Army, Navy and Air Force Supply (although it can raise what topic it likes on these votes) while one of the Consolidated Fund days is traditionally given to backbenchers to raise whatever subjects they wish. Nevertheless, perhaps a third of the time of the House is available for the Opposition to raise whatever subjects it thinks need publicity and to pit its leading figures against those of the Government. Moreover, the Opposition has the right to move the amendment to the Address on the Queen's Speech so that here again it has the choice of ground. Not least, the Opposition can always secure time by tabling a motion of censure against the Government or a Minister, for which the Government is bound to supply time of its own. Above all, the Opposition has the great influence which comes from being able to oblige the Prime Minister to come and face it out with his near equal, the Leader of the Opposition, who is not only at the head of an equivalent great party but who is the claimant for the Prime Minister's place. This is something no American President has to do. He may have to face attacks from a Senatorial Committee but bellicose Senators, however eminent, are not claimants to the Presidential office nor, whatever support they enjoy, can they bring the President down.

Much emphasis is currently placed on the alacrity with which

---

[1] See Strathearn Gordon, *Our Parliament* (Cassell, for the Hansard Society, 6th Edn., 1964), p. 83, for charts showing the apportionment of the Parliamentary 'cake' in this century between Government, Opposition and backbenchers.

Ministers will hurry down to the television studios to be interviewed by commentators who are themselves national figures; and, of course, it is perfectly true that this has given the public a knowledge of politicians and their demeanour which it has never enjoyed, if that is the right word, before. But these are essentially confrontations between men who are not equal: between one who can only question and the other who can only answer (or not answer) the questions put to him: between one who has the status of authority and the other a public standing measured by wholly different criteria. Moreover, a Minister does not *have* to go down to the television studio and if, in a difficult situation, he decides to accept an invitation or seek an invitation to do so, it is because, however disagreeable he expects the interview to be, it suits him on balance to appear. But in the House, when challenged by his opposite number on a motion of censure, he is obliged to appear and face it out on entirely equal ground, however little it suits him. This he must do (or abandon political life) in almost any circumstances except serious illness.

Furthermore, as the presumably alternative Prime Minister, the Leader of the Opposition must, in matters of grave national emergency, be treated as something like an equal and consulted by the Prime Minister of the day, as has been done on almost every grave issue in recent years. The one advantage that television has over the Opposition in the House of Commons is that when a wholly unexpected storm blows up it can bring the Prime (or other) Minister down to the studios (if he will go) *on the night*, whereas it normally takes some days for the Opposition to raise quickly a matter which it wants to debate thoroughly with the Government. This, however, is a disability that the Opposition suffers with the House of Commons as a whole and I refer to this in the final chapter. The Opposition has, it is true, a further power of initiative in the right to put private notice Questions on matters of immediate interest to Ministers after Question Time and, indeed, to intervene in Question Time, though the actual tabling of Questions is left to backbenchers. But this is not a substitute for a speedily arranged full debate. Yet whatever its disabilities, the Opposition does have an influence on the running events of politics which amounts to something more than the challenge it will present to the Government at the next election, when the voters are able to judge the records of both Parties during the Parliament that has gone before. Of course it is true that the next election, and not a particular night's Division figures, normally represents the ultimate sanction that the Opposition can wield against the Party in power. Nevertheless, its impact on the daily evolution of politics is real enough to refute the allegation that its performance in the House of Commons is no more than a charade. If the influence of the Opposition were not a reality *in the present* there might, after all, be no future general election for it to fight.

Chapter Twelve

'Independent' Parliamentary Influence

Irrespective of the party allegiance of its Members, the House of Commons remains jealous of its rights as a body and of the rights of its minorities. Governments of all complexions recognise that it is in their own long-term interest to safeguard the expression of minority views and the Leader of the House, as well as the Speaker, takes scrupulous care to see that small groups with distinctive views have a fair share of the vocal time of the House. On the other hand, minority groups and individual Members can only make themselves heard within a framework of parliamentary procedure which gives the bulk of parliamentary time and the power of initiative to the Government and to the official Opposition—in that order. Further, the right of the Member to speak and vote according to his independent opinion is constantly circumscribed by his obligation to his party and by the demands of his Whips.

The foregoing chapters have shown the considerable influence that may be exerted on a Government's policy-making by its own supporters; and it is right, and logical, that in a political system which makes the Government responsible to the House of Commons, the mainstream of parliamentary influence should flow from the majority party in that House. It has also been shown that the Opposition, as an organised body, may influence the evolution of current politics and has a function which is more immediate and potent than the conduct of a campaign to wrest power from the governing party at the next general election. But the parliamentary dialectic which shapes informed opinion and influences the formation of policy in the places of power, and potential power, is so largely conducted through the hierarchies of the two major political parties that there may seem to be little scope for the exercise of parliamentary influence by the private Member acting independently of party. It is true that the House of Commons still preserves a collective capacity to rise above party, and to speak for the nation, at times of acute need. Yet even when it does so (as it did in 1940) the process is one of bridge-building between sections of political parties acting as such and is seldom based on isolated, independent initiatives. Does this mean, then, that even if Members are more than 'lobby-fodder' in relation to *their own* leaders, the private Member, considered as an individual unit acting outside party allegiance, has no influence worth the name on the affairs and government of the community?

It is self-evident that in contemporary politics there is no place for the Independent Member of Parliament free from party ties; indeed, there has been no place for him since 1945 and little enough room at any time in this century. Nor is there much opportunity for a Member to move between one party and another and still hope for a successful political career. The handful of Members who have crossed the floor since the end of the Second World War (Ivor Bulmer-Thomas in 1946, Raymond Blackburn in 1951 and Alan Brown in 1961) have all been sunk without trace in political terms. A man needs a party organisation if he is to get into Parliament and he must retain its goodwill if he is to stay there. It is also a paradox of the British post-war pattern of politics, in which the Conservative and Labour Parties have been moving closer together in terms of practical policies, that total commitment to a single party, however loudly a Member may disagree with aspects of its thinking, is accounted on all sides a supreme political virtue. Such is the premium thus set on party loyalty that the convert from another party is seldom made to feel really comfortable in his new home. Subconsciously, the question is presumably asked whether he may do again what he has done once. A political career such as that of the young Winston Churchill would not be easy, even for so outstanding a character, in the mid-twentieth century.

Moreover, although the British MP is not a mandated delegate but is a representative who, once elected to Parliament, has as much voting and speaking freedom as he thinks it wise to help himself to, he is dependent on the goodwill of his constituency organisation if he wishes to return to Westminster after the next general election. Even a Member who has built up a considerable personal following after years of active constituency representation under a party flag has virtually no chance of staying in Parliament if he determines to sail under his own colours. Thus Dr Donald Johnson, who had held Carlisle for the Conservatives from 1955 onwards, only managed to poll 1,227 votes as an Independent Conservative in 1964 against 17,049 polled by the official Conservative. (The seat was lost to Labour anyway in 1964 and would have been even if the Conservative vote had not been split.)

Even when a sitting Member does not want to take his freedom, as Dr Johnson did, a local constituency organisation can exert considerable pressure on him if he goes against its deepest instincts and, in the last resort, disown him. The rejection by the Bournemouth East and Christchurch Conservative Constituency Association of Nigel Nicolson as a result of his rebellion against the Government over the Suez affair is the classic example of how strong this pressure can be.

Yet this sort of case is the exception and not the rule. To see local control over Members in proper perspective one has to compare the great number of 'rebellions' by Members of both major parties against their leaders with the very few cases of Members who have been refused readoption by their party organisations. In general, a former Member who has been refused readoption has seldom been penalised for one or even a few acts of definite 'disobedience'. Normally, he is refused readoption only as a result of persistent nonconformity with the general views of his party or, more usually, for what the local activists regard as unsatisfactory personal attitudes in politics. Nigel Nicolson was a case in point. Bournemouth East and Christchurch is an ultra-Conservative constituency and Nicolson's general interpretation of the Conservative creed was such as to make him uncomfortable with this particular Conservative Association. Moreover, the Suez affair was an exceptional incident which stirred deep-rooted, atavistic instincts of national pride in the breasts of a certain sort of Conservative. Yet there were other Conservative MPs who suffered no harm from taking a similar attitude to Nicolson's over the Suez issue, even when they had combined it with other attitudes which were unpopular with Conservative constituency activists. Sir Edward Boyle, who besides resigning from the Government over Suez because he held similar views to those of Nicolson, consistently adopted a 'liberal' attitude on matters of crime and punishment. Yet this did not impede his steady rise in the Conservative hierarchy, whether the party was in Government or in Opposition. Similarly, Left-wing Labour constituency parties accepted with apparent ease the attitude of some of their Members in Parliament after 1964 who enthusiastically supported the Right-wing' foreign policies pursued by the Wilson Government. One such Member who sat for a London seat where the local activists were on the far left of Labour opinion, privately explained his lack of trouble with his supporters on the following grounds. First, it was a matter of personal relationships. Second, his was a marginal seat and the local Labour workers were sensible enough to understand that, while this particular Member might hold it for them, an extremist was much less likely to do so. Third, the local constituency officials were not going to try to push him (and others like him) into a position which might, in the conditions of 1964–6, result in loss of power by the Wilson Government.

If the subservience of individual Members to their constituency organisations is often overstressed, what of the control exercised over Members by the Whips and Party headquarters? Of course, it is true that the leaders of a party in power have great influence over their Members. This influence does not depend, as has been sometimes argued, on the threat of Dissolution which a Government can theoretically bring to bear against insubordinate followers. For Dissolution, in circumstances of a revolt by an important section of the parliamentary party supporting the Government, is likely to be potentially more dangerous to the party leaders than to the rank and file. The outcome is likely to be loss of office for all the leaders— whereas only some of the rank and file are likely to lose their seats in the House of Commons. The real influence of a Government over its supporters in the House is the common interest running through all ranks of the party in power not to vote against the Government on a matter of confidence when the result might be to hand over power to an Opposition, which would be even less satisfactory to the rebels on most counts than to the men in office. (It is frequently argued by parliamentary reformers that the real fault of the present system is the practice of making so many Divisions in the Commons a matter of confidence on which the life of the Government depends. To this question I return in the last chapter.)

Yet allowing for the real influence of a Government over its supporters, the control of the Whips and the Party headquarters of Members of Parliament is, like the control of constituency organisations, also often overstressed. For one thing, though a Government has methods of influencing its Members once they are in Parliament, it cannot control the membership of its party in Parliament. The House of Commons cannot, these days, be 'packed' by the Executive

314

and there have been many instances of able young men for whom the influence of party headquarters was inadequate to secure adoption by a constituency. Thus the composition of a party in Parliament is to a considerable degree determined at the roots of the party in the country—and it is, after all, from parliamentary parties so constituted that Ministers and Prime Ministers are eventually selected. For better or worse, the distinctive characteristic of the British system is that every Minister and Prime Minister has had to run the obstacle race of entry into Parliament in this way and if Party headquarters' influence can help a man to jump hurdles it can guarantee him nothing. A party leadership is not a self-perpetuating oligarchy. It is constantly obliged to take recruits from the mass of the party in Parliament whose composition it cannot control.

Even when a party man is in Parliament, and is subject to the full pressure of his leaders to conform, he is not reduced to the level of a yes-man. The previous chapters have shown the reality of backbench influence over Government policy-making and the frequency with which this influence has been exerted through outright rebellion, or the threat of it. Yet the list of rebellions contains many others besides those used to illustrate the theme of these chapters and frequently constituency or 'area' interests—for instance, the 'cotton' MPs acting together—reach the point of revolt. In general, however, the Whips have not sought to enforce discipline by any elaborate system of punishments and penalties. It is probably true to say that men of safe disposition and small prospects of the highest office have been encouraged to keep in line by the use of Government control over the Honours List—especially in the Conservative Party, where honours are like the long service and good conduct awards in the Army. But there are probably many more Members of both parties who understand that the way forward in politics is not to be found along the unobtrusive paths of safety but rather by a process of self-identification. Certainly, high office is not achieved by tame subservience to a party's leaders. If one examines the records of recent Prime Ministers, it becomes apparent that almost every one has taken what might be regarded as extreme risks in refusing to follow the approved party line in his junior parliamentary years. Wilson twice took a risk—how far calculated, how far impulsive remains for the historians to decide—first when he resigned with Bevan from the Attlee Government and secondly when he stood against Gaitskell 'or the leadership of the Labour Party and received a sharp rebuff

315

less than two years before he himself was elected Leader. Macmillan was perhaps one of the most courageous of the pre-war rebels against the Chamberlain appeasement policy, and a consistent critic of his party's economic policy in the thirties. Eden, for all his delay in doing so, also resigned from the Chamberlain Government. Churchill's whole life was a series of rebellions from his Liberal to his Conservative years. And Baldwin (for all his 'Safety First' when in power) was the arch-rebel—a risk-taker against the Conservative coalition establishment in 1922. Of the Prime Ministers since 1918 perhaps only Attlee, Chamberlain and Douglas-Home did not take serious risks in their early years. But, of course, the argument is not that taking risks is an essential step towards political advantage but simply that it is far from being a way to ruin.

Expulsion from a political party is exceptional: removal of the Whip is fairly quickly followed by its restoration and by and large a talented man is not excluded from office on account of one or two rebellions, though he may be rejected if a party regards him as a congenital rebel or in some personal way as unsound. Perhaps the most effective rebellion of recent years was the two-man stand of Mr Woodrow Wyatt and Mr Desmond Donnelly against the proposal of the Wilson Government to nationalise steel in the Parliament of 1964. There is little doubt that it was this rebellion which stopped the Government from bringing in a Bill during that Parliament. For, though the Government plainly regarded steel nationalisation with little enthusiasm, Labour was committed to it and Wilson had come to office intending to follow Attlee's dictum that a Government should get the really controversial things over in its first year. With the Liberals against the measure, it would have been difficult enough in the circumstances of Labour's narrow majority in the 1964 Parliament. The position of Wyatt and Donnelly made it absolutely certain that steel nationalisation could not pass through that Parliament. After this episode, it would seem that at best a long time will pass before these two Labour MPs obtain ministerial preferment. But this is because of their behaviour in the special circumstances of the Government's small majority in 1964, when these two men were regarded as holding a pistol to the head of the entire Labour Party at its moment of greatest risk. In addition, both earned ill-will as a result of their general attitude and right-wing criticism over a wide field of Government policy. For these reasons the Wyatt–Donnelly rebellion may have consequences which are the exception rather than the rule.

A recent study has analysed in the fullest detail the consequences of all rebellions, great or small, by Members of Parliament against their leaders between 1945 and 1964.[1] It has been found that discipline was used most sparingly. In the last twenty years, no Conservative MPs and only five Labour MPs (four of whom were considered to be crypto-Communists) have been subjected to expulsion. Similarly, although ten Labour MPs have had the Whip withdrawn in this period, no Conservative has been so deprived since 1942. On the other hand, sixteen Conservatives resigned the Whip during this period because they disagreed in some way or other with Government policy. But all who wanted it had the Whip restored to them. A handful either went out of politics voluntarily or (like Dr Donald Johnson) became Independents, tried to hold their seats in that capacity and failed. Opinions varied as to how far the 'Whipless' MPs suffered from social or other pressures from the parties they had deserted during their period in isolation, but such pressures do not seem to have taken an extreme form.

As well as exerting influence on their leaders as policy evolves through 'legitimate' channels, and as well as making demonstrations if their leaders will not heed them, Members of Parliament also act in an 'independent' way in a certain category of issues which usually concern social problems or the grievances of the subject. Thus the abolition of Capital Punishment on a free vote of the House of Commons in the Labour Parliament of 1964 was the culmination of a campaign waged during much of the post-war period by a dedicated group of abolitionists headed by Mr Sidney Silverman. During this period a majority of Labour MPs have favoured abolition and a majority of Conservatives opposed it but opinion crossed party barriers and, for the most part, the state of the law since abolition

[1] Robert J. Jackson, *Parliamentary Discipline in Britain since 1945*, a thesis (unpublished) presented to the Faculty of Social Studies of the University of Oxford, December 1965. I am grateful to Dr Jackson for letting me read his thesis on whose findings I base the observations in this paragraph. Dr Jackson has documented the participation of Members in all rebellions against the policy of their Party's between 1945 and 1964 together with an analysis of the cases of individuals who experienced Party discipline. He also has much interesting information about the Labour and Conservative Party organisations for maintaining discipline and the structure and functions of the Whips Office.

became a serious issue has represented an assessment by the Government of the day of the consensus in the House of Commons.

Thus the Homicide Act of 1957, which distinguished between capital and non-capital murder, represented an attempt by the Government to appease all points of view after a long and difficult period of uncertainty which had lasted for several years. The House of Lords, under the post-war Labour Government, had frustrated an attempt to abolish capital punishment by a clause added to the Criminal Justice Bill which had passed the Commons. A Royal Commission had then been appointed to consider capital punishment and made recommendations which the subsequent Conservative Government did not accept. Early in 1956, however, when the House was debating a Government Motion that the death penalty should be retained, though the homicide law should be amended, an amendment advocating the abolition or suspension of the death penalty was carried by the House on a free vote. This was entirely due to the fact that forty-eight Conservatives voted for it, against the feeling of the majority of their party, and several Ministers abstained. In these circumstances, the Government felt obliged to find time for one of Silverman's abolition Bills which had recently been introduced. After hectic campaigning from both camps, this Bill passed the Commons but was subsequently defeated in the Lords. It was after this that the Government produced its own compromise measure but capital punishment remained an issue until it was abolished (subject to a review after five years) by the Private Member's Bill brought in by Silverman in 1964.

The treatment of capital punishment in Parliament since the war has demonstrated convincingly the power of the private Member's conscience. On this issue, the House of Commons has been consistently 'ahead' of public opinion. It might therefore have seemed that the Conservative Government in 1956, in the sure knowledge that the public, like the majority of Conservative MPs, favoured keeping the death penalty, might have felt safe in following the wishes of the bulk of the Conservative Party. Yet this Government knew that it could not, on this issue of conscience, dragoon its significant 'abolitionist' minority and must compromise with them. It could not simply rest on majority Tory feeling and on the decision of the Lords to flout altogether the alliance between abolitionist opinion in its own party and the majority of Labour MPs. Hence the compromise Bill produced and passed by the Conservative Government abolishing the death penalty except for certain sorts of homicide.

The consistent line adopted by abolitionist Conservative MPs also demonstrated that, when Members' consciences are involved, they will refuse to act as delegates and that their constituency parties do not expect them to do so. On capital punishment, the Conservative Government (itself divided on the issue) could only have recourse to a free vote. In 1964, the Labour Government also allowed a free vote on the Private Member's Bill which ended capital punishment but for a rather different reason. The overwhelming majority of the Wilson Cabinet was in favour of abolition and so was practically the whole of the Labour Party. It would have been practicable for the Government to have taken the initiative and produced its own Bill— even though it would have been right on a measure of this kind to allow a free vote. Yet it was convenient for the Government, especially in view of its small majority, to allow abolition to be carried by a Private Member's Bill. For political leaders apprehend that the public may be less inclined to blame a party in power (in this case the Labour Party) for an unpopular position taken up by a majority of its Members as individuals than it is when such a position is officially taken up by the Government. Similarly, by leaving 'moral' legislation to private initiative Governments are able to avoid giving offence to particular groups in the country whose allegiance is normally divided between the parties. Thus, by not sponsoring legislation for easier divorce or abortion, a Government is able to avoid direct affront to its Catholic minority.

The same tactics will almost certainly always be adopted in matters of religion, as they were in the case of the Revised Prayer Book of 1928. Twice the House of Commons, on a free vote, defeated the new Prayer Book (which was a product of the clergy) because the Protestant majority of the Commons (including non-Anglicans as well as extreme-Protestant Anglicans) objected to the concessions in the Prayer Book to Anglo-Catholic attitudes. (In fact, Parliament's rejection of this Prayer Book has not prevented its use by the clergy since then.) Similarly, free votes of the House of Commons are being increasingly employed where questions of public morality are involved. Faced with the Wolfenden Committee's Report on Homosexual Offences and Prostitution, the Conservative Government had accurately gauged what its followers would, and would not, accept. Accordingly, it implemented the Report's recommendations for dealing with prostitution but it would not propose legislation to lighten the law against homosexual behaviour because it knew that to do so would dangerously affront the feelings of the majority of Conservative MPs. This was an obvious instance of a Government's response to backbench influence—but it might have seemed that if parliamentary opinion moved in favour of changing the law, the Government of the day would produce its own Bill.

Yet in the 1964 Parliament, when public opinion was more prepared to accept this change and when the House of Commons had a majority of Labour MPs, most of whom favoured homosexual law reform, it was still left to a Conservative Member, Mr Humphry Berkeley, to bring in a Bill which sought to liberalise the law on homosexual conduct between consenting adults. Although most Members of the Government, as individuals, favoured this measure, the Cabinet was glad to avoid responsibility for this controversial reform. (In fact, the Bill did not pass into law during the short life of the 1964 Parliament. Further measures of the same sort will obviously be left to the sponsorship of private Members.)

A further instance of the same sort was the introduction of a Bill sponsored by a Liberal, Mr David Steel, in the 1966 Parliament to make abortion easier. Again, most members of the Government probably favoured the measure, including the Home Secretary, Mr Roy Jenkins, and with a Labour majority in the House the Government could be reasonably sure of the passage of any Bills it might wish to introduce to further the evolution of the permissive society. Nevertheless, partly because such a measure was offensive to particular sections of the national community, and also because the bulk of the electorate moves more cautiously than the advance guard of opinion-formers in such matters, the Government was again glad to appear to be on the sidelines.

Thus, at a time when it is fashionable to regard backbench Members of Parliament as ciphers, they appear, in the sixties, to be entering on a new phase in which they have a bigger rôle than ever before in the initiation—often in co-operation with outside pressure groups with which they sympathise—of major measures of a social character. Even where the Government does not connive at them, such measures may, where great issues of conscience are involved, pass the Commons as the Bill introduced under the Conservative Government to abolish the death penalty did. When this happens, the Government is forced to take action. On much less dramatic issues also, the initiative of a private Member, in producing his own Bill at the right time, may stimulate the Government to bring out its own equivalent legislation. The abolition of resale price maintenance was, as we have seen, prompted in this way and so was the existing clean air legislation.

(ii)

Every Member of Parliament is a representative not only of those who voted for him but of every citizen in his constituency. In a wider sense all MPs, individually and collectively, represent all members of the national community, whether voters or not. One of their primary functions is the preservation of civic liberties under the law. With direct access to Ministers and Government departments, and enabled by the privilege of the House to raise in the Commons matters which might not, for fear of legal action, be referred to so freely outside, the Member is the most potent medium through which a citizen may seek the redress of his grievances, however trivial or serious. Most Members hold regular 'surgeries' in their constituencies where they can meet worried constituents: all are lobbied from time to time by discontented citizens at Westminster. In one capacity, the MP is dealing with matters of high policy: in another, he sometimes seems to be little more than an eminent welfare officer. Much of this constituency work he must do personally: it is a notorious commonplace that the research, secretarial and accommodation facilities available for Members at Westminster are derisory, but to some extent this is being remedied and, in the last analysis, it is up to Members themselves to decide how far they wish to 'professionalise' their activities at Westminster. No fundamental principle is involved in determining the precise amount of assistance an MP should have inside the House of Commons.

In the constituencies, however, a wider question arises. There, the Member himself, or his political party, is responsible for his work and the State provides no assistance for him in his capacity as a welfare officer. To some politicians and political observers, therefore, it has seemed desirable for the Member to be officially equipped with local help to remove some of the constituency burden from him. Professor Crick, who very much approved of the constituency work of Members and argued cogently that to relieve them of it would create a sense of alienation between the public and its Parliament, has suggested that each Member should have a trained welfare worker as his local secretary, who should be paid for out of rates. Further, Professor Crick suggested that the Member should hold his surgery not in the party headquarters, to which political opponents may be loath to go, but in a public building.[1] So heavy is the burden of work shouldered by the average Member that the attractions of such a suggestion are obvious. On the other hand, if any scheme of this sort were to be adopted, the greatest care would have to be taken to ensure that the paid official did not act as a buffer between the citizen and the Member and to maintain the citizen's right of access to his MP, however trivial a case might seem to be. It would be only too easy for a local secretary to put off a diffident constituent and it is hard to envisage any trained welfare officer who would not think his time wasted if he were unable to keep at least some problems to deal with on his own responsibility. Yet an apparently trivial complaint, or even a seemingly unreasonable one, may turn out to be one of real political significance—which might be unrecognisable by a welfare officer and discernible only to a politician.

One of the great advantages of the Member of Parliament is that he is in constant personal touch with public opinion: that he is not dependent on what filters through to him by way of a battery of secretaries and officials. Almost certainly he has some benefit also from his ambivalent position as an insider who is also an outsider. On the one hand, the Member has direct access to Ministers, who are likely to be on Christian-name terms with him, and to Government departments. Civil servants are bound to treat the complaints of MPs more warily than those of anyone else in the country, except those of other civil servants. On the other hand, the Member is outside the Whitehall 'establishment' and the creation of an office for each Member, equipped with fairly lavish research and secretarial assistance, might easily result in the formation of a rival Westminster 'bureaucracy' with friendly lines open to Whitehall. As a result of the instinctive understanding that one 'bureaucracy' has of the problems of another, the Member might become less rather than more critical of the conduct of the Civil Service. It is, however, a matter of striking a balance. For when allowance is made for these points, it remains clear that the private Member needs more help if he is to escape from being crushed with overwork and if he is to be sure that he gives proper attention to the examination of real grievances when they come before him.

[1] Bernard Crick, *The Reform of Parliament*, p. 72.

Much may depend upon the quality of individual MPs, to which I shall refer later. Leaving this factor aside, how effective does the procedure of Parliament allow its Members to be in their capacity as instruments for the examination, and possible remedy, of alleged grievances? It is perhaps significant that when the new MPs in the 1966 Parliament were canvassed about their impressions of the House of Commons, a majority believed that they had adequate opportunities to raise constituency matters properly, although most, suffering from the usual disillusion that affects new Members when they discover that they are not, after all, running the country, expressed discontent with their ability to influence important political matters.[1]

The MP has several means of raising with the Government machine matters of concern to his constituents. First, he may write personally to the Minister concerned, or to the department. Such communications may simply involve passing on a constituent's letter with little comment if the Member feels that the matter is either not worth more than formal exploration or is too complicated for him to involve himself in without further knowledge. Alternatively, he may write a letter to the Minister which takes up the case in question with some emphasis. This century has seen a big increase in the volume of correspondence between Members and Government departments.[2] Correspondence is particularly used where a subject is not acceptable as a Question according to the procedure of the House. But a Question is the next means of exploration open to a Member and is certainly to be used when he wishes to gain publicity for the point he is raising. Opinions differ about the efficacy of Question Time. In part, it is a political occasion and both the Prime Minister and senior Cabinet Ministers are subjected to heavily charged partisan Supplementary Questions on major issues of policy. To the outside observer, this use of Question Time for the purpose of scoring Party debating points can seem unprepossessing. Yet it has a probably beneficial effect on the collective psychology of British politics because it obliges even the Prime Minister, the most powerful man in the Executive, to come down to Parliament and answer the attacks of the humblest backbencher—and to answer them within the rules of procedure and custom accepted by the whole House. The author

[1] Canvass of new MPs in *The Times*, June 6, 1966.
[2] D. N. Chester and Nona Bowring, *Questions in Parliament* (Oxford University Press, 1962), p. 105.

remembers a British Prime Minister referring sourly to the lofty unapproachability of President De Gaulle and to the effect of this on the attitude to him of members of his 'Court'—adding the observation that if the President of France had to come down to Parliament twice a week, whatever his other commitments, and stand up to a running fire of Questions, the attitude towards him might be very different. The atmosphere at moments of the sharpest controversy during Question Time reveals the essential closeness of British politics in which the most contentious issues are argued out face to face between the Executive and its critics.

While Question Time gives some MPs a chance to tilt at the men in power, for others it is an opportunity to raise local matters or grievances and to seek information on which the Member can form his own judgment on whether to pursue his point further. Question Time has the further advantage of gaining newspaper publicity for the most interesting Questions. On the other hand, it has its disadvantages, not least of which is the necessity sometimes for a Member to wait several weeks before it is a Minister's turn to answer his Question. His third major option for raising an issue in the House is to do so on the adjournment. Because this takes place late at night it misses newspaper coverage, but even so, if the MP has a good case, an adjournment debate may eventually have a major effect, as in the case of the Thurso boy (John Waters) in 1959. After the debate raised by the local Member, a Tribunal of Inquiry was set up into allegations that the boy had been assaulted by police officers.

Finally, although it cannot be enumerated in the formal processes of the House, a party backbench committee may play a part in securing the remedy of a grievance. An outstanding instance of this was the case of Crichel Down in 1954. This was an instance in which most of the customary devices had been used to secure an inquiry into the refusal of civil servants to allow the former owner of land requisitioned for military purposes to buy it back when he discovered it had not been sold. There were pressures from the individual citizen concerned, constituency pressures, and letters from the local Member to the Minister. But it was the strength of feeling displayed at a meeting of the Conservative backbench Food and Agriculture Committee attended by the Minister, Sir Thomas Dugdale, that was the final straw, causing the Minister to reverse his decision not to hold an inquiry.[1] That inquiry led not only to the resignation of the

[1] Douglas Brown, *The Battle of Crichel Down*, p. 85.

Minister but to the establishment of the Franks Committee to consider the composition and procedure of administrative tribunals. The recommendations of this Committee resulted in the establishment of the Council on Tribunals, which has the function of reviewing regularly the working of administrative tribunals and inquiries.

The relationship of the citizen to the bureaucracy is now at the heart of the MP's function as a protector of civic liberties. If a Member thinks that a citizen or a group of citizens is suffering from bad law, he can seek to get it changed through the ordinary political processes. Despite the shortage of parliamentary time available to backbenchers they are, as we have seen, taking on an increasingly important rôle in sponsoring social legislation. The real contemporary problem is how far the Member can act effectively to defend the interests of the citizen, not against bad law but against the abuses, within the framework of acceptable law, of a bureaucracy which is armed with discretionary powers over an ever-widening field.

This problem falls into two parts. First there is the question of delegated legislation under which administrative authorities are equipped by Parliament with statutory power to make their own orders—in other words, administrative law. Delegated legislation has an ancient history and it is bound to become more extensive as the state provides the citizen with more and more services. Moreover, only by delegation is it possible to ensure proper flexibility in the making of new Orders and rules to adapt the basic law to changing circumstances. On the other hand, the use made of these powers gives rise to continuous anxiety. In some cases, delegated powers have even enabled Ministers to amend the law which grants the power to make orders. In other cases, delegated legislation has appeared to enable Ministers to make decisions of basic principle of a kind which ought to be the business of parliamentary legislation. On other occasions, taxation powers have been delegated—thus diminishing parliamentary authority in the field where it is constitutionally supposed to be supreme.

In practice, the Civil Service, which is so often regarded as distinctively apathetic to Parliament, is more careful of the rights of the House of Commons than is sometimes supposed. For instance, regard for the position of the House of Commons played a part in the discussions within the Treasury which led, in 1961, to the production of the 'regulator' by which a Chancellor was enabled, between Budgets and without the need for a Bill, to raise or lower all indirect taxes by up to 10 per cent. One idea mooted at the time was a 'PAYE' regulator which would enable the Chancellor to impose a straight percentage increase or decrease on every citizen's tax bill between Budgets. This, however, was found objectionable not merely on account of administrative difficulties envisaged by the Inland Revenue but because it was felt that to change income tax by an Order was too great an infringement of the traditional authority of the House of Commons.[1] A similar example was the rejection at the insistence of civil servants in the Treasury of another proposal which would have given the Chancellor power to impose the indirect taxation 'regulator' not as a flat percentage change 'across the board' but in a discriminatory way. It had been suggested that he might be given discretionary power under which he might choose to apply the 'regulator' in some fields but not in others. This, however, was regarded inside the Treasury as giving the Government a discretion to decide as between different sorts of commodities in such a way that the balance of the tax structure would be changed and therefore the rights of the House of Commons infringed. (In fact, the 1964 Finance Act made changes on the lines found objectionable in 1961. A surcharge or rebate could be applied to any one of 5 groups and at different percentage rates—though there could not be simultaneously a surcharge on one and a rebate on others.)

It was to meet concern about the dangers of delegated legislation that the Select Committee on Statutory Instruments was established at the end of the last war. This Committee, consisting usually of eleven members with an Opposition MP as chairman, meets once a fortnight to look at Statutory Instruments which have been laid before the House to see whether they violate any of the limitations of the *parent* Act of Parliament. For the most part, the Committee finds that there has been no such violation but in a few cases it holds up the Statutory Instrument until evidence, written or oral, has been taken from the government department concerned. (The Statutory Instruments Committee has the assistance of the Speaker's Counsel.) Only after taking such evidence in doubtful cases does the Committee, if necessary, report to the House. But its report is not automatically debated and is discussed only if a Member wishes to take it up.

This procedure, which was discussed by a Select Committee on

[1] Samuel Brittan, *The Treasury Under the Tories, 1951–1964* (Penguin, 1964).

Delegated Legislation in 1953, has done something to improve parliamentary control but many criticisms remain. Though its inability to discuss the merits of the case frees the Committee from the charge of partisanship, this is a shortcoming in another respect because delegated legislation does often affect matters of principle. One main question is whether there should be a sessional Committee of the House to examine and draw attention to any unusual or novel proposal in any Bill which delegates legislation. This idea, and some others, were rejected by the 1953 Select Committee. But it seems clear that there should at least be some better means of enabling Members to be clearer, both before and after the legislation of the parent act, about the extent of the rights being assigned to Ministers, or their departments, at the expense of Parliament or the Courts of Law. Equally the volume of these Orders is so great that it is almost impossible to provide time to scrutinise them all. In this, as in so many other respects, the shortage of time is the main problem of the House of Commons.

Yet for all the dangers of delegated legislation, a greater potential encroachment by bureaucracy on the liberty of the individual arises from maladministration. As we have seen, the Franks Committee on the working of administrative tribunals arose from the Crichel Down case, and it produced a Council for overseeing the work of the administrative tribunals which adjudicate between the bureaucracy and the citizen on the application of such procedures as Town and Country Planning or National Insurance. Yet, in fact, no tribunal was actually concerned in the Crichel Down case and the sort of maladministration by overbearing officials which that case did disclose was not within the terms of reference of the Franks Committee. This other sort of maladministration, arising from the ordinary relationship of officials to citizens, has been one of the main reasons for the creation of a new 'officer of grievances', a Parliamentary Commissioner or, more inaccurately, a British 'Ombudsman'.[1] At the time of the 1964 General Election, the Leaders of the Labour Party let it be known that they contemplated setting up some such official. It was clear that they did so partly to reassure doubting voters that, whatever additional degree of state intervention might be found necessary under a Labour Government, they were sufficiently sensitive to the

[1] The case for an Ombudsman was argued in T. E. Utley, *Occasion for Ombudsman* (Christopher Johnson, 1961). This gives instances of the sort of cases which create the need.

rights of individual citizens to provide some additional protection for them. Accordingly, a Parliamentary Commissioner Bill was produced in the 1964 Parliament and reintroduced after the General Election of 1966. The Parliamentary Commissioner was not created to remove from the MP his function of trying to ensure that constituents do not suffer injustice at the hands of the Government. For the Parliamentary Commissioner will act only at the instance of an MP and on a complaint of personal injustice. It is for the Member alone to decide whether a complaint appears to be appropriate for reference to the Parliamentary Commissioner, whose responsibilities cover relationships between the private person and the central Government with important exceptions, including certain stated matters of national or public interest, such as those involving the safety of the state. The Parliamentary Commissioner reports on each case to the MP who referred it to him and is also required to make a general report to the House of Commons each year. It seems likely that this official will usefully provide MPs with some of the additional help they need to fulfil their rôle as guardians of civil liberties.

The essential grievance problem for MPs is how to find out *prima facie* cases of injustice. Once a Member can show that there has probably been an injustice, or when there is a case that catches the imagination of the Commons, the House pursues it indefatigably. Several such cases have occurred in recent years. Three of the most notable took place when Mr Henry Brooke was Home Secretary in the Macmillan Government. The first was the case of a young Jamaican immigrant, Carmen Bryan, who had been convicted of shop-lifting. She was conditionally discharged but, on the Magistrate's recommendation, Brooke's predecessor as Home Secretary (R. A. Butler) had ordered her to be deported. This decision roused a storm in the House of Commons, which regarded it as excessively harsh and contrary to promises given by the Government when the Commonwealth Immigrants Bill passed through the House. So great was the storm that the Home Secretary revoked the order.

Mr Brooke was faced with two other instances of problems arising from deportation orders. One was the case of Chief Enahoro, a Nigerian who had been a refugee from Nigerian justice in Ireland. Enahoro visited London having, he said, received a pledge that he would not be extradited. Nevertheless, at the request of the Nigerian Government he was arrested with a view to being returned for trial in Nigeria for conspiracy against the Government there. In this matter party sentiments about Nigeria were mixed up with strong feeling in the House that Britain should not abandon its tradition of giving political asylum. Some forty backbench Conservatives spoke up against extradition. But after long arguments in the Commons the Conservative backbenchers obeyed their Whips. The argument of the Home Secretary was that it would be an insult to the judicial system of a newly established Commonwealth country not to return Enahoro. The third case was that of Dr Soblen, who had been convicted of spying in the US and who, on his way from Israel to America, slashed his wrist in an aeroplane. Following this attempted suicide, he was landed as an emergency case in England. The question then was whether he should be extradited or, as many MPs wanted, given compassionate asylum in Britain. Brooke decided to restore the position as it was before the attempted suicide and to return Dr Soblen to America. In neither case did the House of Commons manage to change the Home Secretary's mind and it may be argued that these were instances of the Whips predominating over conscience. Yet whatever the merits of the argument, it is probably true that the Conservative majority, however reluctantly, did come to give genuine as distinct from 'whipped' support to Brooke's decisions. It is not necessarily a sign that the House of Commons is incapable of protecting civil liberties if, after debating decisions of the Executive which have caused misgivings, the bulk of the majority party decides in the end that these decisions must be supported.

(iii)

Lack of time on the floor of the House and the monopolising by the Government of opportunities for legislation are, superficially, the chief handicaps of the backbencher in his capacity as an individual and responsible Member distinct from his party allegiance. That this is inevitable in modern conditions seems obvious and there are also strong reasons for suggesting that it is not undesirable either. After the revolutionary curtailment of the backbenchers' share of parliamentary time in the nineteenth century, culminating in 1902, there has been some improvement for him, except during war periods, since then. Since 1950, ten Fridays have been allowed per session for private Members' Bills and ten more for their motions. In 1959, when the Macmillan Government was sensitive to criticisms of

329

Parliament at a time of a large Government majority and at apparently ineffective Opposition, four additional half-days were added for the discussion of private Members' motions.[1]

Private Members must ballot for the use of these opportunities. Otherwise, a private Member can only hope to initiate legislation as an unballoted Bill which must be wholly uncontroversial to stand any change of success, or under the Ten Minute Rule. The latter allows the introduction of a private Member's Bill with a speech of not more than ten minutes by the sponsor and a single opposing speech of the same length. Such Bills, which can only be introduced immediately after Question Time on Tuesdays and Wednesdays, may, if they are unopposed or are successful in a Division, seek a place at the end of a Friday's sitting if there is time. It is obvious that the chances of Bills under either category reaching the Statute Book are remote. But a Ten Minute Rule Bill can be used to make a point to the House at a time when it is crowded and its leading figures present. Frequently, such a Bill is brought in when both the Government and the Opposition frontbenches are full as the House awaits the beginning of a major debate. On occasions, a Government has been pushed into an examination of a problem by the introduction of a Ten Minute Rule Bill; indeed, Sydney Silverman, a Labour backbencher, brought in a Bill for the abolition of the death penalty on two occasions—once in July 1953 when the House refused leave to introduce the Bill, and on a second occasion in November 1955 when Government time was then made available for it to be discussed. It is open to the Government to find time for any Unballoted Bill or Ten Minute Rule Bill if it feels that there is a widespread demand in the House that it should do so.

Nevertheless, legislation is not the most important way in which the backbencher as an individual can influence the Executive. He has Question Time, private contacts with Ministers and, as we have seen, extensive influence through his Party. He brings back to Westminster the opinions of his constituents and, certainly if he is in the Government party, his leaders heed them. He can influence the shape of Bills in the Committee Stage, provided he is willing to undertake the sometimes dull and generally unpublicised morning work that it entails in a Standing Committee. Not all backbenchers are prepared

[1] See Peter G. Richards, *Honourable Members: A Study of the British Back-bencher*, (Faber, 1959) pp. 201 et seq., for discussion of private Members' time.

to sacrifice themselves in this way if it means losing sight of a chance to make a more spectacular if possibly ephemeral impact at Question Time. In the same way, a backbencher can exercise some surveillance over Government administration, finance, the nationalised industries or Statutory Instruments if he is prepared to serve on one of the appropriate Committees. As an individual he can also make a nuisance of himself on the floor of the House and no sensible Minister will antagonise an able Member who can retaliate by causing a loss of parliamentary time. Like-minded backbenchers can combine with each other to influence the policy of the Government, or of their leaders if they are not in the Government, or both. The Victory for Socialism Group and the Suez Group are examples of this sort of activity. They can use the Order Paper for propaganda by putting down Early Day Motions on policy matters and seeking as many signatures as possible for them in order to bring pressure to bear on the Government, or on their leaders if they are in Opposition and wish to do so.[1] Thus the backbencher need not be unoccupied nor does he lack a chance to have his opinions heard.

What the House, considered as a collection of backbenchers without regard to their Party allegiances, does lack is adequate time and opportunity to force a discussion quickly on a topical problem. On innumerable occasions, backbenchers on both sides of the House, from their different Party standpoints, have wanted a quick discussion on some topical issue, often affecting foreign affairs or the grievances of citizens, which the Government does not wish to discuss and when the official Opposition, not wishing to be committed to a categorical statement of its own position, is at best lukewarm. Similarly, backbench Members lack time to discuss Government orders and suffer from inadequate information about Government activities. With the last of these problems I deal in the discussion of Commons' Committees and the financial duties of the House.

[1] For a study of this subject see S. E. Finer, H. B. Berrington and D. J. Bartholomew, *Back-bench Opinion in the House of Commons, 1955–59* (Pergamon Press).

Chapter Thirteen

The Commons' Committees and Whitehall

The twentieth-century case against Parliament on grounds of inadequacy rests to a considerable extent on the twin premises that the House of Commons is no longer capable of controlling adequately either the Government's administrative machine or public finance and expenditure. The remedy almost uniformly suggested for this insufficiency is an extension of the House of Commons' Committees so that specialising groups of Members could concentrate their continuing attention on specific sectors of the bureaucracy and on particular areas of the Government's activity. This suggestion is also frequently presented as if it were the major solution to the larger problem of the House of Commons' alleged decline before the power of the modern Executive over policy.

The premise that Parliament is no longer able to control adequately either public administration or spending partly depends, in turn, on the assumption that there has been a significant change in the balance of power within the Executive in the broadest sense of that term. The balance of power, it is said, has shifted dangerously in favour of the more or less shielded administrators of Whitehall, over whom the House of Commons can exercise no direct control, and at the expense of the politicians in power whom, within the limitations imposed by party loyalty and discipline, Parliament can still ultimately control. Whatever reality may still attach to the concept of *collective* Cabinet responsibility for major decisions of Government, it is argued that departmental ministerial responsibility is inevitably a fiction so far as a large area of a department's work is concerned. No Minister can hope to be responsible for all the acts of his officials, and even where he has a real measure of responsibility for major decisions, he is often voicing *departmental*, as distinct from *political*, policy. Members of Parliament may be able to call the Minister to account, or even on occasions to contrive his dismissal because of the shortcomings of his department. But they can never, even through the Minister, really get at the permanent officials who are said to wield the real power.

With the broader question of the relationship of Ministers to their departments, and with the reality, or otherwise, of ministerial responsibility to Parliament for departmental decisions, I shall deal in the Conclusion. The purpose of the present chapter is to examine the proposal now made for improving House of Commons control over the administration of the Executive and over the public purse by means of specialist committees. The next chapter considers how far it is true that the House has abandoned its traditional control over Supply and how far it has any real control over Government spending. In discussing first the proposals for specialist committees, my object is not to describe in detail the various forms this idea has taken but simply to see whether a reform along these lines would have any *major* effect in restoring the allegedly declining influence of Parliament and whether, as a result, the House of Commons would be able to perform more effectively its traditional function.

Advocacy of an extended House of Commons Committee system has so long a history in this century and has enjoyed such persistent support from political theorists (some of whom have also been practising politicians) that it is tempting to ascribe to obscurantism the refusal of the Commons to act on the advice offered them. Yet some weight must be given to the fact that the Commons have remained reluctant after repeated re-examination of the case for specialist committees. It would be a mistake to suppose that they have been motivated by anachronistic prejudices or that they would willingly be persuaded by a Government, or by their own more conservative elements, to turn aside from such a reform if they genuinely believed it would enhance their influence. Justified or not, there lies behind the hesitation of the Commons in this matter a persistent instinct that a proliferation of parliamentary committees to examine Government work in progress might impede rather than aid the basic political function of Parliament.

A committee, for most practical purposes, is a body to which a more powerful institution commits, or delegates, certain specific tasks or responsibilities. Normally, but not invariably, a committee is smaller than the parent institution and the Committee of the Whole

House is an exceptional instance of a committee whose composition is the same as that of the parent body. A committee is usually in some degree subordinate to the body from which it derives its authority though (as in the case of American Congressional Committees) it may be virtually autonomous in its assigned field—and, in that field, may be more important than the 'superior' institution. A committee may consist of persons drawn from outside the parent body (as when the Government sets up an independent committee of inquiry) or, as is the case with all House of Commons committees, the committee members may be drawn only from the parent body. The function of a committee is usually either to save the time of the larger body or to bring to a particular task the expertise which a limited and compact group can generate over a specific topic to which they devote themselves continuously—an expertise inevitably denied to the larger institution, which cannot concentrate and focus its activities in the same way.

The House of Commons uses what are called Standing Committees (an inappropriate nomenclature) to consider the details of Bills in order to save its time. Though the members of Standing Committees are now chosen on an *ad hoc* basis with some regard to the interest of Members in a particular measure, these Committees do not primarily exist for their expertise. They are constituted to reflect the strength of the parties in the House and when they vote it is normally on a party, rather than an 'expert' basis. They have no permanent existence as specialists in any particular field of legislation.

The Committee of the Whole House, consisting as it does of the entire membership of the Commons, obviously exists neither to save the time of Members nor to bring particular sorts of expertise to particular topics. Its advantages are purely procedural. In particular, it enables a Member to speak more than once, in committee-style, to the same question. This procedure ensures that no Member is deprived of the chance of participating in the discussion of the details of a matter of importance, while preserving the essential faculty of committee members to return repeatedly, if necessary, to the same point. Its style is normally one of small speeches on particular points rather than the single, set speeches used in the House itself. The Committee of the Whole House may sit on a Bill and must sit on a Money Resolution. (As the Committee of Supply, which was abolished in 1966, its theoretical job was to consider and provide the Supply needed to cover Government expenditure and to approve that expenditure.) Under the name of Committee of Ways and Means, the Committee of the Whole House also sits to consider and provide taxation, through the Budget Resolutions. The Finance Bill has also been taken in Committee of the Whole House.

The House also employs a number of Select Committees. One, on Statutory Instruments, has already been discussed. Similar Committees also examine problems of Procedure and Privilege: the Nationalised Industries Committee has been remarkably effective in its limited field. But in governmental terms, the most important are the Estimates Committee and the Committee of Public Accounts. Both of these obviously exist to save the time of the House, in the sense that the full House could not possibly do the jobs assigned to the two Committees. In some sense, however, the Estimates and Public Accounts Committees also have their own expertise to offer. But it is an expertise in the type of inquiry rather than an expertise in the subject matter under consideration. The job of the Estimates Committee (operating through sub-committees) is to examine in detail the Estimates for the current year and to see whether the policy implied in the Estimates might be carried out more economically. In the process it deals with the management and spending problems of many departments. It acquires no great expertise in the affairs of a particular department but it acquires a considerable expertise in inquiries of this nature. Similarly, the Public Accounts Committee, which works with the aid of the Comptroller and Auditor-General and his staff, exists to see that money voted by the House of Commons was spent on the purposes for which it was appropriated. Again, it acquires an expertise in a particular sort of financial post-mortem but ranges widely over the whole field of government.

In its wider processes of government the British nation is notably addicted to committees, whether to run local government, manage community services, or to investigate and pronounce upon great, or minor, national problems. For the representative body of such a nation, Parliament has for several centuries proved itself singularly suspicious of employing committees, in the normal sense of the term, to relieve itself of time-consuming burdens or to provide itself with expert advice. In particular, it has resisted giving those committees it does employ the sort of authority that the committees of legislative assemblies enjoy in other countries, notably the United States. Jealously, the House of Commons has sought to ensure that discussion of policy is never delegated to committees and that no committee should be able to detract from the authority of the House by being empowered to make decisions of substance.

Yet in the sixteenth century, the House of Commons had a very early experience, on which it may have turned its back deliberately, of using committees widely and giving them greater scope in policy matters than parliamentary committees have normally enjoyed in Britain. This short-lived development occurred in the reign of Elizabeth I. At the beginning of her reign, few Bills were sent to committees; at the end of it, virtually all Bills were delegated to committees for discussion and much of the essential debate was transferred to the committees from the House itself.

The use of Elizabethan standing committees was not, however, confined to the study of Bills. Standing Committees specialising on particular matters were established—for instance, on 'griefs and petitions', religion, and privileges and elections. Such 'specialist committees' drafted Bills and to some extent appear to have reflected a growing wish on the part of the House to initiate legislation itself. At this time, most legislation was initiated by the Crown through Privy Councillors and the committee for grievances was, in the words of the historian of the Elizabethan Parliaments, 'calculated to appropriate a share in that rôle for the House of Commons: to provide the House, as it were, with a Privy Council of its own'.[1]

For the most part, however, it appears that the smaller Elizabethan parliamentary committees, which in some respects seemed to anticipate the idea of 'specialist committees' employed in legislatures outside Britain today, were dominated by the Privy Councillors during much of Elizabeth's reign.

It was from this situation, when parliamentary debate appeared to be increasingly relegated to committees, that the House, to preserve the interest of the majority of Members, began to appoint larger committees. The House stumbled upon the device of the Committee of the Whole House when it had begun the practice of letting a large committee meet on the floor of the House. A contemporary explanation (in 1621) of the large number of Members then being appointed to committees was that nowadays 'few matters are debated in the House but are referred to a committee and there debated. So either we must order ourselves to the old course of

[1] J. E. Neale, *Elizabeth I and Her Parliaments, 1559–1581* (Cape, 1953), p. 220.

debating matters before we correct them, or else there is reason for more committees'—that is, for larger committee membership.[1]

The Committee of the Whole enabled the House to be sure that all Members, and not simply the most prominent, or those chosen in the interest of the Crown, could debate all matters and that they did so flexibly. Members could speak more than once to a question, as they could not when the House was sitting as such, and in the absence of the Speaker, who was still primarily a servant of the Crown, they could speak more freely. Some Standing Committees continued through the seventeenth century and the practice, during the Interregnum, of government through executive committees of the House no doubt helped to give the Commons after the Restoration a new attitude towards controlling expenditure and administration through, for instance, the Parliamentary Committee of Accounts.[2] But the idea of Standing Committees to deal with particular areas of policy did not develop—nor did the practice of committing Bills to Standing Committees. In the eighteenth century, private Bills were referred to committees which were often nominated by the sponsoring Member and the system of Private Bill Committees evolved. Yet it was not until the beginning of the twentieth century that the present system of Standing Committees for Public Bills was finally adopted.

In 1848, 1854 and 1861, the Clerk of the House proposed that Public Bills should be referred to small select committees comparable to the Private Bill Committees (discussed in Chapter Two) but this was not acceptable to the Commons. In 1878, Erskine May suggested that Public Bills should be referred to larger Committees of Members, most of whom should sit permanently, but some of whom should be appointed for their particular interest in the subject of a particular Bill. A scheme along these lines was adopted in 1882 for a few years, but did not become normal procedure until 1907. Since 1960, Standing Committees have consisted entirely of up to fifty Members appointed for each Bill, which gives more scope for Members to scrutinise the details of Bills in which they are personally interested. On the other hand, the Committees have no permanent being and they are restricted to the details, as distinct from the principle, of particular legislation. The House has rigorously avoided any system that might enable specialist committees to embrace both legislation and broader policy issues in their field in the fashion of US Con-

[1] J. E. Neale, *The Elizabethan House of Commons*, (Cape, 1949) p. 378.
[2] See p. 363.

gressional Committees. To some advocates of specialist committees in Britain it has seemed desirable that they should be charged with both legislation and government administration in a specified field. To others it has seemed that specialist committees should deal with administration only.

The House of Commons has traditionally preferred *ad hoc* committees for most purposes, and in the nineteenth century, as we have seen, these were used for investigating particular problems, many of which could be regarded as essentially matters of policy, notably in the field of social betterment. Such inquiries have been replaced by royal commissions, special committees of inquiry (to which 'impartial' and 'expert' members can be enlisted) or, sometimes, by the internal Whitehall inquiry which can investigate a problem and report to the appropriate Ministers in privacy and without the intrusion of political debate as it formulates its findings. The unpublished departmental report on resale price maintenance discussed in Chapter Nine is illustrative of a technique of inquiry which enables Government positions to be determined before MPs are formally consulted and which also deprives Members of the basic information on which the Minister has formed his judgment—and therefore makes it more difficult for them to test the validity of that judgment.

The main explanation for the MPs lost position as a participant in *ad hoc* inquiries seems clearly to have been the increased rigidity of party allegiances. The general mid-twentieth-century assumption is that such committees would divide along party lines. It is also held that MPs lack both the time and the expertise to examine adequately many of the 'technical' problems into which a modern Government must commission an inquiry. Though governments of both parties now prefer non-parliamentary investigations, however, there is a certain kind of case in which contemporary politicians, *when in Opposition*, have shown half-hearted signs of advocating that inquiry should be by the House of Commons itself. There is normally no demand for this in such cases as the Royal Commission on the Press of 1961–2, or the special inquiry into broadcasting television under Sir Richard Pilkington in 1960. Nor did MPs make any claims that they should handle the inquiry into the Trade Unions which was assigned to a Royal Commission by the Labour Government in 1965. Yet all these inquiries might have fallen to Parliament itself in the nineteenth century. The sort of case which has produced some demands for inquiry by Select Committee of the House of Commons has been that with political overtones—which is precisely why no Government will agree to it. Thus, on June 21, 1963, when the Prime Minister, Harold Macmillan, was considering what form of inquiry should be established into the security and other problems which had been raised by the Profumo scandal, the Labour Leader, Harold Wilson, let Macmillan know that Labour's first choice would be a Select Committee of the House which would be able to demand the attendance of witnesses and would be particularly equipped to deal with the parliamentary aspects of the case. As a second choice, the Labour Opposition indicated that it would accept, though reluctantly, a Tribunal of Inquiry into the case under the Act of 1921 but it would be totally opposed to a simple inquiry by a judge. However, the last was precisely the form of investigation which Macmillan set up, under Lord Denning. Immediately, Wilson informed the press that the Labour Party might table a motion for a Select Committee which would, for instance, have the power of questioning Ministers into wider aspects of the case than those assigned to the Denning inquiry. In the House of Commons, Mr Wilson accused Mr Macmillan of a 'cover-up' operation.

Yet a few days later, when it met on June 24, the Labour 'shadow' Cabinet decided against tabling a motion calling for a Select Committee of the Commons to investigate the parliamentary aspects of the Profumo affair. The significance of this decision, taken after a week-end of mulling over the problem by Labour leaders, was that they had come to the conclusion that such a move would be a tactical mistake and that it would convey to the public the impression that the Opposition was conducting a vendetta against the Government over the Profumo affair, besides having the effect of closing the Conservative ranks round Macmillan, whose leadership was being generally questioned in his own party.

In short, a (mainly formal) demand for Select Committees of Inquiry by the House of Commons occurs nowadays mainly when there are political implications—in other words, when no Government is prepared to give hostages to its opponents by such an inquiry in which Opposition Members would have an active part. Similarly, security cases are held, by common consent, to demand an external inquiry of some sort, as in the Vassall case in 1962; when the Conservative Government set up a Tribunal of Inquiry, under the 1921 Act, with Lord Radcliffe as chairman. At the most, it has been argued that some MPs might be included in some such inquiries, which would have to be held in secret. In practice all parties appear to have tacitly accepted the difficulty in modern conditions of instituting parliamentary inquiries into any cases which have political overtones—which in practice means almost every case. Even such issues as broadcasting and the alleged monopolistic tendencies in the press may have some political implications.

The contemporary instinct against House of Commons investigatory committees into issues involving controversial policies and political reputations may be sound. Such committees could, on occasions, turn into something like a court of law. On the other hand, the current fashion for seeking new outlets for House of Commons influence by inquiries into the administration of government policy might be seen as a symptom of a contemporary inclination to turn aside from the broader-brush political arguments. It might be argued that, having abandoned hope of effectively controlling the politicians *direct* (through the traditional processes of politics on the floor of the House) the reformers are hoping to find a new way in which the House of Commons might call the politicians to account through the administrators who are suspected of dealing in policy as well as administration. The relevance of this solution depends in part on the answer to the question (discussed in the Conclusion) how far basic policy is the work of the politicians; how far of their permanent officials.

(ii)

Although most advocates of parliamentary reform by extending the committees of the House would disclaim any wish to adapt the American Congressional Committee system in Britain—and would deny that it would be possible to do so anyway—they have received considerable inspiration from the institutions of the United States. In America, over thirty legislative committees, which are specialised and permanent during each Congress, can initiate both legislation and policy resolutions, as well as holding investigations into policy and administration. The fate of the American Government's legislation is in the hands of the appropriate Committee. The Government (that is, the President) and Congress are not necessarily of the same political complexion and even if the President's party has a Congressional majority, the Government's legislation is not necessarily secure against the pressure of particular interests and the effects of cross-voting in Committees. Congress can defeat, or obstruct, the

Government's legislation, knowing that if it does so the President will not 'fall'. For most practical purposes, Congressional Committees are more important than Congress itself and the influence of Committee chairmen is particularly important.

Such a system, suitable for government institutions based, formally, on the separation of the powers of the Executive from those of the Legislature, is plainly unsuitable in the more homogeneous political conditions of Britain. In modern British parliamentary government, the same electoral decision creates both the Administration and the majority party in the House of Commons and makes the two interdependent, and mutually supporting, rather than in counterbalance, for most *normal* purposes. In Britain, the job of the governing party as such is to ensure that the Government continues broadly within the policy lines for which backbenchers of that party were elected to Parliament and for which the Administration (of the same party) was 'elected' (for that is the practical effect of a general election) to Whitehall. Legislative Committees which could challenge, obstruct or overthrow Government policy would plainly be inappropriate in this system. On the other hand, there is an obvious attraction in the idea that parliamentary committees should be able to investigate the conduct of government departments *below* the policy level, and the normal suggestion has been that each department, or group of departments, should be shadowed by a House of Commons Committee—a practice also adopted in post-war France.

An early suggestion of this sort was recorded in the Report on the Machinery of Government in 1918.[1] This made the point that its recommendations for improving the public service would not be fruitful if they disturbed the balance between the Legislature and the Executive. Any improvement in the organisation of government departments should, therefore, be counterbalanced by 'an increase in the power of the Legislature as the check upon the acts and proposals of the Executive'. The suggestion made in the Report was that a series of Standing Committees should be appointed, each charged with consideration of the activities of a Government department. Such Committees would be required to be furnished with 'full information as to the course of administration pursued by the Departments with which they were concerned; and for this purpose, it would be requisite that Ministers, as well as the officers of Departments, should appear before them to explain and defend the acts for which they were responsible'.

[1] Cmnd. 9230, 1918.

As we have seen, two early advocates of an extended committee system along specialist lines (though each produced a different version of the idea) were F. W. Jowett and Ramsay Muir.[1] Lloyd George (like Jowett) favoured Select Committees on the municipal pattern but shied away from the implication that such parliamentary committees should control the affairs of government departments. Ministers, Lloyd George thought, should not be chairmen of parliamentary committees (though they could give evidence before them), and in the affairs of the departments, the Ministers should have 'the ultimate say, subject to what Parliament says'—a muddled observation which exposed the basic dilemma.

L. S. Amery suggested committees presided over by the Ministers concerned and consisting of MPs interested in the work of particular departments. Amery saw no danger that this would lead to a re-production of the American system. This objection, he considered, 'overlooks the fact that the relation of Ministers to committees only reproduces in miniature their relation to the House as a whole, and that Ministers with us, unlike French or American Ministers, are unquestioned masters of the House and are supported in their position of authority by a solid majority there which is reflected in the composition of its committees. My own experience in the offices which I have held is that I should have gained by such regular opportunities of giving information and explaining my policies and of gathering the views of those interested, and that the effect upon the quality of debates would have been equally beneficial.'[2]

Amery's interpretation of the usefulness of specialist committees is a useful indication of the differing purposes they are seen as serving by their various advocates. To Jowett, they were a parliamentary weapon against the Cabinet. To Amery, on the other hand, they were an extra weapon in the armoury of a Minister, and the present author has heard one senior Cabinet Minister in the post-1964 Labour administration privately admit that he would welcome such committees because they would give him an added buttress *against his own departmental civil servants.* Among other pre-1939 advocates of an enhanced committee system was Harold Laski, who accepted that it must be for the Government to initiate legislation,

---

[1] See Chapter Four for their evidence to the Select Committee on Procedure, 1931.

[2] L. S. Amery, *Thoughts on the Constitution* (Oxford University Press, 1947), pp. 53–4.

and who expressed the functions of the private Member as follows: 'The ventilation of grievance; the extraction of information; the criticism of the administrative process; what contribution he can make to debate. In addition to these, he can raise, in private Members' motions, the discussion of large principles which test the movement of public opinion. He can serve on committees of inquiry. I do not myself think that this can be regarded as a small field of action.'[1]

Laski believed, however, that this field should be enlarged without treading on the essential right of the Government to initiate legislation. The job of the Select Committee should be enlarged to scrutinise delegated legislation and to improve, by analysis, by criticism, by suggestion, the work of departments.[2] Although Laski favoured an advisory committee of the House of Commons, which would be attached to each department of state to 'watch the process of administration', to 'make suggestions on policy for examination' and to 'discuss confidentially the principles of Bills before the prestige of the Minister became associated with each clause and schedule of the content', he insisted that such committees should be purely advisory and without executive function. What they would be was a 'valuable safeguard against bureaucracy' and a means of giving Members 'material for understanding which ought greatly to clarify the standard of public debate when the Bill is publicly discussed'.

Even though Laski would have given his committees power to deal with delegated legislation and with the minutiae of Bills, the whole tenor of his argument seemed to be that the authority of the Executive should not be infringed and, by and large, most subsequent proposals for specialist committees have taken roughly the same position. They have sought to distinguish between such a Committee's scrutiny of the administration of policy and the maintenance of Government responsibility for policy itself. But there is another ambiguous argument which falls between the contentions that Committees should not be concerned with policy and that they should be. This is the suggestion that Committees should be able to *advise* the Government on policy—which leaves open the question what authority that advice would carry. Moreover, to call a Minister before such a Committee would immediately be liable to rob the Committee of its crossbench, advisory, independent capacity since its Members would probably break up on party lines—one side supporting, the

¹ H. J. Laski, *Parliamentary Government in England* (Allen & Unwin, 1938), p. 166.   ² Ibid., p. 167.

other attacking the Minister who was 'under fire'. On the other hand, assuming that the Committee called only civil servants for examination, the doctrine of ministerial responsibility would be undermined if these officials were examined on any matter that could be regarded as policy.

The solution most generally proposed for all these problems is that specialist Committees should question only civil servants and only on administration. Such Committees could inform MPs for the purpose of their debates in the House itself and, at the same time, protect the citizen from bureaucratic excesses or inefficiency. Thus in 1959, Professor Hanson and Professor Wiseman put forward a scheme for specialised investigatory Committees which would normally be non-voting and would normally follow the non-partisan approach of such existing Select Committees as the Estimates Committee, Public Accounts Committee and Nationalised Industries Committee.[1] In 1964, as we have noted in the Introduction, Professor Crick also advocated what he called 'Standing Committees of Advice, Scrutiny and Investigation', which emerged in two possible versions. One possibility was for them to be an extension of the existing Standing Committees on legislation which would become specialised and would be given powers 'at least *to debate and discuss*, if not to report upon, the whole subject area of the type of legislation which is sent to them'. However, to merge in this way the concept of the essentially partisan nature of legislative Standing Committees (which are constituted on party lines to reflect the composition of the House) with the non-partisan Select Committee idea (as in the Estimates and Public Accounts Committees) would seem to vitiate Professor Crick's general position that such Committees should not threaten ultimate Government control. Professor Crick's second version, therefore, was more in line with his own basic position and the general fashion in this matter. This was that Standing Committees for legislation should remain unspecialised or, if specialised, 'yet remain limited strictly to the scrutiny and amendment of legislation put before them; but alongside them there could grow up a com-prehensive pattern of "standing" Select Committees covering all areas of Government policy, debating and making occasional reports'.[2] Though there appears to be a certain confusion in Professor

[1] A. H. Hanson and H. V. Wiseman, 'The Use of Committees in the House of Commons', *Public Law*, Autumn 1959, pp. 277–92.
[2] Bernard Crick, *The Reform of Parliament*, p. 164.

Crick's analysis as to whether he wants his Committees to deal with the *principle* of policy and legislation, or to be essentially 'crossbench' and confined to administration, he too shies away in the last analysis from anything that might be said to infringe the traditional position of the British Executive and its relationship to Parliament. It is therefore reasonable to assume that he mainly favoured the crossbench approach, though one must note that, in summing up, he suggests that his Committees may be used by Ministers 'as both sounding boards for future legislation, and as partners in investigating the efficiency of sections of the administration'. The first of these functions would seem to reserve the Committees some say in policy—which after all must determine future legislation. The second seems to imply some support for the idea that Ministers might find such Committees useful *against* their departments—in looking for departmental inadequacy or obduracy—which would be a new development in the relations of Ministers and their civil servants.

(iii)

From academic advocacy of specialist committees, which has been remarkably persistent for many decades, I turn now to the House of Commons' own consideration of the same idea. Arguments for an extended Committee system have been discussed by Select Committees on Procedure since 1931—for instance, in 1946 and 1958. One suggestion by the 1958 Select Committee was that there might be a specialist committee for the colonies. But all the various arguments for and against the notion were crystallised in the evidence given to the Select Committee on Procedure of 1964–5 and in the Fourth Report of that Committee. The Report expressed its view that parliamentary reform should be directed at increasing the efficiency of the House as a debating chamber and that any change should neither supersede the traditional right of the Commons to consider grievances before Supply nor absolve them of their duty to examine Government expenditure and administration. To achieve the latter purpose, the Committee concluded that 'more information should be made available to Members of the way government departments carry out their responsibilities. . . .' This meant that there should be a more efficient system of scrutiny of administration and the Committee acknowledged that it attached importance to the views of academic observers that the machinery of government had failed to keep pace with the increase in the scope of governmental activity. The Committee recommended that a system of inquiry by specialist committees should be built up on the existing Estimates Committee. The principal duty of the Estimates Committee, defined in Standing Order No. 80, is 'to examine such of the estimates presented to this House as may seem fit to the Committee and report how, if at all, the policy implied in those estimates may be carried out more economically'. The proposed new terms of reference were that the Estimates Committee (working through specialist sub-committees) should 'examine how the departments of state carry out their responsibilities and to consider their Estimates of Expenditure and Reports'. These much wider terms of reference did not specifically exclude policy from the ambit of the Committee.

In examining the estimates for the current year, the Estimates Committee picks on a limited number of items for detailed scrutiny. As Sir Laurence Helsby, the Head of the Civil Service, put it in his evidence to the Select Committee on Procedure, 'My impression is that of recent years the Estimates Committee has seldom directed itself simply at the question, "Could this be done more cheaply; in other words, could this Estimate be cut?", and has been more concerned to examine the broader question, "Is value for money being obtained from this expenditure? Are the managerial arrangements under which the expenditure takes place fully effective?" '[1] The Committee, in its Report, took the view that there was also need for investigation of long-term proposals and prospects for expenditure in various fields—such as 'forward looks' and an examination of the 'administrative policy of Government Departments, freed from the considerations of economy alone'.[2]

The Report emphasised the Committee's wish that specialist committees should not become involved in matters of political controversy and that the range of investigations should not go beyond that which could properly be replied to by civil servants. As reassurance against misgivings that specialist committees might be involved in political controversy, the Report cited the view of the Clerk of Committees—that it would be an attempt to put the sub-committees of the Estimates Committee 'on, roughly speaking, the same sort of order of reference as the present Nationalised Industries Committee have'.[3]

[1] *Evidence to Select Committee on Procedure*, Fourth Report, 1964–5, pp. 41–2. [2] Ibid., p. vii. [3] Ibid., p. vii.

While admitting that it is not always easy to distinguish between what are and what are not policy questions, the Select Committee found the work of the Nationalised Industries Committee in producing informative and objective reports, in 'what is politically a highly sensitive field', an example to be followed by specialist committees inquiring into the activities of government departments. The form of the new committees suggested in the Report was that the Estimates Committee should work through 'Sub-Committees each named according to its special subject, such as, for example, "The Sub-Committee on the Social Services" '.[1] Such sub-committees should have additional Clerks to help it and should be able to employ technical and scientific assistance. To a very considerable extent, the recommendations of the Select Committee followed advice tendered them on specialist committees in a Memorandum by the Study of Parliament Group, consisting of university teachers and officers of Parliament interested in this subject.[2]

Thus a moderate version of the long fashionable, but long resisted, recipe for specialist committees was put before the House of Commons by its own Select Committee at a time when great public attention was being directed at the failings of Parliament. Yet it had not been a one-way argument. A minority of the Select Committee, Mr Michael Foot (Labour) and Sir Martin Redmayne (later Lord Redmayne and a former Conservative Whip), in a paragraph which they failed to persuade the Select Committee to adopt, denounced as a delusion the idea that specialist committees were 'a major means of reforming procedure'. They concluded that 'the proliferation of parliamentary committees is not a cure but part of the disease'. Concentration on this issue could block or postpone more urgent, more practicable and more desirable reforms. It was necessary, they said, to restore the authority of the chamber of the House of Commons itself. Debates should be possible over a much wider range and at much shorter notice than is possible 'under its present arthritic procedures' and more specialist committees might make moves in this direction more difficult. More specialist committees would mean that fewer and fewer Members would be available for the House

[1] *Evidence to Select Committee on Procedure*, Fourth Report, 1964–5, p. viii.
[2] The views of this group are set out fully in their pamphlet, *Reforming the Commons*, PEP, Vol. 491, October 1965. (This pamphlet also embodies the group's memorandum to the Select Committee.)

itself. 'Moreover, more "Committees upstairs" are likely to nurture the miserable deception that more and more issues can profitably be "taken out of politics".'[1]

Despite the weight of fashionable opinion in favour of the recommendations in the Report, the Government would not at this time support the proposal for specialist committees when the House debated the Fourth Report, and other Reports from the Select Committee on Procedure, on October 27, 1965. A number of minor reforms were agreed by the House based on the earlier Reports of the Select Committee. These included the establishment of a Second Reading Committee to save the time of the House on what were agreed to be uncontroversial Bills. As an experiment, it was also decided that Ten Minute Rule motions should be taken at the end of Government business on Tuesdays and Wednesdays, instead of 3.30 as formerly. This, however, was an encroachment on private Members' time, not a restorative for the influence of backbenchers, since it relegated to the end of the day, when few Members wish to be in the House, the chance of raising matters which could often otherwise be brought up when the House—and frequently both frontbenches—were full. The experiment, which was by Sessional Order and not by amendment of Standing Orders, was dropped in the next Parliament, and moved to the morning when the experiment in morning sittings was introduced.

The main theme of the debate in the House on October 27, however, was the recommendations of the Select Committee for specialist committees. On this the Government would go no further than to recommend that the Estimates Committee should be allowed to subdivide itself into specialist groups if it wished but should continue under existing terms of reference.[2] The Leader of the House, Herbert Bowden, again made it clear that the main stumbling-block was the fear that the investigations of specialist committees might infringe on policy. 'With the best will in the world, I am afraid that once the terms of reference are widened as suggested—and I know that the Select Committee on Procedure was anxious to avoid this—the necessary detailed examination of Government expenditure and administration is bound to give place to policy discussions. In

[1] *Evidence to Select Committee on Procedure*, Fourth Report, 1964–5, p. xiv.

[2] The Committee was subsequently subdivided into Sub-Committees for Economic Affairs, Defence and Overseas Affairs, Social Affairs, etc.

addition to that, we should lose a valuable part of the procedures on financial control,' said Bowden.[1] Nor did he think that the example of the Nationalised Industries Committee's discussion of the relative value of methane gas and the Lurgi production method, cited in the Fourth Report, was a valid argument. 'This is pure policy,' Bowden stated. The method applicable to a nationalised industry—'a public body which is trading'—was not suitable to a Government department. Was the proposed specialist committee to examine, say, the relative values of one rifle as against another?[2] A former chairman of the Nationalised Industries Committee, Sir Richard Nugent, pointed out that the value of the Nationalised Industries Committees' reports was in reaching conclusions unanimously and he added that, in the case of the report on methane gas and the Lurgi method, unanimity had not been possible—and that therefore the Committee had simply presented the pros and cons without offering the House any conclusions. He saw the nationalised industries as a special field outside ministerial control where ministerial responsibility would not be touched by the Nationalised Industries Committees' reports. 'We have been successful in making reports on these industries only by having great care in not going further into the field where Ministerial policy would be touched.'[3]

The case against specialist committees was most trenchantly made by two left-wing Members of the Labour Party, Mr Michael Foot and Mr John Mendelson. 'Only some academic university professor could consider the present system of committees and conclude that the cure is more committees,' Foot asserted. His first reason for opposing the suggestions in the Fourth Report was that every new committee reduced the time Members could spend in the House. His second was that all topics of debate would be 'hashed and rehashed' before they ever got to the House itself—and by then the subject would either be found 'utterly boring' or Members would be told that those on the specialist committee knew so much more about it, that the rest were not expected to speak. Thirdly, he thought such committees played into the hands of the Executive. 'The cosier the committee, the more likely it will be that we shall have bipartisan politics. Every Minister worth his salt knows how to diddle a committee of that nature.' It was less easy, Foot suggested to a challenger, to 'diddle' the House as a

[1] H.C. Deb., Vol. 718, col. 183, October 27, 1965.
[2] Ibid., col. 287, October 27, 1965.
[3] Ibid., col. 215, October 27, 1965.

whole because there were always one or two who would 'stand out' against the majority. Foot considered that the concept of specialist committees mistook the prime function of Members of Parliament. Of course, MPs must sometimes consult experts and some must be experts—but the main business of Members of Parliament was 'to relate different forms of knowledge—including expert knowledge—and to keep the experts in their place, to know where the shoe pinches for the customers and to see that all questions are approached in a different way from that of the bureaucrats'. Foot considered the specialist committee to be 'a pretentious distraction' from the main problem of reforming the Commons—which was how 'to restore this Chamber as the central forum of debate in the country'.[1] In much the same vein, Mendelson thought that a defence committee (for example) would be taken into the confidence of Ministers and given information that could not be passed on to the House as a whole. Thus far from redressing the balance of influence between the Legislature and the Executive, it would make the position of the Executive much more powerful. Specialist committees, drawing together good and able men from all sides, were a denial of the wisdom of the Commons acquired over hundreds of years—which was that, in the national interest, there should be no blurring of policies, by 'the getting together of people who believe that because they know a few more facts, they can now find a neutral solution to all major problems'. This would deny the function of the House, which was to carry on the great national debate on the great issues of the day.[2]

Thus, though the Select Committee on Procedure had specifically disclaimed any wish to devise a committee system that might endanger the Government's responsibility for policy, the House avoided the modest proposals it made on the grounds, largely, that this danger might result from them. Yet though, for the time being, the matter dropped, it soon became clear that the Government had not entirely rejected the possibility of some steps towards the specialisation of committees. After the 1966 General Election, which gave the Labour Party a large instead of a miniscule majority, the Prime Minister (who when in Opposition had made more or less vague utterances in support of reforming Parliament) suddenly resurrected the idea of specialising committees as a means of giving Parliament a greater participation in the processes of government.

[1] H.C. Deb., Vol. 718, cols. 208–10, October 27, 1965.
[2] Ibid., cols. 246–7, October 27, 1965.

Speaking in the debate on the Address replying to the Queen's Speech, he announced that he thought the time had come for considering an experiment to extend the committee system already used for Estimates, Public Accounts and Nationalised Industries 'over a wider field of public administration'. The Prime Minister said that, accordingly, the Government would 'enter into discussions through the usual channels with the two Opposition parties on the suggestion of establishing one or two new Parliamentary Committees to concern themselves with administration in the sphere of certain Departments whose usual operations are not only of national concern but in many cases are of intensely human concern'.[1] The Prime Minister admitted that there was room for argument about whether there ought to be foreign or defence policy committees and informed the House that he was one who remained to be convinced on the matter. But the Government would start discussions about beginning an experiment with committees to inquire into the administration of certain home departments—the Home Office was a case specifically mentioned by Mr Wilson. The Prime Minister suggested that many Members, not least the newer ones, had a part to play in giving advice on particular social problems.

At the time, the Prime Minister's sudden revival of the idea of specialist committees, albeit in a bowdlerised form, was widely interpreted at Westminster as a gesture particularly intended to appeal to the newer Members of his own party. Many of them were disillusioned about the state of the economy, irritated by their junior place on the Westminster scene and potentially more rebellious than their predecessors of the short Parliament of 1964; simply because the Government's large majority gave them more scope for revolts without endangering the Government's hold on power. No Government wants its prestige damaged by persistent rebellions, even with an assured majority in the Division lobby. In private, the Conservatives freely alleged that the Prime Minister had tossed these ideas out to appeal to the obsession of some of his followers with the machinery of government—but without thinking out the implications. Certainly the highly tentative nature of the Government's approach was tacitly admitted by the Leader of the House, Herbert Bowden, when he came to wind up the Queen's Speech debate a few days later. 'As soon as we have firm proposals we shall discuss them with the Opposition and discuss them with the

[1] H.C. Deb., Vol. 727, col. 76, April 21, 1966.

House.' Bowden saw no point in sending the question to the Select Committee on Procedure. Such committees could help Ministers and help backbenchers; they could give backbenchers a chance to learn about the administration of a department. But it was 'not a question of someone carrying out an examination into a Minister's Department which he should be doing himself.'[1] Bowden was a highly 'conservative' Leader of the House but as a result of a Cabinet reshuffle a few months later, he was succeeded in this office by Richard Crossman, who had a long-standing interest in this sort of problem. Crossman saw value in the specialist committee idea and, indeed, at this time was floating the notion that, if Parliament was to be televised, House of Commons Committees might make a better subject for the camera than the proceedings in the Chamber itself— a point of view apparently prompted by the publicity given in Britain at that time to the televised inquiry of the US Senate's Foreign Relations Committee into the American Administration's Vietnam War policy.

In 1966, Bowden moved from the Leadership of the House to the Commonwealth Relations Office but before he did so, discussions were opened between the Government and the Opposition on the subject of specialised committees. To the Conservatives, these appeared to substantiate their opinion that the Prime Minister was making a gesture towards his own backbenchers but that the Government would be extremely cautious in introducing specialist committees, which would not be allowed to cover departments which dealt with more contentious sorts of policy. In these exchanges, the Conservative Leader, Edward Heath, let the Prime Minister know that the Conservatives would be prepared to support a science and technological committee and also one for *ad hoc* specialised inquiries but was not anxious to go beyond this. As the discussions continued, under the new Leader of the House, Richard Crossman, the Government itself became more cautious. The idea of specialist committees covering the Home Office (which, in fact, became a highly contentious department in 1966 as a result of several sensational prison escapes) or Social Security was relegated to the background and, as part of a package deal of minor procedural reforms, Crossman proposed to the House in December 1966 that two new specialising Select Committees should be established—one on Science and Technology, the other on Agriculture. The House agreed to the creation of these Committees,

[1] H.C. Deb., Vol. 727, cols. 1086–7, April 28, 1966.

both of which would have power to send for persons and papers and would also have power to sit in public during the examination of witnesses, unless they ordered otherwise. Crossman presented the new Committees as a response to the transfer of power from Parliament to the Executive which, he said, had gone too far. The new committees were subsequently constituted and began to hear evidence in public. (Crossman had told the House that there seemed to be no reason why other Committees, such as the Estimates Committee, should not also sit in public if they chose. In fact, security, including commercial security, considerations prevent this and frequently substantial parts of evidence are not published.) It was alleged that there had been some attempt by Ministers to control the membership of the committee on agriculture and, for instances to prevent it from discussing the Common Market problem in 1967. These attempts were not successful. It remains to be seen at the time of writing this book how far these committees form a pattern for others and whether the system will be extended into more controversial fields of government.

(iv)

The following considerations are relevant to any assessment of the case for specialist committees as a major means of reforming the House of Commons. First, many of the advocates of specialist committees have gained attention for their case by linking it to extreme assertions of parliamentary decline. The inference has been that specialised committees were the main solution to the problem of restoring House of Commons control over the Executive to what it once was. Obviously, this argument depends to some extent on whether or not the House of Commons *has* declined in terms of its essential function. But much more important is the dependence of the case for specialist committees on the assertion that the most important acts of the Executive (whether they are called policy or not) now almost wholly escape effective parliamentary control and that the House of Commons has been reduced to a rubber stamp. It would seem that any reform must, if it were to deal with this basic problem, enable the House of Commons to make the Executive more accountable to it for policy and oblige the Government to consult Parliament while policy-making is in a formative stage.

Yet the critics who have made such a strong case for specialist committees on the grounds of this sort of need, have in practice watered down their proposals with the specific intention that they should deny specialist committees any intervention in policy. Most advocates of specialist committees have taken care to emphasise that the committees would confine their attention to administration. To draw attention to the modesty of the proposals is not to suggest that they ought to be more extreme; indeed, they could hardly be so without basically re-shaping the Constitution. But the modesty of most of the specialist committee schemes would at least seem to weaken the argument that they would constitute the major means of making the Government more responsive to the House over funda-mental issues. The complaint is that ministerial authority is now virtually impregnable. On the other hand, the remedy proposed is hedged about with assurances that it would not have ministerial authority undermined.

Secondly, however, it is necessary to take into account the fear that even such modest proposals as those in the Fourth Report might be the thin end of the wedge. Despite reassurances to the contrary, such specialist committees might begin to interfere in policy—with the result either of undermining the responsibility of Ministers to the House *as a whole*, or of causing the committees to divide on partisan lines—thus destroying their essential point. Such fears arise from the belief that it is impossible in practice to distinguish between policy and administration. Are they justified? Many recent advocates of specialised committees dismiss such fears by basing their case for specialised committees designed to shadow departments on an analogy with the normally non-partisan Nationalised Industries Committee.[1] Further, there has been wide (though not unanimous) agreement among advocates of specialist committees that, to preserve the distinction between *policy* and *administration of policy*, only civil servants should be called before specialist committees, leaving Ministers to answer only to the House. On the other hand, policy is involved in all acts of government departments to a degree that it is not at present involved in the acts of nationalised industries which are investigated by the appropriate committee. And if policy questions were reserved for Ministers, it is not clear whether specialist com-mittees could do much that was different in kind from the work of

[1] See, for example, David Coombes, *The Member of Parliament and the Administration, the Case of the Select Committee on Nationalised Industries.*

the present Estimates Committee, though obviously there is a case for enabling the Estimates Committee to do more work of the present kind and of equipping it with the staff to do so on a more specialised basis.

Thirdly, it must be noted that although some suggestions have been made for limiting 'specialist' committees to the job of shadowing the relatively (but only relatively) uncontentious Government departments, such as the Home Office, the Ministries of Social Security and Education, the steam behind the case for specialist committees has come from the belief that the House of Commons has lost control over the *basic* issues of economic, foreign and defence policy. For example, what was judged by some to be the failure of economic policy under the Conservative Governments of the fifties was frequently blamed on the extent to which this policy was manufactured in the closed circle of the Treasury and never subjected to adequate open examination of the sort that a House of Commons Economic Committee might have provided. The following three comments are relevant to this suggestion. It is clear that in the fifties under the Conservatives (or in the sixties under Labour) any Economic Committee would have divided along party lines. To the extent that the Government (or the Treasury) was echoing a fashion for a free economy in the early fifties or a planned economy in the sixties, it is doubtful how far a more effective critique could have been mounted on economic grounds inside such a Committee than was possible outside it. The third comment is that so much of the Treasury's activities, its plans and its assessment of the future must be circumspect to the point of secrecy that it is doubtful whether a House of Commons Committee which was not sworn to secrecy (and therefore separated from the bulk of Members) could perform a useful job in this field.

A House of Commons Defence Committee would suffer under much the same sort of limitation. The author has heard a member of the post-1964 Labour Administration assert that, if only there had been a House of Commons Defence Committee in the fifties, the Conservative defence policy of those years would have been 'laughed out of court'. Whether or not this ought to have happened is a partisan judgment and presumably any Defence Committee would have been limited by being of partisan composition. Moreover, assuming that such a Committee had received much the same technical advice as was available to the Government itself, and was sworn to secrecy, what would have happened to open criticism of the Government by the Opposition's defence experts, who would presumably have been inhibited accordingly?

In practice, these difficulties are now clearly seen and there are few advocates of specialist Defence, Foreign Affairs, or Economic Committees. In the fifties and in the sixties, the basic policies of the Government which were so often cited as calling for House of Commons inquiry were really subjects for political rather than expert criticism. Many of the advocates of specialist committees lent force to their arguments by citing governmental policy failures but they have generally refrained from suggesting that specialist committees should invade this field.

Finally, if by common consent the activities of specialist committees were to exclude all issues of policy, would their operations yield worthwhile results? Sir Laurence Helsby, the Head of the Civil Service, raised this question in the following form in his final words to the Select Committee on Procedure in 1965: 'There could be a point, though I am not saying this point would be reached, at which the system [of specialist committees] became burdensome to departments and might also become a considerable strain on the resources of the House. I would much dislike to see, in these days of scarcity of manpower, a need to spend a great deal of time with embattled experts marshalled on either side and getting down to details of argument which perhaps at the end of the day would not show results really worthwhile.'[1] This doubt connects with the doubt whether, in the cosy communion of expert committees, participating Members might become more sympathetic and less critical of government administration, given that they were required (unlike US Congressional Committees) to assume a non-partisan, 'expert' posture and to refrain from attacking the politics of the Government. Might they not then become almost suffocated in the expertise that bound them to their opposite numbers in Whitehall, understanding too well, rather than too critically, the problems of the bureaucrats? When all these considerations are taken into account, it may be concluded that although an extension of House of Commons' committees to specialise on aspects of administration should be a

[1] *Evidence taken before the Select Committee on Procedure*, Fourth Report, 1964–5, p. 50.

useful facility for Members, they may not be (in the form they seem likely to take) a *major* act of restoration of House of Commons political influence.

As the new specialist committees began to establish themselves, questions remaining to be resolved included their precise relationship to the specialising sub-committees of the Estimates Committee. Another question was the right of the committees to choose their own subjects and areas of investigation. (Having established their right to discuss the Common Market, the new agriculture committee also went on to argue its right to take evidence in Brussels, the headquarters of the European Economic Committee.) In addition, some MPs also felt strongly that committee members should be chosen by selection committees of the major parties representing the backbenchers and should not, as traditionally, be selected by the Whips. One evident danger was over-loading the committees with work; on the other hand, to some MPs it now seemed less necessary that committee members should become experts in their special subjects because the professional experts assigned to the committees could take much of this burden from them. How far the committees on science and agriculture will be a pattern for the extension of Ministry-equivalent committees; how effective they will be in informing public opinion; how far they will prove a substantial addition to House of Commons' machinery, as the Nationalised Industries Committee undoubtedly is, will not be apparent until they have been in operation for some time.

Chapter Fourteen

The Commons' Financial Duty

Public opinion and public support provide the ultimate sanction which the House of Commons is able to exert over the Executive. Under public opinion, however, the final *direct* sanction available to the Commons is to withhold Supply from the Government. For all practical purposes, this sanction now appears to be mythological. It can be argued that it would never be used for two reasons. First, if a Government lost the confidence of the House it would resign without waiting for Supply to be refused. Secondly, if the conventions of the Constitution ever became so tattered that a Government which had been denied either a major piece of legislation or a vote of confidence still refused to resign—then it would not be persuaded to relinquish office by the refusal of Supply. Such a Government, it might be argued, would simply take what it wanted by imposed (and if necessary enforced) taxation. Only national resistance could stop it from doing so.

Such arguments are difficult to refute because the hypotheses involved are wholly remote from anything in our recent national experience. Yet, even in the twentieth century, it is possible to envisage circumstances in which the right to refuse Supply could be a practical weapon for the Commons to use against a recalcitrant Government. A ruthless and determined Government might well try to stay in office after it had been defeated on a major Bill (there have been signs in recent years of a growing doctrine that a Government ought not to be obliged to resign by defeat in the House on a Bill) and might conceivably even resist bowing to a vote of no confidence. A Bill, after all, is not usually indispensible to a Government—but money is. A Government might be prepared to defy the House in a *negative* way by simply letting a defeated Bill lapse and remaining in office, trusting that a lethargic public opinion might let it get away with it. But the same Government might well stop short of taking the

359

positive action of enforcing taxation if the House followed up its defeat of the Government by refusing Supply.

This sort of discussion, in the British political context, appears unreal and theoretical. Yet movements towards arbitrary government in other countries have started slowly from the failure of representative assemblies and public opinion to stand up against the first infringements of political conventions or constitutions. It would be folly to suppose that it would never in any circumstances happen here. For these reasons, as a deterrent (and the important thing about deterrents is that they should never be used) the right to withhold Supply is still an important weapon in the House of Commons' armoury. Though it is never, in practice, refused or reduced under modern party Governments, this is because these Governments adhere to the Constitution. If it ever came about that a Government sought to do otherwise, the refusal to grant taxation could at least be a very effective brake in its path.

The Commons are constitutionally responsible for sanctioning Government expenditure annually, for authorising the necessary Supply and for granting the taxation required to cover both the Government's outlay and (since Keynes) to keep the national economy in balance. After the Government has spent public funds, the House has the further duty of seeing that the money has been used for the purposes for which it has been appropriated.

In the twentieth century, the Commons perform these tasks with varying degrees of effectiveness. The House has virtually no control over the total level of Government expenditure annually nor over the level of Government spending which it sanctions under departmental Votes. This weakness is a reflection of contemporary political realities rather than of a failure of the parliamentary mechanism in the narrow sense. Even though it is now used for other purposes, the mechanism of Supply procedure could still be used to enable the Commons to force the Government to withdraw or reduce the Estimates if the Commons so wished. But in practice, it is not relevant to the function of the Commons to try to force the Government to retreat over the Estimates as such—though it is the business of the Estimates Committee to try to bring about any detailed changes that are likely to ensure better value for the public money that is spent. But motions and debates designed to secure the rejection or the reduction of particular Estimates are largely pointless because the Opposition knows that such motions will never secure the assent

360

of the House since enough Government supporters will never vote for them. Most obviously, of course, Government backbenchers will not take action which would drive their leaders from office. In addition, the items involved in the Estimates have been largely pre-determined by policy decisions which have for one reason or another been accepted by the majority party. The Commons has no more and no less wish to question or overthrow particular spending decisions than it has to challenge the policies lying behind them. The majority party normally accepts the cost of policies to which it, like its leaders, is committed and the Opposition finds it more profitable to criticise the policies rather than to try in vain to secure reductions in the actual sums of money being spent by the Government.

Backed by solid and normally unshakeable parliamentary majorities, Governments come to office committed by their general election manifestoes to particular policies and to the cost of them. Further, as the life of a Parliament progresses, a Government also finds itself adopting policies to deal with new eventualities that were unforeseeable when the election which gave it power took place. By and large, a Government does not adopt policies to meet the contingencies of politics unless it is sure that it can carry its backbenches with it. In this respect too, Government backbenchers, though they may grumble, will pay the price of policies to which they acquiesce. Then there is a wide area of running Government expenditure, both capital and current, to which any Government finds that it has been committed in advance by the actions of its predecessors, even those of a different political persuasion. Such expenditure, based on plans which by their nature must extend over a period of years, cannot normally be cut without losses which most Governments are reluctant to face. Sometimes losses are cut, but Governments frequently 'take on board' the spending commitments of their predecessors—and again the majority party in the Commons accepts the accomplished fact.

Finally, of course, a modern House of Commons, appealing to a mass electorate, is by its nature a spending body rather than a retrenching body so far as most policy decisions are concerned. The majority of the House has been placed there so that a Government of the same complexion shall spend what these decisions cost. It is therefore perfectly logical that when the Commons are called on to vote Supply, the time allotted should be used by the Opposition, not to try to reverse individual Estimates, but to discuss more basic aspects of Government policy that underlie some of them. Since the 1966 procedural reforms, such debates on Government policy and administration no longer take place within the formal framework of the Estimates nominally under discussion.

In short, for Government backbenchers, who approve of their leaders' policies, the consequent expenditure is no stumbling-block. For the Opposition, there is every incentive not to concentrate their attack on detailed spending decisions which they cannot hope to reverse but instead to use the time available to them to gain public attention for attacks on particular areas of Government activity. Yet there is still a perfectly valid justification for *formally* linking these general debates to the processes of Supply. By doing so, the Commons are able to retain in form, and therefore in reserve, their ancient right to demand that grievances should be redressed before Supply is granted and that the Government should be answerable to them for policy. Supply procedure enshrines the still valid idea that, *in some circumstances*, the House of Commons is an 'Opposition' institution. Though it exists to uphold, strengthen, and supply a Government of an acceptable persuasion (which under the modern electoral system is what it gets) it must retain the right to refuse to uphold and supply any Government that was not acceptable to a majority of Members. It can be argued that the reform of Supply procedure in 1966, which removed the connection between the so-called Supply debates and the actual voting of Supply (now relegated to three occasions each year), has made potential control of the Executive more difficult.

There may be other grounds for contending that the House of Commons has lost power before the encroachments of the Executive but it is not relevant to argue this from the contemporary non-usage of the right to withhold Supply. Although the Commons achieved control of the Executive through their control of the purse, they were always primarily concerned with the policy for which they paid rather than the money they had to pay for it. Control of the Government's Supply was the means rather than the end. Of course, the Commons always had a subsidiary and closely related interest in appropriation. Even in the Middle Ages there were regular attempts to appropriate particular grants for particular purposes—notably to tie subsidies for use on stated military enterprises. Under the Stuarts, the idea of appropriation gained a new power; the Commons were concerned that the money they voted should not go to finance the expenditure of the Court but should defray the cost of policies which they wished the Crown to undertake. Yet it is doubtful whether these early essays in appropriation are to be interpreted primarily as indicating the interest of the Commons in efficiency; they were rather a further sign of the Commons' determination to oblige the Crown to pursue certain policies. Provided the Commons in the latter half of the sixteenth century and in the seventeenth century secured the economic, religious and foreign policies they favoured, they were prepared to pay for them. Obviously, appropriating taxation to defray particular policies was a major means of so doing. This is not to say that the Commons were then indifferent to inefficiency in spending or to the misappropriation of funds. Thus, under Charles II, the Parliamentary Commissioners of Accounts carried out a prolonged inquiry into the miscarriages of the First Dutch War and the humiliating presence of Dutch ships in the Medway, and they did so on allegations that money voted for the war had been misappropriated and that there had been corruption. Later, the House of Commons appointed a Parliamentary Committee to inquire into the 'Miscarriages of the Navy'. Both of these investigations (in which Pepys was heavily involved) were plainly designed to get at the king's policies and his policy-makers as much as to investigate the efficiency of spending. In this sense, they too came near to being an early example of the kind of policy-investigation by Committee of the House, which the Commons have normally avoided.[1] But this use of a Committee inquiring into both policy and misappropriation arose in a situation totally different from that which now exists. The majority of the House of Commons was then in opposition to the Crown and had not yet found the means of bringing it under control.

After the Revolution of 1688, which introduced annual parliaments and therefore annual grants, a system of parliamentary control over national finances, which included control and appropriation of expenditure, was built up slowly—a process which continued until half-way through the nineteenth century. First military, then, much later, civil expenditure came under control and appropriation. In the nineteenth century, public finances fell completely under the supervision of the House of Commons and the House came to show a closer interest in retrenchment and in criticising public expenditure. Yet it is easy both to exaggerate the extent and the significance of

[1] For an account of these episodes, see Arthur Bryant, *Samuel Pepys: the Years of Peril* (Collins, 1948), pp. 13 et seq., 259 et seq.

nineteenth-century House of Commons control over the expenditure. Writing in 1867, Bagehot could argue that the Commons had no function in relation to finance that was different from its function in relation to other legislation; indeed, that since an ordinary Member could propose ordinary legislation but only the Government could propose financial legislation, it was less powerful in the financial field. 'The House of Commons . . . has long ceased to be the checking, sparing, economical body it once was. It is now more apt to spend money than the Minister of the day. I have heard a very experienced financier say, "If you want to raise a certain cheer in the House of Commons make a general panegyric on economy; if you want to invite a sure defeat, propose a particular saving".'[1] If this was true in Bagehot's day, it is even more true now. Yet despite a good deal of romanticism in the twentieth-century view of the willingness of nineteenth-century Parliaments to refuse Supply, it is probably true that nineteenth-century MPs were rather more interested than their successors have been in retrenchment and criticism of Government expenditure. This, however, is also reduced in significance when it is related to the political circumstances of the time. In the nineteenth century, MPs were drawn from (and therefore, in terms of interest, largely represented) the small class of taxpayers who were naturally resentful of taxation levied by Governments which had increasing responsibilities to a wider public. Inevitably, nineteenth-century MPs were more vigilant guardians over the spending of *their* money than the modern representatives of a democratic mass electorate can afford to be. But too frequently the contrast between the contemporary House of Commons control of Supply and the control it exercised in the last century is exaggerated. In 1918, a committee of the House reported that there had not been a single case in twenty-five years in which an estimate had been reduced on financial grounds, and that 'so far as the direct effective control of proposals for expenditure is concerned there would be no notable difference if estimates were never presented'.[2]

In other words, we can go back at least to about 1890 and assert that the House has never exerted sanctions against the Government by refusing any Estimates. Yet a certain romantic notion exists that it ought to devote its Supply days to consideration of the actual

[1] Walter Bagehot, *The English Constitution* (Watts Edn.), p. 154.
[2] Quoted in L. S. Amery, *Thoughts on the Constitution*, p. 52.

spending propositions. Thus, on February 20, 1960, Lord Hinching-brooke, a Conservative Member of the House, instigated a backbench rebellion by rising as the Commons were about to devote a Supply day to a debate on Development Districts, and protesting at the neglect of the 'ancient and honourable practice' of debating policy before granting Supply. It was the proposed business of the House to deal formally with the Vote on Account for Civil Estimates, and the Estimates for Revenue Departments and for the Ministry of Defence. Hinchingbrooke protested at the intention of passing Supply of £1,370,537,000 on the nod.[1] He gained some backbench support from both sides of the House and continued his pressure on the occasion of the Consolidated Fund Bill Second Reading on March 16. As a result, discussions between the two sides of the House took place and the Leader of the House, Mr R. A. Butler, reported on July 26 on certain proposals relating to the work of the Estimates Committee, which would enable the House to exercise a closer surveillance over the Estimates.[2] Nevertheless, the argument put forward by Lord Hinchingbrooke which gave rise to them presented a view of the 'decline' of the House of Commons' control of ex-penditure functions which was at variance with the facts.

To sum up, the seventeenth-century Parliament was critical of Government spending because it was, in a sense, in 'opposition' to the Executive though not in the outright fashion of a modern, minority Opposition Party. Finance was part of the process of policy bargaining between Executive and Parliament. In the eighteenth century, because of the close oligarchical relationship between Parliament and the Government, the House of Commons became rather less hostile towards Government spending. In the nineteenth century, new attitudes of financial probity and the interest of Members of the House in retrenchment created a full system of parliamentary supervision over the nation's accountancy—though this did not extend to refusal of Supply to cover Government expenditure proposals.

Now, in the twentieth century, the House, with a Government drawn from its majority party and strictly (for the time being) aligned on the basis of two dominant monolithic parties, can be regarded as effectively in *apposition*, not opposition, to the Executive. The Estimates Committee and the Public Accounts Committee (to

[1] H.C. Deb., Vol. 618, cols. 196 et seq., February 20, 1960.
[2] Ibid., 627, cols. 1922 et seq., July 26, 1960.

whose work I shall return) deal more or less effectively with value-for-money and post-mortem scrutiny of Government accounts. There is little reason for criticising the use of Supply days for general debates on policy and, although there remained until 1966 a strong demand for the modernisation of some of the confusing and ana-chronistic Supply procedure, this was dealt with by the House in December of that year when it acted on recommendations of the Select Committee on Procedure.

Yet in the conditions of twentieth-century government, there has developed a need for a new kind of parliamentary oversight of Government expenditure which the House of Commons is not equipped to exercise (and never has been). It is not so much a matter of arresting a decline as of finding the means to deal with a new need. As we have seen, Supply procedure enables general policy in particular fields or specific spending decisions to be challenged. But in the mid-twentieth century, the financial and economic decisions of Govern-ments have a wider financial and economic implication than they have if considered merely as single acts or aspects of policy, or particular items of expenditure.

It is not simply a matter of deciding whether this or that policy or expenditure is of itself desirable. First, decisions on total expenditure and investment are in many respects to be considered as, *in themselves*, the most important element in Government policy. These total economic decisions determine the direction in which the political, social and economic life of the nation develops. They decide the rate of growth, the level of employment, the extent to which public investment may grow at the expense of private investment (or vice versa), particular growth 'sectors' and, for all these reasons, the changing structure of society. They also, because of their impact on economic stability, impinge strongly on overseas policy and on the nation's international standing.

Secondly, individual policy decisions, and the cost of them, are of interest not merely in their own right but in relation to each other. The Commons may, under the present system, use a Supply day to debate (say) an aspect of the National Health Service. But it cannot easily find the occasion to debate the relative priorities of expenditure within a given total, the total itself or the long-term implications for the economy of preferring expenditure in one sector of public activity to expenditure in another. In a period of acute economic restraint (as in the economic difficulties of 1966, for example), when it has become clear that the rate of growth of public expenditure would have to be checked, the House has had no opportunity prior to the Budget of expressing its views, with knowledge of the Government's thinking, on giving priority to, say, road expenditure as against welfare or defence spending in the planning of cut-backs.

The Opposition may, of course, at any time stage a debate lasting for one or two days on the economy which may take in expenditure. But anyone who has followed such debates in recent years knows that, being held without a detailed statement of expenditure plans by the Government, they are so generalised as to have little impact on the public or on the Government. The Commons cannot expect to determine economic policy. But what is lacking is factual information about the Government's forward thinking and its economic analyses on which Members of Parliament could hold informed discussions on expenditure and planning as it is evolved.

In R. A. Butler's statement on Estimates of July 26, 1960, an approach to this problem was started. The Select Committee was not only to report briefly on the Spring Supplementary Estimates; it was also to examine the principal variations between the Estimates and those of the previous year. Its report on such variations (as distinct from its customary examination of selected Estimates) would provide the House with a basis on which to debate Government expenditure in the autumn. There would also be new opportunities for the Commons to debate reports from the Estimates Committee and the Public Accounts Committee. But all these were, essentially, steps to enable the House to deal better with the costing and efficiency of policy rather than with expenditure policy as an economic tool. More significant in respect of policy was the promise of a White Paper on the investment programme in the public sector, including the nationalised industries, in the autumn.

In July 1961, Lord Plowden delivered a Report on Control of Public Expenditure which the Government had commissioned. The essence of this was the recommendation of 'forward looks' over a four- or five-year period of future Government spending in all sectors and the prospective development of income and economic resources, though the latter would only be possible in broad terms. The Plowden Report also discussed parliamentary control of expenditure. To Lord Plowden, and his colleagues who produced the Report, it seemed that the two new White Papers the Government was then issuing on Public Investment (in the autumn) and Government Lending (in the spring), together with the accounts of the enterprises themselves, were 'suitable and appropriate for the purpose of informing Parliament'. Significantly, however, the Report added: 'There may be a useful prototype here for the development of parliamentary discussion of wider areas of public expenditure, where *what is more important to Parliament is to have the opportunity to express a view on the scale and direction of big blocks of expenditure which are not suitable for detailed individual parliamentary control.*' (My italics.)[1]

This sentence would seem to indicate the essential gap which needs to be filled in Parliament's oversight of the Government's financial and expenditure decisions. The Commons should not be expected to resurrect some fictitious control over finance by going through the empty motions of debating and voting on the Estimates as such (for no majority party will ever bring down its Government for the sake of a few million pounds of public money for a particular project). On the other hand, now that overall spending policy is the foundation of so much other policy, the House should not restrict its interest solely to value-for-money investigations. What it needs is the chance of contributing to the formulation of Government policy by a public airing of the pros and cons, so far as this is politically possible. It is doubtful whether it could do this through a specialist Economic Committee of the House. For this could only be effective, in so politically potent a field, if it could call Ministers before it. This would presumably mean that it would operate on party lines—in which case it would be out of line with the movement of the Commons towards specialist committees which, like the Nationalised Industries Committee, are 'crossbench' in attitude and do not divide on policy according to party interest. The Commons can only fulfil this function by general debates on information put before them by the Government, though it is possible that an Economic Committee of the House might assist such debate if its inquiries could be confined to consideration of matters of fact.

In its examination of parliamentary control of expenditure, the Plowden Report considered it advisable that Parliament should authorise forward commitments; there was a limit to which the Government could make the details of its forward surveys, with all their uncertainties, publicly available. It would therefore be impracticable to have a system of parliamentary control of commitments which went beyond the existing Supply processes. Nevertheless,

[1] Cmnd. 1432 (1961), p. 28.

Plowden still considered that the Government should 'develop means of informing Parliament and enabling it to consider and approve the broad issues of policy involving public expenditure for some years ahead at the time when the effective decisions are taken'.[1] In 1967, it could hardly be said that the Government had shown positive signs of moving in this direction.

Proposals put forward to the Select Committee on Procedure, 1964–5, by the Study of Parliament Group, may well prove to point the direction in which Parliament should oblige the Government to go. To enable the House of Commons to consider the balance of expenditure within the agreed total, the Group recommended first the publication of a Public Investment White Paper annually, before Christmas, and also a Public Expenditure White Paper which would give details of the five-year 'forward-looks'. It also recommended that early in each Session a Select Committee on Expenditure should be appointed, to which the White Papers should be referred. This Committee should 'explore the economic, factual and policy assumptions on which the forecast estimates had been prepared; to draw attention to variations in the Estimates; and to examine their economic implications in terms of availability of physical resources, etc.' It was not suggested that the Expenditure Committee should comment on the priorities of various services but that it should produce material and information to enable the House itself better to debate the priorities and the balance of expenditure. These proposals also advocated a two-day debate on 'the total and overall balance of Government expenditure before the Budget debates'.[2]

Since the Plowden Report nothing has been done to make easier any regular parliamentary surveillance of overall Government spending policy; indeed, it could be argued that, despite the new emphasis on Government planning, the Commons are worse placed than they were. Although a White Paper on Government lending continues to be published in the spring, there has been no regular issue of a Public Investment White Paper in the autumn. Occasional Government White Papers on long-term spending plans have been issued; for example, one in December 1963 dealt with proposed

[1] Cmnd. 1432 (1961), p. 24.

[2] Memorandum submitted by the Study of Parliament Group to the Select Committee on Procedure, 1964–5; Fourth Report from Select Committee on Procedure. The Memorandum is also published in a pamphlet, *Reforming the Commons*, PEP, October 1965, p. 288.

Government spending over the period 1963–4 to 1967–8, and related this to a target growth-rate. Again, in February 1966, a White Paper on Public Expenditure and Planning was issued on the same day as the annual Vote on Account but it was made clear that this was not expected to be an annual occurrence. The Government might argue that the National Plan published in 1965 (but later abandoned) was a new factor in the situation, and enabled Parliament to be better informed about Government forward spending attitudes. It would also no doubt contend that the annual Budget debate enables the House of Commons to discuss Government expenditure as well as other aspects of economic policy. But all these events do not enable the House of Commons to comment on Government long-term expenditure plans in advance of and separate from the annual Budgetary exercise. Most of the economic information given by the Government to the House of Commons relates to the past—not to the future.

The need for fuller parliamentary debate of Government spending plans without detracting from the Government's policy initiative is plain enough. Yet the practical obstacles are formidable. Would it be possible for a Government to place a statement on forward expenditure before the House which could be discussed other than along party lines in a 'Whipped' debate? It would certainly be a complete departure for the Commons to hold a debate without a question being before the House; and might invite an ill-directed discussion suitable for a debating society but not for a representative assembly. Further, there is the difficulty that, up to Christmas, the Government is still making up its own mind about the level and direction of public spending in the forthcoming year. Would an earlier statement on public expenditure, before the Government had decided all its priorities, be practicable? No Government will easily be persuaded to give hostages by allowing glimpses of its half-formulated decisions; and once they are formulated, would any purpose be served by holding a debate earlier than in the normal Budget period? Yet more could be done to enable the Commons to relate more satisfactorily its annual discussion of the coming financial year's spending with spending over the longer term. The President of the United States annually submits a mass of information about his Administration's view of the economic developments of the future and indicates the analyses behind Government economic decisions. Something of the sort ought to be possible here. All that need be said in the present context, however, is that this is the aspect of the Commons' financial duty which is most in need of adaptation to meet the changing demands of government in the mid-twentieth century.

In practice, however, most recent discussion of parliamentary shortcomings in the field of financial control have concentrated on an overhaul of Supply procedure with a view to removing anachronistic forms and obscurities. On December 14, the House of Commons agreed to proposals made by the Select Committee on Procedure, 1965–6, in its Report on Financial Procedure. The essence of these reforms was the removal of antique forms which had no real relationship to what was actually happening in the House when Supply was the business before it. Since these changes, Supply days are rather more easily recognisable for what they are—Opposition days for debating Government policy. Thus an impediment to public understanding of the business of the House was said to have been removed.[1] It had been in the field of Supply procedure that the House was most criticised for 'mumbo-jumbo'—that is to say, 'forms which are based on conceptions which no longer have any relevance to our proceedings', as Sir Martin Redmayne, a former Conservative Chief Whip, had expressed it in the Commons debate on procedure on October 27, 1965.[2]

In seeking changes that would enable 'the real nature of Supply debates—the opportunity given to the Opposition for examining activities of their own choice—to be seen more clearly' the Select Committee had also kept in mind that 'the basis of financial forms must be retained: the House must not give up its right to grant or refuse to grant the money required by the Executive'.[3] Within the limits imposed by this essential condition, the Select Committee produced its plan to amend Supply procedure, much of which, it agreed (quoting the Clerk Assistant's evidence), had become 'little short of farcical'. Detailed reference to changes of a purely procedural nature fall outside this study: it is enough to note that the most important change was the abolition of the former rule that a 'charge'

---

[1] On the other hand, it could be argued that there is a new impediment to understanding, since days are now called Supply days when they do not even formally deal with Supply—while Supply is voted in blocks at specified times of the year.

[2] H.C. Deb., Vol. 718, col. 204, October 27, 1965.

[3] *Report of the Select Committee on Procedure, 1965–66*, Financial Procedure, pp. v–vi.

could only originate in Committee. Coupled with this was the decision that debates on substantive Motions tabled by the Opposition, and motions for the adjournment, as well as the Estimates, could be taken on Supply days. The result was that Supply days were to be taken in the House, sitting as such, and not in Committee. Further, Supply days could be held when circumstances appeared to warrant them, whether or not there chanced to be a suitable Estimate for discussion—though the Opposition's right of debating and voting on an Estimate if it chose would not be removed. The additional flexibility for the Opposition in the choice and the timing of debates, which had previously been to a considerable degree confined to the Estimates season, has a wider implication than the modernisation of Supply procedure. It is relevant to the larger question of giving the Commons more scope to discuss topical issues as they arise, which is discussed in the Conclusion. On the other hand, the decision that the House of Commons now only votes Supply formally, three times a year, and cannot refuse Supply on what is nominally still called a Supply day not only introduces a new, and perhaps 'farcical' anomaly. It might also be held to diminish the sanctions that the House has available to use against the Executive in a constitutional crisis.

(ii)

The non-employment of Supply procedure by the House to scrutinise the Estimates is to some extent compensated for by the work of the Estimates Committee. The first Estimates Committee was set up in 1912 and in the two world wars it was replaced by a Select Committee on National Expenditure. Before the last war, the Estimates Committee was not a success; it seemed to concentrate on duplicating work already done by the Treasury and it was limited in its approach by the need not to intervene in policy matters. Since the war, the Estimates Committee has proved much more effective. It operates through six or more sub-committees and has managed to get down to basic issues of policy-administration and value-for-money. The Committee, consisting of forty-three Members, is empowered to examine such of the Estimates as seem fit to it and to report on economies consistent with policy implied in the Estimates. In practice, however, the Committee is not so much éxamining Estimates that 'seem fit' for examination as investigating those for which it has time. The limitations of so small a Committee are obvious. Moreover, it has no organisation to help it comparable to the substantial staff of the Exchequer and Audit Department whose work, as reported by the Comptroller and Auditor-General, makes the Public Accounts Committee so effective. Indeed, it is difficult to see how the Estimates Committee could be provided with such a body as the Exchequer and Audit Department which, for the purposes of auditing Government Accounts, has representatives in all Whitehall departments and costs the best part of £1m. annually. As the Chairman of the Estimates Committee, William Hamilton, expressed it in 1965: 'We're doing the best we can and really it's little more than sticking a pin in £7,000m. of public expenditure and saying we're going to investigate this or that.'[1] The danger of missing important subjects for investigation is obvious. In 1964, the Public Accounts Committee discovered a big under-estimate in the development costs of the 'Bloodhound' missile, with a substantial profit for Ferranti Ltd., the company developing the guidance system for this missile. A subsequent investigation discovered that the company had made 'excessive' profits of £5·7m. and it was subsequently arranged that the company should repay £4·5m. to the Government over a five-year period. This was a case which, arguably, might have been discovered by the Estimates Committee *before* the event, instead of being left to the Public Accounts Committee afterwards—provided the Estimates Committee was strengthened. The Estimates Committee is further limited in its time by the fact that the Estimates which are produced in February must be passed through Parliament by August. There is plainly a strong case for providing the Estimates Committee with more facilities for doing its present financial job of seeking economies more effectively, and for enabling its sub-committees to specialise in particular types of spending and to employ technical assistance. However, the handicaps under which the Estimates Committee labours in respect of what should be its real work have been obscured by the emphasis laid on specialising committees with a wider brief than a search for economy and value-for-money. As we have seen, it was suggested by the Select Committee on Procedure, 1964–5, that the Estimates Committee should have its terms of reference widened so that it could take on this wider duty. Yet it is arguable that the essential problem is to make the Estimates Committee better able to

[1] Transcript of a series of twenty-five television programmes on Modern British Government, devised by Norman Hunt and broadcast for ABC Television from January 1965.

do the financial and economising job over public expenditure which, by common agreement, the House cannot be expected to do through Supply procedure.

The Public Accounts Committee, aided by the work of the Comptroller and Auditor-General, is by common consent a powerful body whose work in ensuring that public money has neither been wasted nor used for purposes for which it was not intended, is thorough and detailed. The Comptroller and Auditor General has the Exchequer and Audit Department's staff of between 500 and 600 who are continually employed in checking the accounts of Government departments. Basing itself on this skilled work, as well as on its own examination of witnesses, the Public Accounts Committee will often engage in a prolonged written duel with the Treasury, which handles the matter on behalf of the department whose accounts are concerned. If the Estimates Committee were strengthened to anything like this degree, the House of Commons' mechanism for oversight of the details of public spending would be substantially complete.

Sanctioning, appropriating and vetting the Government's expenditure is one side of the Commons' financial duty; the other is consenting to taxation proposed by the Government. (Only a Minister can propose taxation.) There is little complaint about the response of the House to the latter aspect of its financial responsibility. Budget Day is one of the great parliamentary occasions of the year and the contemporary tendency for Governments to act in a budgetary fashion between annual Budgets, or to introduce additional Budgets, has not diminished this interest. The Government is obliged to relate its financial and economic strategy to the taxation it proposes to raise. The House remains vigilant in criticising taxation—so much so that it has continued to take the Finance Bill, clause by clause, in Committee of the Whole House. This, indeed, is one of the perennial causes of complaint by Members, who object to having the floor of the Chamber monopolised by the Finance Bill for a great part of the summer months, during which other topics are deprived of debating time.

Frequently only a handful of interested Members have taken part in the Finance Bill debates; on the other hand, they have all had to be present, often right through the night, to ensure that the Government was not defeated on any of the clauses and that the Opposition voted its full strength. Undoubtedly the irritation caused to the new

Labour Members by the protracted sittings of the House during the controversial Budget of 1965, when the Government only had a minute majority, added fuel to the demand for parliamentary reform which gained such force at this time.

During the Finance Bill Committee stage, Members must, for hour after hour, troop through the division lobbies on clauses in which they have no interest and which they probably do not even understand. It is small wonder, therefore, that there have been repeated demands that the Finance Bill should be sent 'upstairs' to Standing Committee. The Select Committee on Procedure which examined this, and other topics, in 1958 suggested that at least part of the Finance Bill should be sent to Standing Committee and the then Leader of the House, R. A. Butler, seemed to favour an experiment of this sort. One suggestion at this time was for the division of the legislative implementation of the Budget into a Taxes Management Act to deal with purely administrative changes in taxation (this could go upstairs) and the Finance Act proper. In fact, nothing came of this idea. Removal of the whole of the Finance Committee from the 'floor' could be represented as a further step in the decline of the House's ability to control the financial decisions of the Executive.

The use of the Committee of the Whole House to discuss the annual Finance Bill may give the Commons a rather greater chance of amending the Bill when it is produced by a Government with a small majority. Correspondingly, to send the Finance Bill to a Standing Committee in such circumstances might be some protection for the Government. Thus, when the Labour Government of 1964 had only a majority of three or four in the House of Commons, it would have had a majority of one in the Standing Committee. It might, in such circumstances, have been easier to maintain a majority of one, out of, say, thirty closely interested Members on a Standing Committee than to keep a majority of three out of 630 in Division after Division of the Whole House through the small hours. Further, a Government can be far more ruthless in forcing a Standing Committee to sit until its business is through, and to use the guillotine against it, than it would feel able to do in Committee of the Whole House. Indeed, it is notable that an energetic campaign by the Conservative Opposition during the passage of the 1965 Finance Bill did force the Government to make substantial amendments to a Bill which both implemented drastic taxation changes and which suffered from hasty drafting by a Government newly in office. It may be

375

doubted whether the Conservatives would have had quite so much success in a Standing Committee, and, certainly, a Government with a small majority ought to be specially responsive to the House of Commons. For the size of its majority reflects the limited degree of confidence the nation is prepared to repose in it. On this argument, the difficulty the Government had with the Finance Bill (it would have been even greater with a Steel Nationalisation Bill had the Government dared to introduce it in that Parliament) was a tangible example of parliamentary influence.

On the other hand, there are contrary arguments which apply in normal Parliaments where a Government has a reasonable majority. Discipline in the informal atmosphere of Standing Committees is more difficult to impose than on the 'troops' massed in the Commons. On most occasions, moreover, amendments are as easy to obtain (or as difficult) in Standing Committee as in the Whole House. When these facts are taken into account, along with the need for the House to save time and spare its Members the wearisome night-long sittings after the annual Budget, pressure for removing at least part of the Finance Bill 'upstairs' may prove irresistible.

In March, 1967, the Fourth Report from the Select Committee on Procedure, 1966–67, set out the arguments for and against two possible changes. One was to divide the Bill into two parts, dealing respectively with matters of principle and matters of technical detail. The former part would remain on the floor of the House; the technical aspects would be sent to Standing Committee. A Treasury memorandum, however, found strong practical reasons against trying to split the Bill and concluded that the criteria of saving time in the Chamber and avoiding late sittings could only be met by sending the whole Bill 'upstairs'. The Select Committee itself made no recommendation of either course, but all its members supported a suggestion for an experiment in a voluntary 'time-tabling' of the Bill. On May 1, the Leader of the House, Richard Crossman, proposed an order enabling a Minister to move that the business committee should recommend a time limit for completion of the various stages of the Bill. This was passed against Conservative objections. The bulk of Labour opinion would have been willing to go further and send the entire Bill 'upstairs' as part of the general reform of procedure.

Chapter Fifteen

The Public Relations of Parliament

The public is so frequently told that it has lost confidence in Parliament that it may be in some danger of believing that it must have done so. Yet even a cursory examination of public reactions to it over the past century suggests that there has been no loss of interest in the proceedings of the House of Commons and no serious decline in the public's evaluation of it, making allowances for the changes in the mode of politics over this period. More important, however, there appears to be little, if any, substance to the allegations that Parliament has fallen drastically in public esteem since the end of the last war.

The authors of *What's Wrong with Parliament?* began by contrasting the allegedly current decline of Parliament in public esteem with its status at the end of the war. 'In 1945 the reputation of the British Parliament stood as high as ever before in its long history',[1] the authors stated, and they cited the vigilance of the Commons during the war when the Government had been provided with extraordinary powers for the purpose of defending the realm. It was not, perhaps, the best comparison which could be made, since the circumstances of the war years were plainly exceptional. With the normal processes of party conflict in suspension, the backbench Members of the House of Commons were forced, unless they were to concede dictatorial powers to the war-time coalition, to engage in some sort of critical dialogue with it. As we have seen, the very fact that representative leaders of all parties were in the Government made it easier for backbenchers, whatever their political allegiance, to adopt a constructively critical attitude. However, the authors of *What's Wrong with Parliament?*, whose views have crept into the common currency, did not content themselves with a broad comparison of the contemporary state of Parliament with its state in the

[1] Andrew Hill and Anthony Whichelow, *What's Wrong with Parliament?*, p. 9.

somewhat unrepresentative period of the Commons' history at the end of the war. They also called into aid as evidence of a decline in the public interest in Parliament a fall in the 'average daily sales' of *Hansard*, which they set out as follows:

In 1945	8,889
1950	3,384
1955	2,678
1960	2,332
1963	2,170

However, a fuller examination of sales of *Hansard* since the early years of this century reveals a somewhat different picture. Opposite is a table of the sales of daily *Hansards* between 1910 and 1945, the year in which weekly *Hansards* were first published. After 1945 I give two figures—average daily print of daily *Hansards* and average weekly print of weekly *Hansards*. (There are slight discrepancies between some of the figures in the following list, which was provided by HM Stationery Office and the figures provided by Hill and Whichelow.)

These fuller figures suggest that the sharp fall in the sale of House of Commons *Hansards* since 1945–6 in no sense indicates a decline in the public interest in Parliament (assuming that sales of *Hansard* are a reliable indicator) over the present century so far. There has been a substantial rise in *Hansard* sales since the years before the First World War and, even allowing for the fall in sales since the 1945–50 period, total sales in the mid-sixties—taking into account the weekly *Hansards* which only became available in 1946—are well above the average for the inter-war years. The fall in sales since the immediate post-war period is accounted for by the fact that the period from 1945–50 was one of unusual circumstances, which cannot, therefore, be taken as a satisfactory base date from which to measure a rise or a fall in parliamentary prestige. For one thing, it was an intensely political period when the cleavage between the Conservative Party and the Labour Government (the first Labour Government with an overwhelming majority and a mandate for social changes) was sharper than ever before. There was a widespread political interest among the men of the demobilised forces, and the Labour Government's 'New Deal' provoked both enthusiasm and bitter resentment: whatever its merits or demerits it revived a widespread interest in politics—and therefore, also, in Parliament, where the battle between

Daily Hansards (House of Commons)
(average daily print)

Year	No. of copies	Weekly Hansard
1910	162	
1914	303	
1918	919	
In the 1920s and 1930s	normally between 1,000 and 1,300	
1939	1,297	
1940	1,522	
1941	1,793	
1942	2,242	
1943	2,316 (excluding Beveridge debates) 2,593 (including Beveridge debates)	
1944	2,593	
1945	7,111	
1946	6,608	13,438
1947	4,530	13,308
1948	3,989	10,430
1949	3,650	7,845
1950	3,384	7,475
1951	3,256	5,992
1952	3,008	6,084
1953	2,815	3,770
1954	2,673	2,959
1955	2,678	2,645
1956	2,688	2,428
1957	2,557	2,207
1958	2,418	1,772
1959	2,335	1,623
1960	2,332	1,528
1961	2,334	1,474
1962	2,333	1,447
1963	2,202	1,394
1964 (to end of August)	2,174	1,576

379

the two sides was fought out. It is small wonder that, in a period of such intense political activity, the sales of *Hansard* should be high.

But there was another explanation too. In this period of social revolution, when the House of Commons was the forum in which the nation argued out its differences, there was a shortage of newsprint and newspapers appeared in a very attenuated form. Parliamentary reports were necessarily of the briefest and only gradually began to build up again in the 1950s. For anyone who wanted to know what was happening in Parliament (and in a period of heavy and significant legislation many people had a professional interest in knowing the facts) it was essential to read *Hansard*. The same need for *Hansard* did not exist after newsprint had been decontrolled during the early fifties. After the return of a Conservative Government in 1951, moreover, there was an increasing trend towards blurring the edges between the two parties and the period of 'Butskellism'[1] dawned. After 1959, moreover, interest in politics seemed to many people more than ever academic, since it appeared to them that the Conservative Party was established indefinitely in power and that Labour was destined to remain in ineffective opposition. This made much of the parliamentary debate of these years seem unrelated to realities, and therefore comparatively uninteresting. The public admission figures to the galleries of the House of Commons also do not suggest any general decline in interest; they simply show that the public's interest in the House is in direct relationship to the current intensity (or otherwise) of the political argument. At times of high excitement (during the Suez period, for instance, or at the time of the Profumo scandal) the public has flocked to the galleries.

When politics are stale and flat; when there appears to be no political argument worth the name; when it appears that one party is so overwhelmingly entrenched that the Opposition can make no headway against it; when the nation is content and unaroused, as it was in the late fifties, then interest in the proceedings of the House of Commons flags. When politics reach a crisis or when the public's own sentiments are strongly engaged on one side or the other, then its interest in the House revives.

---

[1] A compound of the names of R. A. Butler (Chancellor of the Exchequer and holder of many other offices in the post-War Conservative Administrations) and Gaitskell (Labour Chancellor of the Exchequer and later Labour Party Leader): it signified the similarity of the two Parties' economic and social policies during the early Fifties.

Equally, there is no substantial evidence that the press is less interested in the House of Commons, while television (to which I shall return) has stimulated a much more immediate public interest in politics and politicians. It has been a common complaint of politicians in this century that the press has ceased to give adequate reports of parliamentary proceedings. But those who so complain are not comparing like with like. Of course, the entire press, which now appeals to a mass electorate, does not give the same coverage, in terms of words, to the proceedings in the House of Commons as was provided in the newspapers of the nineteenth century, which were intended for a small, leisured class who made something of a hobby of following politics. Nowadays the essential points of parliamentary proceedings are conveyed, on the whole with skilful and impartial selection, to an audience of millions which, by its nature, does not enjoy the same literacy as the Victorian readers of *The Times*. And to the extent that the 'heavy' newspapers contain smaller verbatim reports of the proceedings inside Parliament than they did then, this reflects a change in the service offered to readers rather than a decline. For one thing, a greater proportion of the time of the House is spent these days in discussing comparatively technical yet very important matters in the details of which the public may be less interested than it was in the broad and more easily comprehensible issues of nineteenth-century politics. It was, presumably, easier to be emotionally involved, and therefore interested, in debates on Irish Home Rule than it is in the technicalities of the recurrent economic crises which have dominated parliamentary discussion since the war and whose specialised intricacy is no less baffling to many politicians than it is to the general public. One of the reasons why people are frequently less interested in the detailed debates in Parliament is simply that the subject-matter of those debates, now extensively dominated by the minutiae of state intervention in a whole host of specialised activities, is *to the general public* that much less interesting —which is not to say that it is less useful.

Another reason for the change is that the press now gives much more attention to parliamentary proceedings in a broader sense than simply reporting what happens on the floor of the House. The press, including the quality press, has to provide a bigger proportion of space for the description, précis and analysis of highly complex Government White Papers which are, essentially, parliamentary business. Newspapers also offer their readers more in the form of political analysis of what happens in Parliament (off as well as on the floor of the House) and in the political parties outside. The press seeks to provide deeper reporting of the processes of government that lead up to important political decisions, while a whole new dimension of newspaper reporting of what is essentially parliamentary politics has been created by the growth of interest in public opinion polling and the study of parliamentary elections.

Political and social conditions have changed so much since the nineteenth century that it is doubtful whether even a major piece of comparative research on the press coverage of proceedings in Parliament could be meaningful. But looking at the reporting of parliamentary politics in the widest sense, one feels doubtful whether there has been any real decline. What is certainly true is that Parliament and the press are interdependent and both interact as guardians of the liberty of the subject. The press is the channel through which Parliament communicates with the public. There follows, therefore, an account of the daily working of the press in Parliament.

(ii)

At 8.27 p.m. on November 18, 1958, all galleries of the House of Commons, including the press gallery, were cleared of Strangers by order of the Sergeant-at-Arms. The Official Report of the proceedings of the House stopped abruptly in the middle of a point of order which was being raised by the Leader of the House, R. A. Butler. How Butler finished his sentence and what happened thereafter we shall never know except from hearsay. *Hansard* baldly states: 'Strangers withdrew', and, so far as the rest of that day's business was concerned, *Hansard* could only supply the Division List, with the observation: 'The following record of the subsequent business is taken from the Votes and Proceedings.'[1] The House of Commons had cut off its normal channel of communication with the public through *Hansard* and the Press.

The House had been engaged on the Committee stage of the Representation of the People (Amendment) Bill and the subject under discussion was the withdrawal of restrictions on the use of motor cars at parliamentary elections. A sharp difference of opinion between the Conservative Government and the Labour Opposition had erupted into an argument over the range of discussion that

[1] H.C. Deb., Vol. 595, col. 1118.

382

should take place on a particular Opposition Amendment. Mr George Wigg, a Labour backbencher with a bent for the ingenious exploitation of parliamentary procedure, had 'purely as a protest' drawn attention to the fact that there were Strangers present. If any Member does this, the Speaker, or the Chairman, is forthwith obliged to put to the House, or to the Committee, the question that Strangers be ordered to withdraw. On this particular occasion, the motion was passed because Members were apparently caught unawares by Wigg's strategem. Had they been a little quicker off the mark, the Conservatives, with their majority, could have foiled Wigg. As it was, the Chairman did not hear any voices call 'No', although Mr Martin Redmayne, a Government Whip, claimed to have done so. In the course of the final exchanges recorded in *Hansard*, the Chairman observed: 'So far as the galleries are concerned, we do not know that they are there.'

Although the Official Report (*Hansard*) is produced by an official body under the Speaker, the publication of the debates of the House of Commons remains, technically, a breach of privilege. The Commons' jealous preservation of their right to exclude Strangers and to debate behind closed doors is rooted in history. In former centuries, the House feared the pressure of Strangers among them, and attempts from the galleries to influence their debates. They feared even more the possibility that the Crown might attempt to intimidate them if it received reports of speeches by Members which were objectionable to it. In the eighteenth century there was a less reputable reason for the attempt to prevent the publication of debates. The House, then representative of a narrow property-owning oligarchy, was reluctant in the age before reform to be accountable to public opinion.[1] Today, when the report of debates is tolerated in practice, there is a practical reason for preserving the right to exclude reporters. By doing so, the House of Commons reserves its ability to debate in secret when necessary, as it did during the last war.

The exclusion of Strangers on November 18, 1958, was not, however, a response to serious need, and there is little doubt that the House rather than the public suffered from Mr Wigg's manœuvre. Deprived of its normal audience of press and public, the House of Commons is like a man dispossessed of one of his crucial faculties.

[1] Erskine May's *Parliamentary Practice*, 17th Edn., edited by Sir Barnett Cocks, K.C.B., O.B.E., Clerk of the House of Commons.

By all accounts, the House got through business unusually fast for the rest of that day. With no audience beyond the Chamber to speak to, many Members presumably doubted the usefulness of speaking. That day the business of the House had been exempted from the provision of Standing Order No. 1 which normally brought the daily sitting to an end at 10 o'clock. A late sitting had been generally expected. In the event, the House adjourned at twenty-nine minutes past ten. This episode provided a useful demonstration both of the need that the modern House of Commons has for communicating with the public and of the ambivalent attitude of Parliament towards the Press at Westminster. The activities of journalists are tolerated because they are needed and, however inadequately, they are facilitated. Nevertheless, the journalists at Westminster are there on sufferance.

The proceedings of Parliament and the conduct of politics in a wider sense at Westminster are conveyed to the public through two main channels. There are first the parliamentary correspondents and reporters, and secondly the political, or 'lobby', correspondents. The first category includes at one end of the spectrum the *Hansard* reporters who provide a verbatim account of the proceedings of the House, although not necessarily a 'full' one in the sense of reporting every aside or interruption. Thus *Hansard* contains no reference to L. S. Amery's call to Arthur Greenwood to 'speak for England' on the eve of the declaration of the Second World War. Similarly, when the House becomes disordered by passion, the often staccato account of interruptions and counter-interruptions conveyed by *Hansard* gives no adequate impression of the scene. And, of course, it is not the function of *Hansard* to do so. The purpose of *Hansard* is to provide, as nearly as possible, a verbatim account of the speeches of Members which is also a lucid account. The *Hansard* reporters, who take turns in covering the proceedings of the House all round the clock if necessary, may check with Members what was actually said, or what Members were attempting to say. As a result, speeches may, in the reading, achieve a degree of grammatical lucidity which was not always apparent in their delivery, although of course *Hansard* should not alter the sense, or what it takes to be the sense, of a Member's speech.

The press gallery also includes the agency reporters who give a fairly full and sometimes a near-verbatim account of the proceedings of the House. Finally, in the category of non-interpretative reporting one must include the reporters on the staff of some national news-papers who provide a long, but not a complete, account of debates, some of which is in direct, and some in indirect speech.

At the other end of the parliamentary reporting spectrum are the parliamentary correspondents whose job is essentially a selective one. Every national and many provincial newspapers have at least one parliamentary correspondent, whose job it is to select, report, and describe those aspects of a debate or discussion in the House which he considers newsworthy for the purpose of his particular newspaper. In some cases, parliamentary correspondents produce an essentially factual account of the words of Ministers and MPs, confining their reports to the main newspoints which emerge. But most also give more or less graphic descriptions of dramatic scenes and clashes of personalities when they occur. Finally, for some newspapers, the job of the parliamentary correspondent is primarily that of a descriptive sketch-writer. His function is to evaluate the proceedings of the House and the speeches of Members; to give his assessment of the success, or failure, of particular contributions to a debate; to indicate, some-times elliptically, which of two political opponents has been the winner in an encounter across the floor of the House; to convey the mood of the House and the impact on it of a Member's speech. Subtly, he may convey his own notion of a Member's sincerity, capacity and intelligence. In doing this job, the sketch-writer provides his own criteria, which, of course, in many cases, harmonise closely with the ethos of his newspaper. At its best, the art of the parlia-mentary sketch-writer is a fine one. Whatever his general opinion of a Member, or of his politics, a good sketch-writer gives each parlia-mentarian his due on each occasion. He responds to the mood of the House in conveying it to his readers. He is not anxious to score points off Members (there have been occasions, however, when descriptive reporters of Parliament have conceived it their duty to act as though they were destructive drama critics and who plainly did not like the collective persona of the House of Commons) and is sensitive to both great and small occasions. Probably the outstanding modern example of such a parliamentary sketch-writer was the late Harry Boardman of *The* (then *Manchester*) *Guardian*.[1] Not every

[1] See, Harry Boardman, *The Glory of Parliament*, Ed. Francis Boyd (Allen & Unwin, 1960). This posthumous collection of reports on Parlia-ment, especially of some of the great occasions, has lost nothing by the passage of time and is important raw material for the future historian.

parliamentary correspondent would fit neatly into one or the other categories I have described. Some might be in one or another category according to the occasion. Nevertheless, all parliamentary correspondents and sketch-writers have as their function the coverage of political activities strictly on the floor of the House of Commons. Reporting and interpretation of politics at Westminster in a wider sense falls to the Lobby correspondents.

About 300 men and women are members of the Press Gallery, although the number on the premises each day is substantially less than this. The daily population in the Press Gallery was put at an average of 170 to 200 people (including telegraphists, messengers and others) in a recent report by a special committee of the Press Gallery.[1] Of the total membership of the Gallery, 116 people are on the official Lobby List of the Serjeant-at-Arms: that is to say, they alone have the right to enter the Member's Lobby, which adjoins the House itself. They also have access to the Ways and Means corridor and the stairs through which they must pass to reach the Lobby from the Press Gallery. They are entitled to be in the Lobby at any time, for the purpose of talking to MPs, except when a Division is taking place. Once a Division is called, everybody except Members must leave and wait in one of the adjoining corridors.

So far as British newspapers are concerned, the Lobby list (which also includes representatives of foreign and Commonwealth newspapers and agencies) is compiled with a strong element of prescriptive right and facilities are granted to newspaper representatives on the basis of historical claims as well as a contemporary evaluation of need. Thus *The Times* is allowed three lobby correspondents whereas most newspapers have only one. As one of *The Times* representatives is the Editor of the newspaper, they have in practice two. Nevertheless, this is a considerable advantage. Most other newspapers (*The Daily Telegraph* is an exception and also has two full lobby correspondents, having inherited the extra one from its amalgamation with *The Morning Post*) have to make do with one 'full' and one 'alternate' lobby correspondent and of these only one may be in the Lobby at any given time. Thus, if a lobby correspondent wishes to enter the Lobby and finds his assistant there already in conversation he must either wait for the assistant to emerge or send him a signal to finish

[1] *Partners in Parliament:* A report by a working party of the Press Gallery, which considered the status, rights and working conditions of parliamentary journalists. (July, 1964)

his conversation. *The Times* and *Telegraph*, however, may have both correspondents in the Lobby together. *The Times* has other advantages too. It has regular access to parts of the Palace of Westminster which other correspondents do not normally enter unless on the way to see a Minister or Member. Equally, *The Times* parliamentary staff has its own special room which facilitates the keeping of records and the communication of the various members of that staff with one another. So has *The Daily Telegraph*. Other newspapers' correspondents share rooms with each other and the staff of some newspapers are scattered through several rooms.

All lobby correspondents' conversations with Members are, unless a Member specifically indicates that he may be quoted, usable for writing on a 'non-attributable' basis. That is to say, political information or opinions that are passed may be used, but the source may not be disclosed. Conversations with Members in the Lobby are primarily of use to political correspondents as a means of sounding the mood and the opinions, of backbenchers. In the aftermath of some major political decision of the frontbench, conversation in the Lobby may give political correspondents a useful insight into the reaction of ordinary Members to them. But a lobby correspondent must know his Member and be able to assess his weight in his party. In the light of his experience, each lobby correspondent must make up his own mind about how representative the views of a particular Member are likely to be. This is particularly important when the reaction to a political situation must be obtained quickly. The first half a dozen Members that a correspondent may chance to meet are not necessarily the most representative or the best guides. He must also learn to discount the rasher reactions of Members under the emotion of the moment and should try to anticipate their second thoughts if he is not to appear ridiculous in cold print the next morning. For the use that a lobby correspondent makes of the material given him depends on his own judgment, and, since he may not announce to the world that this, or that apparently absurd political reaction was given him by this, or that MP, he is himself held responsible for its credibility. But he can skilfully word his report to indicate both that certain views are being bandied about and that he, personally, discounts them.

Apart from the use of Lobby conversations to investigate political mood, the Lobby of the House of Commons may be the place in which a political correspondent chances to meet the very Minister, or

Member, whom he wants to consult for a particular purpose. For the most part, however, a correspondent who wishes to discover the views and intentions of Ministers or leading figures in the Opposition on a particular political issue, will normally choose to consult them elsewhere. He may do so privately but in certain circumstances lobby correspondents act collectively. 'The Lobby Correspondents have a private, un-numbered room where Members and especially Ministers can be whisked away to be interviewed in strict privacy,' as one account of Parliament, in a brief reference to lobby newspapermen, describes it.[1] The collective activities of lobby journalists are, however, confined to an inner Lobby of between sixty and seventy representatives of national and provincial morning, evening and Sunday newspapers. This 'inner Lobby' is a self-administering body, subject to the conditions laid down by the Serjeant-at-Arms, with its own elected Chairman, Secretary and Treasurer. It is on account of these collective activities which have sometimes been represented as an unhealthy 'mystery' that the Lobby has come under some criticism, from journalists who are not members of it and from others who misconceive its function.

Since lobby correspondents are so important a channel of communication between Parliament and the public, it is sensible to be clear about their precise function, their daily job in practice, and to make an assessment of the validity of the criticisms of the Lobby 'mystery'.

In fact, there is little that is esoteric about the general outline of Lobby journalism though there is secrecy and privacy about *particular* conversations and *particular* meetings. Such privacy is an essential and integral part of all conversations that take place between journalists and public figures over the whole range of political activity and is not confined to lobby correspondents. Unless news is to be reduced to a bleak and uninterpreted account of public statements, there must be a good deal of non-attributable exchanges between the press and politicians. Editors, leader-writers and specialist correspondents meet politicians and civil servants, and hear their views: how they deal with them, and how far they are influenced by them, in the columns of the press is a matter for the journalists concerned. Foreign correspondents, defence correspondents and

[1] Roland Young, *The British Parliament* (Faber, 1962), p. 97. See also Lord Hill of Luton, *Both Sides of the Hill* (Heinemann, 1964), pp. 203–6.

labour correspondents have a close and abiding relationship with the Foreign Office, the Ministry of Defence, and the Ministry of Labour respectively. Labour correspondents are also in the closest touch with the leaders of the trade union movement. This sort of relationship is, in fact, essential if there is to be any degree of 'openness' in government. If politicians are to share their thoughts, in some degree, with the public in the process of reaching policy decisions, if the public is to be made aware of the various options, and of the case for one or another method of dealing with a particular situation, then politicians (and sometimes civil servants) must be able to talk freely and non-attributably to journalists in the knowledge that, while the pros and cons of different lines of possible action may be made available to the public, they themselves will not be giving hostages to their political opponents, as would be the case if they could only speak for quotation. So long as we have a party system, politicians know that if they give anything which could be construed as a public commitment before their intentions are finally determined, they are likely to be presenting ammunition to their opponents.

Informal and non-attributable journalism has its pitfalls for the journalist. A journalist who becomes closely involved with the affairs of a particular Ministry develops into a kind of 'expert' himself and he must always beware of the too easy acceptance of the Ministry's 'line', which comes of sympathetic understanding. Nevertheless, a good specialist correspondent has wide individual contacts, forms his own views and does not allow himself to be over-reliant on official collective briefings. Lobby correspondents are to some extent freed from the danger of too great involvement with particular politicians by the simple fact that they have to deal with three rival political parties. At any given moment, it is likely that one or the other of the parties will consider a particular lobby correspondent an 'enemy' because he seemed unduly critical, or unreceptive to the line which the politician had wished to put over.

Sometimes this sort of hostility occurs because a lobby correspondent is finding out too much of what goes on in private backbench meetings. To take two instances, lobby correspondents provoked much anger inside the Conservative Party by the extensive reports of internal dissensions in the Party both in the Suez period and at the time when Harold Macmillan's leadership came under criticism following the Profumo affair in 1963. During the latter episode, some Conservative Members were so angry at newspaper disclosures of bad feeling in the 1922 Committee over the leadership problem that they wrote letters to the press complaining at the reports and throwing doubt on their reliability. At this time, Conservatives were highly sensitive to the damage reports of their internal problem might do to their cause in the country. At the same period, backbenchers, within the author's personal experience, would talk crossly and unrealistically about taking away facilities at Westminster from political journalists. The argument was usually a mixed one: sometimes it hinged on allegations that the press reports in question were inaccurate; sometimes on the claim that they were an infringement of privacy; sometimes on a mixture of both. Since this kind of reporting is indirect, no satisfactory reply to the charge of inaccuracy is possible. But the degree of similarity in the reports in all the newspapers during these crises, together with subsequent cross-checking, suggests that they were generally very accurate. It seems likely that on such occasions the heat of protest relates more to the inconvenience of a particular disclosure than to the degree of accuracy of the report.

This tension between politicians and the press is inevitable. It is natural that MPs should wish to conceal their internal party disagreements from the public. But it is equally understandable that the press should be interested in meetings which, for instance, affect so important a matter as a party's leadership. Politicians themselves sometimes acknowledge press interest in party meetings as legitimate, as when Harold Wilson, as Prime Minister, with the consent of the Parliamentary Labour Party, issued to the press the text of his speech to the party meeting on East of Suez policy after a critical 'private' meeting of the Party in June 1966. On this occasion, however, lobby correspondents, while having the official text of the Prime Minister's speech, had to rely on unofficial reports of what his critics had said which did not entirely suit the Labour critics. To these problems there is no wholly satisfactory answer.[1] If backbench meetings were made public, it is sometimes said, press interest in them would die down. If this proved true, it would only be because, as so often when an institution is thrown open, the decisive discussion had moved behind the scenes elsewhere. And inevitably it is in the decisive discussion that the press is primarily interested. It may be,

[1] The Parliamentary Labour Party, to prevent embarrassing unofficial leakages, decided on June 14, 1967, to give journalists an *official* account of what happens at their meetings.

390

therefore, that the present semi-privacy of backbench meetings represents a tolerable compromise in that it enables the politicians to continue their internal party dialectic without giving on-the-record hostages to their political opponents, while journalists fulfilling their rôle as the public communicators of politics, try to discover what the politicians seek to conceal from the public gaze.

The main work of the lobby journalists is to provide and interpret news, report political trends and mood and to interpret the situation as it is and not as he thinks it ought to be. The briefest account of a lobby correspondent's day (there are, of course, wide variations between one and another) will suffice to show how closely he is tied to immediate news. After a morning spent in reading, or making private contacts with politicians, he may start at the House when it assembles at 2.30. He must read the House of Commons' papers for the day, listen to important Questions or statements, discuss the day's affairs with Members, and amplify as far as he can public Ministerial statements or White Papers by reporting them in context. He may be able to take Ministerial announcements further by explaining to his readers how the policy so revealed may develop, how the political parties may react to it and the views of the official Opposition. He may have to précis and interpret Government White Papers, and must follow backbench meetings. These days, a lobby correspondent's orbit extends beyond Westminster, and beyond Whitehall, to which he also has regular access; for he will be expected to interpret major political speeches made in the country or on television. His day continues until late at night when, at the closing of Public Business, he may have to report on a backbench revolt in an important Division. Several 'stories' each day probably fall to a lobby correspondent, many of them having to be re-written as events develop.

With so heavy a burden of work arising from immediate politics, the lobby correspondent is not primarily concerned to deal with events on a longer time-scale. His first task is to probe into the background of events concerning daily politics and to report on it. Criticisms that he does not dig deeply enough into special situations are therefore largely beside the mark.[1] A newspaper expects its lobby correspondent to provide daily information of interest to its general

[1] An answer to some of the criticisms of the Lobby is given in an article by David Wood, political correspondent of *The Times*, in a special issue of the *Political Quarterly* on Parliament (1965).

readers, not to provide a special service on every subject, however esoteric, of interest to the contemporary historian. If, for some purposes, the lobby correspondent produces too few secrets and not enough information from outside the daily practice of politics at Westminster, so far as the politicians themselves are concerned, he generally produces too much that they would like to keep dark. The lobby correspondent is a mirror of politics and at his best he tries to be an accurate one. In 1938, the then lobby correspondent of *The Times* resigned because his report of Duff Cooper's resignation from the Government was withheld and another substituted under the lobby correspondent's by-line.[1]

Ministers, however, find the 'Lobby' a useful means of explaining their ideas while these are in a process of evolution. They may be prepared to explain to a journalist (so that he in turn can explain to his readers) the options they see before them at a stage earlier than they are prepared to make more categorical statements in the House. Ministers' willingness to answer questions from lobby correspondents which they would not be prepared to answer in the House has been made one of the grounds for criticising the standing of the House of Commons. In fact, the reason is clear: it is one thing to answer 'neutral' questions of fact or probability put by lobby correspondents and quite another to stand up to more or less hostile questions in the House when the Minister's opponents will do their best to force him into a decisive position before he is ready to adopt one. The use of the Lobby in this way by politicians is a perfectly valid exercise, even when 'kites' are being flown. Nevertheless, it does give the Lobby a certain vulnerability. On occasions it suits a Minister to put a case across through the Lobby and what amounts to a Government statement, for which the Government does not take formal responsibility, appears throughout the press on the following day. Thus it has been said that a Prime Minister can use the Lobby to put across his version of a situation: that this is taken by the public as being 'factual' (that is, not partisan) because it is not attributed to its source.

[1] Duff Cooper, *Old Men Forget* (Hart-Davis, 1953), pp. 249–50. *The Times* Lobby correspondent, the Hon. Anthony Winn, who was killed in action two years later, 'duly reported the speech and what had been thought of it. I never saw what he wrote, but it did not accord with the policy of the paper. Not only did the editor suppress it but he inserted a concoction of his own in which the speech was described as a "damp squib" and headed it "From our Lobby Correspondent".' (This was a wholly exceptional incident.)

On occasions, a report of this kind appears, non-attributed, throughout the entire press. Sometimes when it seems later to be proved inaccurate, or not substantiated by events, journalists are angered—as, for instance, when a Government disclaimer of any intention to take deflationary action was apparently hinted to the press on 'lobby terms' in July 1966—a few days before further heavy deflationary measures were announced. Essentially, it is up to the judgment of the individual newspaperman to decide how firmly he believes the information he has been given.

As for the criticism that Ministers may too easily use the lobby to put across their version of events, the decisive fact is that it is unrealistic to expect any journalist not to make use of any news or views of interest given by a Minister in an off-the-record interview. Even if a report of the interview suits the Minister concerned, this consideration would hardly justify the journalist in deciding not to use matter of interest. If one individual were not to use it, others would and no newspaper would willingly give the impression of missing such a report. What a Cabinet Minister says is potentially news, however, and wherever he says it. If there were no 'Lobby', non-attributable news would still remain the essence of political communication.

However, lobby correspondents do try to disclaim personal responsibility for a Minister's non-attributable 'situation report' by using such guide phrases as 'Cabinet Ministers assert . . .' or 'Government circles believe . . .' or 'It is understood . . .'. When a report states that it is made on the 'highest authority' it usually means precisely what it says. Although the reader is liable to ignore such interpolations, or take them as a kind of verbal pomposity, they are an attempt to convey some idea of the status and validity of a particular statement and to indicate how far it represents, for instance, a straight account of (say) a Government's view and how far it is the correspondent's construction from a collation of information from various sources.

This sort of reporting is generally valid and valuable. Yet politicians have had one habit which might to some extent be broken down. On occasions they will speak to lobby correspondents on the normal non-attributable basis, explaining their reaction to some major event, and then go on television repeating the same thing on official record. The result is a wrapped-up story in the press or a report of what the politician actually said on television. It may be that the politicians could be encouraged by political journalists to take responsibility for their own words when they are making what amounts to a pronouncement to the press as a whole, and when it is going to be apparent the next morning that they have done so. While preserving non-attributable contacts where necessary, journalists might, perhaps, encourage politicians to speak at least as freely to the press *on the record* as they are obliged to do if they subject themselves to a television interview. In the television studio, they cannot stop any questions being asked and an audience of millions hears their answers, or non-answers, and judges accordingly. The growing coverage of political events and political issues in special television programmes has greatly improved Parliament's communications with the public. The television cameras are able to bring politicians to talk directly to the public and they are able to cover Party Conferences. Special programmes are quickly mounted on television to cover important national issues immediately they occur and there are few weeks in which the television screens are denied an appearance of some politician. Should the House of Commons decide at some stage to admit the television cameras to cover its proceedings, Parliament would add a new dimension to its communications with the political community on whose behalf it assembles at Westminster. What effect might this have on the character of parliamentary politics and on the public's opinion of the House of Commons?

(iii)

By one vote, the House of Commons declined on November 24, 1966, to accept the proposals of a Select Committee that the proceedings of the House should be broadcast experimentally on a closed circuit. The suggestions of the Select Committee had been recommended to the House by its Leader, Richard Crossman, who took the view that Members should suspend judgment on whether the proceedings should be televised until after the experiment had been completed.[1] Had the experiment been accepted, Members would not only have been able to see complete closed circuit transmissions of their daily business, and have learned what it was like to work under the eye of the cameras: they would also have been able to see specimen edited programmes. The fundamental questions which would presumably have determined their verdict were, first, would the

[1] H.C. Deb., Vol. 736, cols. 1608–9.

394

television of Parliament change the character of the House and if so in what way? Secondly, would it alter the public's opinion of the House—and, if so, in what direction?

The Select Committee on Broadcasting of Proceedings in the House of Commons had spent almost a year in collecting evidence, oral and written, from representatives of the television and broadcasting authorities, independent broadcasters, the Chief Whips of all parties, Members of Parliament and other interested bodies. The basic findings of the Select Committee were summarised in the following sentence: 'Your Committee consider that the House would be wise to agree that its proceedings should be recorded for broadcasting, and that the people should thus be allowed to see and hear their representatives at work, unless it can be shown that to allow cameras and microphones into the Chamber would change the procedure, the character and the atmosphere of the House perceptibly for the worse.'[1] The recommendations of the Committee were summarised as follows:

(1) Continuous live broadcasting of all or most of the proceedings of the House is impracticable and undesirable.

(2) The House could make available to the British broadcasting organisations, for recording and editing by them for use in their radio and television programmes, a feed of all the proceedings of the House. This feed could also be supplied to other interested organisations at home or overseas.

(3) An experiment on closed circuits, in sound and vision, should be conducted for Members of Parliament only. After such an experiment the House should be invited to decide whether or not permanent arrangements for broadcasting should be made.[2]

Almost all the recent advocates of parliamentary reform have also supported the case for televising the proceedings of the House of Commons.[3] Direct reporting of debates and divisions in the House by means of the television cameras would, it is argued, help to restore the public's allegedly waning faith and interest in parliamentary processes and would enable the electorate to see the battles of contemporary politics fought out in their proper arena and not simply re-staged in the artificial setting of television studios. It is

[1] *First Report from the Select Committee on Broadcasting of Proceedings in the House of Commons*, August 1966, p. xxviii. [2] Ibid., p. v.
[3] But see A. Segal, 'The Case for not televising Parliament', B. Crick, *The Reform of Parliament*, Appendix G, pp. 262–9.

said that it would be better for Parliament if the electorate could see the leading political figures of the day confronting each other, and watch Ministers answering Members of the House to which they are constitutionally responsible, than that television politics should be confined to the interrogation of politicians by professional interviewers. Admission of the cameras to the House of Commons would end the unseemly scramble (so it is said) of politicians to the television studios immediately after the vote at the end of a major debate. Television would make politics more 'alive' and (it is variously argued by its advocates) would make no substantial difference to the proceedings of the House or would actually improve them by obliging Members to be more attentive to the real issues underlying debates instead of concentrating so much on scoring party debating points.

Although many academics and newspaper journalists have supported the campaign for televising the House of Commons, probably the main force behind it has come from the practitioners of television journalism, supported by a cross-section of MPs who find the prospect of televised parliamentary performances attractive to them for one reason or another. Yet the campaign for televising Parliament should not be regarded as a 'lobby' in any way comparable to that which brought commercial television into existence or to that which has sought to create commercial sound broadcasting. Indeed, on purely commercial criteria, some of the television companies were privately less than eager to face the additional cost that would be involved in televising the proceedings of the House of Commons. However, those who feel like this could not put themselves at a 'moral' disadvantage, by showing inadequate enthusiasm for creating a new field for television. In general, it is probably fair to regard the campaign for televising Parliament as a natural manifestation of ambition, on behalf of their medium, by executive producers and organisers who believe that the television of Parliament would greatly enlarge the scope of their profession.

The campaign for televising Parliament has rested on two rather different contentions. The first was that the political life of the community and the quality of Parliament would benefit. The second contention was that television should take its 'rightful' place in Parliament (alongside the press) and that the public has established its 'right' (for instance by the television of the Coronation, the Opening of Parliament, Royal marriages, political party conferences and so on) to be present, through the medium of television, at great public occasions. It has not always been clear from this second argument whether the 'right' of the public (implying the demand of the public) to television or the 'right' of television itself to cover all occasions of public interest is the main consideration. But the essence of all the arguments in favour of admitting television to Parliament is that, by admitting the press and the public, Parliament has already conceded the principle that its proceedings are, in normal circumstances, public property. Therefore, it is said, there is no logical reason why television reporting should not also be admitted. Using this argument, the advocates of parliamentary television contend that, if the cameras are still to be excluded, it is up to Parliament to prove a case against admitting them, not for television to prove its case for admission. Furthermore, it is asserted that Parliament could only prove a case for excluding the cameras if it could demonstrate that television would damage the status, efficiency, character or integrity of the House of Commons.

The First Report from the Select Committee itself agreed that no new principle was involved and that the question to be decided was whether 'it would be right to supplement the printed record with the greater directness and intimacy of broadcasting'.[1] The House would, the Select Committee considered, be unwise to condemn television of its proceedings without trial: furthermore, the Committee left no doubt that its own *prima facie* view was favourable to parliamentary television. It favoured edited broadcasts, of a number of types, taken from a recording of the full proceedings. Daily summary programmes would be possible and the Committee hoped that they would be a regular feature; it saw considerable value in weekly summaries; it considered that the House would benefit by the inclusion of excerpts from its proceedings in news bulletins (the fact that they had not been included in the past was perhaps why the House was remote from the public by comparison with other bodies); and it favoured parliamentary television in current affairs programmes. Using the contemporary idiom of public relations, the Select Committee added to the last of these items the observation: 'Here, again, your Committee envisage that there would be a corresponding improvement in the public "image" of Parliament.'

Thus, like most of the other interested persons and committees

[1] *First Report from the Select Committee on Broadcasting of Proceedings in the House of Cormmons*, August 1966, p. xxiii.

that have examined the question, the Select Committee had no doubts that television would improve the public's view of Parliament and considered that the basic problem was whether the character and proceedings of the House of Commons itself would be adversely affected by television coverage. It confirmed that Members were not likely to be physically inconvenienced by the admission of television cameras and that there were no major technical obstacles. But would the cameras change the style of the House; would they encourage Members to speak to the unseen audience, instead of to each other? The Committee considered that provided television transmissions took the form of edited versions there would be no danger of this since Members would not know whether their particular part of the debate was, or was not, being included in the transmission. Provided full broadcasting of the proceedings of the House were avoided, moreover, the character of the House would not be changed in the same way as in Australia. In the words of an Australian politician, broadcasting in that country has introduced an 'element of inflexibility and a lack of continuity into the proceedings which would not exist to the same extent if they were not broadcast'. The private Member, in Australia, is reduced to the rôle of somebody who speaks 'because, and for as long as, it is required to bring the big guns on the air at the right time'.[1]

The Select Committee considered that full 'live' television would be unsatisfactory on general grounds. It also believed that the Australian system of intermittent live broadcasts at pre-determined and regular times was not to be recommended here because it was largely responsible for major changes which had taken place in the Australian Federal Parliament. The edited version, which the Select Committee favoured, would be produced by each broadcasting corporation or company with editorial freedom but it would be fashioned from a common source of raw material consisting of full television coverage of the proceedings of the House supplied by a House of Commons Broadcasting Unit. This Unit would be under the supervision of the House.

This chapter is not primarily concerned with the general argument about the possible effects television of the proceedings of the House

---

[1] A. J. Forbes, MC MP, Minister for the Army and Minister assisting the Treasurer, Commonwealth of Australia, 'The Broadcasting of Parliamentary Debates in Australia', *Journal of the Parliaments of the Commonwealth*, Vol. XLV, No. 2, April 1964.

might have on the attitude and behaviour of Members—whether it would make them more exhibitionist or more responsible and restrained. Every conceivable aspect of this question has been thrashed out in evidence before the Select Committee and elsewhere. In all probability, the advocates of parliamentary television are right in believing that the television of the business of the House of Commons would affect the institution no more than it has affected other public occasions, such as political meetings and party conferences. Television, it is said, has the habit of being absorbed into its surroundings: Members would still speak mainly to the audience they could see. On the other hand, it must be expected that Members would quickly acquire the knack of discerning what sort of contribution would or would not stand a chance of inclusion in television programmes.

But if it is allowed that television would not materially affect the behaviour of the House of Commons, is it equally true that the 'public image' of the House would benefit—or would the public receive a distorted view of it from a potted version of a day's proceedings? This is probably the basic question.

Television coverage of public events differs from that of newspapers in two respects. First, newspapers can allow a greater number of words for the straightforward reporting of facts and speeches. Secondly, the work of the cameras makes the entertainment element in television stronger than it is in newspapers. To say this is not to suggest that television would interpret its job any less responsibly than newspapers do in covering Parliament. If a dramatic incident, based on (say) a clash of personalities, takes place in the House, most newspapers give it banner headlines and front-page treatment. But space allows them to carry as well an extended version, perhaps amounting to several thousand words, which is a précis of the arguments of the debate inside even the popular newspapers. It is not clear that television would be able to inflict on its evening viewers, who primarily demand entertainment or a 'special interest' programme, a comparable 'full report'. Further, in the edited version of twenty minutes or half an hour, there is a strong presumption that the more interesting, because more dramatic, episodes would have pride of place over the summary of the more pedestrian arguments of the debate. The edited version might, in fact, roughly correspond to the newspaper 'sketch' without the extended précis on normal days.

One strong advocate of parliamentary television, emphasising to the Select Committee the importance of the professional character of persons given responsibility for televising the proceedings of the House, observed: 'We do not want the entertainment side of television getting into the act at all.'[1] There is little likelihood that this would happen, but the remark suggests a clearer division between the entertainment element (as distinct from entertainment personnel) and current affairs reporting in television than may exist. There is, after all, an entertainment element in many current affairs programmes; it comes from the face-to-face encounters between conflicting personalities and exists almost apart from the interest of the case they are arguing. Indeed, it exists for visitors to the House of Commons itself. For many, perhaps most, people a visit to the public gallery of the House of Commons is regarded more as a sight-seeing entertainment (on a lucky day they will witness a 'scene') than as an opportunity to study seriously the political issues being debated. However, visitors to the public gallery at least have to sit through a good deal of serious, or pedestrian, discussion in order to witness the dramatic highlights which are a much smaller proportion of a day's proceedings than they could be of an edited version on television.

There are other reasons too why a potted version of a day's proceedings in the House might give a less than true impression of the Commons. As Mr Maurice Edelman, a backbench Labour Member of Parliament put it: 'It seems to me that pictorial editing lends itself much more to caricature than verbal editing because at least with words you are dealing with ideas whereas with pictures you are dealing with all sorts of aspects of the person photographed which are beyond his control.'[2] And the Select Committee considered that working out 'an acceptable technique for choosing ... reaction shots would be one of the most difficult problems facing the House of Commons Broadcasting Unit'.[3] No doubt acceptable techniques could be worked out. Yet it is probably true that the televising of the proceedings of the House, however fairly it is carried on, would stress the personality aspects, rather than the issues of politics. If they are faced with the choice between an entertaining 'personalities' episode or a painstaking account of, say, two worthy but unexciting frontbench speeches which set out the arguments, television editors

[1] Robin Day, *Evidence to the Select Committee on Broadcasting of the Proceedings of the House of Commons*, p. 70.
[2] *Evidence to the Select Committee on Broadcasting of the Proceedings of the House of Commons*, p. 69.   [3] Ibid., p. xxv.

will be liable to use much of their space for the more entertaining and more easily presentable episode. This may do no harm. On the other hand, television will not necessarily bring the real issues of a debate before the public any better than is done now when politicians come to the studio to explain their case rather than to debate with each other.

Parliamentary television may have two further effects on politics which could be more far-reaching than the issues most generally argued about. First it is possible that the Labour Party as such might benefit. Labour has the disadvantage of a larger critical press than the Conservatives have in Britain and however fairly the press reports the facts of Labour politics, there inevitably creeps in a certain criticism whenever reporting is interpretative rather than absolutely flat. Secondly, even when any Opposition has a strong case against the Government, the 'lead' story in most newspapers may be primarily concerned with the *fact* that the Government is going to take certain action. As we have already seen, newspapers are concerned with action, not views, in their reports as distinct from their comment. Television, however, will have to give equal prominence to both sides—to the Opposition's views as well as the Government's actions. It may be, therefore, that television would bring a better knowledge of an Opposition's case and of its leading personalities to the public. If this were to happen, perhaps the biggest benefit from televising the proceedings of the House of Commons would be some reversal of the existing dominance of the Executive in the party battle between elections. As we have seen, the present trend is for the men in power to hold the initiative by means of their command of announcements of decisions and pronouncements of policy made through the various media of public communications. Television might do something to redress the balance in favour of the official Opposition, thus bringing a new significance to the attempts of the Opposition frontbench to influence policy.

Chapter Sixteen

Conclusion (I)

Britain is still a monarchy in the practice of government and not simply because a constitutional monarch occupies the throne, reigning without ruling. It is a monarchy in the sense that the power of the Executive is of a monarchical kind. The Cabinet is the monarchy in commission, with the Prime Minister as First Commissioner. The Prime Minister and his colleagues are heirs to a tradition of authority in government which is something apart from the authority they obtain from parliamentary support, essential though this is to their survival in power. They have a considerable discretion in the conduct of government which Parliament expects them to exercise and they have chief responsibility for initiating policy. The Ministers of the Crown have inherited the tradition of such authority from the Crown itself, but whereas this originally derived from the pretended sacerdotal or hereditary right of the king to wield power as the people's non-elected representative leader, the modern Executive of Prime Minister-in-Cabinet obtains the same sort of authority in a different way.

This authority is nourished by the traditional political climate of the nation, which has favoured strong and unhampered authority, provided it is exercised legitimately and subject to parliamentary approval. The tenacity of the British in retaining monarchical forms, which might have been discarded long since, is itself a symptom of the instinct of successive power-groups to preserve firm and legitimate government representing something more than the dominant faction in an assembly of delegates.

In modern Britain, however, this monarchical extra-parliamentary authority does not depend only on the political climate but, more tangibly, is based on the method by which a Government is obtained. Unlike the old Crown, the modern Executive is, in a sense, a directly elected 'monarchy' as well as being one answerable to the House of

Commons. When the electorate goes to the polls, it is doing two things which are interrelated but which are nevertheless distinct from each other. It is choosing a Parliament to which the Government must be responsible but it is also choosing a Government *as such*— an Executive which is the modern successor to a strong monarchical tradition. In performing the second part of this task, most voters are exercising a clear choice between two alternatives.

By choosing a Government through Parliament, the electorate (in any ordinary circumstances) is effectively preventing any major clash between Government and Parliament. At the same time, in normal twentieth-century conditions, the British Government is something much more than the nominee of a parliamentary majority; it is also the direct nominee of the people and it therefore has the right to back its own judgment on policy matters against parliamentary opinion, even among its own supporters, should this seem to Ministers to be essential. It is then up to the majority party to weigh their dislike of a particular policy against their view of the general policy of the Government or against the consequences of turning the Government out by an adverse vote.

The monarchical discretion of the British Government is a practical matter and its significance can be assessed by comparing the British system with, on the one hand the American, and on the other the system of the Third and Fourth French Republics. The American system is also an elective monarchy; indeed, it is much more of a true monarchy because the executive power reposes in a single man, the President, who for all practical purposes is irremovable for the term of his office. On the other hand, the American President is not elected *through* Congress and he is therefore neither responsible to Congress for policy as the British Government is responsible to Parliament, nor is he similarly assured of Congressional support. American Presidential government can, notably in its legislative intentions, be frustrated by a hostile Congress. Though constitutional conventions make the American system viable, it nonetheless represents a pale reflection of the tension which once existed in Britain between king and Parliament—a tension which was resolved here, not by the separation of powers, but by making Ministers responsible to the House of Commons and therefore chosen from its majority party. In short, though British Government and American Presidency are both 'monarchical', the American President does not enjoy the right to expect parliamentary support on which the British Cabinet relies for its policies so long as the House of Commons is prepared to maintain it in power.

In contrast, the Governments of the Third and Fourth French Republics were essentially non-monarchical; they were, for practical purposes, executive committees of the French Parliament, owing their existence to bargains struck between rival groups of politicians which were as easily dissolved as made. Under such a system, no elector could feel any confidence that he was electing this or that Government; correspondingly, the total authority of a Government under such a system is derived from Parliament and has no other prestige. The essential point of such 'republican' Constitutions has been the destruction of the monarchical authority and the installation of Governments by an assembly composed of as many shades of political opinion as possible. Such Governments could be regarded as no more than temporary nominees of transient parliamentary majorities. In contrast, the British electorate has a strong predilection for trying to choose a strong Government itself but, unlike the Americans who share the same broad tradition, it has kept that Government under control by making it responsible to Parliament and using the House of Commons as an electoral chamber for choosing the Government, with reserve powers to dismiss it by withdrawal of parliamentary support.

It follows that the British Prime Minister and Cabinet have an authority which makes it perfectly natural that they should not be constantly vulnerable either to ejection from office by Parliament or to frustration of its intentions by defeats in the House of Commons. The point must be stressed because, despite repeated and correct assertions by most students of the British Constitution that Parliament has never governed, contemporary criticism of the House of Commons has sometimes seemed to carry overtones of a belief that Members of Parliament once had a more active participation in the affairs of the executive Government than they have today.

The historical sections of this study have shown that Parliament has never (except when driven to adopt a wholly unusual position when the Constitution broke down in the seventeenth century) claimed to govern. Its historical claim, which it made good against kings who were in no sense the nominees of the 'people' (however narrowly interpreted), was to have a Government whose broad policies it approved. Such a Government would then be allowed a plenitude of power (consonant with the traditional liberties of the land) by the House of Commons and would be provided with adequate funds. So long as tension between the Crown and the majority party in the House existed, it was natural that the House should seem more active and its leaders more critical than they are today. But in the seventeenth century, it had leaders who were fighting the Government; once the fight was resolved, the equivalents of Pym and Hampden were to be in the Government—indeed, *were* the Government. It was natural that a Parliament in apposition to the Executive should behave differently to one in opposition to it.

Since Parliament obtained the right to have a Government whose policies are generally acceptable to a majority of the House of Commons, the power to dismiss Ministries has been used sparingly. Even when this power has been used, the House has seldom been acting in an 'independent' capacity against a Government, whether during the period of the unreformed Parliament or after reform. In the eighteenth and nineteenth centuries Governments might fall through loss of their majorities in the Commons. But for the most part, this process should not be seen as the withdrawal of support by an independent House from a Ministry it had ceased to like. It was rather the result of a break-up between the leaders of different factions who had coalesced in Government and who, in parting company from each other, took their followers in the House with them. In particular, changes of Government in the unreformed Parliament took place in the context of a tight political consensus which was not at all like the struggles between Crown and Parliament in the seventeenth century or between the great parties, each representing rival interests, which have dominated politics from the mid-nineteenth to mid-twentieth centuries. Since the House of Commons has known that its majority was elected as a means of putting the leaders of a particular party in power, it has required a rare national crisis or a breakdown of agreement on major principle within the majority party for the House to turn effectively against the Government. The exception to this has been when there has been no clear majority. Yet the idea that the nineteenth-century Parliament made and unmade Ministries persists as part of a wider mythology about the nature of the House of Commons in the last century. These related concepts can usefully be examined by reference to the views expressed by Richard Crossman, the Leader of the House, in the debate on procedure in December 1966.

'... many of our procedures are survivals from a period when parties were weak, when the making and unmaking of Ministries still rested with the House of Commons, not with an electorate based on universal suffrage and when the Cabinet was merely the executive committee of the Commons. Procedurally, we still behave as though we were a sovereign body which really shared with the Government in the initiation of legislation, which exercised a real control not only of finance but of the administration of departments. But, today, not only the House of Lords has been shorn of most of its authority. The House of Commons too has surrendered most of its effective powers to the Executive and has become in the main the passive forum in which the struggle is fought between the modern usurpers of power, the great political machines.'[1] Since this catalogue of assertions would carry widespread assent, it is worthwhile to examine each section of it separately.

Mr Crossman saw clearly enough the distinction between the old House of Commons and the House of Commons which is responsible, through political parties, to a mass electorate. Yet by implication, he appeared to regard the development of the power of the electorate and of parties as having occurred much more recently than actually happened. The truth is that by the latter half of the nineteenth century, the electorate, even though not yet universal, was big and independent enough, and the parties were strong enough, for an independent House of Commons to be a myth. More important still, the main procedures of the House are derived from this later period and not, as Crossman suggested, from the period in which the parties were weak. Most of the procedures which determine the conduct of business in the House of Commons have their origins in Gladstone's procedural reforms of 1882 and the Balfour reforms of 1902, which together tipped the balance of control over the proceedings of the House decisively in favour of the Government of the day. Of course, the basis of Commons procedures had an earlier origin in the sixteenth and seventeenth centuries and were consolidated in the eighteenth; however, it was plainly not these earlier centuries that Mr Crossman had in mind but the middle of the nineteenth, in which there were limited, but not fundamental, procedural advances. How far was Parliament in the nineteenth century a maker and unmaker of Ministries; how far was the Cabinet 'merely' an executive committee of the Commons?

The basis for these assertions appears to be the analysis of the

[1] H.C. Deb., Vol. 738, col. 479, December 14, 1966.

Constitution provided by Bagehot. Thus Bagehot contended that the main function of the House was that of 'an electoral chamber' but in a different sense from the American electoral chamber. For, said Bagehot, the House of Commons 'is a real choosing body; it elects the people it likes. And it dismisses whom it likes too. . . .'[1] Bagehot, however, was writing in 1867, at the very end of a totally exceptional period of about two decades in which the House of Commons, owing to a temporary breakdown of the party system, was making and unmaking Governments (often coalitions) with a rapidity, and it seemed at the time an irresponsibility, which was the despair, not the pride of contemporaries. After 1867, Governments were largely made and unmade by independent electorates which increasingly made their decisions in response to the impulses from the political parties' machines.

Even as early as 1832 party organisations were beginning to achieve a new significance. Before the first Reform Act, it would have been almost as accurate to say that the Governments had made and un-made Parliaments, through the Crown's control of patronage and of parliamentary elections, as to say that the House of Commons made Governments. After the Act of 1832 had taken the power to return a House from the old oligarchy and had given it to a more or less independent electorate, however small, it was obvious that both party discipline and the electorate would have an entirely new significance. But the fragmentation of political allegiances after 1846 concealed the nature of the change and gave the House of Commons an appearance of 'independent' power which was a short-term phenomenon, not a permanent condition of parliamentary govern-ment. A writer looking at the parliamentary scene from the stand-point of a journalist in 1867, as Bagehot did, might understandably conclude from his own immediate past experience that it was the House of Commons which made and unmade Ministries. Similarly, a writer projecting the scene before him at certain times in the 1920s and 1930s might have concluded that a three-party system was imminent and that this would place the power to determine the composition of the Government in the hands of bargaining parties in the House of Commons. Even in 1964–6, accidents or mortality might have removed the Labour Government's fragmentary majority at the wrong moment and have forced it into coalition with the Liberals. Once again, this would have given the appearance of a

[1] Walter Bagehot, *The English Constitution*, ed. C. A. Watts, p. 150.

Government 'made' by the House. On the other hand, it should be noted that at none of these periods was there any illusion about the independence of Members from political parties. The most that can be said is that the Commons always has a residual control over the decision who shall form a Government when the electorate has given no party a clear majority—and the period from 1846–67 was the classic example of this sort of House of Commons control in practice.

The use of this power is the exception, not the rule, and Bagehot instinctively understood that the primary purpose of Parliament was to sustain an effective Government, though he may have over-stressed the elective function of the Commons. For, in discussing the 'elective' function, he suggested that the right reply for a Minister to make to the accusation that Parliament had done nothing in a Session should be: 'Parliament has maintained ME, and that was its greatest duty; Parliament has carried on what, in the language of traditional respect, we call the Queen's Government; it has maintained what wisely or unwisely it deemed the best executive of the English nation.'[1]

Similarly, Crossman's view of the Cabinet as once the 'executive committee of the Commons' is hardly borne out by examination of the historical function of Parliament. It would be better described as the executive committee of (and now elected by) the nation which is subject to the surveillance and approval of the existing House of Commons against which it can always appeal directly to the nation. Further, without entering into the profitless metaphysics of the location of sovereignty in the British Constitution, it is perhaps reasonable to suggest that it has never resided crudely in Parliament, except in the ultimate and final sense that a House of Commons can dismiss a Government (which may, however, have itself reinstated by the electoral will of the people) and in the sense that theoretically Parliament could abolish even itself. But when one is reduced to asserting this sort of residual sovereignty, the rider must be added that its potency depends on the general acceptance by the community of the 'parliamentary idea' and on the maintenance by the community of the power and will to support that idea. So long as the parliamentary idea is sustained, Parliament would not be allowed to abolish itself.

In other words, narrow legalistic notions of the sovereignty of

[1] Walter Bagehot, *The English Constitution*, ed. C. A. Watts, p. 152.

Parliament are not helpful to our understanding of the British Constitution. So long as the parliamentary idea carries conviction, there is reason to believe that the House of Commons would put the liberties of the subject and the survival of the nation above party interest and that, within the disciplines of party, its Members will give expression to these objectives in ordinary times. Thus at moments of potential danger in foreign or economic policy, we observe that Members on all sides normally do not seek to embarrass a Government in the interests of party. For the purposes of bread-and-butter politics, party interest is normally (though, as this study has shown, even then not invariably) dominant.

This situation is viewed by Mr Crossman as surrender by the Commons of most of its effective powers to the Executive and he sees the House as passive while the great political machines usurp parliamentary power. I shall return later to the power of the political machines and of the Executive in relation to Parliament. It is enough to note in the present context that neither the dominance of party nor the initiative of the Executive is new, though it is true that, with the arrival of a mass electorate, the party machines wield a greater influence and that the Executive has a wider field of action. In any comparison between past and present, however, it must be accepted that the House has only been truly itself when it has been disciplined by party. For this assertion, we have the witness of events and of persons who include Disraeli and Bagehot himself who observed of the House that 'party is inherent in it, is bone of its bone and breath of its breath'.[1]

In assessing the alleged loss of parliamentary influence, I turn next to the suggestion that the Commons once shared with the Government the initiation of legislation and had exercised a 'real control' over finance and departmental administration. The present study provides little support for this notion. So far as financial surveillance is concerned, one may cite Bagehot's observation in 1867 that 'the principal peculiarity of the House of Commons in financial affairs is nowadays not a special privilege but an exceptional disability'.[1] The examination of parliamentary control of finance in Chapter Fourteen suggests that the House of Commons now has more effective instruments of financial control than it had in the last century even though these have still not grown fast enough to keep pace with the increasing spending-power of the state and the position of Government

[1] Walter Bagehot, *The English Constitution*, ed. Č. A. Watts, p. 158.

departments as 'businesses'. In the field of administration, new parliamentary machinery may be needed to enable the House to scrutinise the work of Government departments. In legislation, however, we have seen a new rôle developing for the backbencher, acting independently of party, in the sponsorship of social legislation for which Governments do not wish to take responsibility; and this new influence is something greater than backbenchers enjoyed even in the reputedly golden days of the nineteenth-century Parliament.

It may be objected, however, that in the nineteenth century, the private Member had scope for initiating legislation through his sponsorship of the Private Bills of the period covering financial, economic and social issues which would properly be the concern of the Government today.

Yet one may question whether the rôle of the backbencher as a promoter of Private Bills was a true example of the Member's independence in the eighteenth or nineteenth century. His sponsorship of these Bills was, as often as not, a routine job in which he was virtually acting as the agent of the motivating interest. The impact on society of such measures was such as to suggest to British citizens in the twentieth century that the changes they brought about should have been enacted by the Government in the light of the public interest. But the public interest was not held at the time to be involved in the modern sense; the Executive was not normally involved in the same way and it cannot be said that the House was therefore acting independently of the Executive on a matter of public interest. The rôle of Parliament was very largely to reconcile conflicting private interests and to make sure that innovations demanded on one set of private grounds were not wholly offensive to other private citizens as individuals. To put it another way, Private Bills were not an equivalent of the *national* legislation of today; they dealt with private matters needing public sanction and the MPs directly involved were primarily concerned not with the national interest but, like their fourteenth- or fifteenth-century predecessors, with the interests of local communities, or influential figures among them.

The high-tide of the Private Bill in the *private* age of the eighteenth and early nineteenth centuries, when unfettered capitalistic development was at its peak, was hardly characteristic of the legislative history of the House of Commons as a whole. As we have seen, the legislative initiative in Tudor times, in the seventeenth century (except during the revolutionary emergency) and since the middle of

411

the nineteenth century has substantially lain with the Executive. The difference between the twentieth century and earlier periods has been the swift growth of the mass of legislation demanded from the Government—as a result of which the Executive has been obliged to take control of the bulk of the House of Commons time so that the process of governing could be carried on in modern conditions. Even here, however, it must be noted that the trend for the Government to take over the time of the House has been evident since the first Reform Act though, of course, the Balfour reforms of procedure in 1902, supplemented by those of 1945, represent the culmination of this development. But we must be careful not to confuse the greater control over its own time by the House of Commons in the nineteenth century, which appears to have been used primarily for much more lengthy speeches and debates and for Members to raise questions as and when they chose, with a greater participation in the legislative initiative. The handing over of the parliamentary timetable to the Government in the later nineteenth and early twentieth centuries was a necessary means of ensuring that the tradition of a strong Executive should be carried on.

For all these reasons, which have been illustrated during the course of this study, it is doubtful whether the allegations of decline in the influence of the House of Commons can be sustained. On the other hand, it is evident that Parliament needs now, as in all periods, to keep up to date with changes in the structure of society and that, with the enlargement of the scope of government, it has found it increasingly difficult to do so. To the practical problems now involved I shall return—but in the present context there is a different question to be answered. If procedural reforms are needed, does it matter whether the allegations of parliamentary decline which accompany the demand for them are justified or not? It matters because the power and influence of any institution depends on confidence in it and if confidence can be destroyed through over-rigid adherence to existing forms, it can be damaged no less by constant allegations that the institution is effete and powerless, that its Members have no influence and are no more than lobby-fodder for the party machines and that they are of lower calibre than they were.

It is also important to understand why the notion of decline should be so persistent and what its origin is—for only in this way can the challenge now facing Parliament be comprehended. The belief in the decline of Parliament is surely a manifestation of the widespread appreciation in the country that there has been a very real decline in the status and influence of the British nation in comparison with the rest of the world. The accusations directed against Parliament, and against other institutions of government, are also a symptom of a sense of failure in the nation to cope adequately with its reduced rôle in the twentieth century or to solve its economic difficulties and find new forms of influence and citizen-satisfaction to compensate for the loss of imperial prestige. It is highly significant that the first wave of discontent with Parliament arose in the 1920s and the 1930s, when there were also reasons for grave anxiety. The uncanny resemblance between the impact on public confidence and politics of the economic crisis of the thirties and the similar impact of the crises of the 1950s and 1960s has already been described. Since the middle of the century in particular, the nation's self-confidence has been bruised and its energies wasted in the constant battle to sustain a world rôle beyond its reduced resources. The cost of overseas commitments has contributed to obstruct the achievement of economic solvency; in turn, the constant elusiveness of solvency breeds a sense of failure which has combined with inherited faults in the social and economic structure of the nation and has further impeded full recovery from the exhaustion caused by total war waged beyond the nation's resources.

This sense of failure has rubbed off on British governmental institutions but it would be a diversion from the necessary political, social and economic change to assume that the impetus for national recovery can come from parliamentary reform. Why does a nation rise at a particular time in history? Why does it decline? These questions allow no simple answer—not even the answer of economic pressures. There have been instances enough in history (seventeenth-century Sweden might be taken as one example and, even, Elizabethan England as another) when a nation appears to gain a psychological sense of adventure and enterprise wholly beyond anything its economic resources might seem to justify—a mood of advance arising partly from the accidents of personality among its leaders and from opportunity; partly from the confidence bred by success which, like failure, is self-perpetuating. This is not the place for an examination of the social reasons for the malaise in British political life in the mid-twentieth century. Yet it may not be out of place to suggest that the remedies must be generated through new social and political impulses—perhaps reflected through the structure of the British political parties which use our parliamentary machinery— rather than by blueprints for parliamentary reform. For, if the right impulses are generated politically and socially, there can be little doubt that Parliament will respond as it always has.

No political institution has ever owed more to the evolving attitudes of an unusually cohesive nation and less to the political theorists than the British Parliament. The British people, with no fewer human frailties than anybody else, have enjoyed a remarkably peaceful political development. They have been free of violent revolutions (no revolution was ever less bloodthirsty than the English Revolution of the seventeenth century); they have been spared the fear of arbitrary power and, in recent years, the terror of secret police and the concentration camp. Primarily, this is the debt we owe to an inherited political climate in which the parliamentary idea of government by consultation and by the accommodation of conflicting interests has flourished. Parliament has been the prime instrument of consultation. It has also provided a permanent basis for authority which can be respected because it can be seen to be exercised with consultation and with respect to accepted institutions. History shows abundantly that men in society long not only for success, prosperity and the implementation of their wishes, collectively and individually, but also for legitimacy in government and institutions. Parliament provides this legitimacy and were respect for it to be diminished, the parliamentary idea on which many of our liberties and our society of tolerance depend might be in danger.

Yet Parliament has also shown an almost unlimited capacity to adapt itself to social and political change. It has been the means of the peaceful transfer of power from one section of the community to another over the centuries. Power which was once the prerogative of a king and of a small group of magnates is now to some degree shared by a mass electorate. Accidents of history have produced a national temperament and a political habit which have been a seed-bed for stable institutions. In turn, these institutions have allowed successive classes in the community to have a stake in society roughly representative of their place in the community's social and economic power structure. For Parliament has never embodied any constant theory of representative government. It has had no constant composition; its status has varied from time to time; it has allowed both aristocratic and democratic government. For all this absence of clear-cut functional theory, however, Parliament has developed an institutional personality so strong as to be almost unique in government. Though its lineaments have changed so radically over the centuries, there is a sense in which Parliament today is the same institution as the Parliament of the seventeenth or eighteenth centuries with similar attitudes to the conduct of government. This continuity is valuable not only because it provides stability and respect for legal authority but also because of the basic procedural techniques it has evolved which have been tested by time. Of course, the surface of procedure constantly needs renewal and adaptation to make it appropriate to changing circumstances. Similarly, new institutions devised on the drawing-board (so to speak) by contemporaries to deal with specific current problems can obviously be of great value. But the very immediacy of their application may make their valuable life-span a short one. There is a danger in reposing so much confidence in short-term institutional devices that Parliament, which has been forged by the events of a long history, may be regarded as outmoded.

Just because it is geared to more fundamental and permanent needs, Parliament may be found guilty of marginal inefficiency in a particular period. Yet practices of parliamentary government which may seem to be shortcomings in the particular circumstances of today, when respect for forms is at a discount and speed at a premium, may in fact represent great safeguards for the future. Nor should the House of Commons, as an institution, be found wanting because the politicians in it at a particular time have proved incapable of solving the economic or social problems of the nation. Of course, it is the business of the Members of the House of Commons to deal as best they can with such problems; it is equally true that the stability of parliamentary institutions depends on a reasonable degree of success in managing the daily business of Government. Nevertheless, the solution of particular problems is not the basic purpose of Parliament. Its fundamental functions are to preserve legitimacy in government; maintain the freedom of the citizen under the law; ensure that the dialectic of politics never ceases; channel into broad and manageable streams the ultimate choices available to the community; and, above all, to bring the Government into constant consultation with the elected representatives of a community which is governed by consent.

415

Chapter Seventeen

Conclusion (II)

A great deal of the contemporary criticism of Parliament depends for its validity on the accuracy of a set of related assertions, or beliefs, about the nature of other British institutions. Thus the allegation that the House of Commons is now for all practical purposes subservient to the Executive is closely linked with the popular belief that we no longer have Cabinet Government but, instead, live under Prime Ministerial Government of a presidential kind. This 'presidential' Prime Minister, armed with political patronage and with Civil Service and party officials backing him, is said to be able to make his Cabinet and his party in Parliament follow his policies and wishes. Similarly, the assertions of parliamentary impotence are closely related to the belief that ministerial responsibility is a myth which protects, not the House of Commons, but the civil servants who shield behind it. Moreover, the essential decisions of government are said to be taken not by politicians but by civil servants, a freemasonry of non-responsible and virtually immune administrators among whom decisions are evolved without any individual being accountable for them. Their advice and the options they present are said to pre-determine, for all practical purposes, their Ministers' policies.

All this adds up to a fairly formidable mythology which, like all mythologies, satisfies a need and expresses a certain apprehension of the truth but which is not the literal truth. The current mythology of British institutions represents an attempt by students of British politics to understand, interpret and simplify the political phenomena they observe in a period when the decisions and functions of the State have multiplied and assumed a complexity which put them beyond simple political control. In the conditions of mid-twentieth-century government, the older mythology of parliamentary sovereignty over Cabinet Government, which is served by neutral officials who advise but never themselves decide, has rightly ceased

417

to carry conviction. Indeed, the older mythology has made little sense at any time in this century but it once at least seemed a way of rationalising the basic attitudes of government when the responsibilities of the State were fewer and were more susceptible to oversight by the politicians than is possible today. As the old mythology has been abandoned, the urge for a new series of institutional formulae, which is simple and rational enough to satisfy the intellect, has produced a substitute. The new mythology, as we have seen, has gained force from the political and economic problems of Britain and from the urge to discover institutional explanations for national decline.

The new mythology has been useful in that it has forced people concerned with public affairs to look behind the traditional and formal allocation of responsibilities in government to try to determine more accurately the nature of the distribution of power. Its disadvantage has been that it has swung too many people to the false belief that politicians (other than the Prime Minister who is almost removed from this category), and especially parliamentarians, are no more than the front-men for the real decision-makers. These are said to be hidden within Whitehall or to be found in the Party Organisations, where they act as powerful tools of the Prime Minister or (an alternative version) prescribe the decisions he takes by reference to the strategy which they regard necessary for continued power-holding. We must look behind this mythology to discover the facts of contemporary government.

In the light of the findings of this study, I turn now to a final assessment of particular criticisms of Parliament and its relationship with the other institutions of Government. This assessment covers Parliament's relationship with the Prime Minister and the Executive, with the Party Organisations and with the Bureaucracy. In the appropriate context, I discuss some relevant aspects of the contemporary mythology of the other British institutions. It is convenient to begin an assessment of the relationship of the House of Commons to the Executive by considering what the place of the Prime Minister is *within* the Executive.

Is it true that the Prime Minister, for all practical purposes, is the Executive in Britain? Are the members of the Cabinet little more than his dependents, holding office at his will and ground between the Prime Minister and the bureaucrats? What real influence have other Ministers who are individually responsible to Parliament for their departments as well as collectively responsible for Cabinet decisions?

418

The post-war years have produced repeated instances of the primacy of power, or at least influence, enjoyed by the Prime Minister and from these the inferiority and ineffectiveness of the Cabinet have been widely deduced. The decision to make the atom bomb by the first Labour Government, which was taken not in the Cabinet but in the Defence Committee of the Cabinet, is often given as one example. The Suez adventure of 1956 was largely the personal policy of the Prime Minister, Anthony Eden, though other senior Cabinet Ministers were involved with him in its initiation and the Cabinet was kept informed. The decision to try to take Britain into the Common Market in 1961 was essentially that of the Prime Minister, Harold Macmillan. Though he had the support of important members of the Civil Service and of some close colleagues in the Cabinet, as well as of the hierarchy of his Party Organisation, the essential will that finally determined the decision to negotiate with the Common Market was that of the Prime Minister. It was a decision to which both his party, as a whole, and many of his Cabinet had to be slowly and circumspectly converted. The decision of the Labour Government in 1965 to attempt a new approach to Europe also rested ultimately on the Prime Minister, Harold Wilson. He had been personally cool towards the concept of British membership of the Common Market and there were members of his Government who were far more positively committed, as well as others who were positively opposed. But it was Wilson's will which determined a full Whitehall inquiry into the consequences of British membership and non-membership and, following the findings of that inquiry, it was the Prime Minister who led the Cabinet into a new attempt to find means of entry. Again, the Rhodesian crisis in 1965–6 produced what can only be described as a personal policy of the Prime Minister. The Cabinet were consulted but the tactical handling of the crisis devolved almost entirely on Wilson personally. Moreover, any examination of the first seventeen months of Labour Government after the 1964 General Election shows how greatly the Prime Minister was personally responsible for the tone and the decisions of the Government as a whole. It was Wilson's personal achievement to induce Labour to accept certain necessary, if unpalatable, decisions appropriate to a party seriously interested in power-holding—and to abandon the luxury of dogma that might, in view of Labour's small majority, destroy the party's hold on power.

Any Prime Minister has enormous influence because he controls the Cabinet agenda; he can encourage the taking of decisions in Cabinet committees and he can operate through private dealings on policy questions with Ministers in groups or individually. He has a vast power of patronage; he is aided by the Whips and the Party machine and, above all, he has the right to appoint and dismiss members of his Cabinet at will.

Nevertheless, the Prime Ministerial power is not 'presidential'. Britain has a unity of Government, encompassing the Executive and the Legislature, which the Americans have not and the Prime Minister can be removed by Parliament (or even by the non-cooperation of his colleagues in the Cabinet) between elections as the American President cannot. Thus, if Anthony Eden had been American President in the circumstances of January 1957, he would have been irremovable, whatever the state of his health and whatever his commitment to policies which his colleagues had come to see must be abandoned. Even more important, Neville Chamberlain would have been irremovable in 1940.

Further, whereas the American President forms an administration of his personal nominees of any or no party, the British Prime Minister is, effectively, committed to choosing a Cabinet from his own supporters and, above all, his stature is diminished by the fact that he has around him men in the Cabinet who are *potential claimants for his position*. There are prominent members of his own party whom he cannot exclude from his Cabinet or dismiss from it once they are in it—men whose views he must, if they are persistent, heed. Thus, it seems clear that at no time after 1956 could Macmillan have dispensed with Butler, the rival whom he had outpaced for the succession in 1957. Further, even though Butler again failed to obtain the leadership when it fell vacant in 1963, it seems equally clear that Lord Home could not have formed an Administration if Butler had insisted on standing out. During the uncertain week after Macmillan's intended resignation was made known in 1963, the view was expressed by senior Conservatives to the author that any Government that was formed must include Butler—an assertion not invalidated by the existence of an anti-Butler group strong enough to prevent his succeeding to the Prime Ministership. Those close to Macmillan put it to the author that Butler would serve under another Prime Minister because that was the kind of 'political animal' he was —an assertion which leaves much room for speculation about what might have happened had Butler been more forcible about his claims. The same general point was made by other members of the Conservative Cabinet and hierarchy immediately after Home was chosen when they expressed the opinion that Butler could have taken the leadership in 1963 if he had had 'the will'—and it was because he did not possess that sort of will that the party would not accept him. The relevant point here, however, is that any Conservative Government in the Macmillan period had to include Butler. (On the other hand, Macmillan had no difficulty in letting Lord Salisbury resign on a difference of policy, to some people's surprise—but Lord Salisbury had no comparable following among the younger people of the Party and, moreover, he was not dismissed.)

If Butler was an inevitable member of any Tory Cabinet of the later fifties, there were equally figures on the Labour side whom Harold Wilson could not have excluded from his Cabinet between 1964 and 1967, George Brown and James Callaghan (Wilson's former competitors for the Labour leadership) among them. Further, in the period of his small majority, he was obliged to have a much larger Cabinet than he had intended before coming to power. Thus Wilson had hoped to have a Cabinet somewhere between fifteen and twenty-three (the larger figure being the size of the Douglas-Home Cabinet).[1] In fact, Wilson's first Cabinet consisted of twenty-three until it was brought down to twenty-one in January 1967. It is sometimes argued that a large Cabinet is a symptom of a Prime Minister's power; its very size is said to make it more malleable. Yet a large Cabinet may be seen as a symptom of the Prime Minister's need to take in representatives of all shades of opinion in his party—and therefore of limitations on his power. Certainly it was essential for Harold Wilson to consolidate his hold on his party by having a large Cabinet in the circumstances of his tenuous majority after 1964. When out of office, both parties have advocated smaller Cabinets than their leaders have been obliged to appoint when in power.

A Prime Minister is also limited even in his power to dismiss colleagues by the need to retain the goodwill of his followers. Anything that smacks of political 'butchery' damages him in his party and hence his reputation in the country. Whatever the reservations of students of politics about the doctrine of collective ministerial responsibility, it is taken literally enough in the country for wholesale dismissals to give the impression that the Government is confessing the failure of past policies and has been obliged to go into reverse.

[1] *Whitehall and Beyond* (BBC Publications, 1964), p. 26.

Macmillan was irretrievably damaged by the peremptory dismissal of a third of his Cabinet, headed by the Chancellor of the Exchequer, Selwyn Lloyd, in 1962. He also felt it necessary to stress repeatedly that despite Selwyn Lloyd's dismissal (which, it was privately stated, was on account of tiredness), the ex-Chancellor's policies would be maintained. Lloyd's successor, Reginald Maudling, was obliged to delay the process of reflation rather longer than would have been necessary had Lloyd stayed in power in order that the former policy should not seem disowned and this delay was probably detrimental to the economy. When Wilson came to form a Government, he was so haunted by the example of Macmillan's 'purge' that, even when he enjoyed a large parliamentary majority after the 1966 General Election, he was exceptionally cautious about dismissing colleagues—so much so that he was subjected to the opposite criticism that he was not firm enough in removing the less successful members of his Government. Moreover, No. 10 Downing Street was sufficiently disturbed by rumours early in 1967 that Callaghan might cease to be Chancellor of the Exchequer in a coming Government reshuffle, to let it be known that he would stay; the fear was that rumours of a change at the Treasury might suggest a reversal of policy to overseas financial opinion.

When a Prime Minister must operate in a Cabinet of this kind and is restricted in his choice of colleagues, it is obvious that however skilfully he may prepare the ground by private negotiations with colleagues or by the initiation of policies in Cabinet Committees (of which he, or a close colleague, may be the chairman), he cannot, in the last resort, steamroller wholly unacceptable policies through the Cabinet. Very frequently, a situation in overseas or defence policy makes it necessary for the Prime Minister to be tacitly given something like presidential powers of negotiation—particularly, perhaps, when he is negotiating with a President. For instance, the Nassau Pact between the United States and Britain, which gave Britain the Polaris submarine after the American abandonment of the Skybolt project, was negotiated between Prime Minister Macmillan and the President—with the concurrence of the British Foreign, Defence and Commonwealth Secretaries, who had accompanied Macmillan to the meeting. Yet before the Pact could be formalised, it had to be submitted by cable to the Cabinet in London, which acquiesced to it. Since it was obvious that the Cabinet could hardly do anything else, short of disowning the Prime Minister and several of their most senior colleagues, their assent might be taken as a sign of the impotence of the Cabinet when important decisions must be taken. However, the episode can be looked at from the opposite point of view. Unlike the US President, the British Prime Minister did have to obtain Cabinet approval, and had the Pact been tentatively unacceptable in London, Cabinet agreement could have been withheld pending a full meeting on the return of the British Ministers. Further, Macmillan did associate with him a group of his most senior Ministers on the spot and if by any chance this group had refused to accept the Pact (and had backed their refusal with threat of resignation) Macmillan would have been unable to push ahead with it to a conclusion. Finally, we must recall the point already made that the entire exercise was partly designed to meet backbench Conservative opinion which, on this occasion, saw eye to eye with the Government's professional military advisers.

Although the Prime Minister may be an initiator in certain key areas of policy, or take over the handling of a policy when it assumes emergency dimensions, it is obvious that he cannot oversee the whole area of government and that by far the larger part of policy initiation reaches the Cabinet from departmental Ministers. Any individual Minister can ensure that the Cabinet discusses a subject which he is concerned to have discussed, despite the Prime Minister's general control of the Cabinet agenda. Moreover, the Cabinet Secretariat works to the Cabinet as a whole, not to the Prime Minister. For practical purposes, the Secretary to the Cabinet may be regarded as standing to the Prime Minister in roughly the same capacity as a Permanent Secretary of a department stands to his Minister. Equally, the Cabinet Secretariat can act as a vehicle for the transmission of political impulses *from the centre* to the various Cabinet Committees which consider particular areas of policy. Through the Secretariat's network, a Committee may find itself prompted to consider looking at a particular topic on the ground that this looks (to the Prime Minister or his Permanent Secretary) as though it may assume political significance. Even so, the responsibility of the Secretary to the Cabinet and of his staff is ultimately to the Cabinet as a whole and although the Secretariat has been strengthened a little by Wilson, it still has no White House staff. The Prime Minister has no department as the American President has; conversely, the American President has no Cabinet in the British sense and he calls together at moments of emergency only those of his advisers whom he thinks appropriate to the occasion, taking the final responsibility for decisions himself.

The necessarily representative composition of the British Cabinet and the Prime Minister's obligations to it are a symptom of the influence of parliamentary opinion (of the majority party) within the Executive as a whole. The members of the Cabinet are often themselves channels of parliamentary influence. Collectively, the Cabinet is much concerned with parliamentary management and, apart from foreign affairs, parliamentary business is the one constant item on the Cabinet agenda each week. Individually, as this study has shown, Ministers are also obliged to take parliamentary opinion seriously in the preparation of legislation. But, of course, because they are drawn from every wing of the parliamentary party, the members of the Cabinet are, *in themselves*, representative of different shades of opinion within the party. Naturally, the taste for office, so quickly acquired, acts as a deterrent on Ministers who might be otherwise inclined to take a stand in the Government as 'spokesmen' for a dissident section of parliamentary opinion in their own party. The Left-wingers (with the exception of Mr Frank Cousins, who was not a Member of Parliament when he joined the Cabinet) in the post-1964 Wilson Government did not noticeably take risks with their position in that Administration by standing out against policies which they would have resisted had they been on the backbenches. It is undeniable also that the steady rise in the number of MPs holding office in the Government has associated an increasing proportion of the House of Commons with the policies of the Prime Minister and the 'Inner Cabinet' of most influential Ministers. The figures are as follows:[1]

	1900	1930	1950	1960	1966 (Feb.)
Number of MPs holding Office*	33	50	68	65	88
Parliamentary Private Secretaries	9	26	27	36	28
Total number of MPs involved	42	76	95	101	116
Size of House	670	615	625	630	630

* Includes Queen's Household, Whips and Parliamentary Secretaries.

Yet despite this decline in the proportion of the House that is 'free' of Government patronage, it would be wrong to assume that the

[1] D. N. Chester, 'The British Parliament, 1939–66', *Parliamentary Affairs*, Autumn 1966.

424

participants in Government exercise no influence with their colleagues on behalf of the section of opinion which they represent or that they will not, in circumstances which seem to them sufficiently important, risk their office.

Despite the scope that a Prime Minister has to initiate policies and act without full consultations in an emergency (the sudden eruption of the danger of nuclear war might put the Prime Minister in much the same position as the American President), despite the manœuvring which he may employ before the formal settlement of a policy in Cabinet, it remains true that there are many issues of policy, home and overseas, which are not finally decided until the Cabinet has discussed them. Frequently, discussion in Cabinet is difficult and prolonged; sometimes it may not go the way that the Prime Minister would like. Frequently, the Prime Minister does not finally make up his own mind to 'steer' the discussion towards a particular conclusion until he has heard the views of his colleagues. (Votes are not normally taken in Cabinet.)

Nor do the pre-Cabinet discussions of policy which often pre-determine the decisions the Cabinet will reach seriously weaken the position of the Cabinet as the place of ultimate decision for major issues. Pre-Cabinet discussions and decisions take into account the views that the Cabinet as a whole are likely to express and they allow for the firmness with which possible dissenters are likely to hold to their opinions. In other words, the anticipation of reactions is as much part of the process of policy formulation *within* the Executive as it is *between* the Executive and Parliament. Prime Ministers and their senior colleagues do not embark on policies until they feel sure that they can carry enough of their colleagues with them to ensure their success with a particular initiative, or until they are sure that, if there are to be resignations, the departing Ministers will not be likely to attract a dangerous amount of support on the backbenches. Thus the Government as a whole anticipates the reactions of MPs; and the Prime Minister and his closer colleagues anticipate the reactions of other Members of the Government—whose ultimate sanction is that (unlike their American equivalents) they have a place in the House of Commons from which they can continue to fight politically after resignation. They are part of parliamentary influence.

What of the contention that the Cabinet is weakened by the decisions of importance which are taken in Cabinet Committees and which may never come before the full Cabinet for discussion? In fact, the Cabinet Committee system is an inevitable compensation for the large size of the Cabinet and the heavy number of decisions that must be taken by the Executive in one form or another. The Cabinet Committee is a smaller body to which the Cabinet as a whole may devolve particular problems and decisions without abandoning its right to a full discussion and to exercise the last word if it thinks fit. The Cabinet is not a body known formally to the Constitution or one which must be composed in any particular way. The collective responsibility of Ministers in Cabinet to Parliament was a later development than their individual responsibility. Nevertheless, the collective responsibility of the Cabinet remains a reality. It helps to prevent confusion and to create a certain coherence in the actions of the Executive; it establishes a group which can be held responsible for the major actions of government, and one which (even if the disadvantage of size necessitates some devolution of decisions to Cabinet Committees) is far more *representative* than the frequently advocated small Cabinet would be. The smaller Cabinet would also, of course, involve the use of other Committees of the Executive to take major decisions.

The reality of collective Cabinet responsibility is not disproved by the great power of the Prime Minister in modern political conditions; by the support he (and other Ministers) receive from the parliamentary majority; or by the public presentation he receives as a 'President-type' figure at election periods and at other times of intense political activity. Prime Ministerial power must be understood as varying with political circumstances and with the personal fortunes of the man who wields it. Harold Wilson's personal power in the period from 1964–6, when he had to operate with a bare majority in the House of Commons, demonstrated that a Prime Minister has a plenitude of power to deal with emergencies—for this entire period was one of party-political emergency so far as Labour was concerned. On a different level, Rhodesia during much of this period and the defence of sterling in the summers of 1965 and 1966 were governmental emergencies—and the Prime Minister controlled the public presentation of the Government's policies. Similarly, any Prime Minister is bound to have considerable personal discretion in foreign affairs partly because negotiations are so often with other heads of Government who *do* have 'presidential' powers and partly because foreign affairs often involve an emergency in which action by so large a committee as the Cabinet is inevitably inappropriate.

Yet a successful Prime Minister has much greater power than an unsuccessful one. If success snowballs, so does failure or doubt about the adequacy of a Prime Minister. The contrast between the position of Harold Macmillan at his peak and in the last two years of his Administration speaks for itself. Similarly, Sir Alec Douglas-Home, because of the circumstances in which he was elected leader as a compromise, was far less effective in his Cabinet than Macmillan had ever been. Had Douglas-Home been given power, in his own right, at the 1964 General Election, he would probably have become a much more influential Prime Minister. The fundamental fact about the position of the British Prime Minister is that he must operate flexibly within a parliamentary and Cabinet system in which 'power' is distributed and which gives the Prime Minister as much command of the political situation as he can earn. If he has *ad hoc* presidential influence, he is very far from having the powers of a President accountable to nobody except the electorate. A Prime Minister, in varying degrees, is accountable to his Cabinet colleagues, his Party and even, in some degree, to the Opposition. (He considers it his duty to consult with the Leader of the Opposition at moments of national crisis.)

Any Prime Minister who thought he could dispense with consideration for the views of his party in Parliament would wholly misunderstand his position. He would be equally ill-advised to suppose that the so-called 'weapon' of Dissolution would enable him to bring recalcitrant supporters to heel if all the rest of his pressures on them (and their natural inclination not to play into the Opposition's hands) did not suffice to keep them loyal. The general election which followed a Dissolution brought about by a difference of opinion between the Prime Minister and some of his followers would have a greater chance of ejecting the Prime Minister from his office than of depriving the average backbencher of his comparatively humble seat. The Dissolution is not a normal Prime Ministerial weapon, even in reserve, against his own backbenchers. There are frequently times when it is plain enough to backbenchers from the public opinion polls that their Prime Minister simply could not risk it. The Dissolution is a potent weapon in the hands of a Prime Minister for a wholly different reason. It enables him, in the light of the public opinion polls and other reasonably reliable indicators, to appeal to the people at a date (within the constitutional five-year term of a Parliament) which favours his party. Thus the Dissolution, together with opinion-sampling, is a weapon the Prime Minister can use, not against his own followers, but against the Opposition—and, because of the advantage it gives to the Party in power, it may be one of the factors tending to produce longer cycles of power-holding by the political parties.

Nor is the scope a Prime Minister has for changing the policies of his party an indication that he can do with it as he wills. It is, of course, true that a party in power can be brought by its leaders to accept more radical changes in its policy than it would stomach in opposition. Thus the Conservative Party was persuaded to accept economic planning and an incomes policy, as well as converted to the project for entering the Common Market, under Harold Macmillan. Similarly, the first years of the post-1964 Labour Government illustrated the extent to which a party can be brought by the realities of power to abandon, or at least suppress, many of its traditional attitudes. But the appearance of complete Prime Ministerial supremacy may be illusory in both cases. The Conservative Party accepted planning reluctantly and tended to react against it when it entered Opposition. A major conversion campaign was necessary to gain its acceptance of the Common Market policy. It is also arguable that Harold Wilson's redirection of the Labour Party after 1964 was possible only because the party itself was changing both in social composition and outlook. As Labour's new policies developed, they could be accepted by a younger generation of Labour Members as representing the older ideals of the party in a new form that could be reconciled with the demands of power-holding and the changed economic and social structure of 'Britain in the Sixties' in which the mixed economy was generally accepted. Even so, it remained to be seen, as this book was concluded, whether the Labour rank and file would show themselves to have a sticking-point against some of the more extreme reversals of policy by their leaders.

(ii)

From dealing with the relationship of Parliament to the political Executive of Prime Minister-in-Cabinet, I turn to the question of the relationship of Parliament to the Civil Service element of the Executive. Again, it is convenient to clear the ground first by dealing

428

with another contemporary myth—the belief that the essential decisions of Government are taken not by politicians but by Civil Servants. Linked with this is the frequent assertion that the doctrine of an individual Minister's responsibility for a Department is a dangerous delusion which allows officials to shelter behind their Ministers and saves them from being called to account for their actions by Members of Parliament.

Departmental attitudes which can often be tantamount to departmental policies undoubtedly exist. Thus the Board of Trade, by tradition, is a free trade department. 'Single-industry' Ministries like the Ministry of Agriculture and the former Ministry of Aviation also tend towards certain collective attitudes. The Treasury obviously has certain departmental policies for dealing with given situations and which, in those situations, the Chancellor cannot easily ignore. On the other hand, the Chancellor and his Cabinet colleagues are responsible for the basic political decisions involved in accepting Treasury advice. It was essentially a *political* decision not to devalue the pound in 1964 and a different Government might have adopted the opposite course. Once the basic decision was taken, however, it might be said that the Government is largely dependent on the technical advice of its officials on how the basic decision should be implemented.

The decisions to nationalise certain industries or to denationalise them have been political. So were the decisions of the Labour Government of 1945 to establish the National Health Service. The Conservative Government which followed made political decisions to free commodity markets, end rationing, and place greater reliance on the monetary weapon of bank-rate as a means of regulating economic policy. Equally, it was not the bureaucrats who set up the Department of Economic Affairs in 1964 to divide economic responsibility with the Treasury. This was essentially a politician's decision from which a number of consequences important to the economy flowed, some beneficial, some adverse. On the other hand, both politicians and civil servants obtain their intellectual nourishment from the same contemporary climate of informed opinion and the ideas of both intermingle freely. In practice, changes in fashionable opinion frequently presage a change of Government—so much so that a Government that is about to be turned out may be already hesitantly switching course. For instance, trade liberalisation had been begun by the post-war Labour Government before it left office and the Conservatives were logically the party to carry on with this. In much the same fashion, Conservative planning experiments in the early sixties, which went against the grain of traditional Conservative attitudes, resulted from the climate of opinion which was to bring Labour, with its more enthusiastic planning techniques, back to power.

The antennae of Civil Servants are sensitive to advance symptoms of changes of Government and they do their best to prepare themselves for what they anticipate will be the requirements of their new political masters. This preparedness was particularly evident in the months preceding the 1964 General Election when Whitehall Departments kept their lines of communication open to the then Labour Opposition. Subsequently, a senior Conservative politician (who had never been connected with the Treasury as a Minister) asserted to the author that the Treasury had been disloyal to the Conservatives for a year. Whether this imputation is justified may be doubted; nevertheless, the fact that it could be made suggests that the Civil Service does change its attitudes with a change of Government.

Obviously, however, no Minister can be responsible for all the policies and decisions of his officials. Yet it would be foolish to erode the doctrine of ministerial responsibility on that account, for there are many cases in which it is a necessary safeguard. For instance, many departmental decisions result from the tactical requirements of the party in power. During 1963, for instance, there was a steady stream of modernisation plans and announcements of spending commitments by the Conservative Government, and the connection between this flurry of activity and the forthcoming general election was clear. At the time, a Civil Servant observed to the author that he was reaching the conclusion that his salary ought to be paid by the Conservative Central Office. Much the same was true of the period between the 1964 and 1966 General Elections; during this period, senior Civil Servants were well aware that the timing of the election and the Government's small majority determined many decisions taken by the Labour Cabinet. There is nothing wrong with that; but there would be some injustice in seeking to call Civil Servants to account for such decisions and it would be very hard to reach public agreement about which decisions were inspired in this way.

Though it is fashionable to stress the dominance of Civil Servants in the processes of government, it is not a new development. Advising a new Member that he had never known a Government of any party

430

that wanted to do anything, Mr Fitzgibbon, a knowledgeable Irish Member in Trollope's *Phineas Finn* observed: 'The clerks in the offices work for the country. And the Ministers work too, if they've got anything to manage. There is plenty of work done;—but of work in Parliament, the less the better according to my ideas. It's very little that is ever done, and that little is too much.' At least Parliament works today but the function of the 'clerks' appears to have been pretty constant.

While this study was being concluded, the structure and composition of the Civil Service was under detailed examination, and the assertion had been made that officials withheld information from Ministers unless it was asked for.[1] The remedy suggested was that Ministers should be equipped with personal advisers to save them from the position of 'lonely men' among their professional officials. Though these questions largely fall outside the scope of this study, two points are relevant. First, although a weak or inadequate Minister will be mastered by his officials, these same officials normally prefer a strong Minister who takes his own final decisions and who can forcibly present those decisions, reached with his department, in Cabinet. Secondly, there is no reason to suppose that officials wish to stifle their Minister's political impulse but they do warn him of the full consequences of it—aware, perhaps, that when he has that knowledge he will change his mind. This is not wrong; it would be more wrong to allow the politician to go ahead with a scheme devised when he did not have access to all the facts. Nevertheless, some politicians (including Ministers in the post-1964 Labour Government) seems to resent such dampening advice from officials. To counteract it, they recommend—as others have also done—the establishment of a Minister's personal *cabinet* more or less on French lines. If this genuinely took the French form and reinforced the Minister's private office with additional non-partisan talent, such a change would be helpful. If, on the other hand (as the Labour Party evidence plainly implied), a *cabinet* was intended to contain personal sympathisers committed to a particular Minister or a particular party, it is doubtful whether such a change would be desirable. Such adherents might serve only to bolster their Minister's preconceptions and strengthen his will to persist with them without due consideration of all the consequences.

[1] Evidence (published January 1967) of the National Executive Committee of the Labour Party to the Fulton Committee on the Civil Service.

To the extent that *major* decisions are recognisably political and Ministers take responsibility for them, there is little reason to doubt that the House of Commons is still able to exercise surveillance. There remain, however, two linked problems. One is the problem of exercising parliamentary control over the ever-widening process of administration by Civil Servants. Such control may be usefully assisted by the use of specialist parliamentary committees, although it would be a pity if absorption in administrative detail were to divert the attention of MPs from political issues. The second problem is whether (as is so often alleged) the Commons are by-passed by the channels of communication between, on the one hand, the Executive and, on the other, business, professional and other outside interests. Of course, there is nothing new in this communication between Whitehall departments and outside interests, but is it wrong? As the area of Government activity widens, it would seem inevitable and unobjectionable that Whitehall departments should deal bilaterally with interest groups which concern them. Increasingly, the trade unions, professional, industrial and trade associations and other interest groups have close contacts with departments formally or informally, or through advisory committees. To some extent this reflects the increased importance of the Government's administrative impact on sectional interests as distinct from its impact through the passage of legislation. Since the action of Civil Servants in administering the law (which delegates powers to them) is of more constant effect than the passing of new laws, the affected interest groups will naturally turn more to the Departments and less to Members of Parliament. Yet this may be preferable to the development of the House of Commons as a congeries of lobbies.

A large number of MPs are already spokesmen for organised groups in which they may or may not have a personal interest and from which they may or may not receive some remuneration. Many MPs, by the simple fact that they hold other jobs, find themselves speaking with sympathy for particular interests whose position they understand. There is nothing wrong in this; indeed, the composition of the House is enriched by the presence of Members with special knowledge and interests. On July 3, 1965, the Chancellor of the Exchequer, James Callaghan, in a week-end speech at Swansea, said that he did not think of Conservative MPs in the Finance Bill debate as representing this or that constituency. 'I look at them and say, "investment trusts", "capital speculators" or "that is the fellow who

432

is the Stock Exchange man who makes a profit on gilt-edged." I have almost forgotten their constituencies, but I shall never forget their interests. . . .' The speech was referred to the Committee of Privileges, which, having received a letter from the Chancellor indicating that he had not had it in mind to suggest that Members with such interests should take no part in the Finance Bill debates, found that there had been no contempt of the House. In fact, it is normally widely known which MP has which interest. Moreover, most MPs with special interests do not let them prevail against their party allegiance and there is very little cross-voting by parliamentary spokesmen for particular interest groups.[1] The representation of sectional interests, albeit on a pretty haphazard basis, has always been a characteristic of the House of Commons. In the present period, when interest groups are more avid than ever to associate public men with their promotional enterprises, this characteristic of the Commons has probably gone far enough. Certainly the maximum disclosure of MPs' interests, of all sorts, is desirable. The lobbying of more MPs instead of Government Departments (supposing this were practicable) would be bound to extend the scope of the 'interested' MP as such, which would not seem desirable. It is preferable that interest groups should deal directly with Government Departments in matters of administration, appealing to MPs when they are faced with what they consider to be an abuse of power. Equally, it is often better that legislation should be produced by the Departments in consultation with the interests concerned and that it should then be submitted to the House of Commons which should function, not as a body of experts but as a body of amateurs (including some experts and interested persons) representing the consensus of the nation. In this capacity, measuring a particular 'good' against broader criteria, the House can accept, reject and, most important, amend proposals put before it by Government Departments who have worked with the interest groups concerned.

In any case, it would be impossible for MPs to compete with Government Departments in dealing with certain sections of the community, particularly where the Government has an interest in securing consent of external groups to a particular line of policy. Thus, the Department of Economic Affairs attempts to persuade both sides of industry to accept certain planning and wages policies;

[1] Allen Potter, *Organized Groups in British National Politics* (Faber & Faber, 1961), p. 292.

the Ministry of Technology and the Board of Trade act respectively as 'sponsor' departments for a whole range of industries and trades. There can be no question of involving the Commons in this sort of negotiations. The function of the Commons is to express a view on whatever decisions emerge and, though specialist committees may be useful in this respect when the subject-matter is technical, the natural place for the exposure of larger issues to controversial debate is the floor of the House.

(iii)

Within the governmental framework, we have seen a spread of influence and power among the Prime Minister, Cabinet, House of Commons and Civil Service. In normal circumstances, it is virtually impossible to isolate one place and assert that there power lies. But power is also located outside the official structure and, most particularly, in the political parties which are no recognised part of the Constitution.

No politician can hope to survive in Parliament without the protection of one of the big parties. Within the party context, individual MPs have real, if limited, scope for independent action and influence, as this study has shown. But has the dominance of the party organisations in an age of highly intensive public communications reached proportions dangerous to the well-being of Parliament? Further, does the party organisation call the political tune to which parliamentarians, in and out of Government, must dance?

The second question has only to be asked for it to be obvious that the organisation of a party in power is the servant, not the master, of the political leaders. A Prime Minister and his colleagues can persuade both their party organisation and their followers in the constituency to accept policies which would be unacceptable in Opposition. A Government's policy-making is determined partly by pre-election commitments, partly by unforeseen contingencies and partly by the decisions of the previous Administration which an incoming Government may have to take over. But above all, Governments have to take on new policies to cope with developing situations and, if necessary, to convert their followers to them. New policies seldom rise from the grass-roots of a political party. As in the case of tariff reform, which Joseph Chamberlain and a section of his party adopted, and as with the pro-Common Market policy of

Harold Macmillan, new policies frequently originate from outside the party structure and are then given political credibility through adoption by a respected party figure. In this process, the modern research department of a political party may play an important part in sifting new ideas and advising their parliamentary leaders on them. But neither the research departments nor organisational officials can foist policies on their leaders. What they can do is to delineate political attitudes (particularly in Opposition) which their leaders may or may not follow when they are in power. For example, in both their periods in Opposition since the war, Conservative Party strategists have toyed with the idea of introducing differentials to national welfare provisions, based on need, and a modified retreat from 'blanket' social security. In office, however, the Conservative leaders never considered it politically wise to adopt this approach.

A Party Organisation therefore provides the leaders of the party with a powerful instrument for influencing public opinion. It is more influential in Opposition than in office (when the party officials have to compete with the Civil Servants). It is probably (if by Organisation one means the National Executive Committee and its officials) more influential in the Labour Party than in the Conservative, which has no equivalent body determining policy.

What of the control exercised over MPs by the Party Organisations? There is often a certain ambiguity about what is meant by Party Organisation when this control is alleged. Sometimes, the Organisations are loosely bracketed with the Whips—which is misleading because the Whips are essentially the servants of the leaders of the party in the House of Commons at the time. Sometimes the reference appears to refer to party headquarters; sometimes to constituency parties. The matter may perhaps be clarified as follows: a would-be Member of Parliament is dependent on adoption by a constituency organisation. Party headquarters has a list of approved candidates and, (privately) important people at headquarters have candidates they particularly favour. But it is frequently difficult or impossible for these favoured figures to find seats; the choice of candidates depends almost entirely on the composition of the local constituency organisation—and that, in turn, depends on chance or on the particular social structure of the district. Indeed, one of the criticisms against the necessity of party endorsement is that potential MPs are chosen on a haphazard basis according to the prejudices (social, religious and 'public image') of a small group of activists who may represent nobody but themselves.

Once the MP is elected, however, he has a remarkable degree of freedom from his constituency organisations, who have to be tried very hard before they disown him. He is then under control of the Whips (which is another way of saying his own leaders)—but he is himself one of the electors of the leader of the party. He also comes under some propaganda pressure from the Party Headquarters but they, in turn, are always anxious to know what he thinks. As for the Party Conferences, the superiority of the MP over these annual jamborees needs little demonstration. Provided a Party Leader has the support of a sufficient number of his followers in the Commons, he can defy the Conference. This was shown in the Gaitskell defence controversy; it was shown when the Labour Conference of 1966 was confronted with overseas policies by Harold Wilson which it did not like. Equally, it sometimes appears that the Party Conference is more obedient than Members of Parliament—particularly on the Conservative side. Thus the Conservative Members of Parliament consistently took a more critical view of their leaders' Common Market policy in the early sixties than the Party Conference did.

If by Party Organisation one means the official hierarchy, it is obvious that they do not exercise real control over Members of Parliament. For they cannot 'pack' their benches of Parliament with men and women of their choosing and they cannot determine whom their Members will elect as Party Leader. The constituency parties have their moments of individual authority when they choose their candidates. They also pass to headquarters the views of the faithful which are important because the morale of the faithful is important. Yet the constituency parties assembled in Conference are inferior to the body of MPs and they can be defied by their leaders. Finally, the party officials at headquarters serve primarily the party's political leaders, not the men at the grassroots. To say that the MP is dominated by the 'party organisation' therefore means no more than saying that he requires a fragment of the base of that organisation to put him into Parliament and that the apex of the organisation, with the Whips, serves the leader *whom he elects*.

The party organisations, of course, are concerned with public communications and so are Ministers. It is convenient at this point, therefore, to deal shortly with the allegation that the MP is bypassed by the communications between Ministers and the press and television. It is said that Ministers are often more forthcoming with journalists than they are with MPs. Yet the journalist is circumscribed in the questions he puts. As an uninvolved neutral, a television interviewer cannot impute the same sort of political motives in questioning a Minister as may be imputed by an opponent in the Commons. A journalist must concentrate on getting at the bare facts; an interrogator in the Commons is more concerned to make his political case than to elicit simple information. It is, perhaps, not surprising that a Minister's replies to hostile questioning in the House of Commons may seem more evasive than his replies on television.

(iv)

The reality of parliamentary power has five main aspects. First, the influence of the Government's own backbenchers is a corrective to the empiricism towards which all administrations are impelled by the pressures of office. This serves to keep Ministers responsive to the wishes of the majority party and to the political concepts for which that party is in business. The fact that the majority party largely exerts its influence in private is neither new nor damaging. If private party meetings were thrown open to the public, the real arguments would retreat elsewhere—just as in some respects they have retreated from the House because of the full publicity which attends its meetings. Some of the more impressive contemporary debates in the precincts of Westminster take place in private party meetings.

Secondly, the work of MPs acting independently enables the Commons still to act as guardian of the liberties of the subject and to secure the redress of grievances. They have as their weapons Private Members' Bills and the interrogation of Ministers. Thirdly, it is the responsibility of the Commons to guard against administrative abuses on the part of the Executive. Fourthly, the dialectic between Government and Opposition, while reminding the citizen that he will have an alternative choice of Government at the next general election, also contributes to the evolution of political ideas. Finally, parliamentary influence is the ultimate reserve power for use in a national crisis and, on most past performances, the House of Commons can be expected to act above party and in what Members believe to be the national interest when the occasion arises.

We are left now with three final questions. Is the calibre of the House of Commons lower than it was and are talented men either driven from it or deterred from entering it by what they regard as its inadequacy and lack of influence? Is Parliament capable of overseeing administration in its widest sense in contemporary conditions? Should the Commons participate more effectively in policy formulation by being able to debate matters fully and openly *before* irreversible decisions are taken—and, to assist such participation, should there be some retreat from the tradition that a Government defeat entails the Government's resignation?

The facts do not support the assertion that distinguished men leave the Commons because they are disillusioned with it. The authors of *What's Wrong with Parliament?* cited Lord Robens, Mr Kenneth Younger, Sir Geoffrey de Freitas, Mr John Freeman, Lord Shawcross, Mr Hilary Marquand and Mr Chetwynd as examples of men of ministerial calibre who decided to leave the House because of a considerable loss of faith in the importance of the Opposition's function.[1] But, of course, these men left Parliament because of the widespread belief in the late fifties and early sixties that Labour had little prospect of a return to power which would have given them Ministerial office in the discernible future. Can anyone suppose that any politician regards Opposition as more than a second best; as a stint promising the ultimate reward of office, but a stint nonetheless. For men of constructive minds, an indefinite stay on the Opposition front bench is obviously frustrating and it was not surprising that Lord Robens should prefer to become Chairman of the National Coal Board, or that Mr Chetwynd should accept the non-political office of Director of the North-East Development Council, or that Mr Younger should go to Chatham House as Director-General of the Royal Institute of International Affairs rather than soldier on in Parliament with small hope of executive power. Similarly, Mr Hilary Marquand and Sir Geoffrey de Freitas both accepted overseas appointments, the former as Director of the International Institute for Labour Studies, the latter as head of the British Mission in Kenya. Such resignations reveal, not a loss of faith in the functions of Opposition, but the view the retiring Members took of the length of time they would have to spend in Opposition if they remained in the House, or their chances of office if their party achieved power. Sir Geoffrey de Freitas returned to the House of Commons in the 1964 Parliament which brought Labour back to power.

[1] Andrew Hill and Anthony Whichelow, *What's Wrong with Parliament?*, p. 10.

It remains to be seen whether there will be a complementary exodus of Conservatives if their party is subjected to an equally long prospect of Opposition in the sixties and seventies. It is possible that the number of Conservatives who leave the House will be fewer because more Conservative than Labour Members hold jobs which can be reconciled with membership of the House.

What of the separate but related argument that men of great talent do not enter Parliament at all; that the House of Commons is inadequately supplied with industrial or trade union leaders? The reason for their absence is surely lack of time—and here we come to another implicit contradiction between two of the fashionable criticisms of Parliament. On the one hand, it is said that the House of Commons should become more 'professional' and this is, indeed, the present trend. It is the underlying reason for the demand for more Committees and for the introduction of morning sittings. Both help Members to feel that they are doing a full-time professional job. But the farther this trend goes, the less practical it will be for leaders of industry or of the trade unions (the departure of Frank Cousins, the General Secretary of the Transport and General Workers' Union illustrates the point) to give their time to an all-absorbing professional body in which a man's merit may be assessed by the amount of committee work he does and which cannot, except for the men in office, offer positions of comparable power to those they have left.

It is in any case open to question how far it would be an improvement to fill the benches of the House of Commons with more 'top' people from other walks of life, supposing they could spare the time to do a proper parliamentary job. For one thing, politics is a craft of its own and it is simply not true that (say) a prominent industrialist would necessarily make an exceptionally useful MP. It may be true that he would have interesting things to say about his own special field—but he is as well able to say them outside the House as in it. Further, how would such a man find time to do the more trivial chores of constituency work; how far would he genuinely regard himself as the spokesman of the ordinary citizen rather than of his special interest? It is arguable that being a politician is a craft in itself; that men of varying calibre must enter it knowing that some will get to the top and some will not. Politicians must be capable of representing political ideas, not particular kinds of expertise, and able to speak for the conflicting aspirations and interests of ordinary citizens. To do this, it may well be that in the conditions of the contemporary State, they should spend more time at politics—should be less amateur and more professional as politicians. If this is so, it certainly removes much force from the argument that not enough prominent men who are active at the top of other professions are prepared to enter Parliament.

As it is, the calibre of the House of Commons *as a whole* (judged in terms of intellectual interests, which is not the only criterion for assessing political capacity) is almost certainly higher than it was in the 19th century. Where contemporary Parliaments may fall below those of the 19th century is in the men of exceptional ability among MPs. In the 19th century, membership of the House of Commons was the main outlet for the energies of an able man who had the advantages of brain, social status, education and wealth. He could then more easily combine it with such other activities as he pursued. Today, there are rival occupations which may attract the able young Gladstone at the outset of his career more than politics and he may be rather less inclined to take his chance on the Commons as his way to the 'top'. But whatever comparisons may be made with the 19th century House of Commons, it certainly seems probable that the general calibre of MPs now is higher than it was before the second world war. Mr Speaker King expressed his view that 'the quality of Members of Parliament, which is higher on average than ever before in history' was one reason for the contemporary malaise which afflicted Members.[1] If Parliament is in decline, it remains puzzling that, despite all its physical stresses, it remains an object of ambition for so many able men and women.

The demand for reform which would give Members the sense of performing a more useful function is partly explained by the wish of many Members (particularly those in the Labour Party who have left academic and other occupations which cannot be reconciled with their Membership) to obtain job-satisfaction from their parliamentary career. Hence the demand for morning sittings, more committees and greater participation of Members in the work of the Executive. This trend to professionalism is inevitable and it has its advantages. On the other hand, there would be some loss to the community if MPs generally became so professionalised that they were less representative of the ordinary citizen and instead became counter-bureaucrats.

[1] *Second Report from the Select Committee on Procedure*, 1966–7, Evidence, p. 4.

Nevertheless, some improved oversight of Governmental admini-stration is plainly desirable and the new investigatory committees of the House on science and agriculture may set a pattern for the future. Other specialised committees may also be able to call before them Ministers as well as Civil Servants and the practice of taking evidence in public may be extended. On the other hand a fundamental difficulty remains. These committees may be restricted to relatively uncontentious subjects like health and welfare (which could, of course, quickly become contentious anyway). But if it is assumed that committees on the big issues of economic, foreign and defence policy are incompatible with our system, then specialised committees are not a full answer to the main question of how to give Parliament more influence in the major areas of policy, which is really what worries most people. It may be thought that we should grasp this nettle and appoint such committees on more or less American lines. Nevertheless, the strength of the House of Commons has always been that it is not just a debating chamber but a House which votes *on a question* and which can, in the last analysis, bring a Government down. Congressional Committees can be outspoken precisely because they do not have this power; outside their legisla-tive capacity, they are no more than informers of public opinion. Indeed, there is now concern in the United States about the dwind-ling rôle of Congress: a concern which almost exactly reflects worries in the United Kingdom about the efficacy of Parliament.[1]

Part of the answer must surely be to restore a greater reality to debates in the House on matters of high policy. To the extent that lack of time is a difficulty, streamlining Bill procedure (enabling all detailed contents of Bills to be considered in Standing Committee, including the Finance Bill) should help. Members might also take more trouble with speeches and they should, perhaps, think less in terms of deliberately consuming time as parliamentary tactics. (On the other hand, if an Opposition laid too much stress on the fact that Government Bills could not be stopped anyway, it would be a temptation to cease trying to delay or to amend them.)

Part of the answer to the question of how to improve House of

---

[1] See, for example, an article by the Washington Correspondent in *The Times*, January 18, 1967 which observes, *inter alia*, 'Some committees maintain an almost incestous relationship with Government departments and agencies when the interests of members is involved. Then debate is definitely shut off.'

Commons participation in the process of Government decisions must surely be to restore a greater reality to debates in the House on matters of high policy when crises occur. The proposals to relax the restrictions on the interpretation of Standing Order 9 may help in this respect.[1] To relieve the Speaker from being bound by previous interpretations of the Standing Order, the Select Committee proposed that the test of a 'definite matter of urgent public importance' should be replaced by one of a 'specific and important matter which should have urgent consideration'. The extension of the Order to cover subjects in which there is a potential as well as an actual Government interest would, for instance, make it possible for the House to debate overseas questions even where there is not yet any definite ministerial responsibility.

In the twenty years to 1966 there were only fifteen debates under S.O.9 compared with 102 debates in the first twenty years of the century. As guidance to the Speaker, the Select Committee recommended a return to an average of five such debates a Session. Even so, the limitations on the House are clear. Members want to hold major debates when they are appropriate. On the other hand it is recognised on all sides that the Government must be allowed to get its business through. The Select Committee itself stressed that certainty of business was 'a most valuable achievement in a parliamentary assembly'. The Government must not be in danger of losing its planned business for something trivial. Nor, under our system of Government can the Executive be inhibited from taking decisions until it has consulted the House; that would be to weaken its authority at home and abroad. It must take its decisions—and then the House, if it wishes, is at liberty to disown them.

Should it be made more easy for the House to disown at least minor decisions without the Government's being obliged to resign? Would Members benefit by being freed of the pressure from their leaders that a defeat would mean the end of that Administration? The dangers here, I believe, might outweigh the benefits, leading to a situation in which the Government of the day is seen to be able to disregard the wish of the Commons. Already there are some signs that this might happen. In the period of Labour Government between 1964–6, with a majority of only three or four, there were clear intimations from the centre of Government that a defeat on a minor issue would *not* be taken as a reason for Dissolution or

[1] *Second Report from the Select Committee on Procedure*, 1966–7.

resignation—but would simply be followed by a demand for a vote of confidence on general grounds, which the Government could easily have obtained. This trend, I believe, exists; it is not necessarily a desirable one and the House should watch its development.

It is equally noteworthy that the bulk of procedural reforms introduced by the post-1964 Labour Government have had the effect of strengthening the Cabinet's ability to get its business through Parliament more quickly, rather than of enabling the Commons to exercise greater surveillance over the Executive. It has perhaps been easier for the Government to make procedural changes to its own advantage precisely because they were produced in the context of a general discussion on how to restore the influence of MPs. (In any case, all ranks of the Labour Party have generally sympathised with steps to ensure that parliamentary procedure does not impede their party's normally heavy legislative programme.) What is indisputable is that although Ministers can claim to have introduced reforms, the result of these has been to make their own task easier.

Thus, the effect of introducing morning sittings for 'uncontroversial business' on Mondays and Wednesdays (though it originally arose in March, 1965 from the Government's decision to aid a private Member, Sidney Silverman, with his Bill to abolish capital punishment) has been to help the Government to speed up its own business. Although the business which is referred to these morning sittings is supposed to be uncontroversial, there have been a number of arguments between the Government and Opposition over whether particular items (notably ministerial statements) were non-controversial or not. The Government has been open to the suspicion of relegating to the morning sittings (attended, it should be noted, often by no more than a handful of Members) statements of policy which should be made at a time when the full House is normally present.

In the same way, the time-tabling of the Finance Bill, and even more any subsequent decision to send it entirely 'upstairs' (which Treasury Ministers favour), will be of more assistance to the Government than to Members. If Members are spared some late-night sittings and have some free days to devote to more general topics, the question remains unanswered whether they will be allowed to make significant use of this time to debate major issues. Even the speeding up of Question Time, by the reduction of the number of Supplementary Questions, has the effect of making it easier for

Ministers to 'dodge' the really probing interrogation which can arise from a succession of Questions.

So far, the only recent procedural changes which mainly favour the interests of the House as such, are the slightly greater flexibility given to the Opposition in the use it can make of Supply procedure and the establishment of specialist committees, which may be supplemented by pre-legislative committees to associate MPs with the preparation of certain more or less uncontroversial types of legislation. But even with the specialist committees, the Government has been wary about letting them present too great a challenge. It has maintained the traditional method of having the Members appointed by the Whips—which virtually gives the Government the ability to approve the membership of the Committee's majority. Equally, the Government has tried to interfere with the subjects to be investigated by these committees and with the right of the committees to take evidence wherever it chooses.

It is also significant that the topic on which the Government has so far been reluctant to act has been the proposal of the Select Committee on Procedure that S.O. 9 procedure should be loosened so as to restore to the House a greater capacity to debate quickly topical questions of high policy.

In short, the question of procedural changes still revolves round the ancient dilemma of how far they should be designed to make it easier for the Member to call the Government to account, and how far to enable the Government to conduct its business more efficiently. In the end, it is unlikely that the balance of power will be markedly altered as a result of procedural changes.

Indeed, the fundamental trouble with Parliament may not lie in the institution itself or in its procedures. Many of the traditional procedures which have been attacked as mumbo-jumbo do, in fact, symbolise with remarkable accuracy the facts of the Constitution; where they are wholly irrelevant and outmoded, however, they should be removed. Procedure represents no fundamental obstacle to parliamentary influence; it is already changing and can be changed further. Equally, the psychological power of Parliament is repeatedly demonstrated. It is the judgment of the House of Commons collectively on the merits of a man which determines whether he shall reach the top in politics. Nobody who watches the House can doubt its remarkable capacity to assess character. It is a body almost impossible to deceive and singularly unimpressed by oratorical tricks. To master its attention is the mark of some quality in a man. Above all, its influence with the Executive may fairly be judged by the contrast between the general political atmosphere when Parliament is sitting, and the atmosphere when it is not. When Parliament is dispersed and its criticism is silenced, Governments are relieved and they normally enjoy a much more powerful hold on public opinion. Further, despite occasional signs of a certain carelessness on the part of political leaders with the rights of the House of Commons, it is an undeniable improvement in the position of the House that the leaders of all parties (and therefore the potential Prime Ministers) are now elected by the MPs of each party and that the Conservative leader is no longer evolved through the former ill-defined channels of internal 'consultation'.

The essential problem of the House of Commons may lie, not so much in the processes of Parliament, as in the present British party structure. First, because the activists of both parties have been increasingly remote from the electors on whose votes they rely, there has been a growing tendency on the part of political leaders to appeal over the heads of their parties in the House of Commons to the electorate. Both Harold Macmillan and Harold Wilson have done this, though as this study has shown, a leader who loses the confidence of his followers in Parliament may ultimately put himself in some electoral danger.

Secondly, the real arguments of politics have increasingly come to lie across party lines, although it remains true that the fundamental attitudes to society of the two major parties differ sharply from each other. But there is so much common ground between the behaviour in power of either party (the result of trying to achieve majority support in the country) that a widespread disillusion with conventional political arguments is discernible. In addition, the debate between the parties appears to be inadequately representative of the real arguments; this is particularly true over economic policy, and to some extent, it is true of foreign and defence policy. The party-political duel sometimes seems to obscure rather than to illuminate the technical problems of Government. It may be possible to take some of the technical arguments out of conventional politics but that, surely, is only part of the answer. More important, perhaps, is to make the argument between the parties a more genuine one and this may involve gradual changes in political allegiances over the coming years. Whatever changes come about in the parties which

445

operate within Parliament, whatever new procedures are devised, one thing that is clear is that the House of Commons should remain firmly attached to discussing the political decisions of government in a political way. Its function is to keep the Executive in touch with the main streams of political opinion, but it is not within the ability of Parliament, as an institution in a democratic society, to prescribe how that opinion organises and expresses itself through the political parties. The *active* political parties (as distinct from the huge segments of the population which exercise a limited choice in voting for them) may become too remote from public opinion in a wider sense. This has happened periodically throughout parliamentary history. Equally, the dialectic between the parties may cease to connect adequately with the technical arguments being conducted by informed opinion over specific areas of Government activity; the economy and defence are obvious examples. Yet, if the political parties in Parliament do become inadequate representatives of public opinion, the remedy can only arise from the social and economic impulses within the community. It cannot be imposed by Parliament, which is primarily a method of resolving conflicts of interest and opinion in a free society rather than a guarantor that particular political problems will invariably attain an efficient solution.

Footnote References

House of Commons Debates, *passim.*
Sir Ivor Jennings, *Party Politics.* Vol. II: *The Growth of Parties.*
Andrew Hill and Anthony Whichelow, *What's Wrong with Parliament?*
Bernard Crick, *The Reform of Parliament.*
  In Defence of Politics.
Parliament and Government in Our Industrial Society, by a group of
  Conservative Members of Parliament.
Three Dozen Parliamentary Reforms, by One Dozen Parliamentary
  Socialists.
William Rees-Mogg, *Liberty in 1964.*
Christopher Hollis, *Can Parliament Survive?*
Brian Chapman, *British Government Observed.*
Paul Einzig, *The Control of the Purse: the progress and decline of Parlia-*
  ment's financial control.
Jo Grimond, *The Liberal Challenge.*
Arthur Aspinall (ed.), *Three Early Nineteenth Century Diaries.*
Norman Gash, *Politics in the Age of Peel.*
A. H. Birch, *Representative and Responsible Government.*
Benjamin Disraeli, *Coningsby.*
C. S. Parker, *Sir Robert Peel.*
Norman Gash, *Reaction and Reconstruction in English Politics.*
Henry W. Lucy, *Later Peeps at Parliament.*
Walter Bagehot, *The English Constitution.*
William Jeans, *Parliamentary Reminiscences.*
A. L. Lowell, *The Government of England.*
J. Redlich, *Procedure of the House of Commons.*
F. Clifford, *A History of Private Bill Legislation.*
S. H. Beer, *Modern British Politics.*
E. L. Woodward, *The Age of Reform.*
John Morley, *Life of Gladstone.*
Kenneth Mackenzie, *The English Parliament.*
Edward Hughes, *The Changes in Parliamentary Procedure.*
Robert Lowe, *Speeches and Letters on Reform.*
Lord George Hamilton, *Parliamentary Reminiscences and Reflections.*
Peter G. Richards, *Honourable Members, a Study of the British Back-*
  bencher.
Emanuel Shinwell, *The Labour Story.*
  Conflict Without Malice.
Lord Williams of Barnburgh, *Digging for Britain.*
Aneurin Bevan, *In Place of Fear.*
Lord Halifax, *Fullness of Days.*

447

Beatrice and Sidney Webb, *A Constitution for a Socialist Commonwealth of Great Britain.*

Beatrice Webb, *A New Reform Bill.*

A. J. P. Taylor, *English History, 1914–1945.*

Robert Blake, *The Unknown Prime Minister.*

L. S. Amery, *My Political Life.*

Lord Beaverbrook, *The Decline and Fall of Lloyd George.*

Ramsay Muir, *How Britain is Governed.*

Lord Eustace Percy, *Government in Transition.*

Herbert Morrison, *Government and Parliament: a Survey from the Inside.*

George Lansbury, *My England.*

Harold Macmillan, *Winds of Change, 1914–1939.*

Hugh Dalton, *The Fateful Years: Memoirs, 1931–1945.*

Lord Hewart, *The New Despotism: an Essay on Bureaucracy.*

Harry Street, *Freedom, the Individual and the Law.*

Ivor Jennings, *Parliament.*

Harry Boardman, *The Glory of Parliament.*

Earl Winterton, *Orders of the Day.*

Michael Foot, *Aneurin Bevan.*

Francis Boyd, *British Politics in Transition, 1945–1963.*

Ivor Bulmer-Thomas, *The Growth of the British Political Party System.*

R. T. Mackenzie, *British Political Parties.*

Hugh Dalton, *High Tide and After.*

Earl of Woolton, *Memoirs.*

J. D. Hoffman, *The Conservative Party in Opposition.*

Lord Moran, *Winston Churchill, The Struggle for Survival, 1940–1965.*

David Coombes, *The Member of Parliament and the Administration.*

H. H. Wilson, *Pressure Group: the Campaign for Commercial Television.*

Anthony Nutting, *No End of a Lesson.*

Merry and Serge Bromberger, *The Secrets of Suez.*

Nigel Nicolson, *People and Parliament.*

S. E. Finer, *Anonymous Empire.*

D. E. Butler and Anthony King, *The British General Election of 1964.*

The Memoirs of Lord Chandos.

Strathearn Gordon, *Our Parliament.*

D. N. Chester and Nona Bowring, *Questions in Parliament.*

Douglas Brown, *The Battle of Crichel Down.*

Samuel Brittain, *The Treasury under the Tories.*

T. E. Utley, *Occasion for Ombudsman.*

S. E. Finer, H. B. Berrington and D. J. Bartholomew, *Back-Bench Opinion in the House of Commons, 1959–65.*

L. S. Amery, *Thoughts on the Constitution.*

H. J. Laski, *Parliamentary Government in England.*

Roland Young, *The British Parliament.*

Lord Hill of Luton, *Both Sides of the Hill.*

Duff Cooper, *Old Men Forget.*

Allen Potter, *Organized Groups in British National Politics.*

Index

Index

Abortion, 319
Abyssinia, Italian invasion of, 155–6; defeat of, 157
Accounts, Committee of, 337
Acland, Sir Richard, 170
Addington, Henry, 65 n
Administrative law, 327–9
Adullamites, 69
Agricultural Charter, 203
Agriculture, Select Committee on, 353–4
Amery, L. S., 114 n., 165, 166 n., 364 n., 384; and defence, 155; attacks Neville Chamberlain, 168–9; and committees, 343
Anderson, Sir John (Lord Waverley), 306
Anglo-American relations after 1945, 188–90
Anglo-Saxon communities, 32–3
Anglo-Polish Defence Treaty, 165
Anselm, Archbishop, 33
Appeasement, 154–9, 316
Apple Cart, The, 119 n.
Arbuthnot, Charles, 61
Argyll, Duke of, 92
Aspinall, Arthur, 61 n.
Asquith, H. H., (Earl of Oxford and Asquith), 105, 145–6; resignation of, 96; retirement of, 121
Attlee, Clement (Earl Attlee), 150, 185, 277, 315, 316; R. H. Crossman on, 17; and backbenchers' rebellions, 187–201; and conscription, 191–4
Auditor-General, 144, 336, 373
Australia, parliamentary broadcasts in, 398

Back-bench Opinion in the House of Commons, 331 n.

Backbenchers, committees of, 12, 26, 100–1; and the Executive, 12–13; criticisms of, 18–19; independent, 52; in the eighteenth century, 55–6; reverence towards leaders, 91; and taxation, 94; relations with frontbenchers, 101–2; and the fall of Lloyd George, 113–14; contacts between parties, 158, 159; and appeasement, 160–4; wartime influence of, 171–6; and fuel-rationing, 174; revolts of, 179–80, 185–200, 203–91; 315–18, 365; influence of, 179–291; pressures by, 186–200; limits of power of, 271–2; handicaps of, 329–31
Bacon, Sir Francis, 45
Bagehot, Walter, 17 n., 72, 409 n.; on party government, 74; on the Commons, 408, 410
Baldwin, Stanley (Earl Baldwin of Bewdley), 113, 114, 115, 116, 121, 151, 152; and the Labour Party, 98–9; on procedure, 133–4; as Prime Minister, 155; and the Hoare-Laval Pact, 156; resignation of, 157
Balfour, A. J., (Earl of Balfour), 88, 93, 113, 114, 141; procedural reforms by, 407, 412
Barons, the, 33–5
Battle of Crichel Down, The, 324 n.
BBC, 10 n., 185 n., 209
Beaverbrook, Lord, 115, 121
Bechuanaland, 196 n.
Beeching, Dr., 209
Beer, S. H., 82 n.
Berkeley, Humphry, on the Commons, 10–11; and immigration, 281; and homosexuality, 320

451